Critical Essays on
VÁCLAV HAVEL

CRITICAL ESSAYS
ON
WORLD LITERATURE

Robert Lecker, General Editor
McGill University, Montreal

Critical Essays on

VÁCLAV HAVEL

edited by

MARKETA GOETZ-STANKIEWICZ
AND PHYLLIS CAREY

G. K. Hall & Co.
New York

G. K. Hall & Co.
1633 Broadway
New York, NY 10019

Library of Congress Cataloging-in-Publication Data
Critical essays on Václav Havel / edited by Marketa Goetz-Stankiewicz
and Phyllis Carey.
      p.   cm. — (Critical essays on world literature)
   Includes bibliographical references and index.
   ISBN 0-7838-8463-X (alk. paper)
   1. Havel, Václav.   2. Presidents—Czechoslovakia—Biography.
3. Presidents—Czech Republic—Biography.   4. Dramatists,
Czech—20th century—Biography.   I. Goetz-Stankiewicz, Marketa.
II. Carey, Phyllis.   III. Series.
DB2241.H38C75   1999
943.704'3'092—dc21
[b]   98-54637
                                                                     CIP

This paper meets the requirements of ANSI/NISO Z3948-1992 (Permanence of Paper).

10 9 8 7 6 5 4 3 2 1

Printed in the United States of America

To Václav Havel

Contents

◆

List of Illustrations   *xi*
Publisher's Note   *xiii*
Editors' Note   *xv*
Introduction   *1*
    MARKETA GOETZ-STANKIEWICZ

AN OVERVIEW

    Václav Havel in Word and Deed   21
        PAUL WILSON

    Havel's Castle   31
        J. P. STERN

    All the President's Plays   44
        STANISLAW BARANCZAK

    Prague: Intellectuals and Politicians   57
        TIMOTHY GARTON ASH

PERSONAL EXPERIENCES

    Havel's Choice   75
        STEPHEN SCHIFF

    Play on Words   91
        LEWIS LAPHAM

    President Havel   98
        ROB MCRAE

HAVEL'S POLITICAL THOUGHT

Two Democratic Revolutionaries:
Tomáš G. Masaryk and Václav Havel   105
  H. GORDON SKILLING

A Performer of Political Thought: Václav Havel
on Freedom and Responsibility   112
  JEAN BETHKE ELSHTAIN

Václav Havel and The Rhetoric of Folly   127
  KENNETH S. ZAGACKI

Václav Havel's Construction of a Democratic Discourse:
Politics in a Postmodern Age   143
  DEAN C. HAMMER

HAVEL THE PLAYWRIGHT

Havel's *The Garden Party* Revisited   159
  PAUL I. TRENSKY

Havel's *The Memorandum* and the Despotism of Technology   173
  PHYLLIS CAREY

Spectacular Pretending: Havel's *The Beggar's Opera*   184
  PETER STEINER

Václav Havel: The Once and Future Playwright   200
  ROBERT SKLOOT

Delirious Subjectivity: Four Scenes from Havel   209
  MICHAEL L. QUINN

Life under Absurdity: Václav Havel's *Largo Desolato*   224
  DOUGLAS SODERBERG

Variations of Temptation—Václav Havel's Politics of Language   228
  MARKETA GOETZ-STANKIEWICZ

HAVEL IN THE MINDS OF HIS COUNTRYMEN

"That Bourgeois Brat!"   243
  JOSEF ŠKVORECKÝ

The Jubilee   247
  VÁCLAV BĚLOHRADSKÝ

Reflections on Václav Havel   250
  JIŘINA ŠIKLOVÁ

Timely Reflections on a Seemingly Untimely Playwright   255
    ANDREJ KROB

HAVEL ON THE ROLE OF THE PRESIDENT

    The Role of the Czech President   261
        VÁCLAV HAVEL

Glossary   267
English-Language Bibliography   281
Notes on Contributors   285
Index   289

Illustrations

♦

1. About 1967 with Klaus Juncker of the German Rowohlt
   Publishing House who "discovered" the young playwright
   Václav Havel. *Photograph courtesy Klaus Juncker.*   32
2. In 1984 with H. Gordon Skilling in Hrádeček writing
   a letter in support of the Canadian Jan Hus Foundation.
   Photograph courtesy H. Gordon Skilling.   32
3. With his second wife Dagmar during a visit of the German
   Chancellor Helmut Kohl, January 1997. *Photograph by
   Alan Pajer.*   56
4. With Pope John Paul II in the Vatican, March 1994.
   Photograph by Jiří Jirů.   56
5. Queue in front of the bookstore of the publishing house
   Paseka when the volume of the President's speeches *1992
   & 1993* had just been published, April 1994. *Photograph
   by Jiří Jirů.*   90
6. Discussing a play with a group of actors, including director
   Andrej Krob and his wife Anna Freimanová, about 1991.
   Photograph by Tomki Němec.   90
7. With his first wife Olga in Calcutta where Mother Teresa
   had her mission, February 1994. *Photograph by Jiří Jirů.*   128
8. With his second wife Dagmar and President and
   Mrs. Clinton in Secretary of State Madeleine Albright's home
   in Georgetown, May 1997. *Photograph by Tomki Němec.*   128
9. *Audience*, Teatr im. C. Norwida, Jelenia Góra, Poland, 1998.
   Director: Andrej Krob. Jacek Paruczyński (Vaněk). Tadeusz
   Wnuk (Brewmaster). *Photograph by Bohdan Holomíček.*   172
10. *Unveiling* [Wernisaż], Teatr im. C. Norwida, Jelenia Góra,
    Poland, 1998. Director: Andrej Krob. Lidia Filipek-Czarny
    (Vera). Piotr Konieczyński (Michael). Jacek Paruczyński
    (Fryderyk) [Vaněk]. *Photograph by Bohdan Holomíček.*   172

11. *Protest*, Burgtheater-Akademietheater, Vienna, 1979.
S. Fischer (Staněk). J. Bissmeier (Vaněk). *Photograph by
Elisabeth Hausmann.*   210
12. *Largo Desolato*, Yale Repertory Theater, 1990. Director:
Gitta Honegger. Jan Tříska (Leopold Nettles). Julie White
(Lucy). *Photograph by Jerry Goodstein.*   210
13. From a video production of *Temptation* by the Theater on
a Binge (divadlo na tahu). The main role of Foustka is played
by Václav Havel's brother Ivan. *Photograph by Jaroslav Kukal.*   210
14. Visiting (with Olga Havel) Josef and Zdena Škvorecký's
publishing house Sixty-Eight Publishers in Toronto, Ontario,
February 1990. *Photograph by Helena Wilson.*   246
15. Jangling keys as a symbol of the Velvet Revolution on a
balcony overlooking Wenceslas Square, December 1989.
Photograph by Pavel Štecha.   246
16. Walking through the meadows, about 1996. *Photograph by
Bohdan Holomíček.*   260
17. With Marketa Goetz-Stankiewicz in July 1989, about four
months before the Velvet Revolution. *Photograph courtesy
Marketa Goetz-Stankiewicz.*   260

Publisher's Note

Producing a volume that contains both newly commissioned and reprinted material presents the publisher with the challenge of balancing the desire to achieve stylistic consistency with the need to preserve the integrity of works first published elsewhere. In the Critical Essays series, essays commissioned especially for a particular volume are edited to be consistent with G. K. Hall's house style; reprinted essays appear in the style in which they were first published, with only typographical errors corrected. Consequently, shifts in style from one essay to another are the result of our efforts to be faithful to each text as it was originally published.

Editors' Note

The quotations that appear in italics at the beginning of each essay have been chosen by the editors from other texts in this volume. They are meant to make visible a kind of network that connects at a deeper level the seemingly different concerns of the contributors. The editors hope that this network will help reveal and illuminate the basic unity of this volume.

In order to avoid repetition and because of word limitations, some of the reprinted essays have been abridged; missing portions are indicated by ellipses, and necessary editorial changes and explanations are provided in brackets. Certain significant historical and biographical events, however, necessarily reappear in different contexts.

In addition, the editors have, where necessary, corrected mechanical errors and standardized capitalization.

Some of Havel's plays have been rendered into English by different translators. Within the essays, translations quoted are those chosen by the particular author of the respective text. Details on available translations of Havel's work can be found in the English-language bibliography included in this volume.

The editors would like to thank the contributors for their collaboration at all stages of the manuscript; Sigfridur Gunnlaubsdottir (graduate student at the University of British Columbia) for aiding with research and bibliographies, the staff of the library at Mount Mary College in Milwaukee for prompt and careful work, and Anna Freimanová, secretary to President Havel, for patient support and readiness to help.

Introduction

Marketa Goetz-Stankiewicz

In bringing together this collection of critical essays, we have been very much aware that our subject, Václav Havel, differs from most authors treated in this series in at least three ways. The first thought that comes to mind when one tries to talk about Václav Havel is that he entirely escapes classification—academically, politically, artistically. He is a playwright and a statesman, an essayist on political matters and a teacher of moral values; he has created a special form of literature with his *Letters to Olga* and an original rhetorical genre with his presidential speeches. Perhaps one could say that most people know only a small portion of Havel. Drama critics who analyze his plays are not likely to have much knowledge of his speeches as statesman; those who study the great essays of his "dissident" years will probably have only a fleeting knowledge of his plays; analysts of his presidential speeches are not likely to have studied his *Letters to Olga*. But one thing is certain: political scientists, semioticians, cultural critics, historians, theater people, sociologists, linguists, philosophers—Havel could keep them all busy analyzing, explaining, trying to get at the core of what they take to be the most important aspect of this extraordinary mind.

A second characteristic that distinguishes Havel from other writers is that in all his incarnations Havel has had a strong—possibly even unique—impact on fellow writers and others: he is, to give just a few examples, the man for whom Samuel Beckett wrote the dramatic text *Catastrophe;* the man to whom Tom Stoppard (who also translated his *Largo Desolato*) dedicated his *Professional Foul;* the man about whom Arthur Miller felt that they were "each other's continuation"; the man whom the German writer Heinrich Böll called "a rebel, one of the quite dangerous kind, the gentle and courteous kind"; the man who inspired the philosopher Richard Rorty to analyze his concept of "the order of the spirit"; the man who sent the French philosopher André Glucksmann back to the classics to find that he was "a modern Socrates"; the man who caused his countryman Milan Kundera, himself a master with words, to comment on his "magnificent demystification of language."

A third and crucial difference between Havel and other writers is that while this book is being published, Havel is in the midst of an active political situation that, as political situations go, can change from one day to the next. In other words, the story told here is not completed but continues, open to developments the future may bring. This is why our volume should be read not as a conclusion but rather as an opportunity to take stock of a man whose artistic and intellectual impact on our lives was, is, and in all likelihood will be remarkable.

With these initial caveats in mind, our collection represents an attempt to show Havel from various perspectives; to rotate, as it were, aspects of his work before the reader by letting the contributors, who have very different concerns, illuminate them from various angles. The choice of which texts to include was difficult, indeed painful, and the unsettling thought that we were leaving out important and valuable texts never left us. Still, a choice had to be made, and it was made with the best of intentions.

The reader is bound to notice quickly that the contributions are very different in style and mood: there are political analyses, historical assessments, linguistic interpretations, tributes of sorts, critical perceptions, personal memories, generalizations from afar, and detailed examinations from close by. This diversity of approaches again might prove the point that Havel cannot be fitted into one mode of thought, that he elicits a colorful, possibly even untamable, variety of responses. Indeed one might well paraphrase what has been said of another Prague writer, Franz Kafka: Everyone has his or her own Havel.

Since we have tried to show this outstanding man and his oeuvre in context, inevitably some of the events in Havel's life appear more than once (his youth, his early work in the theater, his "dissident" activities, his prison sentence, his meteor-like rise to the presidency of his country after the demise of Communism). The contributions recast these facts in various contexts. We hope that, rather than irritate or bore the reader, these double reflections might provide possibilities for closer scrutiny and deeper insights. Because biographical details are included in many of the essays, we have decided not to provide data and further description of Havel's life in this introduction.

Grouping the essays (some of which had to be shortened) into logical categories has also proven very difficult. Inevitably some could be shifted into other sections because their concerns overlap. As does any more or less mechanistic order imposed on a realm of plurality and bouts of creative intellect, this "order" in a way violates the basic intention of this collection: to convey Havel's consistent striving against the imposition of an artificial system on the fluid diversity of human life and thought in all its manifestations. However, as Havel himself—and surely also each contributor and reader—knows only too well, some form of order had to be decided upon. So we depend on the perceptiveness of the reader not to take the sections as given and watertight compartments but rather as a flexible guide and companion on the journey toward the reader's own conclusions.

A VERY BRIEF HISTORICAL PERSPECTIVE

Before we introduce the essays contained in this volume, it is fitting to provide a short historical overview of the national and international reception of
Václav Havel, playwright and statesman. Havel as playwright for the international stage was "discovered" when a perceptive German publisher, Klaus
Juncker (at the time director of the theater department of the Rowohlt publishing house in Germany), commissioned the first translations (into German)
of Havel's plays and opened, as it were, the doors to the West for a young
playwright who had just delighted and excited Czech audiences with his first
two plays produced at the Theater on the Balustrade in Prague. This was in
the mid-1960s, the time of the political thaw in Czechoslovakia that culminated in the Prague Spring of 1968, which was cut short by the Soviet occupation of the country. From here on Havel became a banned writer at home
while his fame was growing abroad. Translations of his plays into English
(and other languages) followed rapidly. By 1972 his first three full-length
plays had appeared in Vera Blackwell's English translation. The Orange Tree
Theater in London staged the premières of *The Memorandum,* of *Audience,* and
of *Vernissage [Unveiling]* in 1977, and of *Protest,* as well as *The Increased Difficulty of Concentration,* in 1980. Reviews were enthusiastic. *Audience, Unveiling,*
and *Protest* were produced by the BBC in 1977 with Harold Pinter in the
main parts.

Although world premières of Havel's plays after 1968 had taken place in
Germany—mostly in Vienna but also in Hamburg—the plays soon moved
onto the international stage: *The Beggar's Opera* had its première in Trieste,
Italy, in 1976; *The Mistake* in Stockholm in 1983; *Largo Desolato,* in Marie
Winn's translation, at the Public Theater in New York in 1986, and, in the
same year, in Tom Stoppard's adaptation at the Bristol Old Vic in England;
the English-language première of *Temptation,* in George Theiner's translation,
was staged in Stratford-on-Avon by the Royal Shakespeare Company in
1987. *Slum Clearance* was first performed in Zurich, Switzerland, in 1989.

Among the prizes for his literary works that Havel has received are the
United States Obie Prize for *The Memorandum* (1968) and *The Increased Difficulty of Concentration* (1970), the Austrian State Prize for European Literature
(1968), the Palach Prize (1982), the Dutch Erasmus Prize (1986), and the
Peace Prize of the German Booksellers Association (1989). Of the numerous
honors bestowed on Havel after 1989, in addition to many honorary doctorates, only a few will be mentioned: The Danish Sonning Prize for Contribution to European Civilization (1991), the President's Medal of George Washington University (1993), the Indira Gandhi Prize (1994), the Philadelphia
Liberty Medal (1994), the Dutch Geuzenpenning Medal (1995), the Catalo-
nia International Prize (1995), the Future of Hope Medal in Hiroshima
(1995), and the Fulbright Prize, Washington (1997).

It is obvious that, since 1989, Havel the playwright has been overshadowed by Havel the statesman. Apart from the 1990 film version of *Largo Desolato* (with F. Murray Abraham in the lead role) and a production of *Temptation* at the Public Theater in New York (1989), Havel's plays have been limited to smaller and university theaters. As for critical responses in English, Paul I. Trensky (one of the contributors to this volume) supplied a book, *Czech Drama Since World War II* (1978), which discusses Havel's plays in the context of the theater of the absurd; Marketa Goetz-Stankiewicz (one of the editors of this volume) provided a study, *The Silenced Theatre: Czech Playwrights without a Stage* (1979), which has a lengthy chapter on Havel. Goetz-Stankiewicz has also published *The Vaněk Plays: Four Authors, One Character* (1985), a volume that contains eight one-act plays with the Havelesque character Vaněk as protagonist. Three of these plays are by Havel, while for the others three other Czech playwrights borrowed Havel's character—probably a unique occurrence in the annals of theater. Also providing insight into the Czech context, Robert B. Pynsent's *Questions of Identity: Czech and Slovak Ideas on Nationality and Personality* (1994) contains a lengthy chapter on Havel.

Analyses of and commentaries on Havel's plays have been appearing, scattered through journals and other publications, particularly in *Cross Currents: a Yearbook of Central European Culture* (sadly, the yearbook no longer appears). It would be stretching a point, however, to speak of a critical trend in discussions of Havel's theater. The question of whether it is political theater in the narrower sense of opposing totalitarianism or whether his plays have meaning far beyond a certain time and place is part of the more general discussion about the possible or impossible broader appeal of former "dissident" literature once it has lost its concrete opponent (examples of this discussion can be found in several papers in this volume). There is also increasing interest in the way Havel handles language by putting it, as it were, on dramatic display and relating it, unobtrusively, to issues of ethics and identity.

Since 1989 commentaries have centered almost exclusively on Havel's presidential (and inevitably self-written) speeches, which have caused a considerable stir—a stir of admiration rather than analytical criticism. Contributions in this volume provide some insight into the spectrum of reactions. As time passes, interesting commentaries by Czech social scientists, journalists, and philosophers will surely become available in English and will provide a different and fresh perspective.

What remains to be mentioned are two books: an assessment of Havel's first two years as president by the reporter-writer Michael Simmons, *The Reluctant President: A Political Life of Václav Havel* (1991), and the Czech writer Eda Kriseová's biography *Václav Havel* (1993), translated from the Czech.

An Overview

To provide an overview of Havel's oeuvre is obviously not an easy task to perform with a man who seems to have gone through several metamorphoses and yet has remained remarkably consistent in his basic ideas, tendencies, and intellectual makeup. The four essays we have chosen for this section are meant to serve as an informal entrance to Havel's world: An analysis of Havel's thoughts on politics—in theory and in practice (Wilson); a general overview covering Havel's life as well as his writings up to 1990 (Stern); an assessment of his plays as a statesman's writings (Baranczak); a diagnosis, imbedded in a discussion of the context, of the dichotomy president/writer (Garton Ash).

Paul Wilson's essay, which opens the discussion, is an original contribution written especially for this volume. It enables us to listen to a voice that has provided the whole English-speaking world for many years with what Havel has to say—as dissident and as president. Supported by what he calls the "peculiar intimacy that develops between an author and his translator," Wilson guides us through three different stages of Havel's tireless efforts to lead his country through very difficult times—times that exercise heavy demands on a statesman's wisdom and a nation's resilience. First, during the early periods of post-Communist ferment, Havel had to deal with countless remnants of the old system. Second, his appeal for tolerance and the high moral ground he staked out for politics (consistent with the stance of his famous "dissident" essays) could not avoid, and possibly even contributed to, polarization of his country. Despite his eloquent attempts to preserve federalism, he finally had to preside over the breakup (peaceful though it was) of Czechoslovakia. Third, as a result of his "distrust of party politics" and his "belief in nonpolitical consensual politics," he had to deal with protracted political tensions (lasting until the end of 1997) in his relations with his prime minister. Wilson's essay thus extends a bridge between *Summer Meditations,* written in 1991 after only a year and a half of Havel's presidency, and a crucial address to Parliament, delivered in December 1997 at the end of his eighth year of presidency—in Wilson's words, "a thundering critique of the ideology of the marketplace."

J.P. Stern's essay can well serve as an introduction to the whole Czech context as well as to Havel himself. Stern sets the scene with a description of the Velvet Revolution, then casts his eye back to the "betrayal of Munich" and the subsequent suffering and demoralization of the Czech people that lasted until the miraculous year 1989. Stern then introduces Havel and his family, his beginnings as playwright, his subsequent activities in opposition to the coercive regime, and his 20 "prohibited years"—beginning after the collapse of the Prague Spring in 1968—when, punctuated by jail sentences, he wrote his most incisive essays, as well as some of his best plays. Discussing some of these plays, Stern draws parallels to Kafka, Ionesco, and Stoppard, focusing on the typical Havelesque themes that will become apparent in this volume. Finally, aware of Havel's basic concerns that go far beyond those of the Czech scene, the author opens up the vast questions that affect Havel, his nation, and the world in general: For example, can a country free itself from its traumatic past by a single act of self-liberation? Or, what is the country's relationship to its biggest neighbor, Germany? Although several years have passed since these questions were asked and these lines were written, they have lost little of their topicality.

Musing in a lively way on the issue of a writer in the president's chair, Stanislaw Baranczak scans Havel's life to discover as his distinguishing mark the "balance of his moral strength without fanaticism, and pluralistic tolerance without relativism." Weighing the two categories into which criticism has tended to squeeze Havel's plays—the theater of the absurd on the one hand and the political theater of protest on the other—Baranczak shows that the distinction is not only arid but misses the main thrust of Havel's work (Robert Skloot and Marketa Goetz-Stankiewicz pursue similar thoughts). Both types of plays, Baranczak argues, essentially tackle the same concerns. Even the most realistic of Havel's plays, *Audience,* contains an intrinsic pulse of the absurd. *Audience* is, of course, one of Havel's Vaněk plays, and the Vaněk plays represent a one-of-a-kind literary phenomenon—a constellation of plays employing the same protagonist but written by different authors. (Havel's Vaněk plays are *Audience, Unveiling,* and *Protest.*)

In his discussion of Havel's Vaněk plays, Baranczak displays a particularly valuable insight into Havel's multifaceted approach to his characters: Havel the pluralist registers the voices of "normal" people who want to keep their safe jobs, their little comforts, their reassuring sense of belonging, and he does so not with contempt or aggression but rather with a kind of half-sympathetic understanding. Havel the moralist, however, counters this understanding, whereas Havel the ironist, suspended between the two, shows the double bind of the situation. Havel's Vaněk figure, a hapless yet awkwardly serene Sisyphus, loaded down with a thankless and fruitless task, becomes in Baranczak's analysis a centerpiece of tragedy as well as of farce. This kind of existence, Baranczak shrewdly suggests, is close to playing "a role." Tracing this "triangular trap" from the vaněk plays to *Temptation* and illuminating the "exquisitely equivocal character" of Vaněk "in all its incarnations," Baranczak suggests that Vaněk is the locus of the joined forces of Havel the moralist, Havel the pluralist, and Havel the ironist. As Baranczak puts it, each incarnation expresses "something more essential than the need for power: the need for values."

Timothy Garton Ash's "Prague: Intellectuals and Politicians" (tackling the issue of the writer in politics from another vantage point) was occasioned by Garton Ash's attending the PEN Club meetings in Prague in November

1994 as a newly elected honorary member. His colorful picture, a sort of continuation in depth of his essay "Revolution of the Magic Lantern," centers on the timeless yet intensely topical question, "What is an intellectual?" During the Communist rule the dissenting intellectual played the role of the "conscience of the nation." In a relativistic democratic society his task is much more complex. In 1960, Garton Ash muses, if someone had mentioned the theme "intellectual and politics" we might have thought of Sartre; in the 1990s we think of Václav Havel. Indeed, the latter openly speaks about the paradoxical qualities of this combination: Havel is well aware of the "diabolical temptations of power" but stresses again and again the other side of the scale, the "higher responsibility" required of politicians. Garton Ash explores the capacity of twentieth-century intellectuals to rationalize, intellectualize, and philosophically justify their submission to nefarious regimes, and, in the process, he opens up the critical issue of a political leader's responsibility.

In his closer assessment of Havel's individual case, based on deep and widely demonstrated familiarity with the Central European scene, Garton Ash finds that Havel's voice, which had been an extraordinary and much-needed voice in Europe and beyond, and his image as an intellectual in politics have lately become blurred. The mixed picture emerged after Havel's resignation as president of Czechoslovakia and his later election as president of the Czech Republic. Garton Ash explains this rather subtle change by what he considers the most relevant reason: Havel's refusal to choose between the roles of intellectual and politician. (Wilson's contribution, dealing with precisely this critical period, throws additional light on the issue.)

PERSONAL EXPERIENCES

Balancing the overview of Havel's development are essays that recount overtly personal experiences, thereby adding much color not only to the president-in-his-context picture but also to what seems to be Havel's personality. Stephen Schiff's vivacious account of his 1990 encounter with the brand-new president, his equally new advisor, his dressed-to-kill actress-secretary, and his modish office vividly recreates the atmosphere of the first year or two of a democracy-in-the-making within the old Castle walls. Here Havel, as well as his Central European entourage, appear in a gently ironic light. With Schiff we sigh and sit through a lengthy discussion in Czech between president and chancellor (who happens to be a count); amusedly we watch the president tooting a horn to call his staff or writing part of the new constitution between lunch and tea.

However, the ironic tone (which Havel himself would have vastly enjoyed) gives way to a more serious assessment of Havel the president that seems the more insistent because it follows the playful touch of the first pages. The attitude evolves from the skeptical mood of an uninvolved observer to an admiration of the imposing qualities of this unassuming man "in power." At the same time, Schiff reveals the qualities of leadership and political know-how that have characterized Havel's activities from the beginning of his dissident activities.

Lewis Lapham provides a similar progression of skepticism to admiration in his seemingly lightly penned piece on attending what he expected to be "a political analogue of an Academy Awards ceremony" at the Cathedral of St. John the Divine in northern Manhattan. By taking the reader on a brief trip, laced with shades of humor ranging from chilling sarcasm (politicians and "truth") to twinkle-eyed self-assessment (when he watches his own initially cool attitude surprisingly but inescapably change to warmer colors), Lewis Lapham's story appears to be a demonstration of how a text can rise "to an idea higher than itself." This, it could be argued, is what Václav Havel constantly tries to do—and Lapham seems to understand it on the deepest level, or, rather, he shows us how he arrived at this understanding. Here again, Havel inspires a form of hope.

Rob McRae's brief text "President Havel" bears personal witness to an earlier drastic turning point in the life of Havel as well as of his nation. A diplomat with the Canadian Embassy, McRae describes when Václav Havel was elected to the presidency of Czechoslovakia, and McRae himself was standing shoulder-to-shoulder in a jubilant crowd of thousands on a cold, clear day in December 1989. A few days later, on New Year's Eve, the author walked among hundreds of young people dancing around a giant Christmas tree on the Old Town Square while thousands of candles were flickering through the night. The next day Havel gave his first New Year's Day address, which turned out to be most unusual for a new politician: "a tough lesson" that not only described the country's sorry state but also asked its citizens "to shoulder their part of the responsibility of the horrors of the past." We see that the theme of responsibility was there from the very first moment—an extremely important moment in Czech history.

HAVEL'S POLITICAL THOUGHT

The four papers appearing under this heading again come from very different voices. On closer consideration, however, several common themes and perceptions emerge gradually, like submerged figures that appear when the water is let out of a fountain. First, Havel's resistance to ideology of any sort manifests itself in his political work with the fluid values of a new democracy, just as it did—more obviously perhaps—in his past stance as dissident against the rigid ideology of Communism (Jean Bethke Elshtain and Dean C. Hammer develop thoughts on this theme). Secondly, Havel's emphasis on human responsibility—responsibility for oneself, for one's nation, indeed for the world—finds its way into most assessments of his thought. (Most of the contributors refer to this in one way or another.) Finally, Havel's Shakespearean sense of the world as a stage on which we are all actors, for better or for worse, provides a third common denominator for several of the essays. This sense of the theatrical aspect of nearly all aspects of human life is not limited to the playwright; it is also (as Garton Ash, Schiff, and Lapham have mentioned in different ways in this volume) an integral part of Havel's existence as a statesman. Less obvious is the notion that Havel inspires hope—a very different brand of hope from the frantic "we will do a better job than the previous regime" we tend to hear from politicians of all hues in an average Western democracy. Havel's brand of hope is not for a bright, conflict-free future that had been the sanctioned aim of Communism and was related to a philosophical "principle" by the Marxist philosopher Ernst Bloch. Havel's is a kind of hope whose moral fervor is tempered by irony and whose profound sense of responsibility is softened by his awareness of human weakness that includes himself.

Lifting two significant dates out of the jumble of events, the historian H. Gordon Skilling opens his essay by pointing out the importance of 1918 and 1989 for Czechoslovak history, years in which Tomáš Masaryk and Václav Havel, respectively, moved "from being dissidents to being rulers" and tried "to create a democratic state on the ruins of . . . empires." With punching brevity, Skilling's essay scans the profound differences between these empires (Havel himself has voiced a general comparison of this sort): the absolute, semiconstitutional monarchy of the Habsburg Empire still permitted its subject nations a variety of freedoms; the Soviet empire liquidated politics in any real sense and strictly curbed cultural and religious life. Hence, although the two future statesmen developed their first experience of democracy under rather different circumstances, Skilling still draws some illuminating parallels: Neither Masaryk nor Havel regarded politics "as the be-all and end-all of their lives"; both "spoke of 'non-political' or 'anti-political' politics," yet they were aware of the political significance of their activity; both were nonconformists and critical of established institutions but "did not voice their criticism in narrowly national terms but always within a universal framework"; both derived their moral beliefs from a broad philosophical orientation, which led to their espousing unpopular causes; both men and their peoples—a particularly appealing formulation—"had to 'learn democracy' " after the successful revolutions of 1918 and 1989. Masaryk, who had argued that 50 years were needed to build the foundations for a democratic state, did not live to see the demise of Czechoslovakia after a mere 20 years. To extend Skilling's remarks, suffice it to say that Václav Havel, riding the bucking horse of a new democracy in the first quarter of Masaryk's projection, faces a problem-ridden future in his own nation as well as in the world as a whole.

Jean Bethke Elshtain moves into the actual realm of political theory and argues that Havel, departing from Masaryk's confidence in progress, "found a philosophical home in the writings of Jan Patočka." Elshtain eloquently sets up her territory of discussion within the difficult concepts of theory and practice that, as she puts it, form a "central conundrum to many political theorists and philosophers." Touching on Richard Rorty's commitment to contingency and his construction of the concept of "we liberal ironists," she proceeds to illuminate Havel's individual brand of irony (also discussed in Kenneth S. Zagacki's "Václav Havel and The Rhetoric of Folly") as the source of his "refreshing refusal to be captured by one determined side or another" and his ability to defy easy definition, as well as his view of politics as "a sphere of concrete responsibility." Enlarging on Havel's "resistance to the seduction of ideology" (also mentioned in Dean C. Hammer's essay), Elshtain discovers that the antifoundationalism of Rorty and others still remains "wedded to a teleology of progress" while Havel remains a "practitioner of hope" in a tough-minded, unsentimental way. Havel, basing his thought on the Patočkian "humbly respected boundary of the natural world," regards freedom as merged with responsibility. This, Elshtain argues, "yields a distinctly *political* conclusion: democracy is the political form that permits and requires human freedom as responsibility . . . in service to the notion that there are things worth suffering for." Turning to Havel's letters from prison, *Letters to Olga,* Elshtain explores another deep current in Havel's thought, namely, the crisis of human responsibility, which for Havel is simultaneously a crisis in human identity. At the core of Elshtain's argument is the claim that "for Havel, hope, responsibility, freedom and irony are all of a piece," while, one might add, political theorists today tend to pry these elements apart and send them pulling in different directions.

Kenneth S. Zagacki approaches the many-faceted unity of Havel's political philosophy through the mode of irony and highlights what he calls Havel's "bold and profound rhetoric of folly" against the background—classical, Christian, philosophical—of Havel's presidential speeches. Linguistically suspended between repeated certainties of his country's totalitarian past and the need to formulate the vague hopeful shapes of a democratic future, Havel is seen as, first, using irony to project a mirror in which people can both observe and participate and thus "withdraw from a bi-polar view of the world." Havel's call to humility, second, is obviously in stark contrast to any "leader driven by political power, opportunism or mere pragmatic concern." The third aspect of Havel's "rhetoric of folly" is a special form of empathy that is meant to counteract the dangers of resurgent unrestrained nationalism.

Dean C. Hammer's thoughts on Havel's "Construction of a Democratic Discourse" takes on the topical question of what various commentators have called "Havel's postmodernism" (rejection of emancipatory narratives, critique of ideological thinking, and uneasiness with the notion of the intellectual as master). Suggesting that we might read Havel's politics in a less conformist and more fruitful way, Hammer argues that Havel, finding himself in the position of a political leader who is faced with "a dissolved political discourse," actually had to "redefine the identity of the state." This meant that his task began where postmodernism's ended. Here, then, is Hammer's important contribution to the discussion of Havel and postmodernism. By stressing the importance of regaining "control over one's own sense of responsibility," Havel departs from both Derrida's insistence on questioning "the codes inherited from ethics and politics" and Foucault's attack on the "tyranny of globalizing discourses."

Secondly, according to Hammer, Havel turns our attention to the importance of institutions supporting an environment of responsible participation, while postmodern thinkers have consistently held suspect "anything that formalizes human action." This, Hammer remarks, is the privilege of academe but of no use to anyone faced with the actual task of having to create a new constitution, as well as to establish new institutions. Hammer also comments on the magnitude of this task—a two-front battle against two competing notions of politics: the remnants of Communism, which reduces politics to ideological slogans, and the new spirit of faction, a familiar result of democratic government. All this sums up Havel's attempt to "construct a politics in a postmodern world."

HAVEL THE PLAYWRIGHT

The challenge of creating responsible politics in a postmodern age is related to the question of human identity, an issue Havel had long explored in his drama. Seven essays explore this concern and others as they examine Havel the playwright. In his careful analysis of *The Garden Party,* Paul I. Trensky compares Václav Havel with the absurdist playwrights who explore the modern human's identity as an initial vacuum, interchangeable and exclusively formed by the environment. Illuminating the play's meticulously composed verbal structure, Trensky shows that the play's language consists of "a collection of prefabricated clichés" interspersed with false syllogisms and circular logic, misplaced theoretical jargon, and nonsense proverbs masquerading as folksy wisdom. Trensky stresses that what is of basic importance—not just in this play but also in Havel's subsequent plays—is the nonrepresentational quality of the language; in addition, the movement of the drama consists in "changes in tempo, repetition, retardation." In a challenging insight that Trensky provides us early in the game of Havel criticism, Havel's amazing first play could thus be seen as performing a critique of an important tradition of Western thought: its obsession with thinking in categories.

Phyllis Carey's study of *The Memorandum* complements Trensky's reading of *The Garden Party* by examining even further the dehumanizing tendencies in Western thought. Using Havel's analysis of totalitarianism as an offspring of Western philosophical tendencies and as a warning to the West, Carey sees in the bureaucratic mechanisms, the artificial languages, and the human adaptation to systems that *The Memorandum* portrays a domination of the technical that ends up enslaving the human. Even Gross, the main character who expounds on humanistic principles, ends up using those principles as an excuse for not acting humanely: "What is clear is that Gross's identity—like that of the other characters—consists of being a functionary of the system." In her analysis of the interlocking systems of the play and of Ptydepe, the artificial language based on scientific principles that is supposed to make communication more precise, Carey observes that the most sophisticated techniques often become thin veneers for a loss of the human and a regression to the bestial.

In the tradition of its illustrious predecessors, John Gay's *The Beggar's Opera* and Brecht's *Die Dreigroschenoper (The Threepenny Opera)*, Havel's play on the same topic, *The Beggar's Opera*, began with a bang. But in contrast to the first two, the bang of Havel's play came from the underground. Its "illegal" première in a village near Prague in 1975 had serious repercussions for most of the participants. By calling the play "a representation of collective schizo-phrenia" and tracing the social and political background of the event, Peter Steiner provides an illuminating picture of how the regime dealt with "sub-versive" works (Douglas Soderberg calls them "crimes of the imagination") in "normalized" Czechoslovakia. Steiner discusses the phenomenon of commu-nicative duplicity as one of the symptoms of this collective social schizophre-nia. Havel focused his renowned essay "The Power of the Powerless" (written three years after the fateful staging of *The Beggar's Opera*) on this phenome-non. Wrapping a statement in an ideological garment—that is, justifying it officially as worthy and progressive and then undercutting it privately—all this is obviously fertile ground for collective schizophrenia. But there is still "another level to the game of deception": the dealings of the omnipotent and allegedly omniscient secret police. The regime's need to prove this omni-science (ordinarily not all that easy to come by) gave rise to a brand-new regime-sanctioned positive hero, the double agent. Providing an actual live example of such a hero, Steiner plumbs the depths of the quicksand of com-munication and then turns to the artistic mirror of this situation: Havel's *The Beggar's Opera*. The highly entertaining characters that populate the play lie, seduce, manipulate, and pretend, as the audience gradually discovers that no one is to be trusted. Steiner, a knowledgeable, lively guide, takes us through the shifting levels of the play until we arrive at an end that fails to resolve but opens up levels of deception ad infinitum. Yet this seemingly dark ending, pessimistic despite the audience's amusement, ultimately reveals, Steiner sug-gests, an implicit higher order—the order of *play*: "By creating a fictional uni-verse, play splits reality from its representation" and renders possible a mode of "detached reflection." When the curtain falls on *The Beggar's Opera*, the audience's laughter, still lingering in the air, is calmly silenced by thought.

Moving the discussion into the broader context of international theater, Robert Skloot points out that Havel's plays, not having proved to be "good box office," are hitherto practically unknown in America, except for a few productions in university or avant-garde theaters. Having thus set up a sort of empty stage for Havel, Skloot proceeds to draw comparisons with four well-known twentieth-century playwrights: Harold Pinter, Tom Stoppard, Eugène Ionesco, and Samuel Beckett. Skloot sees Pinter as exploring existential freedom and making "confinement a condition of life," whereas Havel, "deeply ideological in both attitude and experience," regards the source of conflict as triggered exclusively by the political situation. Also, Pinter's "wide range of psychological subtexts" distinguishes him from Havel's "very narrow choice of psychological motive." While one may argue with Skloot's assumptions, his juxtaposition of Pinter and Havel raises some intriguing questions about both authors.

Skloot's resourceful comparison of Havel with Stoppard illuminates both playwrights' deep mistrust of all orthodoxy and authority and their shared delight in the liberating power of satirical language. Although Stoppard was born in Czechoslovakia, he did not grow up there. Nevertheless, both he and Havel use the technique of "time slips"—the audience hears words that have lost their objective meaning and witnesses "a world careening out of control." Ionesco's enormous influence on Czechoslovak culture emerging from Stalinism and undergoing the famous political thaw of the 1960s resulted in a wave of literary works, particularly plays, that show, in Skloot's words, "Absurdism with a political face." Finally there are Beckett's clowns who keep waiting for Godot and express the irreducible minimum of human freedom. Havel, too, is seen as part of this tendency, although Skloot's critical stance is that Havel refuses "to extend these wonderful comedies into a more profound and troubling territory" that, according to Skloot, would have had positive results on Havel's playwriting.

Shifting Havel's work into the scholarly context of semiotics, Michael L. Quinn uses the "negative theory" of delirium—a theory of incoherence and a lost sense in communication—to interpret the makeup of Havel's dramatic characters. Quinn, using the development in theory from Shklovsky and Jakobson to Foucault and Deleuze, discusses the nature of Havel's early plays written in collaboration with Prague writers, as well as his early awareness (in the Prague of the 1960s, Ionesco was in the air) of the loss of connection between signifier and signified. The essay subsequently analyzes Havel's plays as variations on the theme of delirium, for example, "the delirious potential of logic" *(The Garden Party),* the "formally imposed confusion" *(The Increased Difficulty of Concentration),* "the political pitfalls of delirious subjectivity" *(Largo Desolato),* "the delirious permutations combining characters, scenes, actions and dialogue" *(The Mountain Hotel),* the recognition that deception is the rule *(The Beggar's Opera).* Havel's dramas, Quinn concludes, show that he manages to attain a careful balance "between the expression of delirious characters and the coherent audience interpretation." This, in turn, means that "our identity is never simply defined in terms of our individual properties. It also places us in some social space." Hence the semiotic theory of mistaken references and distorted messages sheds light on the work of a playwright who would surely disclaim being a practicing semiotician.

When the Yale Repertory Theater staged *Largo Desolato,* directed by Gitta Honegger, in 1990, with the eminent Czech stage and film actor Jan Tříska (who is also a good friend of Václav Havel) in the main role, Douglas Soderberg was the production dramaturge. His "Life under Absurdity" provides Soderberg's reflections about this experience. Leopold Nettles, the fumbling protagonist of *Largo Desolato,* may remind us of Beckett's two clowns who keep waiting, as well as Kafka's Josef K. who does not wait and is arrested. Providing yet another perspective on Havel's absurdism, Soderberg distinguishes Havel's theater, on the one hand, from "absurd theater," where it had been shelved by orderly academics, and, on the other hand, from "political theater," where it had been pushed by supportive reviewers anxious to squeeze out topicality. Although the events of *Largo Desolato* can be seen as rooted in a man's day-to-day existence under a repressive regime, the relevance of the play goes far beyond Communist Czechoslovakia. The restless, anxious, hypochondriac, has-been writer—hapless, helpless, swinging back and forth between his wife, girlfriend, and admiring woman student, swallowing pills, frightened of the doorbell that admits seemingly innocuous but actually dangerous people (or are they seemingly dangerous but actually innocuous?)—no longer knows who he is, for he is trying to be what others want him to be or tell him he is. Relating the tense situation of a suppressed society under Communism to the "free" existence in American democracy where self-censorship is only less obvious, where the rebel thinkers and artists who commit the "crimes of the imagination" are easily caught in Leopold Nettles's Catch-22 situation, Soderberg shows us (as do other contributors dealing with Havel's theater) that, like Havel's other plays, his "dissident" play *Largo Desolato* is no stranger to our world.

Finally, Marketa Goetz-Stankiewicz explores the assumptions of what is meant by "political theater" and shows the basic opaqueness of the concept if applied to well-known plays of Western theater. Goetz-Stankiewicz, raising the issue of the playwright Havel's critique of language—a political topic per se?—centers her argument on the protagonist's linguistic acrobatics in Havel's Faust play *Temptation* as a contemporary average Faust figure seduces (linguistically!) an average woman, Marketa. As in nearly all of Havel's plays—but here harder to detect because not overtly farcical—the pliable instrument of persuasive language is played to the hilt. And it achieves its purpose. Adherents of Havel the author of political plays will detect the seductive quality of loaded language without difficulty. However, as other contributors have pointed out, on closer inspection Havel's language acrobats turn out to be relevant (even "politically" relevant) to our own society. Goetz-Stankiewicz considers these rhetorical outbursts to be subtle examples of double play or a double role—half-concealed and hovering on the flickering borderline of good and evil. Havel's audacious new version of the ancient Faust theme, mingling histrionics with profundity and political insight with philosophical speculation, reveals, as has been noted several times in these essays, deep kinship with Kafka and Beckett. Havel's theater, Goetz-Stankiewicz claims, is "surprising, tantalizing and disturbing for all of us."

HAVEL IN THE MINDS OF HIS COUNTRYMEN

This volume also contains four deeply personal, and thus especially engaging, short contributions from Czech compatriots: a writer, a philosopher, a sociologist, and a theater director. Perhaps they show, once again, that "everyone has his or her own Havel."

The first selection in this section is "That Bourgeois Brat!," written by the eminent Czech writer Josef Škvorecký, who with his wife ran Sixty-Eight Publishers, the first to publish Havel's plays in English. Škvorecký provides three bright flashbacks into the past: the first to the 1960s, the turbulently elated period of the political thaw in Czechoslovakia when Havel, a mere 30 then, showed his courage by a dissenting vote at a meeting of the Writers' Union; the second to Toronto of the 1980s, when Havel (in prison then) received one of the first of his many honorary doctorates; the third to more recent times, with Havel, president now, on a visit to Toronto. So here we have glimpses of Havel the rebel, the prisoner, and the president.

The philosopher Václav Bělohradský, who teaches at the University of Trieste in Italy, recalls an experience in 1979 when Havel's "The Power of the Powerless" struck skeptical Italian students "like a thunderbolt." They strongly responded to Havel's claim that totalitarianism was "a caricature of modern life in general," as well as to his later famous formulation about "living in truth," as opposed to the "meaningless imperative of economic growth" of Western democracies. The image of a generalized abstract promise—be it the stateless society of Communism or the sanctity of progress at any cost—could easily "become another variant of enslavement." Bělohradský sees the struggle with various petrified forms and structures as Havel's basic commitment.

The sociologist Jiřina Šiklová's refreshingly colloquial and lively text comes from the center of Prague as well as from a long and courageous association with the dissident scene under the Communist regime. Against this background, and informed by a perceptiveness that does not become scholastic or speculative but remains, as it were, within the hustle of daily reality, Šiklová provides us with an informal, common-sense diagnosis of the by no means smooth relationship between Havel the president and his people. Šiklová knows the secret connection between popular worship and ready, conformist criticism; she knows that the fostered reduction of people's responsibility under the previous regime was very hard to overcome; she is aware of how soothing and attractive it can be to consider oneself a victim of circumstances, of politics, of the government. And she reminds us of the enormous difficulties and basically stark loneliness a position of power entails. Besides, she also knows that Havel rejects the concept of power as such and that the extreme pressures and demanding tasks that go with his position render petty criticism, to which he has been exposed, irrelevant.

Andrej Krob, the Prague theater director, has, as he says, "lived with Havel's characters for 20 years" in an ever-growing relationship. In 1975 he directed *The Beggar's Opera* in its by now well-known, "illicit," and, under Communism, *only* production in a village near Prague, and since 1990 he has staged several of Havel's plays. Musing over the "timeliness" of events, Krob finds that his 1997 staging of *The Garden Party* has turned out to be his "most timely" Havel production. Stressing the topicality of Havel's first full-length play, the director throws light on its more secret dimensions: for example, how the "teachability" of a man (the protagonist of *The Garden Party*) is connected with his identity. Today the Czech people's "identity," Krob argues, has become two-pronged: on the one hand, it appears that the newly gained freedom from a coercive regime has provided everyone with the identity of decision making, developing one's own talent, and testing one's reasoning powers. On the other hand, however, this newly won identity is newly threatened: giant computers save our memories, assemble evidence, and make up their own universe, which we understand less and less the less it needs us. Havel's plays, his Prague director feels, "are also about this!"

HAVEL ON THE ROLE OF THE PRESIDENT

During a sort of interregnum, late in 1992, between having resigned as the president of Czechoslovakia and deciding to accept the presidency of the Czech Republic, Havel wrote an essay for a Czech journal on the role of the Czech president. This text, until now not available in English translation, is a unique document, summarizing what Havel sees as the values, aims, rights, and tasks of a Czech president. The implications of this document, however, go far beyond the borders of his own country in Central Europe and, in their refreshing avoidance of political jargon, in their unpretentiousness and yet hard-nosed awareness of reality, should be of considerable interest to anyone concerned with the organization of our contemporary world. The essay was made available to us through the generosity of Paul Wilson, and we are most happy to include it here in his translation.

AND FINALLY

At the outset of these remarks we mentioned the variety of views and approaches to which we playfully referred as "everyone having his or her own Havel." Now it is time to point to the profound connections between these various images and distill, albeit in an imperfect way, what seem to us the most significant features of Václav Havel's thought.

Taking helpful and revealing clues from the included essays, we can suggest the following observations: in Havel's dramatic universe people manipulate and pretend, use inflated language and betray, rationalize and use language to conceal rather than to display. But all along we are reminded by the plays' structures that the author uses his characters as musical themes to compose his patterns of human folly. So, as we laugh our way through the plots, we also are stirred to thought, for the playwright's aim, as he has told us, "is not to soothe the viewer with a merciful lie or cheer him up with a false offer to sort things out for him. . . . I'm trying to do something else: to propel him, in the most drastic possible way, into the depth of the question he should not, and cannot avoid asking. . . ."[1]

Turning to Havel's essays and speeches, translated and distributed practically all over the world, we find a rich tapestry of moral admonishments (awareness of individual responsibility); insights into sociopsychological issues (the complex nature of identity); awareness of global problems (the importance of ecology); reasons for strife (rabid nationalism). All this is never presented in a pedantic way, but is steeped in familiarity with human weakness, illuminated by the rainbow colors of knowing irony. Still—Havel's paradoxes are with us—it is hard-hitting, and its thrust finds its aim.

An attempt to look at Havel's life through the grid of the larger cultural patterns of our civilization might open some other venues of approach. As has been variously pointed out, paradox has almost become a trademark of Havel's personality and the course of his life. But the paradoxes one detects when surveying from some distance the less obvious pattern of his life reach further than those he has referred to himself. One can see Havel, for example, as an Antigone figure (a rebel) who has become a Creon figure (the guardian of state law); likewise, he can be seen as a modern Hamlet, preoccupied with large questions of guilt, truth, and responsibility, who finds himself suddenly thrust into the position of Fortinbras, where he has to take charge of pragmatic cleanup tasks; and, perhaps more imaginatively, one can see him as a kind of Sisyphus performing seemingly endless, fruitless labor for many years (as dissident) and then ending up as a sort of Promethean figure, faced with the task of fashioning, out of the clay of his paralyzed nation, new images of the world, a fresh sense of life's possibilities, a restored realization of the nature of duty—in other words, a new humanity.

So who is Václav Havel? We do not pretend that this collection will provide an answer to that question. We hope, however, that readers will close the book with at least the intention of finding out more about this man who is leaving his imprint on the twentieth century and, in all likelihood, beyond.

Notes and References

1.   Václav Havel, *Disturbing the Peace: A Conversation with Karel Hvížd'ala,* trans. Paul Wilson (New York: Knopf, 1990), 199.

AN OVERVIEW

◆

Václav Havel in Word and Deed

PAUL WILSON

{Havel's rhetoric of folly is valuable, too, for its ability to suspend practical discussion and judgment long enough for audiences to re-orient themselves. . . . The role of fool was important for Havel in this regard since folly promoted a certain skepticism about human activity without damaging Havel's moral authority.

—Kenneth S. Zagacki}

. . . Suit the action to the word, the word to the action, with this special obser-vance, that you o'erstep not the modesty of nature; for anything so overdone is from the purpose of playing, whose end, both at the first and now, was and is, to hold, as 'twere the mirror up to nature, to show virtue her own feature, scorn her own image, and the very age and body of the time his form and pres-sure.

—Hamlet, to the players, III.ii.15–20

Recently a colleague at the Canadian Broadcasting Corporation came to me for help in preparing a radio obituary for Václav Havel. He had just been readmitted to the hospital barely a year after undergoing an operation to remove a malignant growth from one of his lungs. By an unfortunate coinci-dence, the Czech Republic was also facing health problems of its own. Prime Minister Václav Klaus, star of his country's much-vaunted privatization pro-gram, had been forced to resign along with several of his key ministers in the wake of a corruption scandal. The role of the president suddenly became cru-cial once more. Against the advice of his doctors, Havel went back to work, doing what he does best: confronting a crisis with eloquence and a sense of drama. On 9 December 1997 he delivered one of his forceful speeches to the Czech Senate and the Chamber of Deputies.[1] It was a thundering critique of the ideology of the marketplace and a resonant reiteration of Havel's belief in the importance of an open, civil society.

Obituaries of famous people are generally prepared in advance, and there was nothing unusual or ghoulish in my colleague's exercise. But I still

This essay was written specifically for this volume and is published for the first time by permission of the author.

found it unsettling to have to think about summing up a remarkable career that was clearly still far from over.

A translator develops a peculiar intimacy with his or her author. Part of it has to do with the intellectual effort of engaging with what literary critics like to call "the text." Far from being a sequence of words on a page, this "text" is actually a living piece of the author's mind, and the trick in translation is to make it live as full a life in the new tongue as it did in the old.

In the case of Václav Havel, this sense of his ideas as living things has only been intensified by the fall of Communism. I began in the early 1980s by translating the work of a little-known writer whose words were meant to give power and hope to people caught in the toils of a totalitarian regime in the middle of Europe. After 1989 I translated many of Havel's major speeches and other writings, but now those same words and ideas, often delivered on world stages, had become agents in a political and economic struggle to build a new democratic edifice on the rubble left behind by totalitarianism. Because of my familiarity with the Czech scene and with Havel's ideas, I watched, perhaps more critically than most, the unfolding drama of Havel's efforts to guide his country through a difficult period of transition. This domestic drama has been in part the story of the collision of Havel's ideas with what he calls the post-Communist syndrome and with political trends and sometimes, as well, with politicians who have tried to take the country in directions Havel has thought wrongheaded. The impact of this drama, or at least of what we have seen of it so far, is rather like the impact of his plays, which often portray good people caught in the complexities and ambiguities of real life, and where their ideas, however good and true they may be, do not always triumph.

The drama begins in November 1989—and at first, there is a fairy-tale aspect to it, one that has not escaped Havel himself, for in his early public speeches as president he often claimed bewilderment, and even shock, at his sudden rise to the realm of "high politics" as he likes to call it. His appearance at the head of a citizens' movement—the Civic Forum—that brought an end to 40 years of Communist rule in November 1989 seemed magical and full of hope. He had everything Western politicians seemed to lack: a clear set of political convictions broad enough to cut across the lines of party politics and the courage of those convictions, for he had gone to prison for them. More than that, his charisma, the aura of a funky Camelot set in the fabled splendor of Prague, the fascination he exercised on intellectuals, artists, pop stars, and politicians, and his unshakable faith in the force of his ideals had made him a hero. He seemed the platonic ideal of a philosopher-king made flesh.

Havel also brought to his role as president a political track record of sorts. As he said in his introduction to *Summer Meditations*, a book he wrote in mid-1991, "When I get involved in something (in my usual all-out manner) I often find myself at the head of it before long—not because I am more clever or more ambitious than the rest, but because I seem to get along with people, to be able to reconcile and unite them, to act as a sort of unifying agent."[2] Havel was alluding here to his experience, in the 1960s, as the editor of a small, radical magazine; as chief spokesman for the non-Communist faction in the Czechoslovak Writers' Union; and, in the 1970s and 1980s, as one of the founders and spokesmen of Charter 77, the first human rights movement in Czechoslovakia and a forerunner of the Civic Forum. All of these experiences were political in the sense that Havel understood politics, as the care and feeding of the immediate needs and interests of a community. He had also learned early on that politics is a struggle best confined to concrete issues, rather than broad principles. It was this understanding of politics that he brought to his role as chief negotiator of the Civic Forum when it sat down with the Communist Party to work out the transition of power. Not surprisingly he was perceived—both by those who worked closely with him and by the general public, to whom he spoke during the mass meetings—as the real leader of the Velvet Revolution, and this perception made him the natural and popular choice for president.

Havel still had to be persuaded to accept the post, but what finally appeared to overcome his reluctance was a principle he had held to all his life and one he often expressed in this straightforward proposition: "It simply seemed to me," he said in *Summer Meditations,* "that since I had been saying A for so long, I could not refuse to say B; it would have been irresponsible of me to criticize the Communist regime all my life and then, when it finally collapsed (with some help from me), refuse to take part in the creation of something better" (*Summer Meditations,* xvi). It was a logical formula lifted directly from one of his early plays, *The Garden Party.*

The collapse of Communism placed an enormous burden on the new politicians of Eastern Europe. Havel was not alone in being shocked and unprepared for what happened when the lid was taken off the Communist pressure cooker. He described the result as "an enormous and dazzling explosion of every imaginable human vice" (*Summer Meditations,* 1). The crime rate soared; pornography flourished; racism—especially directed against the local Roma population—became a major unresolved problem. Party politics replaced the earlier, broader coalitions represented by the Civic Forum and the Public Against Violence—both of which split into smaller, more narrowly political parties. As the process of privatizing state-owned property got under way, there was massive corruption at all levels and people with ill-gotten gains jockeyed for favorable positions in the new economy. Demagogues and populists flourished, for simple solutions often seem most attractive in times of transition. And something that looked like Slovak nationalism began to raise its head, more vocal than deep-seated at first, yet disturbing. Still, Havel continued to believe that, as he put it, "a huge potential of goodwill is slumbering within our society. It's just that it's incoherent, suppressed, confused, crippled and perplexed—as though it does not know . . . where or how to find meaningful outlets" (*Summer Meditations,* 3–4). The job for the new politicians, Havel felt, was to support and liberate this potential. Havel was in fact turning an old adage on its head: it was not entirely true that a country gets the politicians it deserves; a society is also the mirror of the kind of politicians it gets. It is the politicians who set the tone of public life, and if they are vicious, uncivilized, and unprincipled, public life will be vicious, uncivilized, and unprincipled.

Havel's great faith going into his job was that despite the limitations of his office, he could help bring about a positive change in society. "I don't know whether directness, truth and the democratic spirit will succeed," he said. "But I do know how not to succeed, which is by choosing means that contradict the ends. As we know from history, that is the best way to eliminate the very ends we set out to achieve. In other words, if there is to be any chance at all of success," he wrote, "there is only one way to strive for decency, reason, responsibility, sincerity, civility, and tolerance, and that is decently, reasonably, responsibly, sincerely, civilly, and tolerantly" (*Summer Meditations*, 7–8). It was a faith that would, at times, be sorely tried.

By nature Havel is an activist, but his activism is of a special kind. He's a visionary tinkerer; he can imagine the broad outlines of the kind of society he would like to see emerge from the post-Communist ferment, and he has an artist's love of getting involved in the detailed steps necessary to get there. Among the many frustrations Havel experienced in his term as federal president—frustrations that hover beneath the surface of all his published writings since then—was his lack of power to act in matters of crucial importance to the emerging democracy. The first of these problems had to do with coming to terms with the past, dealing with the old regime, or deciding what to do about the old Communists. Czechoslovakia was unique among the countries of Central and Eastern Europe in that the Communist takeover in 1948 was an internal Czechoslovak matter. The Czechs (more than the Slovaks) had a strong indigenous Communist Party, and throughout the four decades of its absolute rule—from 1949 to 1989—it was a mass party, with a relatively high percentage of the population belonging to it. Its grip on society was so complete that in order to hold almost any position of importance, you had to belong to the Party or be beholden to it in some way. That grip loosened during the Prague Spring of 1968, but it took an invasion by the Warsaw Pact to restore it. In 1989 it was still firmly in place, if not in control. And though it finally gave up its claim to absolute power during the Velvet Revolution, its organizational network, its core membership, its statutes, and to some extent even its influence, remained intact, and it continued life as a legitimate part of the new political scene.

Meanwhile many of the former opponents of Communism who had been heroes of the Velvet Revolution—and who constituted Havel's strongest support group—were gradually edged out of public life. The reasons for this were complex. One of them was the eventual bifurcation of the Civic Forum into two separate political parties, one of which, the Civic Movement, contained most of the former dissidents and proved itself politically inept in electoral politics. But there may have been a deeper reason that had to do with a perception among an electorate eager to shed the past that many former dissidents—including Havel himself—were simply too soft on Communism.

The reason for this apparent softness, on Havel's part at least, went back to his earlier thinking about the problem of totalitarianism. In what is perhaps his most famous essay, "The Power of the Powerless," from 1978, Havel examined at some length the complex network of power relations established by the Communists and how intimately involved every citizen was in the mechanisms of power, regardless of how he or she actually felt about Communism. Everyone took part in the rituals by which this power confirmed itself; everyone therefore had a share in the responsibility for the general misery of society. At the time he wrote this, Havel's point was that if enough people revolted—by living according to standards of their own truth, rather than acquiescing in the lies of the regime—the regime would eventually collapse of its own inertia. Havel's analysis was meant to lead to action—not organized, mass action, but to a revolt of individuals, a revolt of conscience.

Once the tables were turned, Havel gave the argument a new twist: it became an appeal for tolerance. In his first New Year's address as president he said, "We had all become used to the totalitarian system and accepted it as an unchangeable fact and thus helped to perpetuate it. In other words, we are all—though naturally to differing extents—responsible for the operation of the totalitarian machinery; none of us is just its victim: we are also its co-creators." Havel hoped this tolerance and understanding would lead to a new kind of democratic activism. "We cannot blame the previous rulers for everything, not only because it would be untrue, but because it could blunt the duty each of us faces today, namely, the obligation to act independently, freely, reasonably, and quickly."[3]

His appeal for tolerance was admirable and consistent, but it did not offer much of a guide to action, nor did it match the popular mood. Many people felt the need for some judicial or political mechanism to help root out those who embodied the old system and were standing in the way of the new. The frustration, expressed most clearly and persistently from "below"—that is, by people from the municipalities outside of Prague where they had to deal with the old Communists on a daily basis—was one of the reasons why so many voters supported parties, like Klaus's ODS, that played a strong anti-Communist card.

There were other, more practical reasons why Havel and the other leaders were soft on Communism: if Communists and ex-Communists were to be disqualified from public life altogether—by whatever means—the country would lose most of the people who had any experience in public administration and in running the economy. On 9 December 1989, at one of the last joint meetings of the Civic Forum and the Communist Party leaders, Havel told his opposite numbers across the table: "As I and many of my friends have often stressed at various public meetings in the last few days, we believe that this . . . was not a revolt against the Communists as such, but against totalitarianism, against the old order. Its aim was human freedom, human dignity. From this point of view, I think it's better to have a person who is a friend of the new order and a member of the Communist Party, than a person who is a friend of the old order, and not a Communist."[4]

Havel was speaking here of the first interim government to be installed by the Velvet Revolution; it was to include both Communist and non-Communist ministers. As it turned out, that government did not meet the approval of "the streets"—that is, of the large public meetings backing the Civic Forum at the time—and it was soon replaced by another interim government with almost no Communist ministers. But the sentiment Havel was expressing here was genuine, not just a negotiating tactic, and he remained faithful to it. As a political position it was both generous and pragmatic. But by consistently staking out the moral high ground, Havel and his allies left the anti-Communist field open to fanatical parties and politicians who were out for blood. Because the center of the political spectrum—which Havel and his allies undoubtedly represented—was unoccupied on the practical question of what to do with the Communists, the issue became polarized. The solution legislators came up with, the so-called Lustration or Screening Law, which denied certain public positions to members of the Communist Party and proven secret police informers, created precisely the kind of divisiveness Havel had striven to avoid.

The second major issue upon which Havel faced an intractable problem was the issue of Slovak nationalism. As long as he was president, Havel's position was—and had to be—on the side of the federation. Before that, however, like so many of his fellow Czechs, he had never given the matter much consideration—at least in his writing—because in his adult lifetime it had never really been a serious political problem. The country did not become a federation until 1969 anyway; before that it had been a unitary state, with a single Parliament in Prague. Granting Slovakia sovereignty and its own assembly in 1969, a year after the Soviet invasion, was an empty gesture under Communist rule, and no one knew this better than the Slovaks themselves.

This is not the time to go into the unfortunate history of the long series of negotiations that took place between the Czechs and the Slovaks after the Velvet Revolution, when many Slovak politicians saw their chance to right some historical wrongs. The beginning, however, is worth mentioning because it seemed so trivial at first. It started in early 1990 with an innocent bit of tinkering on Havel's part: he wanted the official name of the country changed from the Czechoslovak Socialist Republic to something else, preferably just the Czechoslovak Republic. But a major political battle broke out over the new name, revealing some interesting differences in perception. The Slovaks wanted the word Czechoslovakia to be written with a hyphen and a capital *S* on Slovakia. Many Czechs were outraged because the implication was that the two republics were somehow separate but equal, and it evoked memories of the 1930s when the word was spelled that way by proponents of a divided Czechoslovakia, some of whom were Nazi sympathizers.

The irony of the "hyphen war," as it was called, was that each side interpreted the hyphen in opposite ways. The Czechs called it a *rozdělovník*—that is, something that separates or divides. The Slovaks referred to it as a *spojovník*—something that links or joins two components of a word. A further irony was that when the skirmish was over, each side went on writing the name of the country in its own way, and people for the most part ignored the new, compromise name: The Czech and Slovak Federal Republic. So what began as an apparently superficial argument ended as the opening round in a struggle that eventually led to the breakup of the country.

Havel argued vigorously for the idea of a Czechoslovak state. His main arguments, however, came not from politics but from the realm of philosophy and from the thinking he had done about the nature of human identity, particularly while he was in prison in the 1980s. In a speech to the Federal Assembly on 17 September 1990, he traced the roots of the problem to what he called the "unhappy idea of a single Czechoslovak nation." He expressed sympathy for the Slovak frustration with the existing federal system. But, he said, while there is undoubtedly no real Czechoslovak nation, there is a "federal people." He went on to explain his idea this way: "The identity of each one of us is composed of several layers. We are members of our family, of our profession, of our community, of our nation, of our state as a whole, of Europe. And if a citizen of California feels like a Californian, it doesn't mean that he can't, at the same time, feel like an American. When a lesser entity delegates certain functions to a higher entity, this does not mean that something is cut away from the lesser entity, that is, it is not something negative; it also means positive participation in the higher entity. If you will allow me a comparison: if a professor of biology is proud of the department of natural sciences where he works, and at the same time, is proud of the university of which it is a part, there is no contradiction here. It simply mirrors the fact that while his faculty may contribute to the good name of the university, the university at the same time provides the proper environment for the development of the faculty. If we manage to create an analogous situation in our constitutional arrangements, then we can feel a natural pride both in our national identity—as Czechs or Slovaks—and our state identity, as Czechoslovakia."[5]

Havel's argument was a sophisticated one, similar in some regards to the classic federalist arguments made by great American or Canadian political thinkers of the past. But by this time, the political disintegration of the federal state had clearly progressed beyond the point of no return. To be fair, he tried at the same time to persuade the Federal Assembly to put a series of constitutional amendments in place that would give him the political power to intervene should Parliament become immobilized on the question of Slova-kia. But all his proposals were rejected, leaving him powerless to act after the June 1992 elections when a referendum might have stayed the process of dis-integration.

Havel's problems with the legislature point to a third aspect of his thinking as a dissident: his belief in nonpolitical, consensual politics and his deep distrust of party politics. The notion of a nonpolitical politics—of a pol-itics understood at the deepest level as involvement in the life of a commu-nity—was ideal for the kind of opposition Havel and his colleagues offered to the totalitarian regime. But once that regime vanished into history, politics in the narrower and more common sense of the word took hold. Dozens of polit-ical parties sprang up, some of them with ridiculous programs. But serious or frivolous, political parties remain, in a parliamentary democracy, the most effective means of organizing and mobilizing public opinion behind a specific set of policies. Havel does not belong to any political party; as president he must remain above the fray of party politics, and he has always resisted attempts to politicize his office. This position suits his nature and is consistent with his idea of politics as the art of consensus-making. But it has often left him without the practical tools to effect specific changes in domestic politics that could bring Czech society, in practical ways, closer to his vision of what it should be.

That vision is most clearly expressed in *Summer Meditations,* a book he wrote in the middle of his first (and only) term as president of Czechoslovakia. In it Havel emphasizes the importance of our understanding of human iden-tity, a notion that he explores most fully in his plays. He uses a metaphor based on the notion of home—or *domov* in Czech, which suggests something more fundamental than home in English, more like a dwelling place. Havel says that our home is really a set of concentric circles, beginning with one's own room and eventually moving outward to include the whole world. "Every circle, every aspect of the human home, has to be given its due. It makes no sense to deny or forcibly exclude any one stratum for the sake of another, none should be regarded as less important or inferior. They are part of our natural world, and a properly organized society has to respect them all and give them all a chance to play their roles. This is the only way that room can be made for people to realize themselves freely as human beings, to exer-cise their identities. All the circles of our home, indeed our whole natural world, are an inalienable part of us, and an inseparable element of our human identity" (*Summer Meditations,* 31).

Then he delivers his political credo: "I favour a political system based on the citizen and recognizing all fundamental civil and human rights in their universal validity, equally applied; that is, no member of a single race, a single nation, a single sex, or a single religion may be endowed with basic rights that are any different from anyone else's. In other words, I favour what is called a civil society" (*Summer Meditations,* 31–32).

It is over the notion of a civil society that Havel as president has con- *civil soc.*
ducted his most protracted political debate. It has also been the least dramatic because Havel, who in former times was never one to shy away from
public controversy, felt it unseemly for a president to be arguing in public
with his prime minister. But Havel's long-standing disagreements with
Václav Klaus have underlain almost every crisis and every major policy deci- *Klaus V.*
sion made since 1989, with the possible exception of privatization, and even
there they disagreed over methods. Klaus and Havel disagreed over how to
deal with the remnants of Communism; they disagreed over whether federalism could be made to work; they disagreed over presidential powers and how
the Czech president should be elected. They disagreed over enfranchising
charitable organizations, devolving political powers to the regions, reforming
the civil service, and establishing close, cooperative relations with Poland and
Hungary. In this debate, Havel was at a practical disadvantage because
Klaus, the consummate politician, controlled the largest political party—the
Civic Democratic Party—and therefore the legislative agenda. But Havel was
at an intellectual advantage because he could see that beneath the free-
market economics of Klaus there lurked the very ghost the new society was
trying so desperately to exorcise—the ghost of an ideology that encouraged
unbridled economic freedom for those with power (or money) and political
restraints for everyone else. And when Klaus was finally forced to resign after
the scandals he had ignored had grown too large and come too close for com-
fort, Havel literally rose from his sickbed to drive his point home. In the
speech I alluded to at the beginning, he says:

> If I criticize those who have resigned, it is not so much for any particular sin
> they may have committed, but far more for their indifference and outright hos-
> tility to anything that may even remotely resemble a civil society or contribute
> to its creation. In the final analysis, this indifference is precisely why so com-
> mon a democratic event as the fall of one government appears nothing short of
> a Greek tragedy, and to some extent, may even have become one. . . . However
> unpleasant, stressful, and even dangerous what we are going through may be,
> it can also be instructive and a force for good, because it can call forth a cathar-
> sis, the intended outcome of a Greek tragedy. That means a feeling of profound
> purification and redemption. A feeling of new-born hope. A feeling of libera-
> tion. . . .
> Let us therefore understand it as a lesson, a schooling, a test, a challenge
> which may well have come just in time to warn us of our vanity and save us
> from something far worse. ("State of the Republic," 45–46)

In the ledger of history, Václav Havel may well be remembered more for
what he said than what he managed to accomplish, at least in visible, political
terms. But it would be hard, now, to imagine what that tumultuous process of
emerging from the darkness of tyranny would have been like without the bright,
uncompromising mirror he held up to it during the drama of his presidency.

Notes and References

1. Václav Havel, "The State of the Republic," *New York Review* 45, no. 4 (4 March 1998): 42–46; hereafter cited in text as "State of the Republic."

2. Václav Havel, *Summer Meditations,* trans. Paul Wilson (New York: Vintage Books, 1993), xv–xvi; hereafter cited in text as *Summer Meditations.*

3. Václav Havel, *Open Letters, Selected Prose 1965–1990,* selected, edited, and translated by Paul Wilson (London: Faber and Faber, 1991), 391–92.

4. *Zrychlený tep dějin: realné dráma o deseti jednáních* [*The Quickening Pulse of History: A Real Drama in Ten Acts*], ed. Vladimir Hanzel (Prague: OK Centrum, 1991), section 10, 495. (An edited transcript of the negotiations between the Civic Forum, the Public Against Violence, and representatives of the old regime that took place on 9 December 1989.)

5. Václav Havel, "Speech to the Federal Assembly," 17 September 1990.

Havel's Castle

J. P. Stern

{*Masaryk and Havel did not voice their criticism in narrowly national terms but always within a universal framework. Masaryk developed the idea of "humanity" or "humanism" . . . recognizing that the Czech situation was but part of a general world crisis. Havel, too, in condemning totalitarian rule, depicted the faults of this system as an example of universal tendencies.*

—*H. Gordon Skilling*}

The social memory of small countries is punctuated by dates which, as often as not, recall national defeats. When the students of Prague assembled in the late afternoon of Friday, 17 November 1989, to march into the city's main thoroughfare, the Národní Street, the purpose of their officially sanctioned demonstration was to commemorate the fiftieth anniversary of the death of Jan Opletal, a student murdered by the Germans on 17 November 1939; but at the same time they were remembering the death of Jan Palach, another student who, on 16 January 1969, burned himself to death beneath the statue of the country's patron saint, Václav, known as the Good King Wenceslas, in protest against the invasion of Czechoslovakia by the armies of the Soviet Union and three other countries of the Communist Bloc. Now, for the first time in twenty years, "the grown-ups" were taking the students, and the actors who soon joined them, seriously: "our children shamed us into action." By 9 p.m. a crowd of some 50,000 people were moving toward Wenceslas Square. The violence which the police (white helmets, riot-shields and truncheons) and anti-terrorist units (in red berets) used to disperse the crowd led to some broken limbs and numerous concussions, but there were no deaths. This is how Czechoslovakia's "kind of peaceable revolution" began, and it was over, without any further violence, some twenty-four days later. It was not, to begin with, a nation-wide uprising. Both television and radio were slow to begin giving up-to-date news; people had to rely on West German broadcasting stations, and on Radio Free Europe in Munich. In the

Reprinted and abridged from *The Heart of Europe* (London: Blackwell, 1992), 316–30, 405. First appeared in *The London Review of Books* 12, no. 4 (22 February 1990): 5–8.

1. With Klaus Juncker, about 1967.

2. With H. Gordon Skilling, 1984.

provinces they suspected that these were the cavortings of a few crackpot intellectuals in Prague, most of whom had been in gaol anyway.

Václav Havel was not in the city when the uprising started; he was staying in northern Bohemia, at his country cottage, called "Hrádeček," which means "Little Castle." On his return to Prague (probably on Saturday morning), he took charge of events from his headquarters in the basement dressing-room of the Laterna Magica Theatre. His leadership seems never to have been in dispute. The size of the popular support for the students and actors took him by surprise, and he instantly made their cause his own. His next, indeed decisive step was to call a two-hour general strike for Monday the 27th at noon. The call-out, which included the most critical section of the population, the workers in heavy industry and in the mines, was a complete success. By a strange coincidence, the city happened to be full of people from the countryside who had come to attend High Mass to celebrate the canonization two weeks or so earlier, in Rome, of Princess Agnes (1205–82), the daughter of yet another King Wenceslas. (An old lady whose house lies on the steep way to St Vitus's Cathedral put a notice in her window: "Pilgrims are welcome to a night's lodging, but I have only two beds, two eiderdowns and four blankets.") This was the first Czech uprising fully supported by the Catholic Church: a year earlier a petition for religious freedom, drawn up by Augustin Navrátil, a dispossessed Moravian farmer, and endorsed by the ninety-year-old Cardinal Tomášek, was signed by more than half a million people; and an hour after his election as president of the Republic, on 29 December 1989, Havel (no longer in his habitual jeans and pullover but in a neat three-piece suit) attended High Mass celebrated by the cardinal in the cathedral. In a little over a month he had moved from the Little Castle to the big one overlooking the city—"z Hrádečku . . . na Hrad," seven months after his last term in gaol.

The Czechs are a cautious people; they have taken a long time to emerge from the traumas of national defeat. Few of them have been ready to face the fact that, to one side of the "betrayal of Munich" of 1938 by the French (and less directly by the British), the Czechoslovak government's acceptance of Hitler's *Diktat* meant a collapse of everything the country had stood for throughout twenty years of democratic freedom and self-determination. Munich represented the generals' readiness to surrender a highly equipped modern "people's army," without resistance and on the first occasion when that army was called upon to fight; it represented a total collapse of what Havel (among the few who saw the past undistorted by apologies and lies) has called "the spurious realism" of Edvard Beneš, the then president, who, though not consulted, accepted the terms of the surrender. The demoralization which followed that defeat and the harshness and untold humiliations of the German wartime occupation of Bohemia and Moravia (Slovakia chose to become an "ally" of the Germans) explain at least partly the next defeat— this time a moral one: the vengeful fury unleashed by the Czechs on the Sudeten German population after May 1945 (with Beneš's government looking the other way); but they also explain the lack of any effective democratic resistance to the Communist *coup d'état* of 1948, and the failure of the Prague Spring of 1968. Jaroslav Hašek's good soldier Švejk has often been praised for his resilience and cunning, and his ability to survive under adverse conditions: astonishingly enough, in November 1989 the Czechs succeeded (and the Slovaks took their cue from them) precisely because they did not behave like the Good Soldier but chanced their arm; because they behaved like Václav Havel.

Moreover, the Czechs were willing to learn the lesson of their three neighbours, Poland, Hungary and East Germany, that the Soviet Union under Gorbachev was in no mood and in no position to turn Wenceslas Square into Tiananmen Square. This too is astonishing—after all, Czechoslovakia had had bitter territorial quarrels with all three countries since the peace settlements of Versailles and Saint-Germain, and its relations with them went from bad to worse when all three sent their military forces to take part in the occupation that followed the Prague Spring. For Czechoslovakia with its respectable democratic past to be willing to follow on the road to democracy countries with very different political records suggests a commonality of political spirit unprecedented in the annals of Central Europe.

The self-liberation came because there were enough people to follow the students and actors who formed its spearhead—enough people with the courage, perseverance, perspicacity and imprudence of the man whom they later had the good sense to elect as their president. It would be nice to be able to say that in his utter decency, good humour and honesty Havel is "a true representative of the Czech people." So he is. But in all representation there is an element of fiction—a fiction which, in the event, encouraged "the people" to rise to the ethical demands of a charismatic maker of fictions. . . .

Among the qualities Havel shares with Gandhi are a fascination with the law and an occasionally mischievous delight in telling the truth. Whenever he appeared in court he was defended by counsel, often with some skill, yet he took great pains to acquaint himself with the legalities of the indictment; and some of the best and most closely argued writings of this well-organized playwright are the texts of his speeches before the various courts he had to face. His bourgeois good manners were not the least effective of his weapons: "Beware," wrote his friend, the late Heinrich Böll, "here speaks a rebel, one of the dangerous kind, the gentle and courteous kind." He rarely used invective. "The Trial," a *feuilleton* addressed to the chief prosecutor, contains a passage aimed, characteristically, not at the court but at the *je-m'en-foutisme* of those who happen to be unaffected by it. On his way from the Plastic People trial he meets a friend, a film director, and tells him where he has been. Were they up on a drugs charge, the director asks. No, Havel replies, "no drugs were involved, and then I tried to explain briefly what the trial was about. When I finished he shook his head and asked, 'Well, and what else is happening?' Perhaps I am doing him an injustice, but at that moment I was seized by a feeling that this dear man belonged to a world with which I wish to have nothing in common ever again, a world—now listen carefully, Mr Prosecutor Kovařík, what's coming is a vulgarism!—of cocked-up life."

Havel spent altogether almost six years in gaol, two of them doing hard labour, and with several months in solitary confinement. He was never tortured or under threat of execution; but, especially during his first period of imprisonment (1977), he lived under great psychic pressure. His resilience and self-discipline were remarkable. At first he thought life in gaol would provide him with copy for his plays, but he soon found that preserving his own equanimity and making the best of things for those around him took up most of his time and energy at the end of a gruelling day. Two of his friends were in the same gaol and occasionally he and they were able to talk to one another, but his daily contacts were with criminals and "asocial elements" (he and Jiří Dienstbier . . . were given a week in solitary for helping an illiterate Gypsy to write a letter home). For three years his wife's and brother's letters and their visits—one hour every four months—were his only contacts with the outside world. But instead of falling prey to self-pity, he came to see his situation as a challenge to do what none of the characters in his plays succeeds in doing—to make his condition meaningful to himself, and help others to do likewise.

This is what the letters he wrote to his wife between June 1979 and September 1982 are about. He was allowed one letter a week, "strictly confined to family affairs," its exact form prescribed: four pages, no underlinings or deletions, no descriptions of conditions in gaol, no foreign words or quotation marks, and no jokes (punishment is a serious matter!). Couched in an abstract and occasionally abstruse language ("If for instance I wanted to say 'regime', I would have to write 'the socially manifest focus of non-self' or some such rubbish"), these letters are "a cry for fidelity and constancy," they are his attempts "to prevent a breakdown of [my] identity and continuity."

As a boy of sixteen Havel discovered for himself the banned writings of the philosopher Jan Patočka (1907–77), a disciple and friend of Edmund Husserl and a student of Heidegger; later Havel came to know him personally. In December 1976, Patočka joined Havel and Jiří Hájek in founding Charter 77 as "an association of real social tolerance, not merely an agreement for the exclusion of others." Havel's last meeting with Patočka, a meeting which provided the theme of one of Havel's most moving essays, took place in Ruzyně prison while they were waiting to be cross-examined; two months later, after further interrogations, Patočka died of a cerebral stroke. Patočka conceived of human identity as constituted by "a responsibility which is ours, at all times and everywhere," and which surrounds us, like the world, with an "absolute horizon," and whose only real test is in adversity: this, it seems, is the main concept Havel took from his Socratic mentor.

Havel disclaims all authority as a philosopher; his speculations, he says, are no more than "the testimony of one man in a particular situation, his inner murmurings." Yet he is irresistibly drawn to the philosophical reflections that came his way in Patočka's "unofficial seminars." In one of his letters to his wife he tries to discover why a visit from her and his brother didn't go well. Each visit has its own special atmosphere (he writes), made up of the three people's moods, the events that came before and after the visit, their "individual wills" and their "collective will." But all this is merely a "physical preamble" to a "higher order," an order determined by a "collective spirit" with its own identity, integrity, continuity and mood. And this "order of spirit" in turn is part of a higher order still, "an order of Being," which transcends "epochs, cultures, civilizations. . . ." Will he (the reader, and perhaps Olga Havlová too, ask) never come down to earth? "Every work of the spirit," he continues, "is a small re-enactment of the miracle of Being, a small re-creation of the world," and this is especially true of those two spheres of collectivity that are peculiarly Havel's own, the theatre and politics. Moreover (the speculation, now turned metaphysical, continues), no work of the spirit is ever wholly lost, each is registered for ever in the memory of Being; so that every political act, grounded as it is in responsibility acknowledged or denied, is, like every artistic creation, registered in the spiritual experience of mankind as well as in the totality of Being of which mankind is a part. And though he adds, "Our lives are known about," he is reluctant to call on a religious authority in support of that claim; moreover, his liberality of outlook allows him to recognize that most of his friends don't share "the metaphysics" of that conviction.

The greatest challenge to his search for meaning didn't come from the powers-that-be, that increasingly absurd amalgam of Moscow, the Party and its police force, and the army. It came from his friends, who wondered whether his suffering (though he never called it that) was worthwhile, whether he would not be better advised to renege on his beliefs. Embarrassed by the publicity his imprisonment aroused in the West, "the regime" (in effect the president, Husák) was eagerly looking for the least damaging way of releasing him. Would he like to go to America "on a course of study of the New York theatre?" they asked. He knew that the slightest sign of recantation on his part would do the trick, and they almost succeeded. During the interview of 1985 [*Disturbing the Peace*] he recalls his first short imprisonment eight years earlier:

> I didn't know what was happening outside; it was only by reading the [government-controlled] newspapers that I could follow the frenzied campaign waged against the Charter. I was disappointed in my investigators and even in my defence counsel. I was in a strange, almost psychotic turmoil of mind and feelings. I had the impression that, being one of the initiators of the Charter, I had injured a lot of people and brought terrible misfortune on them. I was taking upon myself an excessive responsibility, as though the others didn't know

what they were doing, as though I alone were to blame. In this very unwhole-some psychic disposition it gradually dawned on me at the end of my prison sentence that a trap was being set for me. Certain relatively harmless statements of mine—at least I thought them innocent at the time—in one of my appeals for remission were to be published in a corrupted form in order to discredit me.

In one of the last of these letters to his wife (25 July 1982), from his third and longest period in gaol, he comments unsparingly on this appeal for remission which he had written during his first imprisonment:

Of course, I knew that whether or not I'd be released would be decided by things which had nothing to do with whether or not I wrote the appropriate request. Well—the interrogation was getting nowhere, and it seemed proper to use the opportunity and let myself be heard. I wrote my request in a way that at the time seemed very tactical and cunning: while saying nothing that I didn't think or that wasn't true, I simply "overlooked" the fact that truth lies not only in what is said but also in who says it, and to whom, why and how and under what circumstances it is expressed. Thanks to this minor "oversight" (more accurately: this minor self-deception), what I said came—as it were by chance—dangerously close to what the addressee wanted to hear. What was particularly absurd was my motive in this maneuver, at least my conscious and admitted motive. It was not the hope that it would lead to anything, but merely a kind of professionally intellectual and somewhat perverse delight in what I thought of as my "honourable cleverness." (To complete the picture I should add that, when I re-read it some years later, the "honour" in that clever-ness made my hair stand on end.)

This episode and his understanding of it as an act of betrayal formed one of the fundamental experiences of Havel's life. The experience is incorporated in at least two of his plays, *Largo Desolato* (1984) and in the Faust play, *Tempta-tion* (1985). But his self-understanding is also relevant to his political tactics. Here lies the source of his tolerance—particularly striking among Central European intellectuals—toward those who have succumbed to such tempta-tions; and this tolerance (so different from the attitude of his persecutors, but also of the "reformists" of East Germany) would in due course be recognized by "the people" as legitimating his authority to lead them. From its very beginning, Charter 77 insisted that, as Professor Patočka put it with un-wonted succinctness, "This is not a battle, this is a war!" The Chartists' aims were not single "demos" and isolated "actions," but the continuous unrelent-ing work of enlightening people about their rights and duties; and from this enlightenment nobody willing to participate was to be excluded.

This is Havel's "Postmodernism": in an age still governed by Mani-chaean politics, he refused to accept the Western view that the country was divided into "dissidents"—people concerned to secure freedom primarily for themselves—and the rest of the population, which was waiting to see how things would turn out for "the dissidents" before venturing out into the streets—those streets of Prague "in which [Havel writes] on a Saturday night the only people you met were five secret policemen, five illegal currency dealers and three drunks." (The rest of the population sat at home, watching West German television.)

Here is the element of fiction I mentioned earlier: Havel had no illusions about how things were, yet he acted and wrote (for instance in his letter of May 1975, addressed to "Dear Dr. Husák") as though the public were waiting to be won over to the side of justice and freedom; as though the "dissidents" and "the people" were one. Conscious of the film of lies that had covered national life throughout four decades, he didn't play the moral simpleton. Yet his quiet, unhysterical indictment of the regime was undertaken on behalf of "the people" no less than on behalf of his fellow-dissidents, and it was founded on the belief that people who lie can be made to recognize the truth and speak it. There was that week in August 1968 when he took an active part in the resistance against the invasion in one of the few towns that had stood out and for a while at least had remained unoccupied. The experience taught him that "we never know what possibilities are dormant in the soul of the populace. A whole nation, acting out Švejkian tactics at one time, can bravely oppose a foreign power a year later . . . and another twelvemonth after that can plunge into an abyss of demoralization with the speed of lightning." He didn't and doesn't delude himself into thinking that there aren't worse crimes than lies, or that die-hard ideologists and power-seekers can be turned into liberal democrats. But all the rest, including the trimmers and the Vicars of Bray, can be reclaimed for the common weal. This belief is his strength; and one's fervent hope is that a situation will not arise in which it turns out to be his weakness.

This is a philosophy in which "the lightness of Being" is anything but "unbearable." It is the heavy, bloodstained theory behind Marxist revolutionary politics (the politics of *Darkness at Noon*) that is shown up for the self-seeking farce it really was (and in some parts of our world still is). . . .

"Co se stalo?" "What's happened?" Time and again, one of Havel's plays or the peripeteia of a scene is introduced by that question. It marks the moment when the life of an individual or of a family has been disrupted by a sudden *úkaz* from above, an order that is pointless yet unignorable. And even though "what happens" hardly ever takes the form of what has been expected, and occasionally the answer to the question is, "Nothing, nothing at all," from that moment on everything is senselessly different. In the flat of a "dissident," the secret police are expected, and instead friends come, or a couple of political sympathizers, and their importunate arrival, encouraging patter and well-intended demands, brings with it disruptions which seem worse than any havoc the police may wreak *(Largo Desolato)*. In *The Garden Party* a friend who is well in with the authorities, and has promised to fix things for the son of the family, is expected but doesn't come, and instead his secretary arrives, and reads out a series of telegrams interlarded with her plans for a weekend excursion with [her boss]. Some time later the son, Hugo, turns up after all, but now that he has got the job the family friend promised (having meanwhile ousted the family friend from his place in the *Nomenklatura*), the father thinks he will be too grand to talk to them—and indeed, Hugo is so grand that he isn't their son any more but someone quite different, and of course the garden party where the deal was struck wasn't a garden party at all but an anxious get-together where everybody watched everybody else, hoping for preferment or fearing demotion. The job Hugo has secured in the Inauguration Service involves him in the ceremonial opening of the Department of Liquidation—and *its* first job is to liquidate the Inauguration Service, while its *next* job is to liquidate itself, all under Hugo's direction. "How suicidal our happiness can be!" says Kafka's official—the Inaugurator about to liquidate the case against K.—at the end of *The Castle.*

Life in this society is governed by the mutual back-scratching ideology I have mentioned, the simplest version of which is shown in *Audience* (1975). The play was occasioned by Havel's own time as an unskilled labourer in a provincial brewery, a job he took mainly because it was a convenient and uncompromising way of making a living. The characters have it all worked out to a T: the working-class Head Maltster will help Vaněk (a playwright doing his punitive stint in the brewery) to secure a cushy job in the dispatch office, in return for which Vaněk will help the Maltster to write the weekly report on his (Vaněk's) doings, by means of which the Maltster will placate his friend, Tonda Mašek, who stood by him when he was about to be tried for theft, whereas Mašek needs the report in order to keep the authorities sweet, because . . . Alas, this perfect mechanism fails to work, because Vaněk won't co-operate, *because* he has "principles." This is the cue for the Maltster's Great Speech, and in the whole of Bertolt Brecht's work there is nothing like it. Here speaks the anger and pain of the working man who feels himself condemned to perpetual inferiority by his lack of education and by his very language. He must do without the intellectual's la-di-da words, but even so he knows how to ram home his point:

> Now you wouldn't mind my getting you a warm spot in the storeroom, would you? But when it comes to taking on a bit of this muck I have to wade in every day—no sir! You're all very clever, you've got it all figured out, haven't you? You really know how to take care of your own lot! *Principles!* Of course you've got to protect them, those principles of yours—because you know how to cash in on them, because you're sure to get a good price for them, they're your bread and butter, those principles—but what about me? . . . Nobody's ever going to look after me, nobody's afraid of me, nobody's going to write about me . . . You'll go back to your actresses one day—you're going to show off to them how you rolled out the barrels—you'll be a hero—but what about me? What do you think I've got to go back to? Who's ever going to appreciate what I've done? What have I got out of life? What's in store for me?

Isn't that a speech to tear a hole in the motley, a genuine, even moving challenge to the "master's son" by one of the underprivileged? So it is, except that no sooner has the speech been delivered than it is drowned in a crate of lager and forgotten—and the play can begin all over again.

In *The Conspirators* (1971), Havel's only dramatic reference to anti-Semitism and the Slánský trials of 1952, it's not a cushy job in the warm storeroom that is at stake but the Fate of a Nation. When the conspirators meet (the attorney-general is named after the man who prosecuted Havel in what one hesitates to call "real life," and there is an illiterate censor), each of the four men hopes he will lead the nation in the coming revolution, and the woman (who is or has been the mistress of three of them) encourages each in turn; then each pretends that he thinks one of the others is better qualified for the great task, and again the caballing leads nowhere: it is as though it had never been, and the play ends where it began. What fascinates Havel here is not the "political problem"—these are not Shavian or Brechtian "problem plays" but the self-generated movement of human relations (Act 1: A:B = C:D, Act 2: A:D = B:C, etc.). This sounds a pretty arid formula, yet the plays work, because the problem-parodies they contain are pushed to a point of "absurdity compounded by absurdity" (the phrase is Tom Stoppard's), involving both assertions and losses of identity so complete and so contradictory as to be comic. *The Mountain Hotel* (1976) takes this idea as far as it will go (and perhaps a little further). Not just Rosencrantz and Guildenstern, but nine characters with interchangeable identities are presented, whose Pavlovian reaction (every time the train passes they glance at their wrist-watches) is the only thing they have in common with each other and with what they were an hour or two before. As two more people—the hotel manager and his assistant—are introduced, the scenes get shorter and shorter, dialects, saws and memories float freely from one "character" to the next, answers precede questions, convictions are swapped, identities melt and collapse—the ending is like Madame Tussaud's wax-works on fire.

The loss of personal identity—Havel's central theme with numerous variations—works particularly well when characters are placed in the service of some cause nobody is allowed to reveal as pointless, or of some expectation everybody knows to be absurd. "Ptydepe," the artificial language constructed on the principle of maximum redundancy, which is the subject of *The Memorandum* (1966), doesn't work, not only because it is absurdly cumbersome, but also because, however idiotically abstract its words, they acquire, as they were bound to, emotive connotations and contextual undertones, just like any "unscientific," ordinary language. So the *úkaz* which made Ptydepe the compulsory medium of inter-departmental communication is revoked, and everybody who was involved in teaching it—a whole bureaucratic "machinery"—is discredited and demoted. But no sooner does this happen than "Chorukor," another artificial language, constructed on the opposite principle of minimal redundancy, is introduced. Why? As an assertion of bureaucratic power? But whose power?

The machinery that is at work here is of course that of "the Party," which (a little like the authorities that are said to be at work in the Castle in Kafka's novel) is everywhere and nowhere, and the metamorphosis that goes with power is total: the office boy who becomes the director of a nationalized enterprise assumes the outlook and the jargon of the director he has displaced, at least while he is lording it over everybody. But unlike the powers ascribed to the bureaucrats of Kafka's Castle, this power isn't in the least mysterious: instead it is negotiable, and most of the characters know it to be so. The mimesis of these tragicomedies is perfect: the "Party" (and other self-propelling, self-purposive constructs like it) is the most convenient because the most readily available representative of social entropy or (to use Havel's own, simpler term), of "the world of cocked-up life." As to the relevance of this entropic construct to our national and multinational institutions, the reader or member of the audience is left to draw his own conclusions.

In some ways these characters resemble the figurines of bar football; they all look alike, but if you get close you will see that they are all a little different, each knocked about and damaged in a different place. Nobody is wholly truthful, though almost everybody has a moment of weakness which is also his or her moment of truth. Time and again one of these figures delivers the Great Speech which is meant to sum it all up, like Hamlet's "To be, or not to be," or Lucky's "Given the existence as uttered forth in the public works of Puncher and Wattmann," or the Professional Orator's platitudes in *The Chairs* by Ionesco. And as often as not these speeches turn out to be replicas of the weighty pronouncements of the Great Socialist Panjandrums, the Marxes and Engelses, the Blochs and Lukácses, full of veiled threats and abstract promises, signifying very little. Is there then in the world of Havel's plays nothing that is to be taken seriously? Sex? When not in the service of distraction or professional advancement, it leads to ludicrous disappointment or disaster. True community? The only place where you can find it is in the queue outside the office canteen, whose themes of discourse range from roast goose to goulash.

As Marketa Goetz-Stankiewicz has shown in her splendid study *The Silenced Theatre* (1979), "Vašek" Havel has kept company with a whole bevy of playwrights with similar aims and similar dramatic resources. What is original about his tragicomedies is the single-mindedness with which he places all human relations inside socio-political brackets. Outside these brackets there is a sign saying, "Beware, farce!," and around them there is another set of brackets and another sign, which says, "This is serious, because, though it shouldn't be, this is how life passes here." But as you read that last sentence it grows more faint, until it becomes (to use a word for which Havel has a special penchant) "metaphysical." Cheerfulness is always breaking in: absurdity is an absence of meaning, an absence which, in this theatre, is "inseparable from the experience of meaning." And the only way to escape all those brackets is to escape life; though that happens only once, in Havel's latest play, *Slum Clearance* (1988), in the Oblomov character who takes his own life.

What does the future hold? Will the good-tempered new life last? Havel's relative lack of a historical background may limit him as a playwright, but in the context of the country's social memory it is a blessing in disguise. Of course, he *knows* the national mythopoeia well enough (the liturgy of the great national names, from Jan Hus through Jan Amos Comenius to T. G. Masaryk) but, unlike Milan Kundera, he rejects the *kitschig* notion that appeals to myth as a substitute for political action. He rejects the "small country syndrome" that has led the Czechs and Slovaks more than once into deep unhappiness, into an abrogation of the communal spirit, fear inviting oppression, oppression inviting revenge. Public misery and withdrawal into timid privacy have been the hallmarks of their history on many occasions throughout the last four centuries. Can a country free itself from its traumatic past by a single act of self-liberation? Possibly. After all, history is "us" as well as "them." There is no law of history that condemns a people to perpetual darkness. In the dark years following the destruction of the First Republic, the grave mistakes which preceded that destruction dropped out of the national memory; the monstrosity of the Third Reich obscured the fact that long before Hitler came on the scene Czechoslovakia had no adequate German policy; and the long nightmare of Communism created the myth of an unblemished haven of liberty and fairness. Yet the image of a decent democracy, unique in a region of Europe unpropitious to such things, wasn't all "P.R.": enough of Masaryk's democratic heritage survives for the new republic to build on, and its beginnings are encouraging enough. On his first official visit abroad President Havel went to both parts of Germany, and he wasn't exactly courting popularity in his homeland when, in the course of that visit, he announced the formation of a commission of inquiry into the expulsion of the Sudeten Germans: true, it was an act of surprising political skill and self-assurance; but more than that, it reflected his great moral courage. Together with complete and partial amnesties for all prisoners except murderers and rapists, the proposal to establish diplomatic relations with Israel, an invitation to the Pope to visit the country, an invitation to Frank Zappa to make a film in Prague (presumably in the Barrandov studios in the suburb, the building of which once nearly bankrupted Havel's father) and plans for a sort of Central European summit meeting with the Hungarians and the Poles in Bratislava, the Slovak capital—this is not a bad record for a presidency in its first flush. A single man, however charismatic, cannot ensure that the decencies of a single moment can be perpetuated into an era. Still, Václav Havel, helped by his fiction, can do a lot.

Notes and References

Havel's letters to his wife are published as *Dopisy Olze* (Toronto, 1985); see also *Letters to Olga, June 1979–September 1982,* trans. Paul Wilson (London, 1990), 75, 177, 181, 271–3. The last sixteen letters were published separately as *Výzva k transcendenci* (London, 1984), with a commentary by "Sidonius" and the text of Havel's speech (not delivered in person since he was in gaol at the time) accepting the honorary doctorate of Toulouse University. For a collection of Havel's essays, addresses and interviews of the period 1969–79, see *O lidskou identitu,* eds. Vilém Prečan and Alexander Tomský (London, 1984); I quote from 6, 151. For Havel's December 1968 exchange with Kundera, see 187–200. For the "long distance interview" with Karel Hvížd'ala in 1985, see *Dálkový výslech* (Hamburg, 1989) [translated as *Disturbing the Peace*]; I quote from 8ff., 61, 78, 95, 125, 129, 155, 169. Wherever possible, throughout this essay I have checked my own translations against published ones.

The quotation from *Audience* is from *Hry 1970–1976: Audience* (Toronto, 1977), 265. [The translation used here is by Vera Blackwell.] For *The Garden Party,* see *Ztížené možnosti: Zahradní slavnost* (Purley, 1986), especially 55. In connection with "Ptydepe" in *The Memorandum.* Havel has acknowledged advice from his brother, Ivan M. Havel, a physicist. The uprising of November 1989 is the subject of a brilliant report by Timothy Garton Ash, "Magical Prague," *New York Review of Books,* 18 January 1990, 42–51. The notice "Pilgrims are welcome . . ." is quoted from *Mladý svět,* 36, 51 (1 December 1989), 21. See also Timothy Garton Ash, *The Uses of Adversity* (London, 1989), 193–5, for the petition for religious freedom of 1988.

All the President's Plays

STANISLAW BARANCZAK

{With Arendt, Havel is utterly resistant to the alchemy of "the dialectic" which transforms concrete evils into abstract goods.
—*Jean Bethke Elshtain*}

"SIX ONE-ACT PLAYS BY SIX WORLD LEADERS" was what a [1990] *New Yorker* cartoon envisaged as a canopy advertisement above the door to an off-Broadway theater. The wit is in the arithmetic. The number six suspends the joke precisely between the actual state of affairs and the realm of the improbable. Had the sign said, "TWO ONE-ACT PLAYS BY TWO WORLD LEADERS," we would not laugh, because the estimate would be too realistic. Had it said "TEN ONE-ACT PLAYS BY TEN WORLD LEADERS," we would not laugh, because the estimate would be too fantastic. But six, why not?

Not long ago, there was just one world leader whose resumé included a few plays actually written by him and performed on stage (though their production anywhere near Broadway seems a rather remote possibility). Now there are two: the Pope has been joined by the President of [the Czech Republic]. Who's next? Hasn't a recent article published in a Solidarity newspaper proposed Leszek Kolakowski for the presidency of Poland? Kolakowski, let's not forget, is the author not just of works of philosophy, but also of a comedy he wrote in his spare time. The trend seems to be on the rise. You don't have to be royalty to collect royalties; being the president of a small nation will suffice.

Our amusement at the sight of a playwright becoming his country's president speaks volumes about the declining standards in the West's political life. What's so strange about the election of an outstanding writer from Bohemia? Is it any more consistent with the natural order of things if a much less outstanding golf player from Indiana gets elected to do the same? Weren't Lincoln and Churchill gifted writers? Wouldn't we all be slightly bet-

Reprinted from *The New Republic* (23 July 1990): 27–32. Reprinted by permission of THE NEW REPUBLIC, (c) 1990, The New Republic, Inc.

ter off if our leaders knew how to select a proper word, put together a precise sentence, paint a stirring idea in a well-constructed paragraph?

Admittedly, even though there might be some truth in the tired Shelley line (you know, the one about poets being the unacknowledged legislators of the world), things get a little complicated when a poet, or a playwright, becomes acknowledged as a legislator, a minister, or a president. First of all, the sort of parliament or government he serves is not entirely inconsequential. The sad case of the talented poet Ernesto Cardenál, who lent support to Daniel Ortega's regime by accepting the position of its minister of culture, is just one example of the incompatibility between literature's natural thirst for freedom and despotism's natural desire to suppress freedom. That is a conflict in which something has to give, and all too often it has been the writer's conscience that has given.

Moreover, history provides us with a hair-raising number of examples of humanity's worst enemies, from Nero to Hitler, Goebbels, Stalin, and Mao, who considered themselves, at least before their ascent to power but sometimes also a long time after it, artists or writers. A failed artist or a graphomaniac seems to be particularly good material for the making of a ruthless oppressor; he need only apply his crude aesthetic principle of mechanical symmetry to the unruly and formless human mass.

And even if the political system is a democratic one, and the "acknowledged legislator" or leader happens to be an artist or a writer wise enough to be profoundly aware of human diversity, his success in the world of politics is far from assured. As a writer, his chief strength—the force that made him a "legislator," however "unacknowledged," in the first place—was his steadfast rejection of compromise. As a politician, however, he soon finds out that politics in a democratic society is nothing but the art of compromise.

If it so happened one day that destiny wanted the first president of post-Communist Czechoslovakia [now the Czech Republic and Slovakia] to be a writer, what kind of writer should he ideally be? Let us imagine a group of Czechoslovak citizens gathered secretly in a private apartment in the middle of 1989, taking refuge from their depressing reality by discussing this preposterous question, a question as thoroughly outlandish to them as the seashore that Shakespeare gave Bohemia in *A Winter's Tale*. Any answer would certainly have included the reverse of the qualities we have just mentioned.

First, the literary president should be a writer with an extraordinarily strong moral backbone, someone whose life, like his work, has been dedicated to searching for the untraversable borderline between good and evil; someone, therefore, who would be able to bring the spirit of ethics into his country's national and international politics. Second, the literary president should be a good writer, endowed with the sense of measure and balance that in the sphere of aesthetics is called good taste or artistic skill, and in the sphere of politics translates into a pluralistic tolerance for the natural diversity of people and their opinions. A playwright—someone who shows the world through dialogue—would be a particularly well-qualified candidate: the spectacle of conflicting human perspectives forms the lifeblood of his art.

And third, the literary president should be a writer blessed with a tremendous sense of humor, preferably of the self-mocking, ironic, absurdist sort. For it is only with such a sense of humor that a writer-turned-president would be able to think seriously of making his nation ascend from the depths of the totalitarian absurd toward a more or less rational social organization, while at the same time never taking himself and the miracle of his own ascension too seriously. In short, the ideal president of Czechoslovakia that our depressed friends would have likely dreamed up is this: a genuinely good playwright with a genuinely strong set of moral convictions balanced by a genuine sense of pluralistic tolerance and a genuine sense of humor.

In the middle of 1989, there happened to be one living and breathing candidate who matched this impossibly exacting description. His name was Václav Havel.

"The real test of a man is not how well he plays the role he has invented for himself, but how well he plays the role that destiny assigned to him." This is how Havel himself, quoting the dictum of his friend and mentor, the late philosopher Jan Patočka, reflects on all the twists of fate that made him first Czechoslovakia's most vilified dissident and then its most venerated president. The issue of the "role" (a fitting term in the mouth of a playwright) is crucial in Havel's philosophical system. What he means by that is the responsibility that man, "thrown into the world," accepts by relating his life to the Absolute Horizon of Transcendence (which is defined by Havel, who is reluctant to resort to the vocabulary of theology, as the "Memory of Being").

This kind of outlook, in Havel's case, owes as much to the inspiration drawn from the works of existentialists and phenomenologists as to the inspiration provided by life. *Letters to Olga,* Havel's most detailed and extensive exposition of his philosophy of existence, was written, symbolically enough, in a prison cell—a place to which his "role" consistently led him. It was a place that he converted, ironically, into a stage on which to play, even more eloquently, the same role he had played outside the prison walls. *Letters to Olga* focused on the final outcome of a life, on its complete philosophy. The life that produced this outcome has, in turn, become the focus of *Disturbing the Peace,* a highly engaging autobiographical sketch in the form of a book-length interview. This much-needed book explains how the events of the unbelievable fall of 1989 can be seen as an almost inevitable phase in Havel's lifelong "role," which was both "assigned to him" by destiny and "invented" by himself.

The facts of Havel's life were more or less known in the West even before 1989, mostly thanks to the publicity generated by his trials and his prison sentences. Havel's life was marked by absurd paradoxes early. Born in 1936 into the wealthy family of a civil engineer, he was suddenly a social pariah—the child of a class enemy—in 1948, when Czechoslovakia turned Communist. He was denied access to a higher education, worked for a while as a laboratory-technician, and went through a two-year military service. Throughout that ordeal, he wrote (his first article was published in 1955), and made his presence known in public appearances, such as his speech at an official symposium of young writers in 1956, shockingly critical of the official hierarchy of literary values.

From 1959 on, his life was inextricably linked to theater. He joined Prague's unorthodox Theater on the Balustrade, initially as a stage hand, and ended up as its literary adviser. *The Garden Party,* his first play, premièred in 1963. In 1965 he joined the editorial staff of the monthly *Tvář,* a tribune of rebellious young writers.

Those were heady times of growing ferment and hope, but change was yet to come. *Tvář* was soon closed down by its own editors, unable to continue publishing under the watchful eye of the Party. Between 1956 and 1968, Havel used consecutive congresses of the Czechoslovak Writers' Association as forums for his increasingly critical speeches, but his ideas were staunchly resisted by the well-entrenched camp of Communist writers. In March 1968 he helped establish the Circle of Independent Writers, thus creating a cultural alternative of major importance. Meanwhile his next plays had their Czech and Western premières, and his name became internationally known.

Havel became even better known after the Prague Spring and the Soviet invasion, when he emerged as one of the most eloquent champions of human rights in Husák's police state. His participation in actions of protest and his own analyses of the social apathy induced by Brezhnev's . . . puppets (such as his famous "Letter to Dr. Gustav Husák," which was written in 1975) brought down on him increasingly vicious personal attacks in the official media as well as unrelenting police harassment. On January 1, 1977, Havel joined Patočka and Jiří Hájek as a spokesman for the Charter 77 movement. The rest is a story of interrogations, investigations, detentions, provocations, searches, house arrests, buggings, prosecutor's charges, trials, jail sentences, labor camps, prison hospitals, and, amid all this turmoil, more writing.

As we all know, this particular story has a happy ending, the impeccable symmetry of which—the nation's most persecuted writer turns overnight into the nation's president—looks downright suspicious. Were Havel's life a novel, it might be the most naive piece of literary kitsch in the twentieth century. A clear-headed observer of the world's ways knows that there is no such neat example of virtue miraculously rewarded in real life. Is Havel's life a fairy tale, a dream? The honest and the brave, after all, are supposed to get beaten to death by unknown assailants, to disappear without trace, to be found in the trunk of an abandoned car with bullets in their heads. Havel's triumph is so unequivocally well deserved that it looks utterly outlandish.

And no wonder: this particular writer, again, is a walking paradox. This is true not merely of the course of his life, but also of his inner nature. Havel's role seems to have been delineated from the very beginning of his public and literary activity by his mind's preoccupation with two seemingly incompatible inclinations. His works and his actions reflect, on the one hand, a strong sense of moral order and of the need for justice, and on the other, a good-natured tolerance mixed with an absurd, zany sense of humor. An episode mentioned in *Disturbing the Peace* nicely illustrates the constant coexistence of these two inclinations. At one point early in Husák's rule, Havel took part in a general assembly of the governing boards of the unions of writers and artists, which feared—not without foundation, it soon turned out—that their forcible dissolution was imminent. Havel was included in a three-member committee charged with drafting a strong statement to protest, and to try to deflect, the blow:

> Unfortunately, I was also expected to participate in the opening of a show of paintings by a friend of mine in the Spálená Gallery, on Spálená Street, not far away. I wasn't going to give a serious speech—there were art historians for that —just take part in a little program of verses and songs. This was the dadaist wish of my friend, who loved the way I sang patriotic songs out of tune and gave impassioned recitations from our national literary classics at parties. And so, pretending that I had to go to the bathroom, I fled from the task of writing the historic manifesto and I ran to the gallery opening, where I sang and recited to a shocked audience, then rushed back to the film club to write the final paragraph.

Havel proceeds to note "something symbolic in this accidental juxtaposition." It illustrates, he suggests, certain fusions of a more general scope: the way the Czechs' sense—and more generally, the Central Europeans' sense—of misery about their existence is wed to a "sense of irony and self-deprecation." "Don't these two things somehow belong essentially together?" asks Havel. "Don't they condition each other?" The Central European writer's taste for the absurd, for dark humor, produces in him the saving art of "maintaining constant distance" from the world while never completely disengaging from it. Paradoxically, it is exactly the art of distance that allows you to see your subject from up close. As Havel puts it, "The outlines of genuine meaning can only be perceived from the bottom of absurdity."

In truth, the episode says more about Havel himself than about Central European culture. The distinguishing feature of his life and his art seems to be the nearly perfect balance between the seriousness of his moral imperatives and the boundlessness of his self-irony. That irony is not just his mind's innate inclination. It also stems from his recognition that his own vision of the truth—no matter how scrupulously precise he tries to make it, no matter how much he is himself sure of its accuracy—is still only one of many individual human truths.

It is by now quite obvious how much this balance of moral strength without fanaticism and pluralistic tolerance without relativism has affected Havel's progress along his political path. It is perhaps less clear how this same balance is reflected in his art. There, just as in Havel's politics, the equilibrium of opposites keeps the forces in check, so that the extreme manifestations of each can cancel the other out.

An artist of Havel's sort is truly himself when he submits to his moral impulses, when his work originates from his fundamental objection to the world's injustice. But if that were all it took, the art might easily lapse into dogmatic and self-righteous didacticism, the work would be noble yet tedious moral instruction. Another condition, clearly, must be met. In the arts, the moralist needs to have a sense of humor.

That is not as easy as it sounds. A sense of humor is shorthand for many abilities, from the power to understand others' positions and motivations to the willingness to take oneself with a grain of salt. Only this kind of humor can save the artist from the chronic stiffness of his moral backbone, a disease that is quite common among artists in oppressed societies. It is a disease with which you can live, but not, for instance, dance: you can hold yourself impressively erect, but be too rigid for unrestrained expression. Of course, if the backbone suffers from permanent softening (an even more common affliction), if all that remains is the relativism and the absurdist sense of humor, the effects are even more frightening: when left to himself and to his choreographies, the artist may display much flexibility, but also yield easily to the slightest pressure.

That is why Havel the playwright cannot really be squeezed into either of the two familiar drawers, "Theater of the Absurd" or "Protest Theater." He is too embedded in a stable bedrock of moral principles to fit into the first, and he is too irreverent and self-ironic to fit into the second. More precisely, his plays fall into two different categories, one stemming from the tradition of political theater, the other suggesting some superficial affinities with the Theater of the Absurd. The first category is represented by more or less realistic works such as the series of three one-act "Vaněk plays," inaugurated in 1975 by the famed *Audience. Largo Desolato* [written in 1984] also belongs here. In plays of this sort, realism takes a deep whiff of grotesque exaggeration, but there is no doubt, particularly in the Vaněk trilogy, that the action takes place in Husák's Czechoslovakia and that the characters' behavior is motivated by circumstances of that time and that place. (Unfortunately, the English version of *Largo Desolato,* otherwise excellently done by Tom Stoppard, obliterates this Czechoslovakian specificity by Anglicizing the names.)

The other category, which includes *The Memorandum* and *Temptation,* is represented by plays, usually of greater length and based on more developed plots, that are parabolic rather than realistic. Sometimes they border on anti-utopian fantasy. Instead of a realistic setting, the typical drama revolves around a fictitious institution such as the Orwellian office in *The Memorandum,* complete with watchmen hidden in the hollow walls to keep an eye on employees through special cracks, and the scientific institute at war with society's "irrational tendencies" in *Temptation*. What goes beyond realism, actually, is not so much the setting as the plot's starting device: the introduction of Ptydepe, the artificial language for inter-office communication, in *The Memorandum* and the bureaucratic forms of idolatry of "rational science" that produce the Faustian rebellion of the protagonist in *Temptation*.

The difference between Havel's two types of plays, however, is one of degree. Both deal with essentially the same issues; the parabolic differs from the realistic perhaps only in that the grotesque and the absurd are turned up a notch. But the grotesque and the absurd are intrinsically present even in the most "realistic" of Havel's plays. In the strictly realistic *Audience,* a play that utilizes Havel's own first-hand experience of work at the Trutnov brewery, a socialist workplace that re-educates its employees by making them submit regular reports on themselves to the secret police, cannot help but seem like a profoundly aberrant institution. And it is no less so than the imaginary office in *The Memorandum* that forces its employees to learn a special language, one that would help them produce more precise memos if its utter precision did not make it impossible to use. The only difference is that *Audience* could really have happened in Husák's Czechoslovakia, while something not so blatantly idiotic as *The Memorandum,* but something similar in spirit, could perhaps have happened there.

Another striking similarity between Havel's "realistic" and "parabolic" plays lies in their protagonists. In fact, it would only be a slight oversimplification to say that whatever sort of play Havel writes, a single protagonist by the name of Ferdinand Vaněk always pops up at the center of its plot. The now legendary figure of Vaněk appeared first in *Audience* (to my mind, still the most perfectly executed accomplishment of Havel's wit), [and reappeared] in his next two one-act plays, *Unveiling* [*Vernissage*] and *Protest.* At the same time, the underground success of *Audience* gave rise to a one-of-a-kind literary phenomenon: a constellation of plays employing the same protagonist but written by different authors. ("The Vaněk plays" in that broader sense include pieces written by Pavel Kohout, Pavel Landovský, and Jiří Dienstbier, and they are all reprinted in . . . a handy collection [published in 1987 by the University of British Columbia Press].) But Leopold Nettles of *Largo Desolato* is also, to a large extent, another incarnation of Vaněk, and Vaněk-like characters spur the dramatic action in Havel's "parabolic" plays as well.

What these characters share is a position in society. All of them can be roughly defined as dissidents in a totalitarian state, or at least (as in the cases of Josef Gross in *The Memorandum* and Dr. Foustka in *Temptation*) jammed cogwheels in the otherwise smoothly functioning machine of a powerful institution. This position entails a number of consequences. The most crucial is that the Vaněk-like character represents, obviously, a political and moral minority. He is one of the last Mohicans of common sense, truthfulness, and human decency in a society that has laboriously adopted, in lieu of those simple principles, a Darwinian methodology of survival. Blind obedience to authority, thoughtless concentration on necessities of everyday life, and deepseated distrust of any protester or reformer are the chief precepts of this methodology. Thus Vaněk is by no means a valiant knight in shining armor or a modern Robin Hood whom the wretched of the earth look up to. Despite all the words of cautious support and solidarity that some of his acquaintances occasionally dare whisper into his ear, Vaněk is hated and despised. Hated, because he is "disturbing the peace" of pacified minds; despised, because he is—cannot help being—a loser. The forces that he opposes are too powerful; he will certainly be crushed in the foreseeable future.

Hence the central paradox of Havel's literary universe: it is not Vaněk who, from the heights of his moral purity as a fighter for human rights, accuses the corrupt society of indifference; it is his society that accuses Vaněk of the same—yes, of indifference. In the eyes of a citizen whose main concerns are promotion at his workplace, getting his daughter into a university, and building himself a dacha in the country, Vaněk looks like a dangerous instigator and rabblerouser. What the Brewmaster in *Audience* says to his face would be echoed with equal sincerity by other characters in other plays, had their tongues been similarly loosened by the heavy intake of beer: "Principles! Principles! Damn right you gonna fight for your damn principles . . .—but what about me? I only get my ass busted for having principles!" Vaněk's original sin, all of them seem to think, is his indifference to other people, an attitude that he demonstrates merely by living among them and irritating them with his inflated conscience. He can afford to stick his neck out; we can't.

In specific plays, this reverberating "He can, we can't" is wrapped in different words, depending on the accuser's social status, intellectual acumen, and degree of cowardice. The Brewmaster's argument runs along the lines of social division: you can, but I can't, because I'm a simple worker whom nobody will care to defend and whose protest will go unheard anyway. In *Unveiling,* a married couple of friends who invited Vaněk for the "unveiling" of their newly decorated apartment resort to an argument that reflects their philosophy of life: you can, but we can't, because we need to live our lives to the full, while the pleasures of life apparently do not matter much to you. In *Protest,* a well-to-do screenwriter wriggles out of a moral obligation to sign a petition in defense of an imprisoned artist by invoking sophisticated arguments related to political tactics (he ends up endorsing "the more beneficial effect which the protest would have *without* my signature"), which essentially come down to the following: you can, but I can't, because your career has gone to the dogs anyway, while mine is still something I have to take care of.

These are all voices of human normalcy. Havel the pluralist has no choice but to register them, and even partly to agree with them. But Havel the moralist counters with a more powerful argument of his own: that in a totalitarian society it is precisely the "abnormal" troublemakers who have preserved the last vestiges of normalcy. Theirs is the ordinary human striving for freedom and dignity, the kind that ultimately matters more than the misleading normalcy of a full stomach. And Havel the self-ironist acknowledges, and brings into dramatic relief, the intrinsic irony of the dissidents' position: they may well be the only normal human beings around, but since they constitute a ridiculously powerless minority, their cause, noble though it is, will always be doomed to defeat.

In Havel's plays, Vaněk serves as the central point around which these three lines of argument interlock, forming a triangular trap with no way out. He has no choice but to admit that people have basic rights to food on their tables and to a TV show after dinner. He realizes that his actions make people uneasy or put them at a risk. At the same time, he has no choice; he must stick to his own basic right to follow the voice of his conscience. That is not because of moral haughtiness, but for the simple reason that he is unable to force himself to do things or utter words that he considers wrong or false. In a sense, he lives among his compatriots like a foreigner in Paris: he is aware that all the French eat *escargots,* and he is even able to grasp abstractly their reasons for doing so, but he is physically incapable of forcing the slimy invertebrates down his throat. Finally Vaněk has no choice but to realize his own comical awkwardness. In a society like his, he will always be the odd man out, a laughable exception to the prevailing rule.

The combination of these three necessities makes Vaněk a highly complex dramatic character. This is clear even in the Vaněk trilogy, in which Havel's protagonist is, in terms of sheer stage presence, the least exposed among all the characters. He might seem like little more than a taciturn straight man opposite his rambling and dramatically more developed counterparts. Yet his psychological profile would fill volumes. He is, oddly yet convincingly, heroic and anti-heroic, a centerpiece of tragedy as well as farce. He is never so blindly self-righteous as to forget that, after all, he shares with people their trivial needs, that therefore he is one of them. If his moral backbone is a little more erect than most people's, it is also a backbone that aches.

Vaněk, in sum, is not comfortable with his nagging conscience, and he is not terribly proud of it, either. He realizes how little separates him from the less heroic human mass. In *Audience,* Vaněk, apparently blacklisted, barred from any white-collar job, and forced to take up physical labor in a provincial brewery, does not wish at all to be a martyr; and it is this reluctance that motivates the entire plot. He would gladly swallow the bait of the less exhausting clerical position that the Brewmaster dangles in front of him, even at the cost of the fellow worker whom he would replace. The only reason that he rejects the offer is that the torture of toiling in the brewery's cold cellar is ultimately more bearable than the torture of the nonsensical informing on himself, which the Brewmaster requires as part of the deal.

In *Largo Desolato,* Havel's tendency to endow his dissident hero with anti-heroic features reaches an even greater extreme. Leopold Nettles is a dissident *malgré lui,* one who is not only aware of his weaknesses, like Vaněk, but also doubtful about whether he is up to the task at all. He did not really become a dissident; he was made one. Some of his philosophical writings were denounced by the regime as ideologically harmful, and his quiet life of an introspective bookworm was irrevocably changed. We see him at the point of total exhaustion, on the verge of a nervous breakdown.

Ironically, his new status as a dissident has deprived him of his previous independence. Now everyone, his supporters and persecutors alike, expects something from him. His apartment is visited by an unending stream of friends who worry about his doing nothing, friends who worry about his not doing enough, friends who worry about his doing too much, friends who worry about his worrying. While expecting a secret police search and arrest any minute, he has to entertain his far-from-satisfied lover and at the same time handle a visit from a pair of suspiciously enthusiastic working-class supporters who bear the unmistakable signs of *agents provocateurs.*

When the police finally turn up, their only demand is that Nettles renounce the authorship of his paper. When he refuses, the final blow falls: the police declare that his case has been adjourned "indefinitely for the time being," since it has become clear that his denial of his own identity "would be superfluous." Nettles cries, "Are you trying to say that I am no longer me?" The words aptly sum up what has happened to him. His self has been transformed into (to use the word Havel has applied elsewhere to his own life) a role. A role, in this case, definitely "assigned to him by destiny" rather than "invented by himself," but a role that he has been unable to "play well."

To what extent does Nettles personify the playwright's own doubts? Just as Havel the president is not a man of marble, Havel the dissident was not a man of iron. He has had his crises, his failures, his moments of despair. *Largo Desolato* was written in four days in July 1984, precisely at the low point of a bout of acute "postprison despair." Yet in *Disturbing the Peace* Havel plays down the autobiographical import of his play: "It is not about me, or only about me as such. The play has ambitions to be a human parable, and in that sense it's about man in general."

For Havel, though, writing "about man in general" never means distilling some abstract concept of humanity out of concrete and individual experience. On the contrary, it means portraying man in his concrete surroundings, in the web of his innumerable entanglements, from the metaphysical to the trivial. (*Temptation,* with its Mephistopheles suffering from smelly feet, and its Faust immersed in the vulgarity of power games and sycophancy of his colleagues, is a particularly apt illustration of that range of vision.) Central among those entanglements is the individual's relationship to society and its institutions. In Havel, who is a matchless literary expert on the ironies of totalitarianism, this relationship takes on, as a rule, the shape of the most ironic of oppressions: the constant oppression of the individual by the institutions that he helped create.

Seen from this point of view, Havel's entire dramatic output may not seem to have progressed much beyond, say, Ionesco's *Rhinoceros* or *The Bald Soprano.* The similarities extend even to characteristic techniques in construing dialogue and dramatic situations. Not unlike Ionesco, Havel's favorite device is mechanical repetition. His plays are organized masterfully, almost like musical pieces, around recurring, intercrossing, and clashing refrains, usually utterances from a small-talk phrase book; the more frequently repeated, the more meaningless they are. The Brewmaster's "Them's the paradoxes of life, right?" and similar verbal refrains find their counterparts in repetitive elements of stage action (for example, the way certain characters conspicuously hold hands in *Temptation*). The despotic oppression of language, custom, stereotype, institution, any automatism with which man replaces the irregularity, spontaneity, and uniqueness of his self is a theme that runs through the Theater of the Absurd. Havel did not invent it, he merely transplanted the theme and its corresponding dramatic techniques onto the ground of the specific experience of the inhabitant of a Central European police state.

What he did invent was his counterbalance to the oppressive weight of that experience. That counterbalance is the weak, confused, laughable, and oddly heroic Vaněk, in all his incarnations. Havel the moralist, Havel the pluralist, and Havel the ironist joined forces to produce a deeply human and exquisitely equivocal character. Precisely because Vaněk is safe from the excesses of relativistic immoralism, he is able to help us put things in perspective. Precisely because he is safe from the excesses of dogmatic didacticism and self-righteous seriousness, he remains someone who teaches us something, who has to be taken seriously.

If he is an anti-heroic and comical version of Camus's Rebel, he is nonetheless a Rebel with a cause—and a Rebel with no streak of single-minded obsessiveness. A Rebel essentially powerless, true; but Vaněk's obstinate defense of the core of his humanity expresses something more essential than the need for power: the need for values. In Central Europe in the mid-1970s, it was enough to realize the genuine presence of this need in the human world to begin to believe that "the power of the powerless," prophesied rather than described by Havel in his epoch-making essay of 1978, may one day manifest itself in real life. Last year it did. People very much like Havel's protagonist have woken up the rest of their society and won their seemingly lost cause. The symbolic credit for today's Czechoslovakia is owed not to Švejk, the bumbling soldier and relativistic philosopher of compromise. It is owed to Vaněk.

3. With Chancellor Helmut Kohl, 1997.

4. With Pope John Paul II, 1994.

Prague: Intellectuals and Politicians

Timothy Garton Ash

{. . . *this balance of moral strength without fanaticism and pluralistic tolerance without relativism has affected Havel's progress along his political path. It is perhaps less clear how this same balance is reflected in his art.*

—*Stanislaw Baranczak*}

Imagine a theater critic who is suddenly hauled up from the stalls to act in the play he meant to review. What should he do then? Write the review without mentioning his own part? Appraise his own performance? This is the strange dilemma in which I find myself as I sit down to write this essay. Yet it is a dilemma curiously appropriate to the subject, as will, I trust, emerge. Let me explain.

Earlier this year I received a letter informing me that I had been elected an honorary member of Czech PEN, in gratitude for what I had done for Czech writers in the years up to 1989. I was touched by the gesture. The letter also invited me to attend the 61st World Congress of International PEN, which would be held in Prague in November.

Now there is a great deal to be said against attending any international congress of writers, anywhere, any time. But Prague is a city where writers and intellectuals, especially the numerous banned writers and intellectuals, published only in *samizdat* or the West, had a singular importance up to 1989. This occasion would take place five years to the month after the "revolution of the Magic Lantern," which I described at the time in [*The New York Review*].[1] That had catapulted many of them quite unexpectedly into positions of power, which some retain but others have in the meantime left or lost. Those characteristic post-Communist mutations, dilemmas, and ironies are concentrated—almost as in an archetype—in the person of the writer-president Václav Havel. All this, I thought, might make this particular writers' congress more than usually interesting. It did. . . .

Reprinted and abridged from *The New York Review* 42, no. 1 (12 January 1995): 34–40.

The PEN congress itself was opened by President Havel. Welcoming his fellow writers from around the world "first and foremost as a colleague . . . and only secondarily as a representative of the Czech Republic" he went on to express the hope that our presence would "introduce important spiritual and intellectual stimuli into this sometimes too materialistic and somewhat provincial setting. . . ." Intellectuals, he argued, have a responsibility to engage in "politics in the broadest sense of the word." And not just in the broadest sense:

> I once asked a friend of mine, a wonderful man and a wonderful writer, to fill a certain political post. He refused, arguing that someone had to remain independent. I replied that if you all said that, it could happen that in the end, no one will be independent, because there won't be anyone around to make that independence possible and stand behind it.

However: "I am not suggesting, dear colleagues, that you all become presidents in your own countries, or that each of you go out and start a political party." But we should, he suggested,

> gradually begin to create something like a worldwide lobby, a special brotherhood or, if I may use the word, a somewhat conspirational mafia, whose aim is not just to write marvelous books or occasional manifestoes but to have an impact on politics and its human perceptions in a spirit of solidarity, and in a coordinated, deliberate way . . .

"Politicians, at least the wiser ones," he continued, "will not reject such activity but, on the contrary, will welcome it. I, for instance, would welcome hearing, in this country, a really strong and eloquent voice coming from my colleagues, one that could not be ignored no matter how critical it might be, a voice that did more than merely grumble, or engage in esoteric reflection, but became a clear public and political fact." He then concluded with an eloquent appeal for us all to stand up for Salman Rushdie, for Wole Soyinka, and for Bosnian intellectuals.

Emboldened by this speech, the assembled PEN delegates could begin their usual round of reports, resolutions, and the all-important business of supporting persecuted and imprisoned writers—work in which Czech writers who had themselves long been persecuted or imprisoned could now join. But you could see at once (though I'm not sure how many of the international PEN delegates did see at once) that Havel's speech was as much addressed to the domestic audience. . . .

The next day there was a panel discussion on the very general theme of "intellectuals, government policy and tolerance" in a large hall at the foreign ministry. The most prominent panelist was none other than the writer-premier Václav Klaus. He was joined on the platform by the Hungarian essayist

György Konrád (himself a former president of International PEN, and someone who has written extensively on the role of intellectuals), the Czech novelist Ivan Klíma, writers from Germany, Sweden, and Turkey, and myself. . . .

[Václav Klaus] then opened the discussion with a remarkable short statement in which he announced that in a free country, such as the Czech Republic had now become, the distinction between "dependent" and "independent" intellectuals no longer had any real importance. Some intellectuals were in politics, others not. Expert advice was always welcome. But it made no sense to speak any more about a special role for "independent" intellectuals.

Now the critic was hauled on stage. For this sally could not go unanswered. I began my reply by saying that it was both appropriate and moving to discuss the subject of "intellectuals, government policy, and tolerance" in Prague, where, for twenty-one long years, from the Soviet invasion of 1968 until the Velvet Revolution, some individual Czechs—and Slovaks—had given us a shining example of what intellectuals can do in opposition to a repressive state. The names of Jan Patočka and Václav Havel must stand for many, many more whom I would like to name.

Five years on, however, we happily find ourselves in very different times in Central Europe. What was the role of intellectuals now? I argued, against Klaus, that independence is a crucial attribute of what it should mean to be an intellectual. Not just in a dictatorship but precisely in a liberal, democratic state, independent intellectuals have a crucial role to play.

There should be, I suggested, a necessarily adversarial (but not necessarily hostile) relationship between the independent intellectual and the professional politician. The intellectual's job is to seek the truth, and then to present it as fully and clearly and interestingly as possible. The politician's job is to work in half-truth. The very word *party* implies partial, one-sided. (The Czech word for party, *strana,* meaning literally "side," says it even more clearly.) Of course, the opposition parties then present the other side, the other half of the truth. But this is one of those strange cases where two halves don't make a whole.

The position of a non-executive president or constitutional monarch may, I noted, be a partial exception to this rule. Such a person, standing above party politics, may contribute to setting certain higher intellectual or moral standards in public life. But as a rule there is a necessary and healthy division of labor in a liberal state between independent intellectuals and professional politicians. Arguably this is as important as the formal separation of powers between executive, legislature, and judiciary. It is part of the larger and all-important creative tension between the state and civil society.

Having made my main point about "intellectuals," I commented briefly on the other words in the theme PEN asked us to discuss: "government policy and tolerance." The liberal state—but mainly the legislature and the judiciary rather than the executive branch of government—may sometimes have to limit the freedom of the enemies of freedom. If, say, a private television channel were to mix popular light entertainment with consistent advocacy of the extermination of gypsies, a liberal state should stop it being used for that purpose. If a writer is threatened from abroad with assassination, like Salman Rushdie, the government has a duty to protect him.

tolerance

Beyond this, however, the contribution of politicians in power to "tolerance" lies less in specific acts or policies than in a certain attitude and style of political conduct. No politician likes being criticized. Mrs. Thatcher would often complain about "the media." Her current epigones blame "the chattering classes," which, I noted, is the current English phrase for intellectuals. Yet the closer the politicians can stick to the attitude summed up in the famous phrase "I do not agree with what you say, but I will defend to the death your right to say it," the more secure freedom will be. This, I suggested, is where the business of PEN and the business of prime ministers meet.

Now if these thoughts were expressed around a seminar table at Harvard or Oxford they might be questioned for their simplicity or banality, but they would hardly be thought provocative.[2] Here, with the Czech television cameras rolling and the famously arrogant prime minister locked in this strange intellectual-political wrestling match with his own president, they were accounted so. . . .

Here I need to explicate two issues that were not clarified in the subsequent discussion—partly, I would have to add as a critic, through my own fault. Both were raised by Ivan Klíma, in interventions that effectively supported his prime minister. First, Klíma objected to what he saw as the implication that intellectuals are morally superior to politicians, or somehow possessed of "truth" with a capital T. We have heard too much of these claims, especially in Central Europe, suggested Klíma, in a discussion that we had earlier begun and subsequently continued in private.

Look what a mess intellectuals in power have made of things! Look at the damage done by their utopias! And look what monsters they have been in their private lives! In which connection he quoted Paul Johnson's book *Intellectuals*. The charge about private lives is probably the least pertinent. But there is much in the rest of the indictment. Intellectuals obviously do bear a heavy load of responsibility as architects or accomplices of some of the greatest political crimes of the twentieth century. As George Orwell caustically observed of fellow-traveling intellectuals: "No ordinary man could be such a fool."

Yet I am not making any such high moral, let alone ideological or metaphysical, claim for intellectuals. Many politicians are no doubt better people than many intellectuals. They may also be more intelligent, better read, more cultured. My argument is only that they have, and should have, a different role, which is reflected, crucially, in a different use of language. If a politician

use of lang.

gives a partial, one-sided, indeed self-censored account of a particular issue, he is simply doing his job. And if he manages to "sell" the part as the whole then he is doing his job effectively.

If an intellectual does that, he is not doing his job; he has failed in it. The intellectual is not the guardian or high priest of some metaphysical, ideological or pseudo-scientific Truth with a capital T. Nor is he simply the voice of *Gesinnungsethik* (the ethics of conviction) against the *Verantwortungsethik* (the ethics of responsibility) of the politician, to use Max Weber's famous distinction. But he does have a qualitatively different responsibility for the validity, intellectual coherence, and truth of what he says and writes.

I therefore have an answer to the second question that Ivan Klíma injected into the discussion: "What do you mean by an intellectual?" What I mean is a person playing a particular role. It is the role of the thinker or writer who engages in public discussion of issues of public policy, in politics in the broadest sense, while deliberately not engaging in the pursuit of political power.

I certainly don't mean all members of the "intelligentsia" in the broad sociological definition of "intelligentsia" officially adopted in Communist Eastern Europe; that is, everyone with higher education. Nor do I mean the "intellectuals on the road to class power" of György Konrád and Ivan Szelényi's book of 1974;[3] or the pre-1989 Václav Klaus, an employee of the Czechoslovak Academy of Sciences under President Husák. These were all intellectuals, but in a different sense.

My description of the intellectual's role, which is both a Weberian ideal type and simply an ideal, certainly has more in common with the self-understanding of the opposition intellectuals in Central and Eastern Europe before 1989; of the pre-1989 Václav Havel (who barely qualified as an "intellectual" in Communist sociology, since he had scant formal higher education and for a time did manual labor); of the patriotic Polish, Czech, or Hungarian "intelligentsia"; in their idealistic, pre- and anti-Communist interpretation of their own role. Yet it differs also fundamentally from this. In the "abnormal" conditions that have actually been normality for much of Central Europe over much of the last two centuries, intellectuals have been called upon, or have felt themselves called upon, to take roles that they did not take in the West. The conscience of the nation. The voice of the oppressed. The writer as priest, prophet, resistance fighter, and substitute politician.

Since the liberation of 1989, all these extra roles have fallen away, with stunning rapidity. This is healthy and long overdue. As Brecht's Galileo exclaims: Unhappy the land that has need of heroes. The role of the intellectual as critic of a democratically elected government cannot be equated with that of the intellectual as leader of the opposition against an alien, totalitarian power. . . .

Now obviously, this ideal of the intellectual has never fully been achieved. Indeed, as the twentieth century closes, the catalog of the *trahison des clercs* is a thick volume; the list of those who preserved real independence is a thin one. In our own free societies, we see examples of journalists who have been corrupted by the proximity to power. Academic readers of *The New York Review* will perhaps know, in their own universities, scholars who have politically trimmed their analyses, or at least their conclusions, in the hope of following Kissinger or Brzezinski to a job in Washington. But to say that an ideal has never been fully achieved is merely to say that it is an ideal.

We have Orwell. We have Raymond Aron. We have other writers, academics, and journalists who have maintained a high standard of intellectual independence while engaging in political debate. Even in a free society, there is still an important part to be played by the *spectateur engagé.* By the critic on stage.

And by the playwright on stage? Václav Havel was, of course, the invisible panelist in our discussion. . . .

If you said "the intellectual and politics" in the 1960s, the immediate free association might be "Sartre" or perhaps "Bertrand Russell." Say it now, whether in Paris, New York, Berlin, or Rome, and one of the first associations will be "Havel." If he is right, what he says will be important not just for the Czech lands; if he is wrong, it matters for the rest of us too.

 . . . Three volumes of Havel's speeches have now appeared in Czech, and a Prague publisher has just issued a selection in English, entitled *Toward a Civil Society.*[4] Although the English selection is heavily biased toward his major foreign appearances, and to that extent gives a slightly misleading impression of what he has been doing for the last five years, it does contain the most important and systematic statements of his views since he became president. Havel told me that he regards his presidential speeches as the intellectual continuation of the essays, lectures, and prison letters of the dissident years. "Then I wrote essays, now I write speeches," he said, suggesting that only the form of what he does with words has changed, not the essential content of the intellectual activity.

Certainly as presidential speeches go these are quite extraordinary. Extraordinary in the range of subjects they address, from Maastricht to the Anthropic Cosmological Principle, from European security to the legacy of the Czechoslovak security police, from Kafka to the need for a higher something that Havel cannot quite bring himself to call God. Extraordinary in their literary quality. Extraordinary in their frank and vivid insights based, as throughout his earlier work, on a kind of wry agonizing about his own existential dilemmas. Since his present dilemma—or, at least, one of them—is that of the intellectual in politics, there is much on that in his speeches. And sometimes in unlikely places.

Nearly two years ago, a mutual friend brought me, with the president's greetings, the typescript of a speech delivered in the Asahi Hall in Tokyo in April 1992, and now reproduced in this volume. The speech is devoted to the place of the intellectual in politics. Having described the peculiar post-Communist situation in which "poets, philosophers, singers became members of Parliament, government ministers or even presidents," he proceeds to take issue with "a British friend of mine" who "has said that one of the biggest problems of the post-Communist states lies in the inability of their leaders to make up their minds about who they are. Are they independent intellectuals or practicing politicians?"

Having explained that he understands only too well what I have in mind, he goes on to ask if this may actually be "not a dilemma, but a historic challenge? What if in fact it challenged them to introduce a new tone, a new element, a new dimension into politics?" Based on their specific experience under totalitarianism, might they not inject "a new wind, [a] new spirit, a new spirituality . . . into the established stereotypes of present-day politics?" Faced with the huge challenges of overpopulation, poverty, pollution, ethnic and social unrest, what is needed is a change "in the sphere of the spirit, of human consciousness and self-knowledge. . . ."

Politics is increasingly becoming the domain of specialists, but it should be the domain of people,

> with a heightened sense of responsibility and heightened understanding for the mysterious complexity of Being. If intellectuals claim to be such people, they would virtually be denying the truth of that claim if they refused to take upon themselves the burden of public offices on the grounds that it would mean dirtying their hands. Those who say that politics is disreputable in fact help make it so. . . .[5]

Elsewhere he restates and elaborates on various parts [of his position]. . . .

Perhaps his most remarkable treatment of the subject, however, is a speech he delivered in Copenhagen in May 1991. Here he confronts head-on what he calls the "diabolical" temptations of power. He now finds he writes,

> in the world of privileges, exceptions, perks, in the world of VIPs who gradually lose track of how much a streetcar ticket or butter costs, how to make a cup of coffee, how to drive a car and how to place a telephone call. In other words, I find myself on the threshold of the very world of the Communist fat cats whom I have criticized all my life. And worst of all, everything has its own unassailable logic.

"Someone who forgets how to drive a car, do the shopping, make himself coffee and place a telephone call is not the same person who had known how to do those things all his life." The politician becomes "a captive of his position, his perks, his office. That which apparently confirms his identity and thus his existence in fact subtly takes that identity and existence away from him." This is vintage Havel, probing through a combination of ironical observation and agonized introspection to a larger truth, as he did in "The Power of the Powerless." It hints at a great essay to come: on the powerlessness of the powerful.

Yet the conclusion of this speech is surprising. It does not follow, he says, "that it is not proper to devote oneself to politics because politics is in principle immoral." What follows is that politics requires people of higher responsibility, taste, tact, and moral sensitivity. "Those who claim that politics is a dirty business are lying to us. Politics is work of a kind that requires especially pure people, because it is especially easy to become morally tainted."[6]

He returns to the theme in a speech at New York University in October 1991. . . .

> Of course, in politics, as anywhere else in life, it is impossible and pointless to say everything, all at once, to just anyone. But that does not mean having to lie. All you need is tact, the proper instincts, and good taste. One surprising experience from "high politics" is this: I have discovered that good taste is more useful here than a degree in political science.[7]

(This may be less surprising to anyone who has studied political science). . . .

I have quoted what Havel has to say on this subject . . . because his reflections are always interesting, but also because only through extensive quotation does a problem become apparent. The problem is that what he has to say is often vague and confused, and this analytical confusion reflects a deeper confusion about his own role.

In his PEN speech, for example, he confuses the intellectual's engagement in politics in the broader sense (that is, without being directly involved in the pursuit of power or office) and in the narrower sense (the anecdote about urging his writer friend to take office). But, as I argued against Klaus, the distinction is very important.

The argument in the Copenhagen speech is also confused. Is he saying that politics is or is not a dirty business? If it isn't a dirty business then why should it require exceptionally "pure" people to get involved without being corrupted? Anyway, why should we imagine that intellectuals are any better equipped to resist the temptations of power, to remain decent, upright, uncorrupted, than ordinary mortals? One might well argue, with Ivan Klíma, quite the contrary: the record of intellectuals in power in the twentieth century suggests that they are among the least likely to resist the insidious poison, precisely because they are most able to rationalize, intellectualize, or philosophically justify their own submission or corruption by referring to higher goals or values. Orwell's faith in "ordinary men" may also be misplaced, but the history of Europe in the twentieth century gives us no grounds for believing that intellectuals will do any better.

The argument about the irresponsibility of not taking political responsibility is also a highly questionable projection from the very particular situation of post-Communist Central Europe, and specifically of Václav Havel, to the general one. Of course, in the unique situation of 1989, in countries where the only alternative to the *Nomenklatura* was a new political elite drawn largely from the ranks of more or less independent intellectuals, it would have been shirking responsibility not to take office.

"Someone had to" is, for the year 1990, an entirely valid observation. But even then it could be the polite and, as it were, PC (or, rather, MC—Morally Correct) guise for personal ambition. Lech Wałęsa's *"nie chcę, ale muszę"* ("I don't want to, but I must") has become proverbial in Poland. In any case, this is the particular problem of a particular historical moment: As a new class of professional politicians emerges, there is no reason at all why those intellectuals who do not feel comfortable in professional politics—with its different rules of play, its different way with words—should not return to their desks, laboratories, or studios. . . .

There remains the general claim about introducing a new moral, intellectual, and spiritual dimension into our routinized, specialized, unimaginative party politics: a "new wind," to recall Havel's own simile. At this point, at the latest, one has to turn from the writing to the man. For Havel now differs fundamentally from most writers or philosophers in that the test case of the truth of the propositions he is advancing is himself. As he constantly points out, the test of what Václav Havel argues in these speeches is what Václav Havel does as president (which is, of course, now mainly to give speeches).

So how far has [Václav Havel] achieved the very high goal that he set himself five years ago? Particularly in his first two years as President of Czechoslovakia, the achievement was immense. Through his words and deeds, he both preached and practiced a resolute and morally sensitive moderation, civility, tolerance, and decency that contributed a huge amount to the peaceful, civilized nature of the transition from Communism in Czechoslovakia. There was nothing inevitable about this. Were it not for him, it could have been much messier, dirtier, even bloody. Beyond that, he has been an extraordinary and much needed voice in Europe, and beyond. While the response of West European leaders to what happened five years ago was woefully inadequate, while they fiddled in Maastricht as Yugoslavia began to burn, he has constantly and eloquently reminded us of the larger historical dimensions of what has happened in Europe, and—if one can say this without too much pathos—of our duty.

Of course he did not become Plato's philosopher-king, or even, to take the obvious comparison, a second Masaryk. At times he does seem to hold the peculiar Masarykian belief that Ernest Gellner ironically sums up as "No

State Formation without Philosophic Justification." But he is not a systematic philosopher, and 1989 was not 1918. Yet measured by any but the vertiginous standards he has set himself, the first two years of the playwright-king would be accounted a remarkable success.

Since then, however, and especially since his abdication in 1992 and his return as Czech president in 1993, it has been, to say the least, a more mixed picture. There are many reasons for this, but the one most relevant here is his refusal to choose between the roles of intellectual and politician.

If, when the Civic Forum broke up on the initiative of Václav Klaus in 1991, Havel had allowed himself to be clearly identified with the remaining movement, or some new political movement, or even—perish the thought—a political party, he would certainly have stretched the terms of his office, but he might also have had a real political power base as well as his own charisma and popularity. As it was, he refused to engage in those normal, partisan (and often dirty) politics. His power slipped away. Up came Václav II [Václav Klaus], on whose reluctant sufferance he was, in a quite humiliating way, elected Czech president in 1993, with very limited powers. Havel himself recalls with anger how members of the Czech Parliament openly ignored him, reading newspapers or chatting, while he addressed them. Wryly, but with more than a touch of bitterness, he mutters, in English, the word "clown."

Yet at the same time, his image and voice as an intellectual have become blurred. It's not just the suits and ties (which he says he still feels uncomfortable in), the ceremonial duties and the compromises, such as that on the lustration law. It's not just the privileged isolation from ordinary life, the life in a velvet cage, which he describes so vividly in his Copenhagen speech but which has nonetheless alienated many former close associates and friends.

All that apart, there is simply the plain fact that a president's speeches are not a writer's essays. Text and context interact in a different and much less favorable way. Life contradicts art.

Even the outward form of *Toward a Civil Society* somehow speaks to us of the blurring of the voice that comes from the confusion of roles. The copyright page tells us this book is published with financial assistance from the Czech foreign ministry. Does a book by Havel really need a subsidy to be published? It comes with jacket endorsements from Zbigniew Brzezinski, Eduard Shevardnadze, and one Thomas Klestil, who, readers may like to know, is the president of Austria. Does Havel really need to be puffed by a Klestil? The cover photograph shows a man in a pin-striped suit and tie speaking in front of the yellow-stars-on-blue background of the Council of Europe and the EU. In other words, this book looks just like a professional politician's piece of government-subsidized vanity publishing—which, of course, it definitely is not. But it looks like it.

"The strongest poison ever known came from Caesar's laurel crown," wrote Blake. I do not believe that Václav Havel has been poisoned by power in any normal sense. If mildly infected at all, it is in the rather unusual form of being, so to speak, aesthetically enamored of the theater of high politics—which, as he is the first to point out, is even more the theater of the absurd than the most absurdist of his own plays.

Earlier this year I heard him give a brilliantly funny description of the stage management of President Clinton's visit to Prague, and, in particular, of his visit with Clinton to a typical Prague pub with a typical gathering of typical locals—all carefully identified by the American embassy beforehand, and including the writer Bohumil Hrabal. It was a wonderful foretaste of the book he might write when he ceases to be president. But I must admit that for a moment I did find myself uneasily wondering what the dissident writer Václav Havel would have made of such a stage-managed scene, what subtle lessons he would have drawn about the alienation of the powerful.

Probably the shortest and best retort ever made to Plato's vision of the philosopher-king is Kant's remark that for philosophers to become kings is neither desirable nor possible because "the possession of power unavoidably spoils the free use of reason" *(weil der Besitz der Gewalt das freie Urteil der Vernunft unvermeidlich verdirbt)*. Havel's case is an interesting variation on this eternal truth, because it seems to me that the greater threat to his free use of reason may actually be the relative *loss* of power he has experienced since 1992, a loss that Václav Klaus misses no occasion to rub in. Havel is now fighting to regain some of the lost power, staking out his own political agenda in a series of speeches stressing the importance of education, local government, civic engagement, and so on. He now even seems prepared, at least on some issues, to be a focus for opposition to Klaus, an opposition that is to be found not least within the prime minister's own governing coalition. But to use his "spoken essays" in this instrumental way would seem to be a departure from the standards he has set himself—and simply a sad comedown from his position five years ago.

Anyway, this is not a French-style *cohabitation,* where an executive president with great powers can, as it were, win the political battle. Havel's present constitutional position as non-executive president is more comparable with that of the president of the Federal Republic of Germany, an office held, until recently, by a man whom he much admires, Richard von Weizsäcker. In fact, in *Summer Meditations* Havel wrote that in his dream vision of (as he then still hoped) Czechoslovakia: "At the head of the state will be a gray-haired Professor with the charm of a Richard von Weizsäcker."[8] And as I read Havel's speeches, especially the more recent ones, I notice some similarities—not least in a small but revealing feature of the prose. The most characteristic feature of President von Weizsäcker's style was the rhetorical question. "Of course my office only permits me to ask questions," he would say, before launching a series of rhetorical questions that added up to an extremely clear statement of his own views. Am I imagining things or is Havel increasingly using the same device?

One can take this particular comparison a stage further. It is an open secret that there was considerable tension between the patrician, Protestant, intellectual President von Weizsäcker and the provincial, Catholic, and less ostensibly intellectual Chancellor Kohl. In private, they could be quite rude about each other. In public, some of President von Weizsäcker's elegant rhetorical questions could be understood as digs at the chancellor; some of the chancellor's remarks could be interpreted as barbs in the other direction. But they certainly never descended to anything like the public Punch and Judy show that the Klaus-Havel duel has at times become, with everyone knowing who was the (unnamed) object of each elliptical speech; every occasion being interpreted in that light; and ordinary Czechs sometimes having the impression that if Havel came out in favor of eating spinach then Klaus would be sure to come out the next day against eating spinach. On impeccable neoliberal grounds, of course.

Instead, both Kohl and Weizsäcker scrupulously observed the constitutional proprieties and, at best, tried to turn their differences into complementarity rather than discord. The result was one of the most effective double-acts to lead any European state in recent history. It contributed very substantially to the peaceful achievement of German unity. If the Czech president and prime minister were to achieve such an (albeit uneasy) division of labor, it would doubtless be a great service to the Czech Republic, at home, in Europe, and in the wider world.

To be sure, this, so to speak, Weizsäcker role, would be some miles down from introducing into politics the new spiritual dimension that Havel dreamed, and perhaps still dreams, of introducing. Indeed, as the German example illustrates, in the wider European context it would not even be new. There is also a real question whether the ex-president of Czechoslovakia might not actually have a greater influence in Europe and the world today were he again able to speak with his own unique voice as an independent intellectual. But the die is cast. For another few years, at least, he will go on in the Castle, suffering up there for us; a living exemplar of the dilemmas of the intellectual in politics; condemned, like the central character in one of his own plays, to play out a role that he feels is not truly his own; and haunted and taunted by a slightly threatening character who even bears the same name. Such absurdist tricks the divine playwright plays.

With that somewhat Havelesque reflection, my Prague tale of intellectuals and politics is told, five years, almost to the day, after I told, also in these pages, the tale of the Magic Lantern. Now, as then, I have tried to tell the story as honestly as I can, at the risk of indiscretion and of causing offense. Are there any conclusions to be drawn, any lessons, even? There are, I think, possible implications for the Czech Republic, for the position of intellectuals in post-Communist Central Europe, and finally, and most tentatively, for the place of intellectuals in Europe altogether.

For the Czech Republic the immediate question is: Can the premier and the president possibly achieve the kind of moderately harmonious public relationship that Kohl and Weizsäcker achieved? Almost certainly not. Since this is a new democracy, the constitutional roles are not as clearly defined by law or by precedent. (Good fences make good neighbors.) The two have very different political views of the way the new Czech state should be built. Klaus, the Thatcherite, gives absolute priority to economic transformation, even at the cost of corruption and illegality on the way. "Speed," he says, "is more important than accuracy." At times he seems inclined to Mrs. Thatcher's view that "society does not exist." Havel, whose politics, inasmuch as they can be defined at all in ordinary terms, are those of an ecologically minded social democrat, stresses the importance of culture, local government, civic participation, civil society.

Above all, though, it is the clash of personalities, and biographies. The Tale of Two Václavs is not simply that of the intellectual Havel versus the politician Klaus. To be sure, Havel is a more important intellectual and Klaus a more effective politician. But what makes it so difficult is precisely that both are intellectuals in politics, as the PEN episode nicely illustrated.

This is what makes the story at once unique and representative, for all over post-Communist Central Europe intellectuals are wrestling with similar dilemmas. Many who have gone into and remain in politics will find the dichotomy I present too sharp. The former dissident and former foreign minister Jiří Dienstbier, now the leader of a small opposition party, commented in a newspaper interview after our PEN discussion that while he agreed with my basic argument he did not feel that as a minister he had been working in half-truth. Those, now quite numerous, who after 1989 went into but are now again out of politics, will find it easier to accept such a clear dichotomy. Those who never ventured into politics will find it easier still. But they have their own problems.

The intelligentsia, one of the characteristic phenomena of modern Central and East European history, is now everywhere engulfed in sweeping change. This world of "circles of friends," of *milieux,* where artists, philosophers, writers, economists, journalists all felt themselves to belong to the same group, and to be committed to a certain common ethos (albeit often honored in the breach), was something anachronistic in late twentieth-century Europe—but also something rich and fine. Its extraordinary character was summed up for me in a phrase that Ivan Klíma used in describing how he and his fellow writers had set out to revive the dormant Czech PEN club in 1989. "I was," he said, "authorized by my circle of friends. . . ." The peculiar world of the intelligentsia under Communism was one in which you sought authorization from your circle of friends.[9]

Freedom has changed all that. With remarkable speed, the intelligentsia has fragmented into separate professions, as in the West: journalists, publishers, academics, actors, not to mention those who have become officials, lawyers, diplomats. The *milieux* have faded, the "circles of friends" have dispersed or lost their special significance. Those who have remained in purely "intellectual" professions—above all, academics—have found themselves impoverished. Moreover, it is the businessmen and entrepreneurs who are the tone-setting heroes of this time. Thus, from having an abnormal importance before 1989, independent intellectuals have plummeted to abnormal unimportance.

Yet to say that is to assume that we know what their "normal" importance would be. But do we? Is there any wider European normality in this respect, toward which post-Communist Central Europe might be either moving or contributing? In Britain the term "intellectual" is rarely used, being regarded as something continental and slightly pretentious. The recent coinage "Eurointellectuals" neatly combines both prejudices. Yet, as Lord Byron said of the word *longueurs:* though we have not the word, we have the thing in considerable profusion. And they exist on both left and right—although here, as elsewhere, the right tends to identify the very idea of "intellectuals" with the left.

In Germany, the days of the great public role of writers like Böll and Grass seem to be over. However, some of the country's most interesting political debates are actually conducted by intellectuals, on the *Feuilleton* pages of the *Frankfurter Allgemeine Zeitung* and in smaller journals. Yet here too you have the phenomenon of right-wing intellectuals denouncing "the intellectuals," meaning left-wing intellectuals; in this case for their failure to welcome the unification of Germany.

In France there have been writers and thinkers identified and identifying themselves as "intellectuals," at least since the time of the Dreyfus affair and the *Manifeste des intellectuels.* Yet I doubt that anyone would today venture to write a *Plaidoyer pour les intellectuels,* as Sartre did in 1972. Partly, no doubt, out of an awareness of the awful misjudgments and moral failures of intellectuals in the twentieth century—and not least, French intellectuals, including, notably, Sartre. Partly because there are no obvious new utopias to be embraced—except utopian liberalism, which is a contradiction in terms. Partly, perhaps, because they are too busy appearing on television and generally competing in a crowded entertainment market.

Yet at the same time, there is, in all the major West European countries, a real crisis of popular confidence in the professional politicians, seen to be out-of-touch, self-interested careerists, tainted by corruption. The Italian debacle haunts us all.

In this sense, Havel's call for a new spiritual and moral dimension to be introduced to politics might seem to be relevant, after all, for Western Europe. That was what many in Western Europe felt and hoped at the moment of the Magic Lantern five years ago. But the lesson is surely not that this is a time for intellectuals to enter politics, in the narrow sense of trying to become prime ministers or presidents. No, this is a time for intellectuals to be both resolutely independent and politically engaged—which means, among other things, criticizing prime ministers and presidents. Politely, of course. Constructively, wherever possible. But above all, clearly.

Notes and References

1. See my "The Revolution of the Magic Lantern," *The New York Review*, 18 January 1990, and *The Magic Lantern* (Random House, 1990).

2. A very useful exploration of this subject, partly inspired by Havel's earlier writings, is Ian MacLean, Alan Montefiore, and Peter Winch, editors, *The Political Responsibility of Intellectuals* (Cambridge University Press, 1990).

3. Published in English as George Konrád and Ivan Szelényi, *The Intellectuals on the Road to Class Power* (Harcourt Brace, 1979), Szelényi notes in his introduction that the manuscript was completed in 1974.

4. The full title of the English-language volume is *Toward a Civil Society: Selected Speeches & Writings 1990–1994* (Prague: Lidové Noviny, 1994). A note on the copyright page indicates that this volume is edited by Paul Wilson, with the translations by Paul Wilson and others. The Czech collections are Václav Havel, *Projevy leden–červen 1990 (Speeches: January–June 1990)* (Prague: Vyšehrad, 1990), Václav Havel, *Vážení občané, Projevy červenec 1990–červenec 1992 (Dear Citizens: Speeches, July 1990–July 1992)* (Prague: Lidové Noviny, 1992), and *Václav Havel 1992 & 1993* (Prague: Paseka, 1994).

5. [*Toward a Civil Society*, 195–204 passim.]

6. The Czech original is even more emphatic, saying literally, "All lie who tell us that politics is a dirty business." [The speech, entitled "The Sonning Prize" has since been published in Václav Havel, *The Art of the Impossible: Politics as Morality in Practice*, trans. Paul Wilson and others (New York: Alfred A. Knopf, 1997), 69–74.]

7. [Speech delivered at New York University (27 October 1991), *The Art of the Impossible*, 84.]

8. [Václav Havel, *Summer Meditations*, trans. Paul Wilson (New York: Vintage Books, 1993), 103.]

9. The sequel is amusing. After being instrumental in reactivating the PEN club, Klíma was summoned for interrogation by the security police. Their main concern was that Václav Havel should not become president of Czech PEN. Three months later he was president of Czechoslovakia.

PERSONAL EXPERIENCES

◆

Havel's Choice

STEPHEN SCHIFF

{When does a person live in truth in Havel's sense of the word? Not when he respects some dogma; he lives in truth only when he crosses the boundaries of his own version of the world, finds himself on an alternative map of reality, and is constantly forced to justify his own positions.

—*Václav Bělohradský}*

Amid the black and gold spires of Prague Castle, the dominant sounds these days are the clunk of hammers and the shriek of power saws: everywhere you go, you smell acrid new paint. This splendid city within a city has glowered down at the Czech capital since the ninth century, sheltering Přemyslid princes, Hapsburg emperors, gray Communist dictators. But now, in the wake of the "Velvet Revolution" of 1989, it has been restored to the position it enjoyed during the first Czechoslovak Republic of 1918. It is once again the official seat of a democratically elected president—of a dream-come-true president, a philosopher, a wit, a hero seemingly devoid of pretense and sham: the playwright and essayist Václav Havel.

All the president's men and women work here, too, and even though they've been in place for more than a year now—they no longer slouch around in blue jeans and work shirts—the mood in the Castle still has some of the adolescent giddiness of the first day of school. Everything is newly hatched; everyone runs around looking purposeful and bewildered and slightly dazed. In some wings, the rooms stand empty and expectant; in others, ladders are propped every which way, like pickup sticks, and rolled-up carpets await deployment. Downstairs, in the reception areas, you can still find the glum Communist furniture—squat, rubbery chairs and hulking oak tables—but upstairs there has been a major spiffing campaign. In one restored wing, designed in the twenties mostly by the Yugoslav architect Josip Plečnik, an indoor fountain burbles serenely across from an eyepopping vision: a small room lined floor to ceiling with freshly polished gold leaf. The old socialist-realist paintings in the corridors—heroic Stakhanovites laying

Reprinted and abridged from *Vanity Fair* (August 1991), 124 ff.

bricks and conquering farmlands—have been replaced with landscapes by Czech old masters. Computers have arrived, though no one is terribly deft with them yet, and there are big TVs everywhere, blasting CNN. Outside, in the three vast courtyards, the president's guard marches in majestic navy-blue uniforms newly designed by Theodor Pistek, who won an Academy Award for his costumes in *Amadeus*. Václav Havel isn't just a head of state; he's a man of the theater. He knows it's important to get the sets and costumes right.

Well, sort of right. No matter how hard this government tries—and no one here has gotten much sleep since December 1989—there's something indelibly Ruritanian about the nation it now rules. The new Czechoslovakia feels like an amateur country—you half expect it to be run by Peter Sellers. Forty years of Soviet domination have left a lacquer of backwardness and innocence on every visible surface, and to a visitor from the televised go-go of the West, the beguiling sheen can momentarily obscure the troubles boiling beneath. With its resplendent churches, statues, bridges, and palaces, Prague is so beautiful it's almost comical, like some deliciously quaint Central European theme park. And yet nothing here quite works.

Prices have doubled and sometimes even tripled since controls were lifted last January. Unemployment is soaring. Zealots are driving government officials out of office for having associated, however minimally, with the Communist secret police. Slovak separatists are rioting. The old *Nomenklatura* are still running the most important industries, and people are ranting at Havel for not booting them out of their posts. Foreign carpetbaggers arrive every day to exploit the confusion.

And in the Castle, no one can catch his breath. The old systems have been ripped away, the new ones are not yet in place, and the future is a blur of euphoria and despair. Escorting me at top speed through the corridors, Havel's press secretary, Michael Žantovský, points out the offices of the presidential advisers. This one is a novelist and short-story writer. Here is an architect. Here an actor. This one, in charge of domestic policy and national security, is a screenwriter. The adviser on social affairs is an eight-time Olympic gold medalist in gymnastics. I glance over at Žantovský, who is young and vigorous and wonderfully good-humored, and I think of his various American equivalents. Where but in Czechoslovakia would you find a presidential spokesman who is also the author of his country's only major study of Woody Allen?

And now we round a corner, and there is the president himself, in the middle of some peculiar ceremony. At fifty-four, Václav Havel (pronounced VAHTS-lav HAH-vel) is tiny and roundish, with sleepy-looking eyes, scruffy, ginger-colored hair, and a mustache that looks like a red-pencil scribble on his upper lip; his complexion gives off a vital, orangy glow, as if carrot juice were coursing through his veins. He is standing in the middle of a grand and empty room next to his tall, bulb-nosed chancellor, Prince Karel von Schwarzenberg, and as Nikons flare and video cameras roll, he is receiving some twenty-five remarkable-looking people: the newly appointed rectors of Czechoslovakia's colleges and universities, all gussied up in their ceremonial finery. Most of their outfits are about what you'd expect: red velvet robes, with heavy gold chains round their necks and soft velvet tricorn hats. But the one in the middle, the rector of the art academy, has done himself up as a walking cathedral, and his hat climaxes in three lofty black steeples. When he approaches Havel to receive the official scroll and handshake, he and the president look at each other for a moment and nearly burst into giggles. "They're old friends," whispers Žantovský. "He used to organize Happenings back in the sixties."

But of course. In the new Czechoslovakia, one must never underestimate the Far-out Factor. The generation of dissidents who now find themselves in power remain, for want of a better term, Sixties People, and there was no greater fan of the American counterculture than Václav Havel. This, after all, is the president who has officially received such foreign dignitaries as Frank Zappa, Lou Reed, and the Rolling Stones, who was given a scooter to ride through the Castle corridors when he complained of their length, who, during the first weeks of his term, made televised speeches to the nation wearing a corduroy jacket and a polka-dot tie. When Pistek's new guard uniforms arrived, Havel immediately put one on and yelled, "Let's go scare the cooks," whereupon he descended on the Castle kitchen, giggling and brandishing his new saber.

That was just over a year ago; he's come a long way since. Facing his country's robed rectors in a charcoal suit and a richly striped tie, Havel shifts uncomfortably from one leg to the other, and at times he even appears to be struggling to stay alert, but, for all that, he never seems anything less than presidential: he and the office have plainly met each other halfway. This is a crucial moment in his regime. Everything he does now has national and even international consequences; everything he says is pored over, scrutinized, criticized. In short, the honeymoon is over.

In a way, life was much simpler when he was merely Václav Havel, king of the dissidents. It was easy to maintain a clear conscience when the world was so neatly divided between the devils in power and the saints who fought them. Now every decision demands Solomonic wisdom; every choice is fraught with ambiguity; every step on the road to freedom raises blisters or draws blood. At this midpoint in his first term, Havel is facing obstacles no mere dissident, no matter how celebrated, ever has to face. For the first time, he has real political rivals, most prominent among them the ambitious and charismatic minister of finance, Václav Klaus. For the first time, there have been anti-Havel demonstrations, especially in Slovakia, where Havel came close to being assaulted by an angry separatist mob. Prague's new and astonishingly sleazy tabloids fulminate against him and his administration; meanwhile, some of his programs, like his cherished dream of weaning Czechoslovakia from the armaments industry, have had to be deferred in the wake of vociferous public protests.

And yet Václav Havel remains one of the most beloved heads of state in the world. Conducting ceremonies, he has the aura of a certain kind of theater star—the kind who never quite disappears into his role, but plays it to the hilt nevertheless. If the Czechs continue to adore him even as his free-market economic reforms threaten their pocketbooks, that may be because they see him as one of their own, a man not cut out for his mission but accomplishing it nonetheless—a man who, like Czechoslovakia itself, spends every day rising to the occasion. The paradoxical truth about Václav Havel is simply this: even though the world thinks of him as a writer masquerading, however temporarily, as a politician, the very opposite is the case—inside the writer, an eccentric but world-class politician was always wildly signaling to be let out.

His political persona is uniquely effective. Havel is a sort of European Gandhi: shy and selfless, yet insuperably stubborn; seemingly egoless, yet devoid of moral doubt; cunning and even manipulative, but never toward his own personal ends; conscience-driven, but never condemnatory of those who aren't. "Shyness and courage, both very extreme—that's Havel," says the filmmaker Miloš Forman, who has known him since they were in boarding school together. "It's a strange combination. Because when the Soviets invaded in '68, the question was the same for all intellectuals. Either you stayed and became a persecuted person, or you collaborated, or you left the country. So if you didn't want to collaborate and shit on your own conscience, you had only two choices—emigrate, or become Havel. That's why I emigrated, because I knew that I didn't have the courage to be a hero and a martyr and be sent to prison again and again and again. Havel did."

Unlike many of the other dissidents who were swept into power with him in 1989, Havel has never been a Communist, has never cooperated with any of the governments that have ruled Czechoslovakia since it became a Soviet satellite in 1948, has never espoused any ideology or political theory. Whenever there was an opportunity for opposition, Havel was always one of the leaders; when there were no opportunities, he created them; when he was offered a way out (as in 1979, when he was given the choice of prison or a passport to the United States), he refused. Yet, far from using his record of unassailable virtue to admonish the less virtuous, Havel has used it to forgive and restore. When he ran into one of his former jailers shortly after taking office, Havel shook his hand warmly and asked him how he'd been. And now, as witchhunts threaten Czechoslovakia and potential Robespierres declaim from the rafters, as the new nation rushes to crucify those who once cooperated with the Communists, Havel keeps telling his people that all Czechs and Slovaks are partially guilty, that everyone in some way participated, cooperated, or acquiesced in the old regime—including himself. In the words of Rita Klímová, the Czech ambassador to the United States, "When someone like Havel, who's the least guilty, says that we're all guilty, it's a very, very profound and healing thing to say."

"Havel is a sort of sacred figure here," says Luboš Beniak, the editor in chief of *Mladý Svět,* Czechoslovakia's largest weekly. "Everybody knows he's a very honest man. This is the main difference between him and all the rest. For decades in Czechoslovakia, politics was a dirty business, something an honest man wouldn't get involved in. And all the rest of us, especially people of his age, have changed their stance at least once. Nothing against it; quite natural. But he is the only man who has not changed his philosophy during his whole life. This is why he is so exceptional. He flies above all the everyday troubles, everyday clashes, everyday lies and animosities."

And is he still thought of that way, even as his country faces new economic troubles, nationalist conflicts between the Czechs and the Slovaks, environmental horrors? "The support is not ecstatic like it was before," says Beniak, "but it's still there. You know, sometimes, as a politician, he has made mistakes. But his mistakes all come from the same thing: he sometimes doesn't respect the realities of life. And it's very difficult to say that this is bad, because his whole life is based on not respecting the realities of life. If he respected the realities of life, he wouldn't be president today."

My own unreal day with the president begins around eleven in the morning: Michael Žantovský ushers me into Havel's brand-new reception room, which has just been painted in a style that might make you think Czechoslovakia was run by the Beatles. The painter, a friend of Havel's named Aleš Lamr, has covered the walls with Peter Max-ish blips and blobs in blue, green, and orange. It's difficult to imagine, say, François Mitterrand or George Bush being received in this Yellow Submarine, and more difficult still to imagine them encountering Havel's secretary Bára Štěpánová, a busty hippie in a skintight purple mini-dress, with filigreed white stockings, lace-up boots, and funkily mis-matched earrings. Štěpánová, it turns out, used to be an actress in a theater troupe called the Society for a Merrier Present, which found fame by posing as riot police during demonstrations and mock-threatening the protesters with salamis and cucumbers. It was Štěpánová who presented Havel with his first scooter (it has since been replaced with a fancier one). The president, who needed a secretary at the time, hired her on the spot.

From somewhere deep in the inner sanctum, I hear mysterious noises, like goose honks or maybe the lowing of an asthmatic cow. Štěpánová vanishes behind a door, and a moment later she is leading me through the conference room and into the innermost office, there to meet the president and his chief of staff, Prince von Schwarzenberg. I shake their hands and make ready to wait outside until their meeting is finished, but Štěpánová protests. "You must here," she commands, motioning to a chair across from Havel's. Apparently, I am to remain with the president and Schwarzenberg as they transact the business of the day.

I had asked Žantovský if I might spend some time observing Havel at work—"sort of as a fly on the wall" were my fateful words. I have never been taken more literally in my life. For the next hour I sit alone with Havel and Schwarzenberg, watching them talk and joke and pass papers, all in Czech, and all without so much as a glance at me. For the right reporter, of course, this would be the opportunity of a lifetime, but I am not that reporter: I can't understand a word they're saying. The hour passes slowly—plenty of time to note the huge old map of Bohemia on the wall, the Oriental rugs and the black Josef Hoffmann club chairs, the shiny brass telescope aimed out the window, and a pair of garish imitation-Dali paintings. A massive black bookcase dominates one side of the room, with lots of volumes on art (Breughel, Goya, Titian, Mucha) and several copies of Havel's books *Letters to Olga* and *Disturbing the Peace*. Over in the corner is a small, tacky-looking light-up map of the world, a gift from the current U.S. ambassador, Shirley Temple Black.

The meeting finally ends, and Havel himself accompanies me back to the reception area, zipping along at his customary breakneck speed and, on the way, stopping to tuck an errant lamp cord out of sight, and then to rotate an off-kilter aralia tree twice his height. "He's a very orderly person," says Žantovský. "He devotes a lot of time to aesthetic choices, so he likes to have things in place, the picture in the right spot. And he likes to do it himself, physically." Now he disappears, only to return a few minutes later with two more advisers; I'm not allowed to attend this meeting, because it's top-secret. Has my Czech improved so much?

Another forty-five minutes pass, and then once again I am escorted into the inner chamber, and this time the door closes promptly behind me. I am now alone with Havel, sitting where Schwarzenberg sat only an hour before. The president is eating lunch, and I am being allowed to watch him— silently, I have been warned, unless he initiates some conversation.

He does not. Leaning far over the conference table, Václav Havel devours a small bowl of soup, some beets, and a bottle of Czechoslovakia's most distinguished export, Pilsner Urquell beer. The food in Prague is generally fatty, heavy and tough, and vegetables are hard to come by. But Havel is trying to stick to a regimen. Toward the end of 1990 after about a year in office, his weight ballooned and he grew irritable and despondent; according to Žantovský, he was suffering from chronic-fatigue syndrome. In December he and his wife, Olga, repaired to a health spa somewhere in Germany (the location remains undisclosed), and three weeks later they returned in terrific shape. "He just needed a chance to sleep and take walks, to eat properly and not hastily," says Schwarzenberg. "But it worked. He's come back a new man, running us ragged." Still, the president's people are striving to cut back on his ceremonial functions, to give him more time to think and plan. Žantovský, a trained psychologist, often spends weekends with Havel and his stressed-out advisers at the official presidential country mansion in Lany, teaching them relaxation techniques and rudimentary meditation. And everyone is trying to diet. In fact, Havel's lunch today appears wondrously abstemious until the second course is brought in: beef goulash piled atop a mound of noodles.

Suddenly he rises and, in his characteristic, herky-jerky way, speeds across the room to his desk, where he picks up a large brass bicycle horn about the length of an oboe. Pointing it shakily toward his shut double doors, he spasmodically squeezes its black rubber bulb, and after a few flatulent whimpers it suddenly emits goose honks—the very ones I heard summoning Štěpánová an hour or two ago. I have just encountered the Official Internal Communications System of the President of Czechoslovakia. In comes Štěpánová with tea (the nutritional requirements of flies on the wall seem to have escaped everyone), and, when she leaves, the door closes and the president sits down at his desk. Rummaging through some papers, he begins to write. And write. And write some more. I am now sitting alone with the president of Czechoslovakia, watching him write.

For the next hour, that's all I do. It occurs to me that Havel, famed exponent of the theater of the absurd, is having a little joke at my expense, but I will later be told that nothing could be further from the truth. During his longest prison term, from 1979 to 1983, when he was drafting the missives that would later become his masterpiece, *Letters to Olga,* Havel trained himself to concentrate amid the hullabaloo of a jail cell, and now he is accustomed to being watched and going about his business as if he weren't. But as the minutes tick by, I do wonder just what it is he's scrawling. A major address, maybe? Havel is rare among world leaders in his insistence on composing all his own speeches. They are now, after all, his only literary output, and many of them can stand beside his finest essays. But this is no speech. Scribbling away, mouth-breathing, coughing occasionally (his lungs have never recovered from the bouts of pneumonia he suffered in prison), and pouring himself endless cups of tea, he suddenly stops, looks up at me and speaks, "I must now to write," he says. "Very important we need this new constitution." And then he ducks his head down and goes back to work.

In his stunted English, he's just told me something I wasn't meant to know. However much Czechoslovakia needs a new legal foundation, constitutions are not supposed to be written single-handedly by presidents. Eventually, of course, this particular constitution will be subject to the votes and debates that Czechoslovakia's new democracy demands. But who better to write it than Václav Havel? Ever since Plato and his vision of a Republic governed by philosopher kings, Western intellectuals have fantasized a state like this one, a state led by one of their own. Yet the fantasy has always seemed hopelessly distant. We have come to expect nations to be ruled by mediocrities, by manipulators and glad-handers who have cunningly maneuvered their way into power. Where else in recent memory has a nation been run by its greatest citizen? I am watching the father of a newborn country write its constitution. It is at once the most historic and the most boring hour I've ever spent.

"For me this office is a sacrifice," says Václav Havel, through his translator, "and not the fulfillment of a lifelong dream." It is late at night now, and we are sitting in a dark, smoke-choked Prague *vinárna*—that is, a place where they serve wine instead of beer. Havel is across the table from me, puffing his Multifilter 100s instead of eating, and the rest of the place is empty except for the translator and two bodyguards—a burly man with a scraggly beard and a shapely blonde woman who can't be much older than twenty-five. I've been watching Havel in action for days now, and I can't quite believe all his protestations of distaste for the job he's undertaken. His gusto is too much in evidence—and so is his odd but undeniable political flair. After a lifetime of opposing power, how must it feel for him now to possess it?

"The power naturally is accompanied by certain advantages," he murmurs in his distinctive monotone. (Although Czech is generally spoken with almost no inflection, Havel's voice is unusually deep and lilting, and even a benighted outsider can hear the music in it.) "Nowadays, it is impossible that there would not be a table for me in a restaurant, or a ticket to the theater or cinema. And I've discovered that despite my high salary I usually don't have to pay the bill in a pub. There are lots of people who can arrange things for me, so that I don't have to worry about ordinary tasks, and from this point of view my life is, of course, much more comfortable." He pauses for a moment and smokes, holding the cigarette between his thumb and index finger like Erich von Stroheim. "On the other hand," he says, "I can now imagine how easy it is to be corrupted by power. I understand why so many people love power so much."

Still, it must be difficult for a man who has spent his life battling the obvious lies and injustices of a Stalinist regime to be thrust into a position where decisions have more to do with nuances of policy than with the stark contrast between good and evil. After years of inhabiting a black-and-white world, how is he managing all these shades of gray? He studies my face for a moment, and then, dropping his eyes, leans rakishly into the table. "You know, everyone is always facing some dilemmas," he says. "I used to have dilemmas in the opposition and I'm facing analogous dilemmas now. For example, I used to have the dilemma of whether to say everything I wanted to say openly and risk imprisonment or whether to be more cautious and phrase things in a more careful way and reduce the risk. And nowadays I am faced with exactly the same dilemma. For example, should I be the first in the world to recognize officially the Baltic States and thus risk immediate interruption of Soviet oil supplies and the subsequent total collapse of our economy? Or should I take into account the circumstances and express my deeply felt opinion more cautiously? It is exactly the same dilemma in a slightly different form."

Now he lifts his eyes to mine and shoots me a shrewd look, and I realize he has just performed a bit of political *legerdemain*: without actually jeopardizing his country's oil supply he has used me to declare to the world his interest in recognizing the Baltic States.

In fact, the more time I spend watching Havel, the more I realize he is far from the political naïf he pretends to be. "He always says that he is not a politician," says Ambassador Rita Klímová. "He's new to the job, and he just has to do the best he can. Fine. But I also think he has a wonderful nose for politics. And if he had grown up in a normal society, not like Czechoslovakia, he might very well have gone into politics. His plays were perceived by everybody who saw them as very political, even though they were plays of the absurd. He was able to negotiate with the Communists this very smooth transition to power without one window being broken, not one car being overturned, not one Molotov cocktail being thrown. That's a politician. And he's very good in his international dealings. When he spoke to the United States Congress, that was unbelievable—the Congress getting a lecture on philosophy and standing up to cheer. We're still living on that; it still has not evaporated."

Havel began launching adventurous political initiatives the moment he took office. Although new Czech leaders had traditionally paid their first state visit to Moscow, Havel made a beeline for Germany, where he visited East Berlin (symbol of the soon-to-be-reunited Germany) and Munich (symbol of the disastrous Munich Agreement, which led to the Nazi dismantling of Czechoslovakia). Earlier he had made public (if unofficial) noises about apologizing for the brutal way in which the Czechs had expelled Germans from the Sudetenland after World War II. And while these initiatives outraged many Czechs, who have never forgiven Germany for the depredations of the Third Reich, Havel knew that his popularity at home so early in his term would let him get away with it—and he knew that it was worth the candle. On the international stage, his German diplomatic mission was a masterstroke. It signified that Czechoslovakia would now be turning Westward instead of Eastward, and it offered a powerful invitation to the richest country in Europe to view its impoverished neighbor as a valuable—and aidworthy—ally. "He's not the best of troubleshooters," says Žantovský, "because he gets involved too fast; he doesn't see the dangers of embroiling himself in a political conflict. He never wants to tell people, 'It's none of my business—you sort it out yourself.' But under our system, it's not the president's job to run the country day to day. That's what the prime minister is supposed to do. It's like the French system—the president is supposed to be above it and reconcile dilemmas. And as a rule Havel is much more farsighted than most of the other people in the political sphere. He can see beyond the problems of the day to the consequences, to what comes next. And this is very precious and rare and important. Even though his way is unconventional, in nine cases out of ten, it works."

Take, for instance, the sticky situation that engulfed the Salzburg Festival in July 1990. Havel had accepted an invitation before the revolution, believing at the time that he would never be allowed to leave Czechoslovakia.

Then, after taking office, he learned that Austria's president Kurt Waldheim, who so infamously concealed his Nazi past, would be in attendance. "Many of us told Havel, 'No way. You shouldn't go,' " says Žantovský. " 'This is a losing issue,' we said. 'Bad press and nothing to gain.' But in the end he decided, 'Well, I shook hands with Yasser Arafat, and I shook hands with Jaruzelski. I'm not a hypocrite. I can't see any reason why I shouldn't shake hands with Waldheim. There's no proof that he did more than tell a lie. So I'll go and I'll tell him in public what I think of people trying to revise their personal histories.' And he made a speech in which he did just that, and it was marvelous—the perfect solution to a political problem. He was criticized in *The New York Times*, but everyone else thought we pulled it off."

And what about those notorious meetings with Frank Zappa, Lou Reed, and the Rolling Stones? The president lights another cigarette and flashes his gap-toothed grin. "In our former conditions," he rumbles, "rock music acquired a special social function. And that's connected with the fact that culture and arts in general fulfill a different role in our country than they do in the Western world. Under a totalitarian regime, politics as such are eliminated and the resistance has to find substitute outlets of expression. One of those substitute channels was rock music. That's why its role here was more significant than it is where it's a part of general consumption. And when, for example, Lou Reed came here, I took him to a club and there was a band playing there called the Velvet Underground Revival. And he was absolutely amazed, because he had never met in the U.S. a band that knew his old songs better than he did. They handed him the old *samizdat* editions of his songs, and when this 'tough guy' saw them, he almost had tears in his eyes."

But wait a minute. What kind of head of state even cares about Lou Reed's tears? Isn't Havel a little more celebrity-crazy than he's willing to admit? "All my life, I've been in a silly way timid around famous personalities," he replies. "But now I'm in a situation where I am visited by famous people, and as someone who has always been curious, I enjoy meeting them. If you like to listen to rock and you're visited by the Rolling Stones, you're not going to hide in a closet."

There's something almost too perfect about answers like these, and it occurs to me that I'm experiencing what one of his acquaintances has described as the Havel Effect: from a distance, he appears incredibly warm, intimate, and chummy; up close, he's strangely opaque. "There is a side to Havel that's closed and difficult," says William Luers, who was the U.S. ambassador to Czechoslovakia before he became president of the Metropolitan Museum of Art. "He's a somewhat distant person, about his personal life, about sharing human aspects. He loves to have people around to talk to, but I don't think you'd find many who say they really know him. I don't think he's given to being intimate with people."

Indeed, there's a strangely studied quality about Havel, as though he doesn't dare trust his responses without first passing them through the sieve of his conscience, where every conceivable implication can be examined and judged. The order one feels in his writing—in his plays' mirror-like symmetries and in the cautious, stepwise motion of his essays—that order is there in his presence as well. His is the meticulousness of a man of the theater, a man aware that things must be presented in a certain sequence, that effects are achieved through circumspection and parsimony and control. "I think he's compulsive about his mission," says Luers. "He does have the capacity for pleasure. He likes to have fun, he likes women, he loves to gossip, he likes to drink, he likes to smoke, he likes the excitement of celebrity. But what he's really devoted to is tying together the intellectual and cultural threads of his country and relating them to the wider world. That's his mission, and it's a full-time occupation for him."

In fact, the more we talk, the clearer it becomes that something in him loves being president of Czechoslovakia—if only for the chance it gives that theatrical mind of his to stage the birth of a nation in all its regalia. Running the country remains Havel's guiltiest pleasure—and no one can get him to admit to it. The closest anyone has come, says one friend, is this: "He told me that when he gets up in the morning some days, he groans and says, 'Oh my God, do I still have to be president?' And then by dinnertime he's feeling 'God, I love being president' again." . . . What he doesn't love is the sudden disappearance of his privacy. The world is constantly peering over [Havel's] shoulder now. "One wrong sentence I would say here into your tape recorder because of fatigue would be enough to cause a complication," he moans. "This could never happen to me in the past."

On the world stage, too, the limelight has a peculiar effect. "I quite suddenly arrived in a situation where I had to talk, negotiate, and even make friends with people I had known for many years only from the television screen. And what I discovered was how very important are the politicians' personalities, behavior, opinions, and so forth. The relations between nations are often influenced by the relations between their leaders—which was rather surprising to me. I'll give you a fictional example. It might happen that my minister of foreign affairs will plan a foreign trip for me at a time when I am totally exhausted, feeling empty. So during the visit, I won't be sociable enough. I'll be yawning. Three days later, I'll read in the press that relations between our two countries have cooled."

And there is something else that's "difficult for me to come to terms with," he says. He stares down at his hands, which are small and hairless and oddly delicate. "In a number of professions, you can immediately see the results of your work. If you're a bricklayer, you see the wall you've built, and if you're a writer, you can see the book you've written. In politics, your work is never visible enough. And that's what I don't like. The only result of my presidency that's visible at first sight is the new uniforms of my castle guards."

He's being far too modest, of course. The changes his administration has wrought are already visible everywhere. On the magnificent Charles Bridge, whose statues have studiously ignored the Vltava River beneath them since the early eighteenth century, string quartets play Dvořák, and guitarists warble old American country tunes—here, where, under the Communists, music performance was officially banned. Painters sell paintings, craftsmen sell knickknacks, and, strangest of all, a few entrepreneurs peddle souvenirs from the bad old days—Soviet-army hats, belts, and medals. New magazines and newspapers are on sale everywhere—three hundred periodicals have been launched since the revolution—and in the bookstores the works of once banned authors have gone on display. The Czechs line up to ogle them: Josef Škvorecký, Ivan Klíma, Bohumil Hrabal, Pavel Kohout, and, of course, Václav Havel. The president's picture hangs in groceries and barbershops, often on posters with a Czech slogan that translates as "Truth and love will triumph over lies and hate." Open-air markets have popped up all over, and you can buy strawberries, melons, mangoes, and other formerly unheard-of delicacies at unheard-of prices, of course. And near the Old Town Square, an incongruous sight: the stolid women of Pařížská Street peering into the exotic windows of Christian Dior. . . .

It seems almost unimaginable now that this city, the ebullient capital of free-spirited Bohemia, should have been the center of one of the gloomiest and most repressive of the Warsaw Pact regimes—and one of the cruelest to dissidents. Where, one wonders, did Havel's courage come from during the dark years? Ask him and he merely shrugs. "I have never considered myself a courageous person," he murmurs. "But life and my nature put me in situations in which I had to behave either as a coward or a noncoward. I managed to behave as a noncoward, and that's all there is to that so-called courage of mine."

But that answer's not good enough. Even if he managed to be a "noncoward" when circumstances forced him to choose, that scarcely explains the times when there were no such circumstances, when something drove him to speak out against the injustices he saw even though everyone around him remained silent. By 1989, Václav Havel had spent a total of five years in prison. Why was he so willing, time and time again, to put himself in harm's way? He clears his throat and stares into the table. "It's fear of my conscience," he says, "or God, if you want. I've discovered that the qualms of conscience are among the worst states of mind I can imagine. In a way it's easier for me to be in jail than to be out of jail but feeling remorseful."

And so, even though his plays and essays were regarded as a provocation and were banned in his own country, he continued to write them, and they continued to be performed and published all over the world. Which meant that his fame among the international intellectual community burgeoned; every time he was arrested, people like Philip Roth, Tom Stoppard, and Harold Pinter took noisy note.

Was the writing as admirable as its author? Not really. The plays have a chilly technical perfection, but not much life: they're theater-of-the-absurd allegories, thumbnail sketches of totalitarian bureaucracies whittling down their minions like so many pencils. The best ones—especially *The Memorandum* and *Temptation*—dissect the institutional distortion of language, and they have a witty sting. But Havel's love of order obtrudes: the repetitions and symmetries in his plays feel arid, the characterizations superficial and bland.

Havel's essays, the finest of which appeared last spring in the Knopf collection *Open Letters* [1992] are richer [Havel has since published *The Art of the Impossible* (1997)]. Their forthrightness and generosity of spirit can be moving, and there's something exhilarating about the dogged way Havel sniffs and digs at his ideas until every bony chip has been unearthed. Here too, the strongest meditations are about language, and also about the insidious nature of official lying—about the way every unquestioned falsehood drops the temperature another degree, until in the end freedom itself is frozen in its tracks. But Havel the stylist can be clunky and overemphatic, and he doesn't cover much ground that the great anti-totalitarian thinkers—George Orwell, Arthur Koestler, Hannah Arendt—haven't already excavated. As Irving Howe has written, "It would not be hard to name a dozen Central and East European intellectuals who write with more flair and provide more original analysis."

And yet something draws us to Havel anyway. That paradoxical combination of heartfelt humility and brick-wall moral conviction is as plain in his written voice as in the public man, and it's enormously appealing. What makes us read Havel's writing is not the prose itself, but the man we glimpse behind it. And that's why his finest works are two almost accidental self-portraits, *Disturbing the Peace,* the book-length autobiographical interview conducted by his friend Karel Hvížd'ala, and *Letters to Olga,* the prickly, moving collection of letters he wrote to his wife during his longest spell in prison, from 1979 to 1983. Reading *Letters to Olga* is like witnessing the messy genesis of a secular saint—one who smokes and drinks and womanizes, one who irritably upbraids poor Olga for everything from her hairdo to the feebleness of her correspondence, one who spends page upon exasperating page misinterpreting Heidegger's phenomenology (by way of Havel's mentor Jan Patočka) and manages nevertheless to create a stirring and coherent political philosophy that has become the foundation for every decision and policy he's set forth since. Despite his own protestations to the contrary, Havel the writer was always merely Havel the politician waiting to be born. . . .

In fact, far from being an unlikely president, Havel now seems to have been almost inevitable. Given the inspiring purity of his political record and the complex web of alliances he had managed to build over the years, he was so clearly the boss of a sort of dissident machine that it now seems naive to have thought someone else could take the reins of post-revolutionary Czechoslovakia. Had any other dissident become president, Havel would still have been the most powerful political figure in the country, just as Lech Wałęsa was in Poland even after Tadeusz Mazowiecki became prime minister. . . .

Indeed the trait that Havel's critics find most irksome is the very one that helped make the revolution possible: his penchant for attracting friends and bringing people together and his fierce loyalty to those friends, particularly the ones who now advise him. "Have you ever seen so many advisers?" one Czech insider complains. "Havel likes to be nice to his friends, and so he surrounds himself with his buddies—this is a government of buddies. Many of them are incompetent, and I'll tell you another thing. Most of them drink too much."

"You have to understand," says one friend of Havel's, "these people were the outcasts of society. They had a limited circle of friends; they were not allowed to travel; they were well read and well informed, but their intellect was much larger than their experience.

"A lot of them were intellectuals whom the government had kicked out of their jobs, so then they became window washers and stokers. Well, after twenty years as a window washer, they can't go back to what they were before. Being a window washer has changed them. They can't govern."

But then, they probably don't have to. Most Havel watchers think it's he who advises his advisers. "He's an exceptional man," says a Czech who works in the government, "but he's also very weak. He needs approval from the people around him, and he did all along. Havel has interesting ideas, you know, and the advisers are there to confirm what he says." On the subject of his advisers, at least, Havel stands firm. "I feel comfortable ruling with those friends I have surrounded myself with," he says. "If someone doesn't like them, he's free to replace them. But he would have to replace me as well."

No one wants to do that. At this point in the life of the new Czechoslovakia, Havel is almost universally perceived as irreplaceable. But what happens in the summer of 1992, when his term ends? He's always said he'd like to step down as soon as he can, as soon as his mission is finished. "I'd like to return to the play I was writing when I became president," he tells me a little wistfully. "I was already about two-thirds through the first draft and then I threw it away because I thought that with the revolution the subject [the inner life of an aging dictator] had become irrelevant. Now I've discovered that in fact it is very relevant—but the play is in the wastebasket. And as far as my presidential experience is concerned, if I were to write some kind of memoir, I'd wait until much later, so that I would be able to see these events from the right distance."

He finishes his glass of wine, stubs out his cigarette, and stands up suddenly, signaling his bodyguards with his eyes. But wait a minute. Before he goes, I have one last question. Will he run again?

Havel slumps back into his chair and considers a moment. And then he leans toward me. "If I said I was not going to run and the people of this country heard about it, it might incite feelings of disappointment and frustration," he says. "That would be like playing a trick on my colleagues, and it would be a very unproductive step to take from the point of view of the performance of my office." He pauses and looks slyly into my eyes. "And if I said I was going to run again, I'm not sure I'd be telling the truth."

And with that artful paradox, he is off, racing out into the night with that peculiar speed-skating shuffle of his. As he goes, I realize I've been watching a kind of performance—that, indeed, Václav Havel now spends every day of his life performing. Perhaps the most unpleasant part of this job that he claims to despise (but seems to adore) is having always to be, at every moment, Václav Havel—not the Václav Havel he sees when he looks in the mirror, but the Václav Havel his country now depends on: the unswerving, fearless, unimpeachable Havel that his own conscience created. No wonder he complains of the responsibility. No wonder he fears the mistakes that come with fatigue—let alone with the roistering boho life-style he left behind when he ascended to the castle. In meeting the demands of destiny, Havel has, in a way, left the realm of humanity. He no longer has any margin for error.

And does he really believe that he will step down next summer, will return to a quiet life of playwriting? Does he think the public eye will simply shut and leave him in peace? So he says. But I can't help feeling that he will run again in 1992, that he is still, when all is said and done, *the* man. And maybe, in his heart of hearts, nothing could please him more. In Czechoslovakia, his beloved counterculture has become the central culture; the bohemians have taken over Bohemia; the losers have finally won. This enchanting country in the center of Europe has finally welcomed its outcasts back into the fold. Who else but the king of the outcasts should lead it home to the Western world?

"We need to keep Havel," says a Czech friend of his, "and I'll tell you why. I have been giving my son some horse-riding lessons. And, you know, I put him up on the horse and he sat very well up there. He said, 'You see, Papa, I can ride.' But the horse was standing still.

"This is the way it is with our new freedom. What happens when the horse begins to move, or, worse, when it begins to run?

"Democracy is a very big horse. You cannot learn to ride it in one day."

5. Queue for books in Prague, 1994.

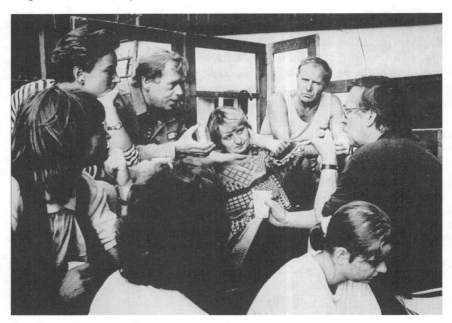

6. Discussion with actors, about 1991.

Play on Words

LEWIS LAPHAM

{After the ceremony {at York University in Toronto in 1982, awarding an honorary doctorate to Václav Havel, who was in prison} another fresh honorary doctor, the jazz legend Oscar Peterson, leaned over to my wife and whispered into her ear: "Tell Mr. Havel, I'm with him all the way!"

—Josef Škvorecký}

The world of politics is always twenty years behind the world of thought.
—John Jay Chapman

On a rainy Thursday night in late February, at the Cathedral of St. John the Divine in northern Manhattan, a choir of celebrities staged the political analogue of an Academy Awards ceremony in honor of the president of Czechoslovakia, Václav Havel, and on the way uptown in the subway I wondered if I could expect to see Ivana Trump and the Solid Gold dancers. The invitation listed the names of some of the illuminati scheduled to appear on the program (among them Warren Beatty, Henry Kissinger, Meryl Streep, and Sting), and the sum of their collective Q ratings foretold an evening decorated in pious tinsel. In Czechoslovakia, actors and playwrights maybe have an aptitude for politics—the Civic Forum, Havel's first constituency in Prague, met in the basement of the Magic Lantern Theater—but in the United States the arrival of more than two or three celebrities at the scene of a political event ordinarily means that whatever meaning that cause or question once might have possessed already has been broken up into photo opportunities and sold for scrap to network television. Because I had admired Havel from a distance, for both his courage and his eloquence, I was reluctant to see what I knew of the text of his life translated into an advertisement for the moral beauty of somebody else's social conscience.

The venue of the cathedral compounded my sense of foreboding. The place is known for the trendiness of its sentiment, and during a long and reluctant acquaintance with its spiritual repertoire, I have become accustomed to doves of peace fluttering through the sacristy, aging guitarists playing Bob Dylan songs in the apse, minority dance troops performing to choral works dedicated to the memory of the lost counterculture or the Twelve Nations of the Sioux. Every autumn, to commemorate the Feast of St. Francis, the bishop bestows his blessing on pets and small animals, and one year, in the crowd of children holding their dogs or their rabbits or their birds, I remember seeing a pale and presumably sardonic child walking up the steps of the west portico with a pet lobster on a long, embroidered leash.

Thinking about the lobster and the doves of peace (some of which had been festooned with red and blue ribbons), I walked the few blocks from the subway to the cathedral in a state of mind by no means friendly to the evening's diversion. Between Broadway and Amsterdam Avenue, I refused to give money to three different beggars, annoyed with myself for being so foolish as to take part in a spectacle that I could imagine Tom Wolfe describing under the rubric "Radical Czech."

But when I fumed north at the corner of 111th Street and saw the crowd standing in the rain outside the cathedral, a much bigger crowd than I had expected, it struck me that maybe I had been too quick and easy with the smart jokes. From what I could tell by looking at the patient and serious expressions on the faces of the several people nearest me at the end of the line, nobody had come for the publicity. I was relieved to notice the absence of limousines and photographers, and while I waited for the cathedral to open its doors, I had time to reflect on my own reasons for taking the uptown train.

On January 1, a few days after Havel took up his duties as president of a country lately released, like himself, from captivity, he had given an extraordinary speech to the Czechoslovakian people. Reading the text in the paper, I had been moved by the force of his words in a way that I hadn't thought possible. The man apparently was trying to tell the truth, and because I had never heard an American president try to tell the truth, the effect was both violent and shocking, as if somebody's anarchist cousin had fired a pistol in the midst of a cocktail party meant to raise funds for the New York Public Library. Almost two months later, I could still remember the opening lines of the speech:

"For forty years," Havel had said, "you have heard on this day from the mouths of my predecessors, in a number of variations, the same thing: how our country is flourishing, how many more millions of tons of steel we have produced, how we are all happy, how we believe in our government. I assume you have not named me to this office so that I, too, should lie to you."

The American public, of course, pays its politicians (and pays them handsomely) to tell as many lies as might be necessary to sustain the romance of the afternoon headlines, and yet here was a man—on his fourth day in office and not yet familiar with the silver tea service and the comforts of power—willing to risk the loss of his newfound privilege for something as plain and unprofitable as the truth. For an American politician, Havel's opening statement would have been—quite literally—impossible. American politicians long ago gave up the burden of speaking in their own voices or forming their own words. Their owners and speechwriters don't permit them to take idiot chances with any text that hasn't been approved by the investment committee.

Havel proceeded to make matters worse by informing his fellow citizens that they were all responsible for their own troubles. "It would be very unwise," he said, "to think of the sad heritage of the last forty years only as something foreign, something inherited from a distant relative."

Havel went on to say that the Czechoslovakian people—himself among them—had become "morally ill" because "we are used to saying one thing and thinking another," because "we have learned not to believe in anything, not to care about each other, to worry only about ourselves."

In the mouth of an American politician, Havel's words would have been condemned as blasphemy (because, as everybody well knows, nothing is ever America's fault), and as I stood outside the cathedral that evening in New York, I called to mind the scene in Washington on the previous day, when Havel had addressed a joint session of Congress. Again he had made the point that politics was about the willingness to say what one meant, about finding a language in which to express not only the theory but also the practice of liberty. He began by recognizing the absurdity that is often synonymous with improvisations on the theme of freedom:

"The last time they arrested me . . . I didn't know whether it was for two days or for two years. Exactly one month later, when the rock musician Mikhail Koscak told me that I would be probably proposed as a presidential candidate, I thought it was one of his usual jokes."

As recently as October 27 of last year, Havel had been an outlaw, imprisoned by one of the most repressive Communist regimes then still extant in Eastern Europe. By profession a playwright, he had invented too many characters who voiced too many opinions deemed offensive to the wisdom in office, and he had spent five and a half of the last thirteen years in prison. The period of enforced silence prompted him to reflect on the nature of political power, and so, standing before the members of the House and the Senate, he had said, "A person who cannot move and live a somewhat normal life because he is pinned under a boulder has more time to think about his hopes than someone who is not trapped this way."

Although he acknowledged the military and economic victories of the United States in the years after the Second World War, he didn't think that the triumph of capitalism was quite as triumphant as it had been made to seem in the pages of the *Wall Street Journal*. Nor did he think that the Western nations had come to the end of history:

"We still don't know how to put morality ahead of politics, science, and economy. We are still incapable of understanding that the only genuine backbone of all our actions, if they are to be moral, is responsibility—responsibility to something higher than my family, my country, my company, my success."

The assembled senators and congressmen, most of them illuminated with the smiles of self-congratulation, interrupted the speech with five standing ovations and repeated shouts of "Bravo." If their effrontery had been staged in a theater—in a play by Dürrenmatt, or Havel, or Beaumarchais, or Brecht—the scene would have played as bitter comedy. Not one American politician in twenty-five has read both the Constitution and the Bill of Rights; not one in fifty knows of any higher good than "my interest, my party, my success"; not one in a hundred finds any connection, whether logical or allegorical, between what he says and what he means.

The last of the day's light faded before the cathedral doors opened, and as the line lurched slowly forward I fell into conversation with the woman next to me, a librarian at Columbia University who was writing a monograph about Shakespeare's surprisingly thorough knowledge of music and the law. She didn't share my suspicion of the American governing classes or my too easily awakened anger at their insufferable hypocrisy, and on my way up the cathedral steps I noticed that my humor had been amended by her delight in words, and I found myself wondering what had become of the lobster that had so cautiously made the same ascent.

I found a seat in the nave, about half the distance between the west door and the pulpit, and as the immense and dimly lit neo-Gothic space gradually filled with people come to pay their respects to a brave man, I studied the mimeographed program and guessed at the weight and length of the camera boom placed in the crossing between the transept and the nave. Among other spectacles and diversions, the revised edition of the program promised remarks by Miloš Forman and Eli Wiesel; readings from Havel's speeches by Paul Newman and Gregory Peck; songs by Dizzy Gillespie and Roberta Flack; and a good many orchestral performances of music by Dvořák and Mozart. The camera boom, fifty or sixty feet long and balanced with a block of lead, was so large and so prominently situated that it dwarfed the human figures in the cathedral. It looked oddly prehistoric, as if it were some sort of monstrous and omniscient insect. The rights to the evening's entertainment had been awarded to Czechoslovak television as well as to the American Public Broadcasting System. Across the aisle, about four rows nearer the camera and the pulpit, I noticed one of New York's wealthier literary agents in conversation with an author noted for his patriotic fictions on the theme of America the Invincible and America the Good. They looked as sleek and soft as otters, both of them expensively manicured and glittering with gold jewelry. It occurred to me that neither would have had much trouble serving the Communist *ancien régime* in Prague. Nor, if the times demanded a change of ideology and a rearrangement of the political furniture, would they find it difficult to serve any other state (fascist or monarchist or social democratic) that generously rewarded them for their hired loyalty and praise.

I was estimating the likely speed of their change of costume when Havel entered the cathedral through a side door, forty-five minutes late, invisible in a crowd of friends, dignitaries, and Secret Service agents. He was so far away that I was aware only of blurred movement, as if I were watching a wind passing through distant grass. Although almost nobody else in the cathedral could see him any better than I, the entire congregation, maybe as many as 4,500 people, instinctively rose and applauded.

The program began with a fanfare played on a herald's trumpet and the ringing of the cathedral bells. Miloš Forman spoke a few words of welcome to his longtime friend and fellow dramatist, Placido Domingo sang an Agnus Dei written by Bizet, and Paul Newman read a brief passage from one of Havel's reflections about the difference between the uncomfortable truth and the expedient lie.

Newman read the lines with an emphasis and inflection better suited to a bad movie, and yet, much to my astonishment, I felt myself infiltrated by a feeling of irrepressible hope. If I had come to mock the proceedings as a work of synthetic glitz, I was mistaken. The words rang true, even in a voice as false as Newman's, and for the next hour I was filled with an elation as reckless as that of a truant child. Listening to the voices in the cathedral (Susan Sarandon reading Havel's letters from prison, Arthur Miller addressing Havel as the first avant-garde president), I thought that it might yet be possible to invent or discover a new politics expressed in a language capable of telling a straight story. The Brooklyn Philharmonic Orchestra played a passage from Mozart's *Don Giovanni* (which was first performed in Prague in 1787), and I thought, If the Czechs can slip the bonds of cynicism and cant, then might not the Americans make good their own escape? All that would be required would be a few people willing to say what they meant and to bear the responsibility for their own voices. The music shifted into a major key, and I could feel myself shrugging off my accustomed wariness as if it were an old and heavy coat. I glanced across the aisle at the well-stuffed literary agent, and in the enthusiasm of the moment, I understood that on a rainy Thursday night in upper Manhattan, the dogs of selfishness, ambition, and greed had been brought briefly to heel. For the time being, at least, maybe because of a trick of the light or the abruptness of the modulation away from a minor key, I thought I saw the agent's expression of habitual avarice softening into the lineaments of conscience and thought.

The camera that had reminded me of an insect reappeared in a completely different kind of metaphor. The crane and boom moved so effortlessly—gliding forward and drawing away, rising and falling in a slow, dreamlike motion—that I could imagine it as a living soul, weaving the thread of immortality on the loom of time. The image was more in line with what Havel had been trying to say. More than anything else, we have need of a believable story, because without a believable story we have no means of connecting the past to the present, the dead to the living, the citizen to the state, the now to the then.

So great was my excitement with the prospect of the feats of the political imagination that might yet be performed with a new company of actors under the direction of a new theater management that my era of good feeling, again to my astonishment, survived the entrance of even so famous a fool as Henry Kissinger. Until Kissinger appeared in the pulpit, the evening had passed without embarrassment—the music was good, the emotion genuine, the speakers brief and to the point. The instant Kissinger's name was announced, the ceremony lost a good deal of its optimism. The entire sum of Kissinger's life and work testifies to the success that can be chiseled from a degraded politics with the journeyman's tools of presumption, dishonesty, and betrayal. A man seated directly behind me screamed, "Murderer!"; I could hear people shouting boos and cat calls elsewhere in the cathedral. Prior to Kissinger's sententious homily on the text of the Cold War, all the speakers had tried to describe the shape of an idea larger and higher than themselves, looking, at least figuratively, upward. Kissinger looked down, condescending to bestow on the congregation the favor of his advice. Instead of talking about Havel, he talked about himself. "When I was in Prague in 1968," he said, "I tried to warn my good friends the Czechs, but they wouldn't listen to me. . . ." He continued in the same manner for more than five or six minutes (nobody else having spoken for more than one or two minutes), and the effect was turgid and pompous.

Kissinger was followed by Gregory Peck and by Lukas Foss conducting the Largo from Dvořák's *New World Symphony,* and for a moment it looked as if the evening might regain its balance. The chance was lost with the appearance of Barbara Walters and Saul Bellow. Like Kissinger, Walters and Bellow spoke, adoringly, of themselves. Walters said that she had been thrilled to be in Prague last Christmas, in time for the wonderful, thrilling experiences associated with the collapse of a Communist regime. Bellow was glad to know that when Havel was in prison he had remembered to read Bellow's novel *Herzog.* As a reward for Havel's intelligence and taste, Bellow had brought an autographed copy of the novel *Herzog,* which he hoped the obviously perceptive president of Czechoslovakia would accept as a token of his, Bellow's, esteem.

The evening collapsed inward on itself like a dead star, and it ended on a sustained note of mummery—with the presenting to Havel of a meaningless "spirit of freedom award," with the passing around of candles for everybody in the cathedral to light, and with the playing of Aaron Copland's disingenuous *Fanfare for the Common Man.*

Havel didn't give a speech. He explained that because he didn't spend the afternoon in prison he hadn't had time to compose his thoughts, and he confined himself to saying thank you in a voice obstructed by obvious emotion and a heavy accent.

Even so, I counted myself fortunate, and I left the cathedral in high spirits, willing to consider the possibility that even Henry Kissinger and Barbara Walters might one day learn to doubt their own magnificence. It was still raining, but more lightly, and I figured that if all of us were at fault for the shambles of the American enterprise, then I had as much of an obligation as everybody else to try to find the words, or the rush of words, that could be bound to the task of telling a believable story.

President Havel

ROB MCRAE

{I do not remember T. G. Masaryk, but I think people also did not read him, and they loved him unreservedly only after his death. An ideal is such a lovely thing! It does not require a lot of space; it can fit into a very small apartment of a prefabricated house.
—Jiřina Šiklová}

The day of Václav Havel's election to the presidency was clear and cold. The Ambassador was invited to attend the ceremony on December 29 [1989] in the historic Vladislav Hall of the Prague Castle, where the Federal Assembly would vote. With everything I had been through over the last year, including Havel's trial in February, I decided that I could hardly sit back and watch the event on television. I went down to the Castle and found a huge crowd jamming the square in front of the large iron gates. There were parents with children on their shoulders, couples arm in arm, and flags and banners that gave the event a festive atmosphere. The cold provided the usually smiling Czech faces with some particularly rosy cheeks. I made my way slowly through the crowd and finally managed to squeeze in through the main gate. Loudspeakers outside broadcast the ceremony to the crowd. It would be followed by a mass in St. Vitus Cathedral, located within the walls of the Castle itself.

The Castle grounds consisted of a series of courtyards opening on to one another. They led to the Cathedral and to the main entrance of the Castle itself. The crowd outside the gates and in the courtyards was standing shoulder to shoulder. I made it as far as the second courtyard. There were banners and the red, white, and blue Czechoslovak flags everywhere. Some people were standing precariously on the rim of a large baroque fountain in the middle of the courtyard, waving a sheet that said "Havel for President." The courtyard itself was a soft white and beige color, its architecture a monument to the Habsburg baroque style. Yet somehow Prague Castle was more gentle and whimsical, as if purged of its German, northern baroque antecedents.

Reprinted from Rob McRae, *Resistance and Revolution: Václav Havel's Czechoslovakia* (Ottawa: Carleton University Press, 1997), 191–95.

I gave up trying to get to the inner courtyard and the Cathedral. There were just too many people. I was a little concerned that the crush on the inside would become intolerable as more and more people tried to move forward. As at the demonstrations in the bad old days, I was still looking instinctively for a quick exit if needed. I contented myself with staying amidst this jubilant Czech crowd in the second courtyard. They were out to witness the culmination of their struggles over long years, a victory over the forces that had sought to humiliate the basic sense of decency in every single one of them. Now that was over, like a bad dream, and they were filled with irrepressible joy.

The election in Vladislav Hall went off without a hitch. First, the Federal Assembly, under Dubček's chairmanship, voted for Havel. The many Communist deputies voted for him too and it was unanimous. The next step was part of an old tradition. An official of the Federal Assembly was dispatched to bring Havel to the hall. He had been watching the proceedings on TV in an adjoining room. When he saw he was elected, he decided it was finally time to put on a tie. As he was escorted by the parliamentary official down a long corridor I wondered if Havel was thinking about the many times he had previously been escorted to a police station for interrogation. When he arrived at the entrance of the hall, Dubček in his capacity as President of the Federal Assembly accompanied him down the center aisle. Havel was wearing a new navy blue suit. He made a short speech. I noticed he looked a little uncomfortable in his new suit, but even this was refreshing. I do not think any of us could believe that what we were witnessing was actually happening. Then Havel made his way to the main balcony of the Castle to say a few words to the crowd outside. This was followed by the mass in St. Vitus Cathedral celebrated, appropriately enough, by Cardinal Tomášek.

For the first time it suddenly dawned on me and on the crowd around me that this magnificent Prague Castle, the seat of Czech kings, belonged to them again. It had been the domain of the Nazis during the war, and then of the Communists after 1948. The people who had suffered both had been forbidden to enter its grounds. Husák had turned the Castle gardens into his own private domain. The Communist army guards posted everywhere had only served as a reminder that some Communists were more equal than others, and that Communists in general were more equal than anyone. Now the sun shone in a clear sky. I think at least some of the people standing in that courtyard were relishing the moment when they had finally thrown out the impostors. Havel was a worthy successor to the line going back to Masaryk.

It was clear from the start that he did not regard position and power as an end in itself. I think that there was also a populist element in him, reflected, for example, in the way Civic Forum identified itself as a movement rather than a party. One of the first things that Havel did as President was to throw open the doors of the Castle to the citizens of the country, a populist touch reminiscent of U.S. President Andrew Jackson. On January 1 [1990],

children from the neighborhood were running up and down the long halls of
Prague Castle, while their parents gawked at the huge glass chandeliers and
paintings. None of them had seen any of this before. The Spanish Hall took
one's breath away with its rococo cherubs and scintillating cut glass reflecting
a white and gold panorama. It was just too sensuous for words.

As Havel came out on to the balcony on the day of his election, a roar of
approval burst from the inner courtyard and spread to each successive courtyard, echoing off the walls. It swept by me and there were cheers and the
muffled sound of mitts and gloves clapping. He spoke briefly from the balcony. I thought to myself that somehow the fairy tale had come true. Everything now seemed so easy and so light. There was no problem too great that
could not be overcome. I looked at the children, thinking how lucky they
were to have escaped the idiocy of the past forty years, to have escaped the
subterfuge, and the psychological and the real violence perpetuated by dictatorship. Now freedom lit up their future like the warm rays of this December
sun. These children, at least, would be whole and undamaged. As I stood in
that courtyard, I inwardly rejoiced for them and for their parents.

New Year's Eve fell on the Sunday. It was two days after Havel's election. I went down to the Old Town Square with Ole Mikkelsen, my friend
from the Danish Embassy. We imagined, rightly, that there might be some
special festivities to mark the beginning of this New Year. Lynn and I had
known Ole and Anne-Marie from the first days of our arrival in Prague. Our
children were in school together, and we had shared some adventures and
some good times during this amazing period in our lives. Ole had been with
Pierre [Guimond] and me, and a friend from the American Embassy, Cliff
Bond, on our ill-fated trip to Jan Palach's grave in January, 1989. I think
that, following that escapade, Ole's Ambassador was none too happy about
the notorious company he was keeping.

Soon after that confrontation with the StB, the executive assistant to the
Communist Foreign Minister Johanes had asked me if NATO had chosen
Canada to give Communist Czechoslovakia a hard time. Or did it just come
naturally? I said it was the latter. In any event, as Ole and I came into the
Old Town Square on New Year's Eve in that remarkable revolutionary year,
we found that people were literally dancing in the streets. A giant Christmas
tree lit with winding strings of white lights towered above the crowd in the
middle of the square. Young people danced around it to the sound of traditional Czech folk music. A hot air balloon moored by a rope rose and fell,
bobbing just above the songs and laughter of the crowd.

There were a lot of young people. They were dancing what looked like
Czech reels, spinning around arm in arm. Czechoslovak flags were draped
over the black statue of Jan Hus. There were some handpainted sheets that
called for free elections and the end of the Communist Party. Hus seemed to
be supportive. Candles were burning everywhere, and some of the young people put them on the cobblestones and danced around the flickering flames.

The flames lit up the flushed faces of others sitting around in a circle, clapping their hands. It was cold, but this was a celebration, and it was a celebration about being young and alive and being totally and fantastically free. Not that they, or I, understood what that meant. But they definitely felt it here and now and it would be seared into our memories no matter what happened after. They danced all night until they dropped.

Havel's New Year's Day address in his new role as President of the Republic was unlike any by a politician, ever, anywhere. It was by turns sobering, philosophical, and determined. It was called "For a Humane Republic." Havel began by saying that he had not been elected to lie to people. He then went on to describe how the country was not flourishing, how in fact the economy, the educational system, and the environment were all in an advanced state of decay. He added, "But this isn't the most important thing. The worst is that we are living in a contaminated moral environment. We have become morally sick because we have got used to saying one thing and thinking another. We've grown accustomed not to believe in anything, not to notice one another, to look out for ourselves only." Havel described how the regime had exploited and demeaned both human being and nature. He said that everyone had got used to a totalitarian system, accepted it as a fact, and thereby kept it going. "In other words, all of us—each to a different degree, naturally—are responsible for the functioning of the totalitarian machinery; none of us are just its victims, but all of us are at the same time its co-creators."

This was a tough lesson to deliver at the height of the revolution. Yet I think people were sufficiently big-hearted then to accept it. The admission was, for a time, liberating. But it did not quench the thirst for justice and for revenge, which would resurface barely six months later when the search for collaborators would begin in earnest. Nonetheless, at this moment, Havel was asking everyone to shoulder their part of the responsibility for the horrors of the past, and to participate in the making of the future. He said he was encouraged by two things brought to light by the revolution: the totalitarian system had not been able to erase human striving for something higher; and the humanist and democratic traditions of Czechoslovakia were seemingly only asleep.

Havel emphasized that, at last, "both our nations [Czechs and Slovaks] have straightened their backs by themselves" without the help of, or dependency on, a larger power. He referred to the fact that Masaryk based politics on morality and hoped that this approach, at the crossroads of Europe, might constitute a specifically Czechoslovak contribution to international politics. He then set out his main priorities. The first was, of course, free elections. But the second, significantly, concerned Czech and Slovak relations. Here Havel said that his task was "to see to it that we go into the elections as two genuinely autonomous nations which mutually respect each other's interests, national integrity, religious traditions and their symbols." He added that he felt a special obligation to ensure that the interests of the Slovak nation be respected. Havel emphasized the need to improve the lot of the disadvantaged and minorities. And he wanted to humanize the army, while strengthening the role of Czechoslovakia internationally as a country of peace and tolerance.

But his most controversial initiative was the declaration of a relatively broad amnesty for prisoners. His argument was that the system of justice had been less than perfect under the [Communist] regime. He wanted to give the people who had been subjected to it a second chance. This gesture made sense against the background of Havel's own five years in prison, and it recalled the amnesties granted by kings at the time of their coronation. However the rise in crime during the first year of his presidency, due to many factors, would in the public mind be associated with Havel's amnesty. In fact people were going to find it difficult, generally, to live up to his demands for tolerance and understanding, at a time when political and economic change was sensitizing them to their vulnerability in the new order.

HAVEL'S POLITICAL THOUGHT
◆

Two Democratic Revolutionaries: Tomáš G. Masaryk and Václav Havel

H. Gordon Skilling

{In fact, far from being an unlikely president, Havel now seems to have been almost inevitable. Given the inspiring purity of his political record and the complex web of alliances he had managed to build over the years, he was so clearly the boss of a sort of dissident machine that it now seems naive to have thought someone else could take the reins of post-revolutionary Czechoslovakia.

—Stephen Schiff}

Two great dates in Czechoslovak history, 1918 and 1989, stand for remarkably similar achievements—the overthrow of a dominant Empire, the establishment of Czech and Slovak independence, and the attainment of a democratic state and society. Although many political forces produced these results, the role of leadership was a significant factor and was assumed by two persons, Masaryk and Havel. Both carried out difficult and courageous struggles for liberation and freedom and then faced the responsibility of trying to create a democratic state on the ruins of the empires. Both moved from opposition to power—from being dissidents to being rulers.

This essay is intended to be no more than a preliminary outline sketching out parallels and contrasts between these two men and between these two revolutions, widely separated in time, and conducted under greatly different circumstances, and yet representing a strange repetition of history. It cannot claim to be a definitive scholarly appraisal, with theoretical implications, but represents only a tentative hypothesis of some recurrent similarities in Czech and Slovak history. The analysis will be confined largely to the period before victory and the attainment of power.

Masaryk and Havel, in spite of many differences, had much in common. Both were intellectuals, Masaryk an academic scholar, a historian and

First published in Leslie Miller, K. Petersen, P. Stenberg, K. Zaenker, eds., *Literature and Politics in Central Europe: Studies in Honour of Marketa Goetz-Stankiewicz* (Columbia, S.C.: Camden, 1993), 15–21, and appears here courtesy of Camden House, Inc.

philosopher, Havel a creative writer, a playwright; each of them was more comfortable in the world of ideas than of practical life. Masaryk was born in lowly circumstances and was accustomed to hard labour and relative poverty in his earlier years. He was, however, able to enjoy university training, in Vienna and in Leipzig, and could speak and read a number of world languages. Havel, born in a well-to-do family, was denied university training under the Communists and worked manually in his early years and again in the sixties and seventies. His knowledge of languages and the outside world was much more limited. Havel suffered what Masaryk never experienced— long years of imprisonment and constant police harassment.

The situation in which the struggles for independence and democracy were carried out was vastly different. The Habsburg Empire, for all its deficiencies as an absolute, semi-constitutional monarchy, did permit its subject nations to enjoy, at least in some degree, the advantages of democratic life— freedom of association and expression, an electoral and parliamentary system, a fully-developed array of political parties and associations, a free press, an independent cultural, religious and educational life, and broad national rights. Czechs and Slovaks were not fully satisfied with their lot and subjected the Austrian policy to severe and constant criticism. What they principally lacked was political independence, the right to have their own autonomous system of decision-making, within or outside the Monarchy. Within these limitations Czechs and Slovaks, and in particular Tomáš Masaryk, could carry on their activities with relative freedom and develop a democratic political culture.

The Soviet imperial system was of a fundamentally different character, denying not only genuine national independence to its subject nations but also even the rudiments of democratic life. For more than forty years politics in any real sense was liquidated—there were no elections with any meaning, no parliamentary life, no independent political parties or associations, no free press, and cultural, educational and religious life was strictly curbed. Czechs and Slovaks who sought freedom, including Václav Havel, had to act in a semi-conspiratorial fashion through independent and *samizdat* activities and were subject to constant persecution by the authorities. They could not practice politics in any real sense and could only derive democratic experience in the surrogate politics of dissent.

In these circumstances Masaryk and Havel were but two actors in a broad spectrum of political activity. The former (Masaryk) was but one individual politician in a wide political spectrum of many parties and organizations, contending for a share of power in a relatively open society. The latter (Havel) acted within the narrow confines of a small band of independent spirits grouped together in Charter 77 and in other civic initiatives, who could carry on their activities only at great personal cost in a closed society. Under these widely different conditions both men exerted a substantial influence but only over relatively restricted circles of society. Masaryk, as a political leader, undoubtedly had an immense impact on his contemporaries but never suc-ceeded in rallying a large proportion of the population to his cause. Havel was a leading and influential figure within the relatively small dissident move-ment, but because of official propaganda and censorship could not mobilize widespread public support.

Both Masaryk and Havel were profoundly political in their outlook, although neither placed politics in the centre of his activity. Masaryk was a political scientist who wrote extensively about democracy and public affairs; he was also a practitioner of politics—although not a very successful one—for a quarter of a century, forming his own political parties and serving in the Austrian Parliament in Vienna.

Havel was a much less political man, having never been a member of a political party or elected to public office. Although he was primarily a writer and amateur in political thinking, he showed an acute understanding of the nature and meaning of politics and modern society, not only in his plays but in his *samizdat* essays. Within Charter 77 Havel showed himself to be a mas-ter of the art of persuasion and compromise among his fellow dissidents and one of their most eloquent spokesmen.

Neither Masaryk nor Havel regarded politics as the be-all and end-all of their lives or of social activity. In spite of Masaryk's active political life, he always expressed the belief that the fulcrum of national development was not political, but cultural and economic. The individual played a crucial role in the performance of what he called *drobná práce* (small scale work). Havel evoked Masaryk's example in this respect, and used the same word to describe Chartist activity. In a situation in which repression prevented overtly political activity, Havel and his colleagues placed the main stress on indepen-dent cultural work by individuals and groups. Although both spoke of "non-political" or "anti-political" politics as being the essence of their activity, they were fully aware of its profound political significance.[1]

Both Masaryk and Havel were persistent dissenters and nonconformists, critics of conventional wisdom, established institutions and customary prac-tices. In his work and political activity Masaryk presented a systematic cri-tique of what he regarded as the evils of society both at home in Bohemia and in Austria-Hungary, including the foreign policy of the monarchy. At the same time his criticism was constructive, pointing to concrete reforms which ought to be introduced. Masaryk viewed the role of the Czechs as a small nation whose fate was closely linked with a democratic Europe. Havel, too, in his own medium of the play, and later in his political essays, presented a searching critique of Communist institutions and practices in all their aspects, and in his essays set forth ideas of reform. He also dealt with the international context of Czech politics, condemning Soviet rule in Central Europe, includ-ing the invasion of 1968, and urging the return of his country to Europe. In defense of human rights, he and fellow Chartists appealed to international public opinion, to the governments of the world, and to the Helsinki process.

Masaryk and Havel did not voice their criticism in narrowly national terms but always within a universal framework. Masaryk developed the idea of "humanity" or "humanism" to describe the objectives which the Czechs should strive to achieve, recognizing that the Czech situation was but part of a general world crisis. Havel, too, in condemning totalitarian rule, depicted the faults of this system as an example of universal tendencies. Sharing Masaryk's humanist approach, Havel shunned narrow nationalism and sought to disclose "something universally human . . . about people in today's world, and about the crisis of modern-day humanity."[2]

The attitudes of both Masaryk and Havel were derived from a deeply moral attitude to the world around them. Each placed the principal responsibility on the individual to act as a citizen whatever the personal costs of such an action. The individual, although apparently powerless in the face of state power and social pressures, had the capacity to influence the course of events and the duty to follow the moral imperative of his conscience. Both denounced falsehood and "living the lie," and urged the pursuit of truth, no matter how hazardous and unpopular. Truth was the crucial criterion of the individual's actions and should be the principal objective of his behaviour. Said Havel: "I think that to speak the truth always makes sense under all circumstances."[3]

Both Masaryk and Havel derived their moral beliefs from a broad philosophical orientation. Masaryk was a professional philosopher, thoroughly conversant with the entire history of thought and developing his own eclectic philosophy of realism. Havel did not consider himself a philosopher but became increasingly philosophical in his approach. In his political essays and in his letters from prison, he sought constantly to define his personal identity and to formulate his convictions of the meaning of life. Like Masaryk, although in a lesser degree, Havel was concerned with the social question in its broadest sense, and was willing to call himself a socialist. Like Masaryk, Havel rejected Marxism for its materialist outlook, for its dogmatism and for its advocacy of violence.

Their beliefs were based on religious feelings, even though these were not identified with any church or body of religious thought. Masaryk had broken with the Catholic Church and became ostensibly a Protestant, but he was not a churchgoer and he subjected all Churches to searching criticism. His was a profoundly personal religion—a belief in God and immortality, and a deep conviction of the importance of religion in the life of the individual. Havel was even less "religious" and much more secular in his outlook. Although born a Catholic, he had no religious affiliation. Nonetheless, in his writings, he often expressed a belief in a universal order and a supreme authority above ordinary men. Just as Masaryk perceived the crisis of the contemporary world as resulting from a breakdown of universal religious faith, Havel believed that the crisis of modern man—manifested in the loss of inner identity and of responsibility to the world—reflected the "loss of God as a kind of absolute and universal system of coordinates."[4]

In acting according to their convictions and refusing to conform to political and social rules, Masaryk and Havel showed great personal courage and suffered the consequences of espousing unpopular causes. For instance, Masaryk, in the trial of Hilsner, defended an ordinary Jew in the face of prevalent anti-semitic attitudes in Austria and in Bohemia. Havel took up the cause of the rock music group, the Plastic People of the Universe, without regard for popular lack of sympathy for these young nonconformists. Masaryk conducted an unrelenting struggle against the Catholic Church and its dogma, whereas Havel fought a ceaseless war against the Communist Party and its ideology. As a result Masaryk had to endure the obloquy of his fellow Czechs, bitter attacks by anti-semitic journalists and by the Catholic hierarchy, and discrimination by the Austrian authorities. Although he was brought before the courts several times, the maximum penalty was the payment of small fines. However, his entire career was put into jeopardy and he was tempted several times to emigrate to America.

Havel suffered much more severe persecution by the Communist regime. He was deprived of the right to pursue his career as a playwright for many years. Although offered the chance of release from prison by emigration, he refused. Havel did not suffer popular opprobrium but was hardly known to the general public and received little active support from them. Both Masaryk and Havel stood their ground courageously and eventually emerged from their ordeals as popular national heroes.

The struggle for freedom and independence took very different courses. In Masaryk's case the objective was sought abroad, through emigration in 1914, at the risk of his entire career and with the sacrifice of his family. The outcome was determined largely by a persistent effort to win diplomatic support from the allied governments for the cause of Czechoslovak independence. Although Masaryk had abjured violence in his writings, he resorted to armed force in the form of the Czechoslovak legions, to contribute to the destruction of the Austro-Hungarian Empire. Domestic support was at first limited to Masaryk's closest allies but broadened to include the population as a whole in the closing months of the war. Success was attained only after many years of war.

Havel's struggle for liberation was conducted entirely at home and without the use of violence. In the moment of crisis in 1989, small independent movements, such as Charter 77, took the lead in opposing the Communist regime and received the support of the overwhelming part of the population, which expressed itself in massive street demonstrations. Havel was thrust into the role of leadership and guided the continuing popular unrest and negotiations with the Communist authorities. International support manifested itself in the simultaneous popular movements in neighbouring countries and by the avoidance of interference by the Soviet Union. Independence was achieved in a few days, or weeks at the most, and without the use of force of any kind.

It is too early to continue this comparative analysis into the period which followed the success of the democratic revolutions in 1918 and 1989. Suffice it to say that both men, and their peoples, had to "learn democracy," in the former case with the advantage of several decades of limited democratic experience under the Habsburgs; in the latter case without the benefit of any such training under Communism. In each case the mental attitudes of the past had to be overcome—in Masaryk's words, it was necessary to "de-Austrianize" Czech and Slovak thinking and acting. As Havel put it, people had to overcome the legacy of decades of Communism and to de-communize their thought and behaviour. Each of the two leaders enjoyed immense personal popularity at the time of his assumption of high office but was confronted with the difficult and unaccustomed task of exercising power.

Their relative success in fulfilling these tasks would have to be the subject of another essay. In some ways it seemed as though the efforts of both Masaryk and Havel came to naught. Masaryk had argued that fifty years were needed to build firm foundations for the new democratic state, but it was granted only twenty. He did not live to witness the destruction of his handiwork in 1938. The democratic revolution of 1989 had only two and a half years to achieve its goals; unlike Masaryk, Havel had perforce to preside over the liquidation of Czechoslovakia as a single state.

Yet the inter-war Republic did lay firm foundations for a new democracy. Masaryk showed himself capable of taking effective political action and of guiding Czechoslovakia towards a stable democratic society which survived for twenty years while neighbouring states in Europe succumbed to Fascism and authoritarianism. The free market system was successful in producing a highly productive economy and an advanced welfare state, but in the end it could not escape the catastrophic effects of world depression and international crisis. At first it seemed that Masaryk had won over many of the Slovak and German citizens to the legitimacy of the new republic. Recognition of the Slovaks as part of the ruling Czechoslovakian nation did not, in the end, appease the growing desire for recognition as a separate national identity and for self-government. The granting of widespread democratic rights and national rights to the Germans could not in the end counteract the appeal of national unification with Germany and the diplomatic and military pressures of Nazi Germany to achieve this goal. The ultimate collapse of the state in 1938 came as a result of outside forces, Nazi aggression and Western weakness of will, but it was also caused by serious faults in the structure of the state, which Masaryk had created. Nonetheless the integrity of the state was re-established as a result of the war, and the democratic values for which Masaryk had stood were partially restored in 1945 and again in 1968, and more fully in 1989.

Havel, as President, in a little more than a year and a half, contributed to the rebuilding of a democratic system and to the creation of conditions for a market economy to replace the disastrous totalitarian system which had governed the country for four decades. He was less effective than Masaryk in translating his highly moral approach into practical politics. Although much was achieved in effecting a transition to democracy, Havel alone could not overcome the fragmentation of political life and its highly polemical character. His prolonged efforts to establish an authentic federal system with very extensive powers for the two republics could not mask the erosion of Slovak faith in a single state and the expansion of the belief in Slovak sovereignty or, for a substantial minority, in total independence. Havel's greatest triumph was an international one, restoring Czechoslovakia to the forefront of world affairs and, like Masaryk, winning admiration and even affection for his personal role.

Nonetheless, the end of the united Republic did not mean the loss of other gains of the revolution. In the Czech Republic a firm foundation had been laid for democracy and a market system, and for a state capable, although reduced in size, of surviving in a dangerous world. In smaller, weaker and internationally isolated Slovakia, the future of democracy and a prosperous economy, indeed its very viability as an independent state, seemed, at the time of writing, more problematical.

In the perspective of history the two democratic revolutions, led by Masaryk and Havel, suffered the fate of many other great revolutions, meeting with profound setbacks and temporary defeats, but could not be said to have failed completely. They did lay foundations for eventual, though by no means certain, triumph of their guiding ideas. Whatever the outcome, and whatever their faults, Masaryk and Havel will stand out in the eyes of the world and of their citizens at home as two of the greatest figures in the history of their country, of Central Europe, and of the world.

Notes and References

1.   See Václav Havel, "Politics and Conscience," trans. E. Kohák and R. Scruton, *Václav Havel or Living in Truth,* ed. Jan Vladislav (London: Faber and Faber, 1987), 155.
2.   Vladislav, ibid., xvi.
3.   Quoted in Vilém Prečan and Alexander Tomský, eds., *Václav Havel: o lidskou identitu* (London: edice rozmluvy, 1984), 223.
4.   Quoted in Prečan and Tomský, 238, 349.

A Performer of Political Thought:
Václav Havel on Freedom and Responsibility

JEAN BETHKE ELSHTAIN

{There should be . . . a necessarily adversarial (but not necessarily hostile) relationship between the independent intellectual and the professional politician. The intellectual's job is to seek the truth, and then to present it as fully and clearly and interestingly as possible. The politician's job is to work in half truths.

—Timothy Garton Ash}

The problem of human identity remains at the center of my thinking about human affairs. . . . All my plays in fact are variations on this theme, the disintegration of man's oneness with himself and the loss of everything that gives human existence a meaningful order, continuity and its unique outline. . . . As you must have noticed from my letters, the importance of the notion of human responsibility has grown in my meditations. It has begun to appear, with increasing clarity, as that fundamental point from which all identity grows and by which it stands or falls; it is the foundation, the root, the center of gravity, the constructional principle or axis of identity. . . . It is the mortar binding it together, and when the mortar dries out, identity too begins irreversibly to crumble and fall apart.

—Václav Havel, *Letters to Olga*

Anyone who claims that I am a dreamer who expects to transform hell into heaven is wrong. I have few illusions, but I feel a responsibility to work towards the things I consider good and right. I don't know whether I'll be able to change certain things for the better, or not at all. Both outcomes are possible.

—Václav Havel, *Summer Meditations*

Reprinted from Ian Shapiro and Judith Wagner DeCew, eds., *Theory and Practice: Nomos XXXVII,* The Yearbook of the American Society for Political and Legal Philosophy (New York University Press, 1995), 464–82.

Theory and practice, or *theoria* and *praxis,* as they are sometimes couched, thus drawing attention to the classical lineage of both the categories and the vexations they deed us, form a central conundrum to many political theorists and philosophers. The distinction is, for many past and present, made exigent precisely because there is a gap between that which we can theorize and that which we can realize. Now, to some, this gap is part of the human condition. We always aspire to more than we can attain so it behooves us to keep our feet on the ground and not to engage in theoretical or wishful overreach. To others, this gap is, quite simply, unacceptable. They yearn for a more perfect order; a fullness of political being; an amplitude of justice or equality or wisdom; a state of unity and never-ending brotherhood and sisterhood, perhaps. For those who thus pine, the distinction between aspiration and "reality" may come to seem an unacceptable blot on the fortunes or misfortunes of humankind.

Many of our great movements of social and political yearning derive from one version of such recognitions. I think here of the anti-slavery movement, especially the slave's expressed desire for freedom, for that which is denied. But, alas, a good number of political and social catastrophes can be traced to this aspiration should it become a relentless drive to overturn any and all distinctions between that which is and that which, in theory, ought to be. In this latter case, our practices are always struggling to catch up to our theories and, in the process, much overturning and gnashing of teeth and shedding of blood may be inevitable. So one revolutionary story goes. This leads to my central concern, one that moves through this essay and helps to frame my interpretation of the work of Václav Havel. Havel, for me, represents an exemplary figure in part because he simply refuses to be drawn into the theory/practice dilemma as it is usually posed, thus opening up fresh ways of thinking; in part because he very delicately (for that is his way) summons up the best that is in us without stirring up the beasts that are always lurking at the same time.

Havel helps me to understand my own problem with the theory/practice problem, namely, that the issues at hand are too often so abstractly couched. It is difficult to get a handle on what, precisely, is at stake. I refer to the dilemma as it has been presented to me by political philosophers committed to the notion that the presumed divide or tension between theory and practice could be quite overcome in some future perfect world of transparent human relations and human communication. The theory/practice dilemma was such only because there were barriers in the way of instantiating in practice an abstract theoretical understanding. One variant on the Marxist project was particularly given to an odd combination of deep cynicism about the present, with its distorted relations, consciousness, and practices, by contrast to some future moment within an emancipated human community. In that future community, presumably, no theory/practice dilemma would persist because distinctions, boundaries, and tensions would have melted away and a "oneness"—that oceanic feeling Freud described and mocked so effectively—would have triumphed. The individual would be at one with himself or herself, the social order cured of its previous dissensions, conflicts, and divisions.

Dreams of this sort die hard. The notion of "positive transcendence" of estrangement will always beckon. Thus, one version of the theory/practice conundrum holds that the dilemma itself exists only because we live in a world of flawed and imperfect social forms. Once the universe is administered a stiff dose of the right medicine and cures itself, no dilemma—no distinction of this sort or of most other problematic sorts—will persist. This, of course, is a quite unbelievable political fantasy, believed in devoutly because it promises an overarching *Weltanschauung* of the sort described and decried by Freud, "an intellectual construction which solves all the problems of our existence on the basis of one overriding hypothesis which, accordingly, leaves no question unanswered and in which everything that interests us finds its fixed place."[1] Before practice can be perfect, or nearly so, one requires a theory that explains all, determines all, and can be enacted more or less in toto.

Now, one might have thought those committed to ridding us of foundational superstition would resolve this dilemma, falsely couched within totalizing theories, by pointing out that the world is a dense and rather intractable place, that our practices can never be made perfect any more than our theories can explain all that wants explaining or help us to understand all that requires understanding. Not necessarily so. Take, for example, Richard Rorty's treatment of the theory/practice vexation. For him, too, it simply ceases to be a question because one jettisons the "theory" end of the pole. However mistakenly cast this may be in Marxist and critical-theory formulations of the problem, eliminating the question altogether does not seem terribly helpful. But Rorty is deeply committed to insouciance. This is how it works. Rorty reassures us that things are pretty much moving along as they were meant to. The committed "contingentist" understands this; therefore, he also understands that even those who *claim* that their political actions and their very identities are imbricated with a set of deep theoretical or philosophical understandings are simply mistaken about their own project and the nature of its entanglement with such understandings.

Rortyanism requires that we all join the ranks of an army of contingent "we's." For Rorty contingency is what one is left with when one rejects the correspondence theory of truth and similarly eschews any strong convictions concerning the nature of reality. Rorty links his commitment to contingency to a rough-and-ready progressivist teleology (even though he cannot permit himself teleological arguments, he relies tacitly on Whiggish history) when he claims, as but one example: "Europe gradually lost the habit of using certain words and gradually acquired the habit of using others."[2] Aside from the peculiarity of granting agency to a continent, what is at work here appears to be a conviction that although there is nothing intrinsic or essential about anything that has happened, or that led to the construction of "we liberal ironists," we are still in pretty good shape if we endorse a loose liberal utopia in which things pretty much continue to move along the way they have been moving because the contingencies seem to be on "our side." At least this is the way I interpret a statement such as: "A liberal society is one which is content to call 'true' whatever the upshot of such encounters turns out to be."³ The encounters in question here are basic good guys versus bad guys stuff in which, over time, the good guys appear to be winning, more or less. Given the blithe certainty of Rorty's commitment to contingency with progress, it is, perhaps, unsurprising that he should claim that those who claim they require certain philosophical understandings or metaphysical commitments in order, in fact, to understand and to commit are making a big mistake. In a review of the work of Jan Patočka, Václav Havel's philosophical mentor and himself a signatory of Charter 77, Rorty allows for the possibility that we might find ourselves enthralled by—or in thrall to—an unconditional moral obligation grounded, he says, in groundless hope. In criticizing Patočka—and Havel—he endorses unconditional obligation but severs it from, indeed he mocks, the identity out of which such obligation grows, on the account of Patočka and, as we shall learn shortly, Havel as well.

But it is hard for Rorty to sustain this maneuver, even as verbal foreplay. He writes: "Non-metaphysicians cannot say that democratic institutions reflect a moral reality and that tyrannical regimes do not reflect one, that tyrannies get something *wrong* that democratic societies get *right*." But just one sentence further, Rorty claims: "Patočka's conscience led him to do the right thing."⁴ How does Rorty know this? How can he claim that Patočka, a dissident in danger, stripped of the reasons he himself proffers for doing what he did, would have done what he did without those reasons and the beliefs to which they gave force and fervor? He can claim it, in part, because he endorses his own version of practice being unproblematic in relation to theory; indeed, what is problematic, on Rorty's view, is assuming there is any problem, or question, or deep dilemma at all.

I will argue or, perhaps more accurately, display the ways in which the thought of Václav Havel and his actions as a dissident/president fall through the grid of Marxist and critical theory formulations of the theory/practice relation and, as well, offer a powerful alternative to anti-foundationalism, with its evasion or excision of the question. For Havel concerns himself not only with the immediate—the ways in which he enacts thought, his role as a performer of political thought—but the ways in which current enactors are, at one and the same time, re-enactors who must take responsibility for the past without repeating it. As he noted in his first speech as President of a (then united) Czechoslovakia, "It would be unreasonable to understand the sad legacy of the last forty years as something alien, which some distant relative bequeathed us. On the contrary, we have to accept this legacy as something we committed against ourselves. If we accept it as such, we will understand that it is up to us all, and up to us only, to do something about it."[5]

Let me begin by situating Václav Havel in relation to a number of current political possibilities and positions. It is, perhaps, Havel's misfortune to have become a hero.[6] The upshot is that various partisans representing entrenched positions of the sort Havel himself disdains now vie either to identify themselves with Havel or to insist that Havel "really" belongs to them—whether democratic socialist, or mainstream liberal, or more free-market capitalist. There are those who emphasize his skeptical ironic stance and see him as a leading exemplar of a modernist, perhaps even a post-modernist temperament. Others appropriate him to a distinctly religious sensibility. Such moves to secure Havel, to pin him down, are rather beside the point. With Hannah Arendt, indeed in identical words, Havel declares that he is going to say what he has to say, do what he has to do, think in an unfettered way save insofar as all serious thought takes place against a "horizon of Being," without regard for labels, without checking in first with the guardians of political correctness (whether of the left or the right) to be sure he hasn't crossed some line or other.

Consider the following exchange between Hannah Arendt and Hans Morgenthau:

HANS MORGENTHAU: What are you? Are you a conservative? Are you a liberal? Where is your position within contemporary possibilities?

ARENDT: I don't know. I really don't know and I've never known. And I suppose I never had any such position. You know the left think that I am conservative, and the conservatives sometimes think I am left or I am a maverick or God knows what. And I must say I couldn't care less. I don't think that the real questions of this century will get any kind of illumination by this kind of thing.[7]

Now Havel from a little manifesto entitled, "What I Believe":

I refuse to classify myself as left or right. I stand between these two political and ideological front-lines, independent of them. Some of my opinions may seem left-wing, no doubt, and some right-wing, and I can even imagine that a single opinion may seem left-wing to some and right-wing to others—and to tell you the truth, I couldn't care less.[8]

It is precisely this refreshing refusal to be captured by one determined side or another that helps to account for the freshness of Havel's "take" on theory and practice. Mind you, he doesn't discuss action in relation to thought in precisely those categories, understanding, surely, that this might commit him to a lot of other things from which he seeks to be free. Suffice it to say that Havel defies easy definition. Here one begins. But to end on this irenic note would be a serious cop-out. What makes Havel an exemplary performer of political thought is the way he works the boundaries of various commitments and modes of thought and inquiry; the care he takes to locate himself, and the politics of his own society and of our time more generally, in a permanent *agon,* a never-ending contestation between tradition and transformation.

In a discussion in Prague, on September 25, 1992, Havel responded to questions about politics and "public space" by reiterating his longstanding view that politics is a sphere of concrete responsibility, just as the theater is a concrete institution in which characters enact positions. Real life, he continued, is bound to be richer than any politics. There is always a dramatic reduction from life to politics and one must exercise freedom within finiteness. One can never know enough to make an absolutely sure, certain, clean-cut decision about much of anything. One must try to pretend that behavior is decent "after all," acting always in a mode of "as if" in order to get things to proceed decently. Asked to comment explicitly on a theory/practice question, Havel simply avoided the dilemma as presented. He was enjoined to explain how he fit into the distinction to be marked between an ethics of intention and an ethics of consequence. Given that Havel avoids both pure intentionality and pure consequentialism, I (for one) anticipated that his response might be to work the theoretical turf between these alternatives, or to explain the way he puts intention and consequence together in a fruitful mix. But instead he told a story. Imagine, he suggested, two scenes: the politician with the expert, on the one hand, and the politician with the ordinary citizen, on the other. A decent politician can always find an expert to inform him of certain things or to do certain things. Far more important is the relation of the politician to the ordinary citizen, for politics is a special kind of vocation and one drawn to this vocation should be more urgently committed to the citizen, with his or her complex but non-expert understandings. This way of doing things makes people nervous because we hanker after experts to solve problems. But the search for solutions in this way invites ideology and ideology is absolutely the worst way to hold things together. Inventing ideologies and utopias is easy, too easy, but we must follow a more complicated course, he suggested.

What, then, is this more complicated course and how does it help us to think in supple ways about how political thought may be performed in a manner that keeps ideas alive and practice robust? What follows is a general discussion of the contours of Havel's reflections on responsibility, reflections that put on display his resolute commitment to a worldview that rejects latter-day Protagorean efforts to make man the measure of all things. For Havel, free responsibility is an outgrowth of a commitment to live "in truth" and that commitment, in turn, is inescapably shaped by a loss of metaphysical certainties coupled with an equally sure and certain insistence on the need for a "higher horizon," for a transcendental or suprapersonal moral authority which alone can check the human will to power, an anthropocentric arrogance that threatens the human "home."[9]

Because Havel is mostly talked about and treated as a trendy playwright-president who would as soon entertain the Rolling Stones as heads of state, it seems best to proceed chronologically in order to unpack the rhythmic continuities in his thought. As a thinker, to press a metaphor familiar to students of political thought, for all his foxiness, there is a rather stubborn hedgehog at work and it is the fusion of solidity of being—living in truth—with irony that makes for Havel's uniqueness and, as well, ideally suits him as a guide through the miasma of the *fin de siècle*.

Havel is deeply indebted, in a rough-and-ready way although more systematically than he sometimes seems to allow, both to the phenomenological tradition of Husserl and Heidegger as "translated" by the great Czech philosopher, Jan Patočka, mentioned above in my criticism of Rortyan antifoundationalism, and to Masarykian humanism. Shaped by the overlapping of many movements and traditions, Havel places himself under no obligation to systematize or, for that matter, to synthesize. He is not only temperamentally unsuited to the logic-chopper's or Hegelian "over-comers" task, he is opposed on principle to both sorts of efforts—the former because it issues into a penury and niggardliness of thought; the latter because it promotes ideology whose dead-hand soon closes over "life itself." Havel notes the "intellectual and spiritual" dimensions of his own cultural identity as a complex but very specific amalgam of many currents, many forces:

> We live in the very centre of Central Europe, in a place that from the beginning of time has been the main European crossroads of every possible interest, invasion, and influence of a political, military, ethnic, religious, or cultural nature. The intellectual and spiritual currents of east and west, north and south, Catholic and Protestant, enlightened and romantic—the political movements of conservative and progressive, liberal and socialist, imperialist and national liberalist—all of these overlapped here, and bubbled away in one vast cauldron, combining to form our national and cultural consciousness, our traditions, the social models of our behavior, which have been passed down from generation to generation. . . . We are like a sponge that has gradually absorbed and digested all kinds of intellectual and cultural impulses and initiatives.[10]

Departing from Masaryk's "positivist belief in progress," Havel found a philosophical home inside the general themes offered by Patočka, a philosopher nearly unknown outside the Czech Republic.[11] For Patočka, philosophy begins once life is no longer something that can be taken for granted. The alternative to a world of certain meaning is not subjectivism, however, but another sort of engagement with the world, specifically with the *life-world* rooted in a distinctly premodern sensibility but which the modern sensibility must knowingly affirm and grant as "that which is"—something objective and tangible—in order to get out of a perverse preoccupation with self-absorbed wishes, preferences and feelings.

The contrast points for Patočka's (and Havel's) thought, then, are a mechanistic and austere rationalism, on the one hand, and a perfervid, labile romanticism, on the other. A central preoccupation in a world which ceases to "respect any so-called higher metaphysical values—the Absolute, something higher than themselves, something mysterious"—necessarily becomes the self—human identity—and, with it, the nature of human burdens and responsibilities appropriate to this self. There are philosophers who hold the everyday in contempt as womanish stuff, a potion that dilutes the bracing tonic quaffed by real thinkers. Not so Patočka and Havel. Both begin with philosophy "from the bottom," and from a "humbly respected boundary of the natural world." Both view the self as one who, while passing away, has an identity and a unique and independent purpose. We become acquainted with others through acts of responsible surrender to that which is required of us rather than supererogation or arrogation. One begins by taking the natural world for granted as the horizon of doing and knowing—a horizon which is always there and against which we define our own being.

Freedom in this scheme of things is not the working out of a fore-ordained teleology of self-realization; rather, freedom comes from embracing that which it is given one to do; the "secret of man," writes Havel, "is the secret of his responsibility." This responsibility consists, in part, in a knowing rejection of God-likeness and mastery. For when man takes on this hubristic role, he becomes the sole source of meaning in a world rendered dead and meaningless. Man exceeds his strength and he becomes despairing, a destructive Titan ruining himself and others.[12] We are not perched on top of the earth as sovereigns; rather, we are invited into companionship with the earth as the torn and divided beings we are. Even our duty is not one. Havel is so committed to the need to strip our practices of theoretical hubris, he insisted that the draft of the constitution for the new Czech Republic refer to man as part of the universe rather than as "the master of everything."

The fusion of freedom and responsibility worked out in Patočka's phenomenology yields a distinct but definite *political* conclusion: democracy is the political form that permits and requires human freedom as responsibility, not as an act of self-overcoming, nor pure reason, but in service to the notion that there are things worth suffering for. Patočka, it should be noted, remained a theist throughout his life: without God the world, he insisted, is quite literally unthinkable. For this reason the atheist is more likely to be dominated in a rather uninteresting way by a particular construction of theism than is the phenomenologist who articulates explicitly the horizon of his or her thought. Although Havel evokes God, especially in his later works, he is reticent about the status of his own relationship to theism and considers that belief in a "personal God" is not the pressing philosophic question. What gives urgency to this matter for Havel is the fact that once the supra-human is repudiated or forgotten and man crowns himself lord and master of all he surveys, the world loses its human dimensions. If this be theism, he might say, then make the most of it.

Tracking the question of responsibility in Havel's most famous political essays as well as his *Letters to Olga,* the casual or careless reader might be tempted to jettison the philosophical frame within which Havel nests his own understanding of responsibility as unnecessarily cumbersome, a clumsy and even redundant accessory to an otherwise very straightforward insistence upon accountability. But this would be a mistake. On this score Havel is quite insistent. Humans confront nothing less than a general crisis that manifests itself in many ways and this crisis is, at base, spiritual. Something is "profoundly wrong," for the horizon of thought itself is increasingly beclouded, even despoiled; the order of nature (yes, nature) is ruptured and the result is estrangement, demoralization, and indifference. We face a crisis of human identity and this crisis *must* be understood—can only be understood—when projected against a shrinking screen emblematic of a declining human awareness of "the absolute." Human reason has wrenched itself free from human *Being* and the results are both tawdry and tragic.

The argument continues in this vein: the world is possible only because we are grounded and once this world of "personal responsibility" with its characteristic virtues and marks of decency (justice, honor, friendship, fidelity) is ruptured or emptied, what rushes in to take its place is politics as a superannuated "rational technology of power" whose exemplar is the manager, the *apparatchik.* Humans play god and the wreckage intensifies. Man finds himself "in the rut of totalitarian thought, where he is not his own and where he surrenders his own reason and conscience."[13] Man lives within a lie; he gives himself over to the social auto-totality and he or she who does so surrenders identity and responsibility falters.

Responsibility within Havel's philosophical thematic flows from the aims of life "in its essence" which are plurality, diversity, and independent self-constitution as against the conformity, uniformity, and stultifying discipline of the social auto-totality, which not only abandons reality and assaults life but corrodes the "very notion of identity itself." To live within the truth is to give voice to a self which has embraced responsibility for the here and now. "That means that responsibility is ours, that we must accept it and grasp it *here, now,* in this place in time and space where the Lord has set us down, and that we cannot lie our way out of it by moving somewhere else, whether it be to an Indian ashram or to a parallel *polis.*"[14] The only "solution" to the crisis Havel sketches is to deepen human responsibility in and through hope for the moral reconstitution of society. And this reconstitution can only come about through a radical revision of the relationship of human beings to the human order: trust, openness, solidarity—if these three do not abide; if we cannot rehabilitate such values, our rootedness in the life-world, which alone gives rise to openness and dynamism and plurality, is "forgotten" and, along with it, responsibility falls into forgetfulness, down something on the level of consciousness akin to the "memory hole" in Orwell's *1984.*

In *Letters to Olga,* Havel is insistent that his evocation of responsibility not be conflated with conforming to convention, or following the rules. If anything, responsibility, rooted and concretely construed, imposes far heavier burdens of freedom on one living in truth than rote, rule-governed behavior allows. Responsibility—acceptance of the risks of free action—forms the very basis of one's identity; any mode of thought that reduces human responsibility to the extent it does shrinks the horizon of human possibility. This responsible self must act in a kind of twilight, never knowing for certain what the outcome of his or her deeds may be. Responsibility is not only vouching for oneself but taking on the task of neighborliness.

A crisis in responsibility (the "intrinsic responsibility that man has to and for the world") is a crisis in human identity and human integrity.[15] To assume "full responsibility" is not to lapse into dour moralism, nor to universalize a kind of giddy and boundless compassion, but to take up the very specific and concrete burdens of one's own time and place. Havel himself sums this up nicely in Letters 142 and 143 of *Letters to Olga:* "The crisis of today's world, obviously, is a crisis of human responsibility (both responsibility for oneself and responsibility 'toward' something else) and thus it is a crisis of human identity as well."[16] Also:

> Love, charity, sympathy, tolerance, understanding, self-control, solidarity, friendship, feelings of belonging, the acceptance of concrete responsibility for those close to one—these are, I think, expressions of that new (or more precisely, continually renewed and betrayed by all of human history) "interexistentiality" that alone can breathe new meaning into the social formations and collectivities that, together, shape the fate of the world.[17]

Let me now focus on a central fault-line in Havel's work, namely, his lively acceptance of paradox coupled with his rejection of fixed categories. Such a philosophic stance and existential temperament is most often associated with a repudiation of foundationalism or theism in our epoch. Not so in Havel's case. Stubbornly (here the hedgehog), he reiterates time and time again his conviction that rootedness alone gives birth to an authentic paradoxical outlook, an awareness of irony that cuts to the bone rather than appearing as froth on the latest wave to hit the shore. Unembarrassedly, Havel speaks of his "mission," the need to "bear witness" to the "terrors" of his time and to "speak the truth." He rejects words that obscure rather than illuminate (like "socialism") and with this goes an "antipathy to overly fixed categories, empty ideological phrases and incantations that petrify thought in a hermetic structure of static concepts."[18] He would, I believe, argue that this very particular and pointed blend of belief in the need for an "absolute horizon" for thought and action alone offers a certain block against the speciousness of ideology with its illusory identities and excusatory functions, hence against the deadliness of that terrible and seductive (and ultimately false) hope embodied in the word "utopia."

Utopianism—the vision of a "radiant tomorrow"—yields inevitably to an impersonal "juggernaut of power," hence to that ethical crisis which marks late modernity and requires an ethical-political reconstitution grounded in authentic hope—the humble and simple hope for trust, openness, and solidarity. On this score Havel has been consistent and insistent for nearly three decades—from his earliest "dissident" writings to his most recent presidential "meditations." With Simone Weil, Albert Camus, Hannah Arendt, George Orwell, Czeslaw Milosz, and other independent thinkers of this century (their numbers, alas, are not legion), Havel scores utopianism as a

> typically intellectual phenomenon—the greatest revolutionaries were all intellectuals. It is an arrogant attempt by human reason to plan life. But it is not possible to force life to conform to some abstract blueprint. Life is something unfathomable, ever-changing, mysterious, and every attempt to confine it within an artificial, abstract structure inevitably ends up homogenizing, regimenting, standardizing and destroying life, as well as curtailing everything that projects beyond, overflows or falls outside the abstract project. What is a concentration camp, after all, but an attempt by utopians to dispose of those elements which don't fit in?[19]

In response to those who parry by suggesting that a life without utopias would be horrible and unthinkable, would reduce life (as one of Havel's interlocutors put it) to "hopelessness, despair, and resignation to the daily corruption and absurdity," Havel replies by contrasting "openness towards mysteriously changing and always rather elusive and never quite attainable ideals such as truth and morality, and, on the other hand, an unequivocal identification with a detailed plan for implementing those ideals which in the end becomes self-justifying."[20] Hope is not the same as joy in the certainty that things are going well, or the willingness to invest in enterprises that are obviously headed for success, but, rather, an ability to work for something because it is good, not just because it stands a chance to succeed. Hope is definitely not the same as optimism. The over-intellectualizing ideologue and revolutionary forgets this in his zeal to get everything right and in order.

The theme of *trahison des clercs* is nothing new. What adds freshness and piquancy to Havel's project is that he has personally paid the price for his resistance to the seduction of ideology and that he does so, not in the name of a restorationist ideal, but in the name of an elemental, forward-pressing, yet limited ideal of free responsibility. Havel's "higher horizon" opens up rather than forecloses on genuine political possibility. In Havel's world, individual responsibility deepens and expands to the extent that utopianism—giving oneself over to a *Weltanschauung*—is eschewed.

Havel often muses on (and is bemused by) the "genuinely human." For our very humanness to come into sharp focus our worlds must be shaped and formed against a horizon rather than sunk in an immanent sea. That is, the human dimension cannot be derived from a flatness of being, a world cut and dried to our own measure, but stands out and takes shape from externality. This externality should not be construed as absolutely Other, as utterly transcendent—and here things get tricky—but should and must be *recognized* as absolute and supra-personal. Identity and responsibility are shaped, molded, and hammered out of the material of a world understood against the frame of a horizon of Being. This prevents or serves to guard against a blurred, all-purpose, and limitless collapse into universal empathy which promotes, finally, a vapid because unbounded pseudo-responsibility for everything everywhere.[21] In order for our lives lived among others on the horizontal plane to bear fruit, we must resist fusion with the auto-totality which is nothing more nor less than the socio-political expression of a world without a supra-personal horizon of Being against which to measure itself.

To those who argue, as Rorty does, for example, that Havel and his mentor, Patočka, really do not require what they themselves claim they require—a transcendental horizon or grounding for thought, action, and responsibility—Havel might insist that Rorty and many contemporary anti-foundationalists in fact rely on what Hannah Arendt called *bannisters* for their thought. That is, for all their anti-foundationalism they remain wedded to a teleology of progress, a nearly unbounded faith in the possibility of enlightenment in that glorious epiphany once the debris and clutter of metaphysical thought is swept away once and for all (hence the "more liberal" a policy or thought or whim can be said to be "the better"). This attitude often gets coupled to an utter insouciance concerning power. The tacit bannister to which such thinkers cling remains intact but it is a stairway not to heaven but to yet another utopian hell.[22] With Arendt, Havel is utterly resistant to the alchemy of "the dialectic" which transforms concrete evils into abstract goods. There is a beyond and that is why the here and now, this moment as a concrete slice of all moments, takes on such shimmering vitality and importance.

Havel's response to those who claim his own thought is murky and unrealistic and will not survive a move into the realm of practical politics is complex, amounting to something akin to an invitation for them to help him take stock in order that his own words not become empty clichés. The process of enacting thought in a situation of murky uncertainty—for society is a very "mysterious animal with many hidden faces and potentialities"—can never yield transparent translations from the "mysterious" to the pragmatically clear. No one knows the full potentiality of any given moment, for good or for evil. Hence the importance of the "purely moral act that has no hope of any immediate and visible political effect" for such an act can "gradually and indirectly, over time, gain in political significance."[23] One must be patient and not so excessively result-oriented that the humanly possible work begins to look tawdry and unworthy. Havel tells one interlocutor that he tries to "live in the spirit of Christian morality," not as a doctrinalist but as a practitioner of hope who attempts to see things "from below" in a tough-minded, not sentimental way. His unabashed embrace of life is precisely an embrace of a post-Babelian world in which there are wondrous varieties of human "homes," identities, languages, particular possibilities, but there is as well a trans-particular world framing our fragile globe united perhaps only in its travail. Real hope is not hope for some "happy ending" or for glorious heroes to save the day but hope that human beings, in taking responsibility for a state of affairs (in the broadest sense), might "see it as their own project and their own home, as something they need not fear, as something they can—without shame—love, because they have built it for themselves."[24] Havel shares the basic gospel hope that all might have life and might have it more abundantly.

For Havel, hope, responsibility, freedom, and irony are all of a piece and to lop one bit off in order to better serve our purposes will not do. What makes Havel such a fascinating performer of political thought is that he provokes the complacent, mocks the smug, tweaks the arrogant, and suffers without excusing the weak. In his rejection of the petrified politics deeded us by the legacy of the French Revolution and a century of total wars, Havel helps us to move into a future dis-illusioned, hence paradoxically free.

I think he would agree that a central task of political philosophy for our time lies in recognizing what has happened for what it is. What has happened for what it is in Europe, at this point, is the definitive collapse of an attempt to rebuild human society on some overarching ideal or *Weltanschauung*. What has been undermined is the comforting myth that we have transparent and direct instruction and relations. Europe, Havel noted in Prague, has entered the long tunnel at the end of the light. The problems which lie before it could not be more exigent and will not be dealt with in a kind of lightning flash. One must continue to perform political thought, not knowing how the draw ends nor, with any finality, who—or what—is its author.

The last words shall be his:

Genuine politics, politics worthy of the name, and in any case the only politics that I am willing to devote myself to, is simply serving those close to oneself: serving the community, and serving those who come after us. Its deepest roots are moral because it is a responsibility, expressed through action, to and for the whole, a responsibility that is what it is—a "higher" responsibility, which grows out of a conscious or subconscious certainty that our death ends nothing, because everything is forever being recorded and evaluated somewhere else, somewhere "above us," in what I have called "the memory of Being," an integral aspect of the secret order of the cosmos, of nature, and of life, which believers call God and to whose judgment everything is liable. Genuine conscience and genuine responsibility are always, in the end, explicable only as an expression of the silent assumption that we are being observed "from above," and that "up there" everything is visible, nothing is forgotten, and therefore earthly time has no power to wipe away the pangs brought on by earthly failure: our spirit knows that it is not the only one that knows of these failures.

If there is to be a minimum chance of success, there is only one way to strive for decency, reason, responsibility, sincerity, civility, and tolerance: and that is decently, reasonably, responsibly, sincerely, civilly, and tolerantly.[25]

Notes and References

1. Sigmund Freud, "The Question of a *Weltanschauung,*" *New Introductory Lectures, Standard Edition* 22 (London: Hogarth Press, 1964), 158.

2. Richard Rorty, *Contingency, irony, and solidarity* (Cambridge: Cambridge University Press, 1989), 6. My general argument is that Rortyanism is all contingency, finally, as authentic irony is dependent upon deeper reflections and recognitions than Rorty permits himself, even as solidarity demands a much "thicker" account of the self. Portions of this paragraph and one or two others are drawn from my essay, "Don't be Cruel: Reflections on Rortyan Liberalism," in Daniel W. Conway and John E. Seery, eds., *The Politics of Irony* (New York: St. Martin's Press, 1992), 199–218.

3. Ibid., 52.

4. Richard Rorty, "The Seer of Prague," *New Republic* (July 1, 1991): 37.

5. Václav Havel, "The Art of the Impossible," text of the first speech as President of Czechoslovakia, *The Spectator* (January 27, 1990): 12.

6. I draw liberally upon my essay, "A Man for This Season," *Perspectives on Political Science* 21, no. 14 (Fall 1992): 207–11 for my analysis of Havel's political thought.

7. See Melvyn A. Hill, *Hannah Arendt: The Recovery of the Public World* (New York: St. Martin's Press, 1979), 333–34.

8. Václav Havel, *Summer Meditations,* trans. Paul Wilson (New York: Knopf, 1992), 60.

9. What follows relies on my reading of Havel's works in English. I will provide notes only for longer quotations. The works I will draw upon include Jan Vladislav, *Václav Havel or Living in Truth* (London: Faber and Faber, 1987); Václav Havel, et al., *The Power of the Powerless: Citizens against the State in Central-Eastern Europe* (Armonk, N.Y.: M. E. Sharpe, 1985); Václav Havel, *Letters to Olga,* trans. Paul Wilson (New York: Henry Holt, 1989); Václav Havel, *Disturbing the Peace* (New York: Knopf, 1990); Václav Havel, *Open Letters: Selected Writings, 1965–1990,* trans. Paul Wilson (New York: Knopf, 1991); and Havel, *Summer Meditations.*

10. Havel, *Summer Meditations,* 125–26.

11. Patočka's works, or selections from them, have only recently appeared in English. See Erazim Kohák, ed., *Jan Patočka: Philosophy and Selected Writings* (Chicago: University of Chicago Press, 1989).

12. This is the theme of Patočka's essay, "Titanism," written in 1936, and it echoes persistently throughout Havel's work. See 139–45 of the Patočka collection.

13. Havel, "Politics and Conscience," in *Living in Truth,* 151.

14. Havel, "The Power of the Powerless," *Living in Truth,* 104.

15. See *Letters to Olga,* 266–68.

16. Ibid., 365.

17. Ibid., 371.

18. *Disturbing the Peace,* 9.

19. Havel, in an interview conducted by Erica Blair, trans. A. G. Brain, *Times Literary Supplement* (January 23, 1987), 82.

20. Ibid.

21.   Havel's pointedly ironic rejoinders to Western peace activists is a prime example of his rejection of an immanentist politics of empathy. See "An Anatomy of Reticence" in *Living in Truth.*

22.   See Rorty's review of Patočka's work in *The New Republic,* as noted above, in which he claims Patočka was mistaken about the need to ground his political commitments in certain ethico-philosophical claims.

23.   Comments from *Disturbing the Peace,* 109, 114–15.

24.   *Summer Meditations,* 128.

25.   Václav Havel, "Paradise Lost," *New York Review of Books* (April 9, 1992): 6, 7.

Václav Havel and The Rhetoric Of Folly

KENNETH S. ZAGACKI

{With an intellectual playfulness and unerring sense for the histrionic that might deceive us about the seriousness of the topic discussed, the playwright takes us through a spectrum of philosophical questions about truth and falsehood, reason and rationalization, good and evil.

—Marketa Goetz-Stankiewicz}

Post-Cold War Eastern and Central Europe was racked by the transition from totalitarianism to democracy, the struggle of moral conscience over political opportunism, and the tension between national civility and violent nationalism. M. Kondracke observed that even as the collapse of Communism in Eastern and Central Europe brought about the ascent of "bourgeois, consumerist, mixed-capitalist, welfare-state democracy," a new set of conflicts based on economics, race, religion, and nationality was emerging from the cauldron of geopolitical change. The imposing challenge was to prevent these conflicts "from leading to mass destruction; and, eventually, to make humankind one democratic family."[1]

In the midst of this post-Cold War clamor, Václav Havel came to power. His goal was remarkably idealistic, to establish a new post-Cold War world, a sort of "one democratic family." The rise of Havel to the Presidency of Czechoslovakia represents an astonishing ascent to political authority. . . . Describing Havel's dramatic odyssey, T. B. Farrell has written that "It is unlikely that any of his fictionalized characters ever played a more improbable role than the one he was about to perform. Once a witness to this moment of transformational history, he was now to enact its central interpretative part."[2]

This essay argues that Havel "enacted" history's "central interpretative part" by offering a bold and profound "rhetoric of folly." Bold because he assumed the difficult task of defining, to both Czechs and Westerners in general, the direction of the post-Cold War world in a way that avoided the

Reprinted and abridged from *The Southern Communication Journal* 62, no.1 (fall 1996): 17–30. Reprinted with the permission of The Southern States Communication Association.

7. With Olga in Calcutta, 1994.

8. With Dagmar and the Clintons, 1997.

Realpolitik of many political spokespersons. Profound because Havel encouraged an unusual reversal of thinking about the new world order and the role of citizens within it. Havel's rhetoric described future policy and all of human action as originating from the lowly position of the fool. Rather than boasting about the achievements of his people or his own administration, Havel was first and foremost concerned with the folly of the human endeavor, with people, nations, and governments in their human state, restrained and frequently made ridiculous by their limitations or attempts to overcome them. And yet, Havel showed that folly is a kind of lived wisdom, a source of strength, motivation for overcoming despair and moving toward hopeful human action. Moreover, folly was a way of transforming common sense assumptions. As S. K. Foss says, "The effectiveness of the fool depends on the ability to hold a mirror up to the traditional social order . . . showing that reality as it is experienced could very well be different."[3]

Investigating Václav Havel's rhetoric is important because it illustrates how the comic mode of discourse might encourage peaceful persuasive practice, especially during periods of great social or historical turmoil. Indeed, fools are often held in esteem because they can cope with perplexing and particularly demanding phases of transition.[4] The power of Havel's rhetoric of folly is found in its ability to provoke certain creative transformations at an opportune moment, through its metaphorical and meta-morphic potential. Havel's opportune moment was the closing of the Cold War, a time during which he tried to restore "to the contemporary world a sense of human dignity and personality largely eclipsed both in Marxism and in prevailing currents of Western thought."[5] He thereby sought to reclaim for himself and his audience a lost world and its gentler virtues of humility, compassion, and moral responsibility. These virtues in turn provide the commonplaces of Havel's speeches, and work to overcome the anxiety of his audiences during a time of political unrest and possibility. Havel's virtues are derived from what he sees as the fundamental nature of human Being, yet these virtues respect the concrete realities of present circumstance. For Havel, these virtues originate in the limited disposition of humanity, its state of folly. But Havel's rhetoric gives birth to hope. "Our dignity," Richard Rorty writes about Havel's discourse on humanity, "does not come from being potentially in touch with the infinite, it comes from our finitude."[6]

Thus, between the crushing historical absolutes posed by totalitarian regimes and the troubling uncertainties of a democratic future, Havel's rhetoric of folly relied on a different logic, a social grammar of dialectical *irony.* Through irony, Havel claimed that power was obtained through weakness, strength through vulnerability, wisdom through ignorance. Havel proposed irony as a means of easing the passage to an uncertain geopolitical future. Essential, too, was *humility,* a constant awareness of the frailties of the human condition and the desire to work with rather than ignore those vulnerabilities. In Havel's rhetoric, humility, and the mindful moral action it engenders, overcame the political paralysis caused by Communist oppression, along with the political opportunism that frequently attends political revolution. As Timothy Garton Ash cautioned, in the post-Communist environment, "the drumbeat" of political opportunism could drown "the whisper" of moral conscience.[7] Finally, Havel's rhetoric was *empathic* and represented a fitting response to the unbridled eruption of anti-semitism and other forms of (hyper)nationalism that have historically plagued much of Europe. Havel himself has written that the post-Communist transition "is fertile ground for radicalism of all kinds, for the hunt for scapegoats, and for the need to hide behind the anonymity of a group, be it socially or ethnically based."[8] Empathy allows one to assume the perspective of those who might otherwise be neglected from (or persecuted by) the observer's allegedly "superior" vantage point.

In what follows, the concept of folly, as it emerges in the Western tradition and as it operates in Havel's public discourse, is explored. The implications of such a rhetoric are also examined.

FOLLY AND IRONY

Unlike tragedy, which has typically dealt with individuals in their godlike embodiment, the comic appreciation of folly has been more realistic, celebrating the spectacle of human failure and weakness. . . .

[M]editations on comedy date much farther back. The Greek word for folly, *moria,* along with its cognates, denoted a physical or intellectual deficiency of persons in their conduct and actions. . . . Examples of folly in classical Greek imply a kind of madness as well as an external control by a power which confuses individuals.[9]

In the New Testament, St. Paul imbued folly with a metaphorical and meta-morphic function. The metaphorical character resulted from an irony, from the transferring of the usual negative meaning of folly to a positive meaning. In I Corinthians 4:10, for example, Paul was proud to be "a fool for Christ's sake." . . .

Folly, according to Paul, therefore involved a complete reversal of human standards, expectations, and conventional wisdom; it entailed a paradoxical manner of thinking, an irony. . . . God's power was not demonstrated with forceful signs from above; it showed its strength in the word of a weak cross. God's wisdom was not displayed with scientific certainty or absolute dogmas; it established its knowledge in the word of a foolish cross. Reversal of human values, of human ways of being-in-the-world, therefore constituted the folly of Christianity. In other terms, Paul meant that Christianity involved a contradiction, what J. Kellenberger calls the "absolute paradox."[10] The cross was a supreme paradox, an objective uncertainty of the greatest magnitude that was an absurdity to reason. It signaled a disjunction between transcendental claims and the exercise of worldly sovereignty, divine manifestation without grandeur. As a result, the world was perishing with its wisdom of proof and rationality.

This metaphorical, ironical feature of folly is treated in the writings of Ernesto Grassi . . . and Kenneth Burke. . . . Sensing the failure of Europe's intellectuals and the death of the Enlightenment, Grassi's hope was that by choosing the humanistic perspectives of Erasmus (and Vico) over the rational paradigm of Descartes, he could recover the power of the word as connected to and based in the creative imagination. Grassi's selection of the humanities over science, the imagination over the rational, is rooted in Erasmus's vision of folly. As Grassi says, "To live in folly is the profound reason for existence."[11]

In *Folly and Insanity in Renaissance Literature,* co-authored with Maristella Lorch, Grassi deals extensively with the theme of folly. Here Grassi owes much of his understanding of folly to Erasmus's classic text, *In Praise of Folly.* . . . Erasmus's was a meditation on the foibles of humans and on their ability to learn adequate answers to the enduring theological problems. In Erasmus's view, folly and all of its ignorance were, ironically, sources of religious strength. . . . The power of *moria* [the uncovering of all beings] opens up the immense stage of the world with the unfolding of its paradoxical play of comedy/tragedy. The principal actors are humans; folly is the divine director; and the outcome of the play depends upon the actors' willingness to embrace the claim of folly.

Two kinds of folly present themselves to the actors: one is the folly of insanity, the other folly is viewed as a god. Insanity results when actors lose sense of the value of life. The theme of the play concerns their attempt to cope with the environment. As long as actors remain under the spell of divine folly, they survive. In fact, Grassi claims divinity for the power of the word, a metaphorical and meta-morphic power: "Only in the word can I find myself again in that I recover my world from nature." . . .[12]

The power of the word, then, grants new insights and the hope of eternity to the actors. However, the tragic element now comes into play. As Grassi notes, "We are actors in an uninterrupted game which bears witness to the metaphorical nature of reality. Not only the different eras but also the different languages are born, exist, and perish."[13] But the illusion is maintained by the spell of folly. In other terms, a deep spiritual identification with the common community of humanity casts its spell of survival over the actors. Only in this way can humans avoid insanity.

According to Kenneth Burke, people employ "frames" or symbolic structures by which they impose order upon their personal and social experiences. Comedy is one such frame, supplying an entirely new, charitable way of approaching persuasion and cooperation. Burke claims that by acknowledging the role of chance in history, comedy encourages not passivity or determinism but maximum consciousness of who people are, of why they act as they do, and of the often disguised, faulty motivations behind human behavior.[14] In addition, Burke suggests that comedy often entails an ironic understanding of events. Irony arises in the first place when one tries, by the interaction of terms upon one another, to produce a development which uses all the terms. . . . Wisdom, to use another example, can only be comprehended once it is seen ironically, as stemming from folly. Wisdom cannot be obtained without folly. "Folly and villainy are integral motives, necessary to wisdom and virtue."[15]

Folly and Irony in Havel

Havel, too, sees folly as a fundamental part of human existence, the recognition of which leads to an enlightened, ironic understanding of human affairs.[16] In light of the post-Communist transition, Havel claims that folly enables humans to survive, to change, to cope, and to appreciate their existence because it produces a mirror which allows people to be observers of themselves as actors: "It seems to me that if the world is to change for the better it must start with a change in human consciousness, in the very humanness of modern man. . . ." "[Individuals] must discover again, within [themselves], a deeper sense of responsibility toward the world, which means responsibility toward something higher than [themselves]."[17]

For Havel, the exigencies of the post-Communist world required transformational thinking and a resulting concern for the larger plight and direction of humanity in a scene of dramatic change and constitution. To encourage such a transformation Havel wished others to see a kind of folly in history, thus opening the human world and looking beyond what had been passed down from the past to an alternative truth or possibility for the future. This ironic perspective became particularly useful for Havel when considering the future of the Soviet Union and its former satellite states, like Czechoslovakia. How would the United States and its allies respond to their one-time Communist enemies? How would the transition from totalitarian rule to democratic government take place within the old Soviet bloc? Many of Havel's speeches speak to these issues; his address to the American Congress, on February 21, 1990, replies in a way that is clearly ironic.

Billed as a request for American aid to the newly liberated Czech nation, Havel's speech employs irony to caution about the limits of government power. He suggests that attempts by totalitarian governments to maintain power and to impose particular historical inevitabilities, ironically, brought about their demise. Havel used the example of his own unlikely rise to power to make this critical point. For here was the humble playwright and political prisoner of the oppressive Communist regime, who, ironically, ended up presiding as leader over the very nation in which he was imprisoned, over the very individuals who had only shortly before incarcerated him. . . .

Havel admonished that no government stands forever, no power is beyond reproach, that even chance may override the best of human intentions. In his speech, Havel expressed the folly, unacknowledged by the Communists, of assuming that history can be completely controlled. So listeners were left with Havel's "temperized" stand as a warning about future democratic change. They were encouraged to celebrate the new, fertile democratic time, but to recognize that such moments pass quickly from sight.

Havel also employed irony to disclose a new way of thinking about the post-Cold War world. He argued that the United States, which had for decades struggled against Soviet expansion, could now precipitate the complete destruction of the Soviet Union, and then its eventual resurrection as a democratic state. He posed the irony in this form: "How can the United States of America help us today? My reply is . . . paradoxical. . . . You can help us most of all if you help the Soviet Union on its irreversible, but immensely complicated road to democracy. . . ."[18]

Thus, for Havel, withdrawing from a confrontational, polarized Cold War picture of foreign policy to a more conciliatory post-Cold War stance would allow the United States to move toward a new world order, an entirely unique mentality. In this scenario, all nations, including the Soviet Union, were redeemable. Havel described this new order:

These revolutionary changes will enable us to escape from the rather anti-quated straitjacket of this bipolar view of the world, and to enter at last into an era of multipolarity. That is, into an era in which all of us—large and small—former slaves and former masters—will be able to create what your great president Abraham Lincoln called the family of man.[19]

These remarks once again underscore the transformational power of folly through irony. Certainly the objection might be raised that assisting former enemies is not original to Havel, that since the Second World War American foreign policy has been based on this principle. And yet, in the year 1990, it was unclear whether the Soviet Union was merely a "former" enemy or whether it still presented a formidable threat to geopolitical change. Perhaps more importantly, Havel is reacting to the arrogance of power, the possibility that some leaders in America might interpret the Cold War victory as metaphysical justification for foreign policy decisions. The recognition of folly prompts a different response. For folly entails not only an appreciation for the fragility of power, even for the might of the United States, and more than mere praise and blame. It is an intense "spiritual identification with the common community of humanity," an identification which allows "humanity to survive.". . . .

Furthermore, [since they were] dehumanized by decades of oppression, Havel wished to restore human dignity and trust. As Raymond Aron observes, in totalitarianism, "individuals lose their organic ties that bind them to their families, their neighbors, their companions at work or in poverty . . . no one any longer trusts his neighbor."[20] Havel desired that the resulting new world order would benefit the downtrodden and the unacknowledged, the forgotten and dispirited masses of Eastern and Central Europe, and not just the powerful and the rulers.

Thus, Havel's discourse was important for establishing a new sense of order, community and international bonding. . . . Out of suffocating totalitarian ashes would rise a new democratic fire, a world where all persons could be treated with greater dignity, made part of "the family of man."

FOLLY AND HUMILITY

This kind of irony, with its "temperizing" tone, is what Kenneth Burke has in mind when he identifies irony as the trope best adapted to dialectical thought because it always signifies the contingent nature of any statement or temporary resting place. . . . "[T]rue irony," argues Burke, "irony that really does justify the attribute of 'humility,' is not 'superior' to the enemy."[21]

In order to explain further how folly is linked to humility, Erasmus's three negative judgments about the claim of folly can be considered: 1) Life is a ludicrous comedy because the actors do not realize that they have submitted to the spell of *moria.* 2) Since life is an empty masquerade, history becomes the highest tragedy. 3) Unmasking the actors would prove to be insanity. The only hope is to remain under the spell of folly. Any attempt to arrive at the truth will lead to insanity. This awareness of the tragic interpretation of life and human history is the basic theme of Erasmus, although there remains, in the teaching of Folly (*Stultitia*), the recognition of social hope. . . .

For Grassi and Lorch, meaning emerges through folly, not in rational thought. "Insanity" occurs when individuals assume that rational knowledge is all there is and all that is required. Grassi and Lorch maintain that only when under the claim of folly, one is most in touch with the human condition. Insanity arises "whenever man is incapable of meeting that which we can name the 'claim' of Being. This is always manifest for man in a concrete situation, urging him to the appropriate response so as to meet the claim made of him."[22] Under the claim of folly, however, rhetoricians are encouraged to speak and believe in the possibility for positive change. The implication, then, is that humility derived from folly does not mean one must give up hope or close down options. On the contrary, to observe "human affairs as folly is to achieve an ontological insight into what is possible in any situation; that is, to see all as folly is to realize that things are never what they seem."[23]

Folly and Humility in Havel

Havel's address to Congress is clear about the salvation of humanity being connected with, among other things, the power of "human meekness" or humility.[24] By humility Havel means a person's ability to understand oneself and what one has done too clearly to be inclined to exaggeration.[25] Humility is gaining a proper perspective on the limits of human influence. For Havel, folly is a useful impediment to vanity, an invitation to humility. Thus, Havel's unpretentious leader is always questioning and reflective, always knowing that his acts could, at any moment, bring about his downfall. And yet, the resulting skepticism is not disabling or cynical, but a source of moral strength, of moral action. "When I find myself in extremely complex situations," Havel declared in an interview in the Czech magazine *Mladý Svět*

> I worry about whether I'll be able to sort them out. But I wouldn't want this to sound as though I'm just a bundle of panic and misery and lack of self-confidence. On the contrary, this constant self-doubt and constant uncertainty are what drive me to work harder and try harder.[26]

For Havel, then, skepticism leads to self-knowledge: "If I've accomplished anything good, then it's mainly because I've been driven by the need to know whether I can accomplish the things I'm not sure I have the capability for."[27]

A similar sense of humility is conveyed during Havel's speech at the Hebrew University, in Jerusalem, on April 26, 1990, where the president was awarded a degree honoring his commitment to democracy and human rights. Havel admitted to a profound "paradox," one illustrating the deep humility—the folly—of the rhetorical stance which informed his status as President. . . .

> It's a paradox, but I must admit that if I am a better president than many others would be in my place, then it is precisely because somewhere in the deepest substratum of my work lies this constant doubt about myself and my right to hold office.[28]

For Havel, weakness was strength while strength was weakness. From this ironic reversal flowed humility and then, wisdom:

> The lower I am, the more proper my place seems; and the higher I am, the stronger my suspicion is that there has been some mistake. And every step of the way, I feel what a great advantage it is for me as president to know that I can at any moment, and justifiably, be removed from the position.[29]

This call to humility is important. Against the image of the leader driven by political power, opportunism, or mere pragmatic concern, Havel situates himself as a clown of sorts. The "lower" he is, "the more proper my place seems." And yet, this modest stance gives way to wisdom, . . . For Havel's own example shows that humility engenders the sort of moral reflection and responsible moral activity that liberates the actor from the numbness imposed by totalitarian rule. As Raymond Aron has written, during political oppression, ". . . individuals become frantic or resigned, prisoners of an implacable fatality, the playthings of an inhuman force."[30]

For Havel, though, humility is a powerful reaction to this "implacable fatality," a mode of consciousness necessary for liberation. His discourse discloses the qualities of hope and surrender; Havel came to humility almost against his will. He illustrates that the world cannot be overcome, but, as in his own ordeal, the suffering that comes around can be endured with faith. Indeed, although Havel cautioned against both collective and individual hubris, his resulting sense of humility did not fall into a damaging political fatalism or philosophical inertia.[31] On the contrary, speaking to Congress, he forcefully argued that individuals triumph over material conditions, what amounted to a *coup de grâce* to the Marxist notion that material structures determine consciousness and action. "Consciousness precedes Being," Havel asserted, "and not the other way around, as the Marxists claim." As such, "the salvation of this human world lies nowhere else than in the human heart, in the human power to reflect, in human meekness and in human responsibility."[32]

Therefore, Havel's discourse on folly encourages a consciousness of human frailty and "meekness" which places Havel and his audiences in a position to transcend themselves and to act in unique ways. . . . [He] appears to use humility to open a heretofore impossible realm of political possibility. In his vision, the post-Cold War world could "escape from the rather antiquated straitjacket of this bipolar view of the world, and to enter at last into an era of multipolarity."

FOLLY AND EMPATHY

Humble and looking "outside" itself, folly encourages rhetors to imagine (through *ingenium*) things other than they are, to assume the perspective of others. In other terms, a rhetoric of folly entails empathic communication or what Kenneth Burke calls "identification." By empathic is meant the ability to understand and integrate basic human nature, to identify one's ways with the ways of another. For Burke, identification is a means of "acting together"[33] that emerges out of the ambiguities of substance or the fact that individuals are by nature divided from one another. Both division and unity exist at the same time: each person remains unique and therefore isolated from others, even though they share a locus of motives, ideas, or attitudes. Despite the condition of separateness, then, identification occurs when the interests of individuals are joined. . . .

Ernesto Grassi insists on the alignment of folly with empathy. He observes that in the absence of folly, contemporary lives become divorced from their social, corporate selves: "Contemporary men feel the need for values that can unify their lives. But the source of this need lies in man's original nature as a human being and not in his momentary situation."[34] Paul, too, discusses empathy. . . . In Paul's notion of folly, suffering was not something God made up to his people. Rather, Christians were encouraged to endure suffering in a way that was less self-indulgent, more disciplined, more compassionate of others, just as Christ had experienced his suffering on the cross. One might say that Christians were invited to display greater empathy for the suffering of others. In other words, for Paul, the deeply ironic logic of folly was only apparent in its empathic function for believers and not in its words, syntax, or evidence.

Folly and Empathy in Havel

Empathy was vitally important for Havel because the dangers of unrestrained nationalism and its resulting ethnic and political divisions were everywhere apparent, especially in Yugoslavia and parts of the former Soviet Union. There was, additionally, the need to console those who had labored under the subjugation of Communist power and to articulate further the virtues most conducive to reducing division. Havel recognized these exigencies and chose to address them in many ways, not the least of which was his condemnation of anti-semitism. In his address to "The International Conference on Anti-Semitism in Post-Totalitarian Europe," delivered in Prague, on May 21, 1992, the President conveyed empathy, not simply by identifying with the suffering of holocaust victims, but by casting his empathy as a profound form of metaphysical shame. Havel admitted to a strange paralysis whenever asked to comment upon the endless suffering of the Jewish people. This paralysis "proceeds mainly from a deep—I would even say a metaphysical—feeling of shame. I am ashamed . . . of the human race, of mankind, of man." At first, Havel distanced himself from Jews by identifying with the acts of their persecutors. Yet, he moved closer by offering a consolatory gesture, reinterpreting the abstract shame personally, and giving his Jewish audience a greater sense of his own participation in their plight:

> I feel that this is his crime and his disgrace, and thus also *my* crime and *my* disgrace. It is as if that paralysis suddenly threw *me* to the very bottom of the perception of human guilt and of *my own co-responsibility* for human actions and for the condition of the world in which we live and which we build.[35]

Of course, the possibility for empathy occurring turned on two acknowledgments: first, on the notion that while Havel himself had no real responsibility for the suffering of Jews, his own personal account of responsibility made him seem sympathetic to the Jewish fear that non-Jews would forget the Jewish past. Essentially, Havel's claim that "guilt" had driven him to be accountable "for human actions and for the condition of the world in which we live and which we build," established him in a position of empathy. . . . Moreover, Havel refused to put the blame on a single subject or locate the sin in an event or an act of origin.

Equally significant is that Havel himself, along with other Czechs, were the victims of persecution, a theme explored at length in his address to Congress. Here, the President meditated on the "horrors" of Communist oppression, horrors that Americans "fortunately [had] not known." Still, he once again exposed the dialectical tension between oppression and freedom, between despair and hope. Havel argued that the horrors of Communist oppression "have given us something positive: a special capacity to look . . . somewhat further than someone who has not undergone this bitter experience."[36] In other terms, the lowly, persecuted fool possesses true wisdom.

Hence, Havel's "bitter experiences" placed him in an especially credible position to understand the suffering of Jews or any other oppressed group which, as a result of its oppression and suffering, felt divided or estranged from other individuals. In this way, Havel could identify with and console his audiences because he could, in a sense, countenance his own origins. . . .

A kind of humility also occurs in Havel's Prague speech, in his appreciation for the limits of human action against intolerance and racial hate. [In 1992] Havel warned against an uncritical faith in democratic institutions and procedures. The President was certainly optimistic about the prospects for democracy. However, Havel also knew that journeying down this road was "immensely complicated," a path ridden with folly. So the recognition of folly here produced humility and caution: "It is extremely dangerous for the new democracies to underestimate the manifestations of anti-Semitism, to play them down, to fail to take action against them and, to remain silent about them."[37] Nevertheless, even as Havel conceded the folly of human endeavor against hate, from this folly emerged empathy, compassion, and reassurance. For Havel's rhetoric occupied a symbolic space beyond the clear racial animosity of the past and the uncertainty of the future. . . .

THE QUEST FOR HOPE

What can be learned from Havel about folly as a mode of discourse for the contemporary world? Havel's rhetoric is nearly devoid of deliberative and forensic content, which no doubt accounts for criticisms often directed against Havel's way that "he does not support any concrete political program. He is an intellectual to such a high degree that . . . he [will not] be able to pursue one."[38] A related criticism is that Havel remains too detached from (or ambiguous about) transcendent sources, and overly attached to irony. After all, the folly of the cross, as Paul would have it, is not a story ending on Good Friday, or else the Christians would literally be simple fools. Thus, it could be claimed that Havel's folly fails as a deliberative mode, something required of any political leader, in not offering audiences a grounded choice, other than acquiescence to the folly of history. This is not to underplay the tremendous difficulty, as Havel seemed to see most clearly, of restoring a moral view of the world in the wake of the collapse of a cynical, state-centered ethic. But moderation, empathy, and moral awareness, this criticism implies, are not the only virtues a great leader requires.

On the other hand, the deeper significance of Havel's rhetoric may lie in its recovery, through ironic and epideictic means, of a differentiated experience of reality out of the suffering of the people of Central and Eastern Europe. Havel's irony is a powerful trope because it is both metaphysical and pragmatic. It uses the potency of the closed linguistic category, and the power of the open form. Irony has both an empirical (communal) and a transcendent dimension.

Also, Havel's rhetoric demonstrates that while important, a strictly deliberative rhetoric is never enough during periods of significant change. In fact, Havel's rhetoric of folly was precisely what was needed for a transitional movement because it reaffirmed values that had been discouraged during Communist rule. But Havel did more than praise and blame; he disclosed hopeful possibilities, not only for proper civil conduct, but for the very survival of humankind. His discourse was not simply emotional but more like what Sullivan calls a "suprarational rhetoric that goes beyond the rational capacity to confront an individual's being with the radiance of Being." This kind of epideictic speech "operates during the opportune moment under inspiration to bring presence to a single vision."[39] In Havel's case, he unveiled human frailty, especially in light of the intractable forces of history, as a fundamental aspect of human Being. But he did so in a way that made it seem as though weakness is strength, as though both individual and collective action are meaningful and can result in productive futures that are as yet undefined.

Havel's rhetoric of folly is valuable, too, for its ability to suspend practical discussion and judgment long enough for audiences to re-orient themselves, to reconsider what is before them as well as what is left behind. The role of fool was important for Havel in this regard since folly promoted a certain skepticism about human activity without damaging Havel's moral authority. Given the unpredictability of historical change and yet the quick rush to impose political order—experiences which Havel himself had witnessed in the most profound of ways—folly cautions that seemingly permanent political fixes, even past political successes, often turn into political disasters.

Finally, the stance of folly can enhance a leader's rhetorical flexibility, making the rhetor seem both inside and out of society at the same time, but also allowing for a greater range of controversial topics to be discussed. Indeed, the move toward folly must always acknowledge "that no individual can soar above the crowd for very long. With our reconciliation to the worldly order of necessity, is our reconciliation to the crowd as well."[40] Yet, as one of the few who could pronounce on folly, who had achieved complex ironic reversals, humbling personal insights, and strong identifications based in his own experience, Havel himself stood beyond his audiences, as a moral harbinger of possibility, of the way things had been and the way they might be. This more transcendent position, in turn, enabled Havel to say what many refused to consider, to see through to the opposite perspective. The fragility of the human condition forced not only a reassessment of the Other (e.g., the defeated Soviets, the Jews, the downtrodden masses), but a necessary and difficult reminder that one could never be certain that one's own position was right.

Notes and References

A version of this paper was presented at the annual meeting of the Speech Communication Association in San Diego, CA during November 1996, where it was named the top paper in Rhetoric and Public Address. The author would like to thank the editors, Karen Foss, Rod Kennedy and Andrew King for their valuable contributions to this essay.

1. M. Kondracke, "The World Turned Upside Down," *The New Republic* (September 1989): 29.
2. Thomas B. Farrell, *The Norms of Rhetorical Culture* (New Haven: Yale University Press, 1993) 267.
3. S. K. Foss, "The Logic of Folly in the Political Campaigns of Harvey Milk," *Queer Words, Queer Images: Communication and the Construction of Homosexuality* (New York: New York University Press, 1994) 10.
4. Ibid., 9.
5. E. Sandoz, "The Politics of Poetry," *Modern Age* 34 (1991): 20.
6. Richard Rorty, "The Seer of Prague," *The New Republic* (July 1991): 36.
7. Timothy Garton Ash, *The Uses of Adversity: Essays on the Fate of Central Europe* (New York: Random House, 1989) 12.
8. Václav Havel, "The Postcommunist Nightmare," *The New York Review of Books* (May 1993): 8.
9. Of course, the dialogues of Plato are filled with many confused truth-seekers whose states of ignorance and weakness Plato regarded as natural to the human mode of being. The classical Greeks realized that the "paradox, burlesque, and ribaldry" of comedy could be emancipatory (See M. Charland, "Norms and Laughter in Rhetorical Culture," *The Quarterly Journal of Speech* 80 [1994], 342). Folly played a role in later Christian antiquity as well. P. Brown has contrasted the Greco-Roman *paideia* of the upper classes (the pagan literary and political education tempered by common experience of provincial governance) as a claim to leadership with the "living faith" of the monks living in the countryside. According to Brown, this "living faith" was used by the bishops as an alternative claim to both sacred and secular authority in consolidating their power in the third and fourth century empire. They frequently organized the monks to scare the authorities in Antioch and Constantinople. Finally, the emperor recognized that his power base was no longer held by his loyal provincial aristocrats through shared

paideia, but directly from God and sanctioned by the bishops, and exemplified in the wild devotion of the monks. As the emperor became a divinely sanctioned human, his legitimacy rested in the folly of desert monks and the simple believers. In other words, the monks, in all their simplicity possessed wisdom. (See P. Brown, *Power and Persuasion in Late Antiquity: Towards a Christian Empire* [Madison, WI: University of Wisconsin Press, 1992]). Later in the Middle Ages, folly occurred in the ritual irony of the medieval church, which included celebrations such as the Feast of Fools, Easter Humor, or the Feast of the Ass during which a carved donkey was carried in procession. M. M. Bakhtin has noted that during the Middle Ages and into the Renaissance, folly in the writings of Rabelais and in the form of "Carnival celebrated temporary liberation from the prevailing truth and from the established order; [they] marked the suspension of all hierarchical rank, privileges, norms, and prohibitions. Carnival was the true feast of time, the feast of becoming, change, and renewal" (see M. M. Bakhtin, *Rabelais and His World* [Cambridge MA: M.I.T. Press, 1968], 10). The 15th century philosopher, theologian, and mathematician Nicolas of Cusa claimed that a person was wise only if he or she were aware of the limits of the mind in knowing the truth. Shakespeare is well-known for frequently giving characters lines that endorsed folly, as when Bottom discovered that method was to be found in madness. Meanwhile, along with Erasmus, the great Renaissance philosopher Montaigne appreciated the folly of the human endeavor. He quoted Paul: "The simple and the ignorant, says Saint Paul, raise themselves to heaven, and take possession of it; and we, with all our learning, plunge ourselves into the infernal abyss" (See *The Complete Works of Montaigne: Essays, Travel Journal, Letters,* trans. D. M. Frame [Stanford: Stanford University Press, 1957], 367). In the Romanticism of the 19th century, folly comes down in the character of Wagner's Parsifal, the heroic "pure fool" whose innocence conferred healing power and allowed him to attain the Grail that had eluded older and wiser knights.

10.   J. Kellenberger, "Kierkegaard, Indirect Communication and Religious Truth," *International Journal of Philosophy and Religion* 16 (1984): 153. The theological implication of what Paul was saying when he spoke of *moria* was that knowledge of God is not obtained through wisdom but through faith in the saving action of Christ on the cross. Here, the move to faith, which, philosophically speaking, was seen as foolish, was really wisdom. In I Corinthians 1:20, Paul wrote, "Has God not made foolish the wisdom of this world?" He meant the "foolishness" of what was preached, and that is (verse 23) "Christ crucified." The foolishness of the cross came from its being above reason and capable of apprehension only to those who entered into the God's covenant through faith. Ordinary foolishness was below reason, but the cross was really above it. Thus Paul was using folly as the great reversal mentioned above, as an irony. Those who entered into Christ's death knew that what appeared to outsiders as foolishness was really God's wisdom. They also knew—since everything is reversed in irony—that it was those who rejected Christ who were genuinely foolish. The worldly think that human wisdom can obtain God, but if they were truly wise they would recognize the logical impossibility of this. How can one who is created know that which is uncreated?

11.   Quoted in S. K. Foss, K. A. Foss, and R. Trapp, *Contemporary Perspectives on Rhetoric* (Prospect Heights, Illinois: Waveland Press, 1991), 164.

12.   Ernesto Grassi, *Rhetoric as Philosophy: The Humanist Tradition* (University Park: The Pennsylvania State University Press, 1980), 112.

13.   Ernesto Grassi, "Why Rhetoric is Philosophy," *Philosophy and Rhetoric* 20 (1987): 75.

14.   See Kenneth Burke, *Attitudes Towards History* (Los Alto, California: Hermes Publications, 1959).

15.   Kenneth Burke, *A Grammar of Motives* (Berkeley: University of California Press, 1969), 515.

16.   Jan Vladislav, for instance, mentions that Havel "bases his view on the fact that one should look at life honestly and realistically and that one must take account of man with all his weaknesses and imperfections." See J. Vladislav, editor, *Václav Havel or Living in Truth* (London: Faber and Faber, 1987), ix.

17. Václav Havel, *Disturbing the Peace: A Conversation with Karel Hvížd'ala*, trans. Paul Wilson (New York: Alfred A. Knopf, 1990), 11–12.

18. Václav Havel, "Address by his Excellency Václav Havel, President of the Czechoslovak Socialist [sic] Republic," *Congressional Record* (February 1990): 393.

19. Ibid.

20. Raymond Aron, "The Essence of Totalitarianism according to Hannah Arendt," *The Partisan Review* 3 (Summer 1993): 369.

21. Burke, *A Grammar of Motives*, 514.

22. Ernesto Grassi and M. Lorch, *Folly and Insanity in Renaissance Literature* (Binghamton, New York: Medieval and Renaissance Texts and Studies, 1986), 48.

23. Ibid., 5–7.

24. Havel, "Address," 394.

25. In his conversation with Karel Hvížd'ala, for example, Havel's humility is evident when he expressed concern about the "arrogant anthropocentrism of modern man, who is convinced he can know everything and bring everything under his control. . . ." See Václav Havel, *Disturbing the Peace: A Conversation with Karel Hvížd'ala.* 11–12.

26. Václav Havel, "Uncertain Strength: An Interview with Václav Havel," *The New York Review of Books* (August 1991): 6.

27. Ibid.

28. Václav Havel, "On Kafka: An Address at the Hebrew University in Jerusalem on April 26, 1990," *The New York Review of Books* (September 1990): 19. [Also in *The Art of the Impossible*, trans. Paul Wilson and others (New York: Alfred A. Knopf, 1997), 31.]

29. Ibid.

30. Aron, 369.

31. In this respect Havel is perhaps similar to Kierkegaard. The latter argued that by embracing the absurdity of the human condition an individual must adopt an attitude based in "fear" and "trembling." Nevertheless, such an attitude does not mean that the person denies civic duty: "a concrete self . . . stands in reciprocal relations with [his/her] surroundings, these conditions of life, this natural order. This self which is the aim is not merely a personal self but a social, civic self." See Søren Kierkegaard, *Either/Or* (Anchor Books, 1959), 219–220.

32. Havel, "Address by his Excellency . . ." 394.

33. Kenneth Burke, *A Rhetoric of Motives* (New York: Prentice Hall, 1950), 21.

34. Quoted in J. M. Krois, "Comments on Professor Grassi's Paper." In *Vico and Contemporary Thought,* eds. G. Tagliacozzo, M. Mooney and D. P. Verene (Atlantic Highlands, N.J.: Humanities Press, 1976), 187.

35. Václav Havel, "Message to the International Conference on Anti-Semitism in Post-Totalitarian Europe," *The New York Times* (June 1992): A15, emphasis added.

36. Havel, "Address by his Excellency . . ." 394.

37. Václav Havel, "Message to the International Conference on Anti-Semitism in Post-Totalitarian Europe": A15.

38. Quoted in T. Omestad, "Ten-Day Wonder," *The New Republic* (December 1989): 20.

39. Dale L. Sullivan, "Kairos and the Rhetoric of Belief," *The Quarterly Journal of Speech* 78: 329.

40. Thomas B. Farrell, "Rhetorical Resemblance: Paradoxes of a Practical Art," *The Quarterly Journal of Speech* 72 (1986): 16.

Václav Havel's Construction of a Democratic Discourse: Politics in a Postmodern Age

DEAN C. HAMMER

{Havel disclaims all authority as a philosopher; his speculations, he says, are no more than "the testimony of one man in a particular situation, his inner murmurings." Yet he is irresistibly drawn to the philosophical reflections that came his way in Patočka's "unofficial seminars."

—J. P. Stern}

In a 1990 article in *Philosophy Today,* Caroline Bayard suggests that an affinity exists between Václav Havel and the postmodern intellectual. In looking primarily at Havel's literary works, Bayard argues that Havel, like the postmoderns; rejects grand "emancipatory narratives" and adopts, instead, a pluralist ethic that privileges no particular discourse. Along these lines, according to Bayard, the heroes in Havel's plays resolutely reject absolutes, and, instead, subvert the brutality of Communism with humility, quietness, and an "obstinate individualism." The Havelian hero refuses to privilege any discourse, even his own; instead, "the unresolvable heterogeneity of phrases must be accepted."[1]

In reading Havel's works, though, particularly his political writings and speeches, I am struck not by his postmodernism but by precisely how his writings serve as a critique of postmodernism. As Bayard suggests, and I will extend her argument in the first part of this essay, there is much in Havel that appears postmodern, including the rejection of emancipatory narratives and the emphasis on human plurality. But while Havel and postmodernism walk the same path, at least for a while, they do not share the same reasons for this journey. The focus of postmodernism has been on a thorough critique of institutions and discourses, postponing any extended discussion of the possibility of constructing a political discourse that answers their concerns. Havel, on

Abridged, originally published in *Philosophy Today* 39 (1995): 119–30. Reprinted by permission of DePaul University.

the other hand, begins with an interest in how to construct just such a politics. What is necessary for this politics, according to Havel, is an "authentic subject" able to act responsibly, yet this is precisely what is missing in postmodernism. This is no small issue, for the postmodern rejection of these assumptions makes it a stranger in the construction of politics.

A POSTMODERN HAVEL?

There are three characteristics of postmodernism that Bayard highlights in Havel's literary works: the rejection of emancipatory narratives, a critique of ideological thinking, and an uneasiness with the notion of the intellectual as Master. I will explore each of these elements, drawing upon Havel's writings and his political speeches during his years in dissent and since becoming President of Czechoslovakia (now the Czech Republic). Havel does, indeed, maintain a continued allegiance to these ideas, but as I will argue it is an allegiance that Havel uses to construct, not deconstruct, a modern politics.

Postmodernism brings to politics a healthy distrust of what is referred to as the "emancipatory" or "salvation narrative." Jean-François Lyotard, in his controversial monograph, *The Postmodern Condition: A Report on Knowledge,* defines postmodernism "as incredulity toward metanarratives," narratives governed by a telos of human redemption.[2] In large part this is an attack on the Enlightenment project that, while promising human liberation through the application of reason, has actually resulted in totalitarianism, oppression, and violence. Such emancipatory narratives have found their expression in Marxism-Leninism, Fascism, apartheid, and colonial oppression as well as the suppression of sexual, ethnic, and political difference.

The reason such narratives result in oppression derives from what Jacques Derrida sees as a desire in Western philosophy to ground human action in metaphysical certainty. Human development is depicted in these emancipatory narratives as the development of Being, a Being that is seen as always present whether in a theological narrative of human redemption or a Hegelian dialectic of the unfolding of Spirit.[3] This search for metaphysical certitude results in the creation of ideologies; that is, fixed systems of thought that create "value-oppositions" that "subordinate these values to each other."[4] Ideology, as it is premised on this metaphysical tradition, thinks in terms of binary opposites: truth/untruth, positive/negative, normal/abnormal, good/evil.[5] Rigid boundaries, thus, are established that elevate that which is good, truthful and normal and subordinate that which is deemed evil, false, and abnormal.

This rejection of grand narratives leaves the postmodern intellectual in the curious, if not difficult position, of rejecting his traditional role as Master, the guardian of reason, while still "being unwittingly the sustainer of canons, the representative of an elite who appropriates the production of knowledge in order to bring the species to perfection." The intellectual, rather than claiming to express some totalizing unity or truth, must, instead, be tolerant of different positions and recognize, as well, the existence of the different roles one may assume, whether that be "citizen, creator, teacher, or critic." It becomes the role of the intellectual, then, to testify to the "unresolvably heterogeneous" nature of discourse as individuals have their "own stakes, strategies, addressees and addressors."6

Havel, too, rejects utopian narratives and ideological systems. In *Summer Meditations,* a book written the year after becoming the first President of a free Czechoslovakia, he talks about the "kind of politics and values and ideals I wish to struggle for." Yet, he is careful to point out that he is not "entertaining" the hope that this struggle will "one day be over." He does not seek to create "a heaven on earth in which people all love each other and everyone is hard-working, well-mannered, and virtuous, in which the land flourishes and everything is sweetness and light, working harmoniously to the satisfaction of God." The "arrogance" of such "utopian rationality," which privileges itself above all other considerations, becomes dangerous as it "liquidate[s] everything that did not fit, that exceeded its plans or disrupted them."7

Havel has a similar intolerance for ideological thinking. He defines ideologies as "closed, ready-made systems of presuppositions about the world" that differ from utopias in that they do not necessarily promise a harmonious end. At one point he writes that "Right-wing dogmatism, with its sour-faced intolerance and fanatical faith in general precepts, bothers me as much as left-wing prejudices, illusions, and utopias."8 As President, Havel has had continually to confront the voices of faction, "small-mindedness, defeatism, nostalgia, baseness, provincialism, and isolationism" as well as the "many expressions of racial or nationalist intolerance, anti-semitism, political extremism, repression of minority rights, xenophobia, and even fascism."9

There are several practical reasons why Havel rejects ideological thinking, including the difficulty of governing a society torn apart by separate and hostile interests. But for Havel, ideological thinking, as it seeks to provide a system for understanding human action, is fundamentally inconsistent with his conception of human action and thought. Havel, writing in an open letter in 1978, suggested that "life, in its essence, moves toward plurality, diversity, independent self-constitution, and self-organization."10 In structuring his own life, he discusses how he has always attempted to "think independently, using my own powers of reason, and I have always vigorously resisted attempts to pigeonhole me." This refusal to systematize life has allowed him to remain "open to everything interesting or persuasive." Contrarily, ideological thinking, which through its dogma and assumptions "deems itself more clever than life itself," is actually for Havel "an attempt against life itself."

Life, for Havel, is simply more plural, nuanced, contingent, and open-ended than can possibly be grasped by an ideological system. Ideologies are nothing short of the "extreme expression of the hubris of modern man, who thinks that he understands the world completely" and thus feels that he can "run the whole world."[11]

Even as President, Havel has not set himself up as a Master who claims a privileged access to truth or the guardian of a totalizing ideal. He, for example, steadfastly opposed a law that would have prohibited former Communists from holding office. Furthermore, while arguing for the importance of national integration, he argues for a multiplicity of domains or "homes." There is not a singular home, a singular source of identity or experiences. One's home, instead, "can be compared to a set of concentric circles," consisting of one's house, village, family, friends, profession, workplace, country, region, and the world as well as "my education, my upbringing, my habits, my social milieu." There can be no privileging of one of these realms over the other, no hierarchical ordering of more important and less important homes. Instead, society must be properly organized to "respect" all the realms "and give them all the chance to play their roles." Only with such freedom can people "exercise their identities" and thus "realize themselves freely as human beings." As these circles are an "inalienable part of us," and by this Havel means that the identity of home is "a basic existential experience," to be deprived of any aspect of one's home is to be "deprived of himself, of his humanity."[12]

But while rejecting a privileged access to the truth and recognizing the multiplicity of human identity, Havel does not similarly reject the possibility of speaking for reform. On the contrary, he suggests that this struggle between an orientation to "the world and eternity against people who think only of themselves and the moment" is an eternal one that takes place not only between individuals but within each of us. "It is what makes a person a person, and life, life." There will always be the ambitious, the irresponsible, and humans will never "stop destroying the world." And he freely admits that he may be unable to change things for the better but, he concludes, "There is only one thing I will not concede: that it might be meaningless to strive in a good cause."[13]

In one sense, the cause Havel speaks of overlaps with postmodernism in their respective desires to challenge discourse that privileges itself. After laying bare the discursive practices that shape our thinking and identity, though, postmodern theory seems silent as to what to do with the knowledge obtained. It is in this sense that Havel's project differs so fundamentally from the postmodern one. For Havel, part of the cause for which he is struggling is to construct a democratic political discourse from the rubble of Soviet domination, a discourse grounded not simply in critique but in the existence of an authentic subject able to make judgments.

THE POLITICS OF POSTMODERNISM

Given the sheer volume of postmodern writing that has subjected political discourse and institutions to a sustained critique, surprisingly little has been said about what a postmodern politics should actually look like. Bayard, in her article on Havel, makes a couple of references to a postmodern politics that goes beyond its critical stance. In addressing at one point the role of intellectuals she suggests that they bear a certain responsibility to society. Repeating a phrase that is commonplace in postmodern writing, she notes that "one must be answerable for civic and ethical responsibilities, but such viewpoints only call for 'local and defensive interventions.' "[14] While Bayard makes no attempt to explain the meaning or implications of this statement, it would seem that a postmodern politics in this guise is at root a politics of resistance. Responsibility becomes a local responsibility (though the parameters of what makes something local are impossibly vague) to critique forms of power, including discourses, that claim any grounding in truth or reason. The closest Bayard comes to describing a postmodern politics is in referring to its "pluralist ethics." This means that one must be always cognizant of the heterogeneity of speech and of the different grammars operating within different narratives. What is less clear is how one constructs a community both premised on and protective of this notion, let alone how the community sorts out what it will and will not do.

If we turn to a book that more directly attempts to link postmodernism to politics, Michael Shapiro's discussion of the political implications of postmodern textual readings, there is a similar reluctance to sketch what a postmodern polity would look like. In concluding his book, Shapiro summarizes what his objective has been: "Moreover, my concern is with the recovery of politics, not rational steering mechanisms, where politics is understood as a recognition that we are always involved in a struggle to, as Paul Virilio has put it, 'extract life from death.' " To explain this, Shapiro continues, "And 'life' is seen not simply as a matter of duration and 'policy,' thereby a matter of protection—for the 'burrow' is as much a prison as it is a shelter—but an intense encounter with death; it is living with danger rather than merely a consuming of frightening data."[15] I am struck by the contrast between the "defensive" politics of Bayard's postmodernism and the much more aggressive, intense encounter with death that makes up Shapiro's, but I am no more clear about how one constructs a community on these premises.

There are similar problems with one of the most political of postmodern theorists, Jacques Derrida. I say he is one of the most political because he has continually made forays into the political realm, writing about the problem of violence and apartheid in South Africa, resisting attempts by the French government to decrease the teaching of philosophy in the secondary schools, and speaking out on issues of human rights and feminism. In reaction to some of his critics who point to the nihilistic consequences of deconstruction, Derrida has responded that "deconstruction always presupposes affirmation"[16] and is "at the very least, a way of taking a position, in its work of analysis, concerning the political and institutional structures that make possible and govern our practice, our competencies, our performances. Precisely because it is never concerned only with signified content, deconstruction should not be separable from the politico-institutional problematic and should seek a new investigation of responsibility, an investigation which questions the codes inherited from ethics and politics. This means that too political for some, it will seem paralyzing to these who only recognize politics by the most familiar road signs."[17] That deconstruction has political import as it calls into question different positions, as it seeks to be subversive of established authority, as it reveals the variability, if not self-contradicting aspects, of boundaries we as a society have accepted, is undeniable. But a politics of subversion ultimately devours itself, leaving a nihilistic abyss in its path. Derrida has spoken of a "democracy to come," one which celebrates difference.[18] But he never speaks to the particular institutional forms and language this would take, how a community would act together and make decisions together, and how its members would be responsible to each other. What is missing from Derrida is, as one commentator has pointed out, "how can we 'warrant' (in any sense of the term) the ethical-political 'positions' we do take?"[19] Derrida's response: "I must confess that I have never succeeded in directly relating deconstruction to existing political programmes" is revealing of the gap between postmodernism and constructive political engagement.[20] The reason for the gap is because the radical openness created by deconstruction cannot allow for a foundation of political commitment because such foundations, at the point that they become accepted, must be resisted. One's commitment, by Derrida's own reckoning, must come from outside a postmodern suspicion of language and institutions.[21]

Michel Foucault's work stands out as a model of scholarly inquiry as he has sought to respond to the difficult questions his own writings have raised. Much of Foucault's work has been focused on exploring what he sees as the historical production of truth. Truth, for Foucault, is constructed by discourses which claim on the one hand a "unitary body of theory which would filter, hierarchise and order" knowledge while on the other hand seek to disqualify all other knowledges as illegitimate.[22] Foucault's genealogical approach has focused on revealing the power relations that underlie our discursive practices, seeking to rupture these totalizing discourses by recalling local knowledges that reveal the struggle of these discourses to become dominant. The point, as Foucault is quick to reveal, is not that local knowledges contain truth and universal knowledges do not; rather, local knowledges, as they are less implicated in the power relations that control our lives, can rupture the "tyranny of globalising discourses."[23] The interest of Foucault, and the aim of philosophy, thus is emancipatory—to discover points of resistance of forms of power through an ongoing critique, thus freeing us from totalizing discourses.

A question that arises in Foucault's work, and one that he sought later to address, is who was being emancipated. If all knowledge, including knowledge of the self, is bound up in discursive practices and constituted historically, then emancipation becomes a peeling away of the layers of an onion that reveals, ultimately, nothing at its core. In Foucault's later work, *The History of Sexuality,* he seeks to address this issue by focusing not on the historical constitution of the subject but on how we constitute ourselves as subjects.[24] What Foucault seems to arrive at is a notion of a self that we create "as a work of art."[25] The self-constitution of the subject, free from totalizing power, becomes the ontological starting point for human action.

While Foucault has provided an ontological foundation from which to engage in a critique of discursive practices, what this translates into politically becomes less clear. Politics appears as a form of ongoing critique; discourse, as it inherently participates in power, is to be distrusted; and institutions, as they become formal instances of power, are always to be questioned. Foucault seems to confirm this when he suggests that his work has largely involved "problemization," which he takes to mean "the development of acts, practices, and thoughts that seem to me to pose problems for politics."[26] His interest is not in providing political answers to problems but to "open up problems that are as concrete and general as possible, problems that approach politics from behind and cut across societies on the diagonal, problems that are at once constituents of our history and constituted by that history." Foucault's political ethic becomes an ethic of resistance.[27]

Foucault does address the issue of the creation of a community, but it is strikingly ancillary to his discussion of the ethical subject. The possibility of a "we," Foucault suggests, must be the result of (and not precede) the "problemizations" one poses to politics. But this "we" would seem to be a rather unstable one, a "necessarily temporary result" since as Foucault notes elsewhere politics can never answer these questions "completely."[28] What is troubling in this formulation is that there is no clear indication of why one would expect a "we" to arise out of such questions, or on what basis such a community could be constructed. This incongruity between the "I" and "we" results from a postmodern subject who can always say "no" but has neither reason nor basis to say "yes." We can read Havel's politics as an attempt to answer to this incongruity, not by grounding politics in certitude but by arguing for a responsible subject who is able to make decisions about the future.

HAVEL AND THE CONSTRUCTION OF POLITICAL DISCOURSE

Half a century of Soviet control had left a previously vibrant Czechoslovakian state with neither a constitutional framework nor political and civil habits upon which to build a democratic society. Jiří Musil sets the historical stage that confronted Czechoslovakia in 1989: "It was necessary to define and re-define the identity of the state, specifying the citizens' rights and obligations, deciding on the structure and rules of the representative democratic bodies, the administrative and regional structures of the state, and on scores of other issues defining the constitutional frame of a modern society. The old, disinte-grating mechanisms of central planning had to be replaced by measures which would lead to a market economy. Principles had to be laid down for the difficult maneuvers incorrectly defined as economic reform, when in fact a total economic restructuring, of unprecedented extent and intensity, was required. A reliable social and cultural framework for these new societies had to be built—a framework that involved nothing less than the creation of a civil society."[29]

Havel himself recognized this task, making references over and over again in his political speeches to a Czechoslovakian "nervousness, confusion, impatience and many times even hopelessness."[30] The reason for this sense of drift, as he revealed in a speech to the Czech Parliament, is "the loss of the old and the absence of the new course" that "awakens in many people a feeling of emptiness . . . and frustration."[31] In a speech at George Washington Univer-sity directed at his Western audience, Havel pointed out how the years of Soviet rule had left the Czechs without the traditions or values necessary to provide a foundation for a new political system.[32] In a sense, Havel had to start with an already dissolved political discourse, collapsed beliefs, and the breakdown of all traditions; his task began where postmodernism's ended.

In addressing the feeling of emptiness in the Czech people and the recourse of many to different strands of fanaticism, Havel has sought nothing less than a rethinking of what it means to be political. "One cannot be con-tent with sociological explanations of this atmosphere and take refuge in the hope that it is all only transitory and temporary. One cannot even count on better legislation and more effective use of state power to resolve everything." Instead, continues Havel, "We need something more: To patiently breathe a new spirit into politics."[33] As he wrote on an earlier occasion, "After decades of artificial uniformity, our society needs to learn how to think of itself in political terms once more, to restructure itself politically."[34]

This restructuring has two components. First, it requires the creation of a "conceptual environment," one that "will provoke individuals, independent scientific institutions, businesses, the interested public and lastly government departments to think strategically and take better account of what is possible from a long-term perspective and what is not."[35] Second, it requires the establishment of a constitutional, legal, and economic framework that is sup-portive of this new conceptual environment. I will treat each of these compo-nents in turn.

Throughout his years in dissent as well into his presidency, Havel has been unremitting in confronting traditional conceptions of politics. His speeches and writings read with an impatience towards parochial, short-sighted, and opportunistic factions who press their claims upon the state and society. Havel, instead, envisions the political realm as involving the much broader discussion of "where we stand, what opportunities we have and where we ought to go."[36] More important than any specific set of questions or particular answers, Havel's concern is with the creation of an environment that can actively engage in these questions. Politics becomes, ultimately, the realm in which the people of the community in all their different roles are involved in "lively and responsible consideration of every political step, every decision; a constant stress on moral deliberation and moral judgement; continued self-examination and self-analysis; an endless rethinking of our priorities."[37]

We cannot help but pause when Havel talks about politics as involving moral deliberation. These are words that Havel never hesitates to use, yet they sound odd (if not dangerous) to postmodern ears. Politics' "deepest roots," Havel notes, "are moral because it is a responsibility expressed through action, to and for the whole." This responsibility has a "metaphysical grounding" in that "it grows out of a conscious or subconscious certainty that our death ends nothing" but that "everything is forever being recorded and evaluated somewhere else, somewhere 'above us,' " in what Havel calls "the memory of Being." Conscience, responsibility, and ultimately politics, rest upon the "silent assumption" that words and deeds are recorded in memory that lasts beyond human life and, in some sense, is impervious to our attempts "to wipe away the sharp disappointments of earthly failure: our spirit knows that it is not the only entity aware of these failures."[38]

Havel seems less concerned with the exact nature of this Being than that individuals have a sense that something exists beyond them to which they may be answerable. This memory may be an eternal Being but for Havel it may also be history, not as an unfolding but as a record of our actions and a testament to our life. Rejecting the suggestion that one can "with impunity navigate through history and rewrite one's own biography," Havel argues that there is an integrity to history that must be faced.[39] Unable to change this record, we seek to subvert it by lying to ourselves and others. But the toll for this subversion is a high one as we are always aware of the possibility of being caught, of being held answerable for our deeds and our refusal to admit to these deeds. Indirectly addressing Kurt Waldheim, President of Austria and former Nazi collaborator, but also speaking to his own nation, Havel suggested that "Too often in this corner of the world, fear of one lie leads only to another lie, in the vain hope that it will cover up not only the first but also the very practice of lying." Even in areas where the masking of the past is seen as a safeguard to freedom, "there is no full freedom there where freedom is not given to the full truth." Through the falsification of the past, "many here have made themselves guilty. Yet we cannot be forgiven, and in our souls peace cannot reign, as long as we do not at least admit our guilt. Confession liberates." In particular, it liberates us from "fear." Havel, thus, spells out the task of the Czechs (and other Europeans): "Let us try then to free this sorely tested region not only from its fear of the lie but also of its fear of the truth. Let us at last look sincerely, calmly and attentively into our own faces, into our past, present and future. We will reach beyond its ambiguity only when we understand it."[40] Havel's desire is not to dwell in the past; rather, his suggestion is that we can talk responsibly about the future only when we have accepted responsibility for our actions in the past.

Ideologies act much like historical lies in that they provide to people "an illusion of an identity, of dignity and of morality while making it easier for them to part with them." In an elegant discussion of how the Marxist-Leninist system worked in Czechoslovakia, Havel talks about the meaning of a sign a local grocer placed in his shop window, "Workers of the world, unite!" when, in all likelihood, neither the grocer nor those who read the sign agreed with or cared about the semantics of the statement. The message of the sign, though, lies beneath the specific words, conveying the public message, "I am obedient and therefore I have the right to be left in peace." Havel notes that if the grocer had been told to display the slogan, "I am afraid and therefore unquestioningly obedient" then "he would not be nearly as indifferent to its semantics, even though the statement would reflect the truth." Instead, the grocer would be "embarrassed and ashamed to put such an unequivocal statement of his own degradation in the shop window, and quite naturally so, for he is a human being and thus has a sense of his own dignity." What the original slogan provided was a guise, a way for the shopkeeper "to conceal from himself the low foundations of his obedience, at the same time concealing the low foundations of power. It hides him behind the façade of something high. And that something is ideology."[41]

Ideologies, as they pretend to offer something "suprapersonal and objective," enable "people to deceive their conscience and conceal their true position and their inglorious *modus vivendi,* both from the world and from themselves." What ideologies do most of all, and this takes us to the meaning of authenticity for Havel, is that they absolve us of our responsibility. Ideologies serve as "a veil behind which human beings can hide their own fallen existence, their trivialization, and their adaptation to the status quo." While diminishing the individual, ideologies at the same time "provide people, both as victims and pillars of the post-totalitarian system, with the illusion that the system is in harmony with the human order and the order of the universe."[42]

In unravelling historical lies and exposing ideological thinking, Havel's interest is in the recovery of the authentic self, an attempt first and foremost to "regain control over one's own sense of responsibility."[43] Responsibility is born of a resistance to totalizing discourses, but the reason for such resistance is because ideological and utopian discourses strip the individual of the moral freedom to act responsibly and, thus, politically. Departing from postmodernism, Havel's resistance, then, becomes recovery, the regaining of the responsible self.

The second component of this political restructuring involves the "technical aspects of building the state."[44] I turn to Havel's writings on this issue because it stands in such sharp contrast to postmodern scholarship. There is in postmodernism a reticence about the role of institutions born in part of a suspicion of anything that formalizes human action. There is, consequently, a focus on the raising of questions, postponing any serious inquiry into the possibility of constructing institutions.

Such are the privileges of academe, but for Havel such critique admits of no end. New problems can always be found, new questions can always be raised. Faced with the actual task of having to create a new constitution, though, Havel pushed for a two year (as opposed to four year) mandate to complete it. In his words, speaking as an individual who has sat through one too many meetings, "To drag out the 'revolutionary' phase, to prolong some of the improvisational measures (including the absurd business of gluing amendments and addenda to the Communist constitution), to delay the creation of something as basic as a new constitution, could have fatal consequences for our nascent democracy." Endless questioning would simply result in an "extended period of uncertainty and confusion" which only breeds "a state of general anarchy and frustration, and a permanent social crisis."[45]

In crafting these institutions, which is itself a political task, Havel turns our attention to the importance of institutions in supporting this new conceptual environment of responsible participation. Not surprisingly, Havel argues for the creation of certain democratic institutions, such as representative bodies chosen by popular elections, but he adjusts these institutions to the particular needs as well as traditions of his society. . . .

[In] economic matters, Havel argues for the establishment of a market economy. Havel describes the market economy as "a system in which complete independence and plurality of economic entities exist within a legal framework, and its workings are guided chiefly by the laws of the marketplace. This is the only natural economy, the only kind that makes sense, the only one that can lead to prosperity, because it is the only one that reflects the nature of life itself." This is a rather curious statement given that the market is at best usually seen as a cruel necessity for economic efficiency and rarely elevated to the status of a moral institution. What the market does for Havel, though, is answer to this twin demand of human plurality and responsibility. On the one hand, a market contains an openness that allows for continued invention and innovation as well as new directions for human activity, all unguided by some predetermined end. Furthermore, the market economy "in which everything belongs to someone" means that "someone is responsible for everything." In contrast, a centralized economic system subjects all economic life to "one central voice of reason" that claimed to be "more clever than life itself" by proclaiming what should and should not be done. But, for Havel "The essence of life is infinitely and mysteriously multiform, and therefore it cannot be contained or planned for, in its fullness and variability, by any central intelligence."[46]

It is in this same spirit that we can read Havel's political vision. Politics is reducible to neither particular institutional forms nor resistance to these forms. Instead, politics becomes the realm in which citizens raise questions about the direction of the community and deliberate about the role institutions will play and have played in moving in this direction. Politics, thus, makes institutions the outcome of human action and, in turn, makes individuals accountable for the creation and maintenance of these institutions. In this way, the people who comprise a community cannot hide behind institutional demands any more than they can disguise their responsibility by an appeal to ideology.

Havel is very much aware of the magnitude of this task as he must conduct a two-front battle against two competing notions of politics: the remnants of Communism which reduced politics to ideological slogans, and the new spirit of faction which, as James Madison noted, is an inevitable result of democratic government. Even supporters of Havel have pointed to the seeming futility of his enterprise. But his project has not been futile. Instead, there is a realism and freshness to Havel's project as he has sought to link his political discourse to particular institutional forms, and there is an importance to his project as he has suggested how one may construct a politics in a postmodern world.[47]

Notes and References

1.   Caroline Bayard, "The Intellectual in the Post Modern Age: East/West Contrasts," *Philosophy Today* 34 (Winter 1990): 292, 296, 297.
2.   Jean-François Lyotard, *The Postmodern Condition: A Report on Knowledge,* trans. G. Bennington and B. Massumi (Minneapolis: University of Minnesota Press, 1984), xxiii-xxiv.
3.   See Jacques Derrida, "Structure, Sign, and Play in the Discourse of the Human Sciences" *Writing and Difference,* trans. Alan Bass (Chicago: University of Chicago Press, 1978), 279–80. Also see Richard J. Bernstein, *The New Constellation: The Ethical-Political Horizons of Modernity/Postmodernity* (Cambridge: MIT Press, 1992), 175.
4.   Jacques Derrida. *Limited inc.,* ed. Gerald Graff (Evanston: Northwestern University Press, 1988), 93. Derrida does not use the term "ideology" here.
5.   See Bernstein, *Constellation,* 176.
6.   Bayard, "Intellectual," 293–95.
7.   Václav Havel, *Summer Meditations,* trans. Paul Wilson (New York: Vintage Books, 1992), 16, 62.
8.   Ibid., 66.
9.   Václav Havel, "October 28 Speech in Vladislav Hall," CTK National News Wire, 27 October 1993; "Havel Diagnoses Czechoslovak Ills, Reviews Successes," CTK National News Wire, 1 January 1992.

10. Václav Havel, "The Power of the Powerless," October 1978, in *Open Letters. Selected Writings 1965–1990*, ed. Paul Wilson (New York: Alfred A. Knopf, 1991), 134.

11. Havel, *Summer Meditations*, 60, 62.

12. Ibid., 30–31.

13. Ibid., 16–17.

14. Bayard, "Intellectual," 294, quoting Lyotard, *Le Tombeau de l'intellectuel*, 20.

15. Michael J. Shapiro, *Reading the Postmodern Polity: Political Theory as Textual Practice* (Minneapolis: University of Minnesota Press, 1992), 139.

16. Interview with Jacques Derrida, in Imre Salusinzky, *Criticism in Society* (New York: Methuen, 1987), 20.

17. Derrida, "The Conflict of Faculties: A *Mocholos*," 56, quoted in Bernstein, *Constellation*, 186–87. See also Derrida, *Positions*, trans. Alan Bass (Chicago: University of Chicago Press, 1981), 41–42, 89–91.

18. Quoted in Bernstein, *Constellation*, 217.

19. Bernstein, *Constellation*, 191.

20. Richard Kearney, ed., "Dialogue with Jacques Derrida," *Dialogues with Contemporary Continental Thinkers* (Manchester: Manchester University Press, 1984), quoted in Bernstein, *Constellation*, 213.

21. Bernstein, *Constellation*, 214.

22. Michel Foucault, "Two Lectures," *Power/Knowledge: Selected Interviews & Other Writings 1972–1977*, ed. Colin Gordon (New York: Pantheon Books, 1980), 83.

23. Ibid.

24. For an insightful discussion of this, see Kyle A. Pasewark, *A Theology of Power. Being Beyond Domination* (Minneapolis: Fortress Press, 1993), 35–39.

25. Foucault, "On the Genealogy of Ethics: An Overview of Work in Progress," in Hubert L. Dreyfus and Paul Rabinow, *Beyond Structuralism and Hermeneutics*, 2nd ed. (Chicago: University of Chicago Press, 1983), 236.

26. "An Interview with Michel Foucault," in *The Foucault Reader*, ed. Paul Rabinow (New York: Pantheon Books, 1984), 384.

27. "Politics and Ethics: An Interview," ibid., 376.

28. "Interview," ibid., 384–5.

29. Jiří Musil, "Czechoslovakia in the Middle of Transition," *Daedalus* 121 (1992): 180.

30. "Havel Diagnoses," CTK National News Wire, 1 January 1992. In his 4 July 1994 speech in Philadelphia, Havel extends this sense of uncertainty to, in his words, "the postmodern world." *The Buffalo News* (10 July 1994): 8.

31. "Extracts from President Havel's Speech to the Czech Parliament," CTK National News Wire, 23 February 1993.

32. "Czech President Speaks at George Washington University," CTK National News Wire, 22 April 1993.

33. "Extracts," CTK National News Wire, 23 February 1993.

34. Havel, *Summer Meditations*, 61.

35. "Extracts," CTK National News Wire, 23 February 1993.

36. Ibid.

37. Havel, *Summer Meditations*, 20. While Havel has been characterized by some as an idealist, the questions Havel addresses are quite pragmatic. In a speech before the Czech Parliament, for example, he set out some of these questions now facing the Republic: "Will we be primarily a transit country and will we thus support the modernization of airports, highways . . . and the development of the necessary infrastructure? Will we orient ourselves, according to some prognosis—more towards a certain regional autonomy of economic life, or will we go the way of rapid integration into supranational units? To what degree do we invest in tourism and support everything that can make it a powerful source of prosperity? Will we bank on the resourcefulness of our people and support small and mid-sized producers and businessmen?

What perspectives do our electronic and radiotechnical industries have? What will we do about our aircraft industry? What possibilities does our heavy industry sector have?" ("Extracts," CTK National News Wire, 23 February 1993).

38.   Ibid., 6.

39.   This concern with memory is fascinating in view of Milan Kundera's work on memory and forgetfulness. For Kundera, life involves the struggle of the individual against the tyranny of forgetfulness as the loss of memory allows for a remaking of one's past. It is this past, though, that gives identity to the individual.

40.   "Heads of State Call on Waldheim," *New York Times* (27 July 1990): A6.

41.   Havel, "Power," 133.

42.   Ibid., 133–34.

43.   Ibid., 153.

44.   Havel, *Summer Meditations,* 19.

45.   Ibid., 22–23.

46.   Ibid., 62.

47.   My thanks to William Marty, Kyle Pasewark, Susan Strandberg, and Heather Wolak for their useful comments.

HAVEL THE PLAYWRIGHT

◆

Havel's *The Garden Party* Revisited

PAUL I. TRENSKY

{By communicating about a communication disorder, Havel theatrically reframes the double-bind predicament of those locked in the primary frame and offers to them for inspection his reframing.

—Peter Steiner}

No other living Czech author is better known in the West than Václav Havel. Many are familiar with his name primarily due to his association with the dissident political movement in Czechoslovakia. {In the late seventies,} the so-called Charter 77, a sort of a declaration of human rights of which he was co-author, attracted world-wide interest and caused once again his prolonged detention. But since the mid-1960's Havel has been also the most frequently staged contemporary East European playwright in the West. The critical acclaim of his works, written mostly in the absurdist mold, has been as pronounced as their success with the public. For example, his *The Memorandum,* produced in New York in 1968, received the prestigious Obie Award, and Martin Esslin, the famous theoretician of absurd drama, called him "one of the most promising European playwrights of his generation . . ."[1] Only Havel's first three plays, however, were staged in his native country. After the Soviet intervention of 1968 his plays were banned in Czechoslovakia, but they continued to be produced abroad.

In spite of the relatively large number of plays Havel has written, many who are intimately acquainted with his work regard his first drama, *The Garden Party* (*Zahradní slavnost,* 1963) as his masterpiece. It was staged extensively in continental Europe, in particular in Germany, but it never received so much attention in English speaking countries, very likely because of a not too felicitous translation. *The Garden Party* is a many-layered, complex work. It is perhaps the greatest satirical play exposing the bureaucratization of life and deformation of intellect by a totalitarian social system that has ever come from the pen of an East European dramatist; but at the same time it may be

Reprinted and abridged from William E. Harkins and Paul I. Trensky, eds., *Czech Literature Since 1956: A Symposium* (New York: Bohemica, 1980), 103–18.

159

viewed as a commentary on modern man's predicament in general. This play, and in particular its language, will be the concern of this article.[2]

The principal character of the work is Hugo Pludek, and, in the stratum of the action, the play deals with his overnight success. As is the case with most absurd dramas, there is no plot, intrigue, or conflict in the traditional sense of the word in *The Garden Party*. At the beginning of the play Hugo is a nobody whose indifference towards his future angers his ambitious parents. They induce him to take the opportunity to secure a respectable position through the influence of Kalabis, an official of the Liquidation Office, an old acquaintance of Hugo's father. Hugo is to meet the important man at a garden party organized by the office, but upon his arrival, he learns that Kalabis is absent. Nevertheless, Hugo quickly draws attention to himself by easily adjusting to the peculiar way of thinking of the officials, and in no time becomes the leading figure of the Liquidation Office. This is only the beginning of his career. With equal facility he storms the rival Inauguration Office and finally becomes the head of a brand new institution, the all-powerful Central Committee for Inauguration and Liquidation. His swift career is, however, realized at the expense of his personality. The outstanding feature of Hugo is his ability to adapt to his surroundings, through which alone he is able to succeed in the world of bureaucracy. As he is constantly forced to assimilate to the new milieu, he gradually destroys his own self to such a degree that he ceases to be aware of his original identity. At the end of the drama Hugo does not even recognize his parents, nor do they recognize him. He has become a different, faceless being.

The play is based on the traditional theme of the degradation of man by his lack of principles. Hugo is a sort of Julien Sorel, with his two rival offices paralleling Sorel's army-clergy dilemma. Unlike Sorel, Hugo ends up victorious by being able to adjust himself to both, but his success takes the inevitable toll. The techniques of *The Garden Party*, however, have little in common with the traditional drama or novel. Hugo, while trying to adapt himself, mutates directly into other personalities. The decomposition of his ego is realized not merely on the psychological level, but in the very structure of the drama. The essential dramaturgical device of the play rests in a direct character metamorphosis, which is, in general, widely used by the absurdist playwrights. In Jean Genet's plays, for example, the device of metamorphosis is still masked by the Pirandellian play-within-play technique. Thus in *Les Bonnes* [*The Maids*], Solange and Claire alternately impersonate each other, as well as their mistress. The game develops, however, into the complete absorption of the person into the impersonated object, as the tragic denouement of the play demonstrates. The situation is further complicated by Genet's demand that the role of the maids be played by male actors. A more direct destruction of traditional conception of character is achieved by Ionesco, whose plays exhibit, in general, an affinity with Havel's. "We shall get rid of the principle of identity and unity of character and let the movement and dramatic psychology take its place."3 This statement is made by one of Ionesco's characters in *Victimes du devoir* [*Victims of Duty*], but expresses without doubt the playwright's own views. In his plays characters merge, fall apart, double, exchange places, change their sex, etc. At the end of *La cantatrice chauve* [*The Bald Soprano*], for example, the Smiths turn into the Martins and vice versa. In *Tueur sans gages* [*The Killer Sneers*] the concierge mutates into Mother Pipe, the Architect into the Police Commissioner, and later into a Patrolman. In *Le rhinoceros* [*Rhinoceros*] people are afflicted by a disease which transforms them into a herd of pachyderms. The *metamorphoses* are symbols not so much of the multifarious nature of man as of the illusiveness of his personality. Havel shares with other absurdist playwrights the conception of modern man's identity as a vacuum; consequently, man can become anything at any time, depending largely on the influences to which he is exposed. All his characters are soulless, mechanical creatures who are formed and defined only by their environment. The human world is an impersonal world in which individuals are exchangeable.

Lacking a real plot, conflict or set of characters, the play rests on a highly complex verbal structure, and it is actually the language which is its primary moving force. This aspect of Havel's play is also identifiable with the absurd theater in the West, which has substantially changed the role of language in the structure of the dramatic genre. Jean Vannier, in his pioneering article on the theater of the absurd, written in 1956, defined the movement as "a theatre of language where man's words are held up to us as a spectacle."4 In the traditional theater the role of language was largely secondary. It served merely as a vehicle for expressing the ideas and emotions of the characters, for the elaboration of the theme and conflict, and as a necessary link between the stage and the audience. In a theater which accredits to characters no inner life, however, words cannot be used just as projections to the outer world. Language not only ceases to enhance character development, but the opposite becomes the fact, and characters are made the vehicle of language. Words form people by filling their inner void until human speech stops functioning as a means of communication and becomes a form of social behavior. And since language no longer serves to express ideas, it also has to be contentless. Indeed, the long dialogues in *The Garden Party* are nothing but a collection of prefabricated clichés which the characters repeat over and over, or the more creative ones intertwine and twist, but seldom does the human mind exhibit more originality than a perfectly functioning linguistic computer. Language is the symptom of the alienation of man, but in a much more intense way than, for instance, in Chekhov's plays. It points up not only the impossibility of communication between people, but the very corruption of intellect by language. People cannot understand each other because they simply do not say anything. The play presents language as a proliferating object of monstrous energy. Words constantly threaten to take over and play with their victims at their whim.

The first act of *The Garden Party* is a parody of the family drama. The stock situation and the cliché language of the soap opera are studiously burlesqued in order to unmask the bizarre nature of the petty bourgeois world which this genre glorifies. Of course, Havel's conceptions of the bourgeoisie are based not on political factors, but on moral ones. In his play the spokesman for bourgeois morality is Pludek-father, who is appalled by the nonconformist appearance of his elder son, Petr, and puts all his hope in his more ordinary yet apathetic younger son, Hugo. Pludek's complacent sense of purpose and propriety is, however, only a thin layer masking his inner void, which betrays itself in his hopelessly futile attempts to verbalize his creed concerning the messianic role of the middle class. All his endeavors to explain to Hugo his philosophy of life constantly slip out of gear: "No historical epoch can exist without the middle classes, but the middle classes can exist independently of all epochs. And even without them! . . . The only country that doesn't need any middle classes is Japan because there are enough Japanese even without the middle classes."[5]

The humorous effect of Pludek's speeches (and basically of all the characters' speeches in the play) is based upon the discrepancy between the form and the content. Pludek's posture is completely self-assured, showing great faith in his ideals, and at superficial reading the statements even give the impression of having been carefully chosen; yet he says absolutely nothing. The sentences nullify themselves as they originate. From the dramaturgical point of view, the function of the phrases lies precisely in their meaninglessness. The abject way in which people speak is hyperbolized to such an extreme that its absurdity comes fully to the fore. Circular logic and false syllogisms are constantly present in the dialogue. Thus, for example, in the dialogue between the parents concerning the expected visitor, Kalabis, the necessity of his arrival is "proven" by the following sequence of thoughts:

> MRS. PLUDEK: He should have been here by now—
> PLUDEK: He was probably detained.
> MRS. PLUDEK: How come, detained?
> PLUDEK: Perhaps he met somebody, and was carried away with conversation.
> MRS. PLUDEK: But whom?
> PLUDEK: A friend from his youth—
> MRS. PLUDEK: You know he had no youth!
> PLUDEK: He had no youth, but he had friends in his youth. Am I not after all a friend from his youth?
> MRS. PLUDEK: He couldn't have met you!
> PLUDEK: See! He'll come for sure! (19)

The most conspicuous feature of the first act is the use of nonsense proverbs. Ionesco's use of this device, especially in *The Bald Soprano,* was probably the main source for the Czech author, who, however, extends its symbolic significance. Proverbs are considered the deepest emanation of popular wisdom. Concentrated in their phrasing, vivid in their imagination and compelling in their logic, they are among the most distinguished verbal accomplishments of man. If their use becomes automatic, however, the speaker often ceases to perceive their content and easily distorts them. In *The Garden Party* the distortion of proverbs is symbolic of the downfall of traditional values. Pludek-father, in order to support his conservative philosophy, uses a large number of statements which have the ring of proverbs, yet, under a closer scrutiny, turn out to be conglomerations of semantically unrelated words. For example: "Not even the afternoon witch carries grain to the loft by herself"; "Not even the hussars of Kolin go to the woods without dog collars"; "I fed my chipmunk so long that my pipe fell into the reeds"; "He who quarrels about mosquito screens can't dance with the she-goat at Podmokly"; etc. Unlike the examples in which the destruction of language is based upon the illogically chosen sequence of otherwise "correct" sentences, the destruction of meaning is here within the sentences themselves. The trick played here is simple. The statements have all the formal features of proverbs—but in other respects the combination of words is purely mechanical. So the first example above ("Not even the afternoon witch . . .") is modelled upon the so-called "plain truth proverbs." The beginning of the sentence with the familiar ["Not even . . ."] creates in the context of Pludek's tirades the expectation of a proverb, which is further strengthened by the syntactical pattern, as well as by the use of words from uncommon lexical strata (agricultural society and folk mythology). A more complicated feature here is again the syntactical structure, the "He who" pattern typical of proverbs. The second clause of the sentence, however, is taken almost intact from a well-known saying concerning avarice: "He would rather dance with a she-goat than give a penny." The total unrelatedness of the first half to the second creates the effect of comical frustration on the part of the listener.

Proverbs show instability even in the peculiar world of the Pludeks. Pludek-mother takes one half from each of two unrelated pseudo-proverbs used earlier by her husband and creates a new one, "Not even the afternoon witch goes to the woods without a dog-collar," while Pludek-father quickly uses the other two halves: "Have you ever seen the hussars carry grain to the loft by themselves?" In the world of the Pludeks every turn of speech is possible, since their language is governed not by thought, but only by grammar. A correct use of proverbs would be as meaningless as their distortions.

The great originality of Havel's talent finds its full expression especially in the subsequent acts, when the play acquires the character of a political satire. All the features of the avant-garde dramaturgy are retained, but, while continuing to be a general critique of modern mechanized society, the play goes on to expose the absurdities of the socialist system in particular. The second act is an easily recognized allegory on the institutionalization of private life in present-day Czechoslovakia, while the third act lampoons the monstrous bureaucratic machinery of the country. The connection between the first act and the succeeding ones is made not only in the stratum of the action (Hugo's adventures), but in the ideological stratum as well. There are unmistakable parallels between the home life of the Pludeks and the outside world. Life guided by the socialist ideal turns out to be as soulless and degenerate as that of the petty bourgeois. It is governed to an even larger degree by opportunism and conformity, with people acting and speaking as senselessly; the only difference actually is in the replacing of one type of verbal gesture by another. The "conservative" maxims of Pludek-father are superseded by the mechanical repetition of official statements, slogans, and ideological clichés.

Both acts are strictly actionless, and language again carries the movement of the play. The dominant feature of the second act is the dispute over whether the Large Dancing Floor is larger than the Small Dancing Floor, during which Hugo learns the phraseology of the new milieu and asserts his supremacy in the subsequent controversy concerning the importance of art versus technology. The third act, which takes place in the Inauguration Office, consists solely of disputes involving bureaucratic matters. The antagonists of Hugo are the He- and She-Secretary and Plzák in the second act, and the Director in the third.

Individual members of both offices could be identified with different forms of the Communist regime. In the humorless pedantry of the representatives of the Liquidation Office, one can recognize the era of the 1950's whose effects, of course, were very much alive when the play was written, while the greater permissiveness of the representatives of the Inauguration Office reflects the new wind of the period of thaw. But Havel by no means attempts to place one above the other, and shows rather that they are two different manifestations of the same absurd principle. The call for a "full life" turns out to be as devoid of substance as the dedication to abstract ideals.

There are some basic differences in the speech mannerisms of the individual characters. They all have their particular lingo, except for Hugo's, which is in constant flux. The language of the He- and She-Secretary is characterized by an excessive literariness. Both speak as if they were citing a prepared text; their language is dry, precise and complex. It reflects ideological textbooks, official party polemics and directives, which are used by them in a routine, mechanical manner. The grotesque unnaturalness of their language is especially evident in their references to mundane subjects, such as when they describe the entertainment facilities at the garden party in the style of an official memorandum:

SHE-SECRETARY: You are present at the main entrance B 13. You can buy here a general admission card, which will provide you with the right of free movement throughout the entire topographical extent of the garden as well as with the right

of visitation of all attractions organized within the framework of the garden party
of the Liquidation Office—

HE-SECRETARY: As is, for instance, the discussion with the Chairman of the
Development Department concerning liquidation methods, given in the area of
the Little Pond—

SHE-SECRETARY: An amusing quiz from the history of the Liquidation Office
given in pavilion No. 111—

HE-SECRETARY: Or the narration of humorous stories from the experience of the
Fifth Division that were recorded and will be narrated by the Head of the Fifth
Division—(25–26)

The divorcement of their speaking habits from reality is total, yet their
rhetoric is so fluent that they can easily transpose any fact into their abstract
world. Thus, Hugo's attempt to point out the faulty organization of the party
is virtually dissolved in an avalanche of ready-made phrases which actually
ignore entirely Hugo's simple and logical argument:

SHE-SECRETARY: At first glance it appears to have some logic—

HE-SECRETARY: Unfortunately, purely formal—

SHE-SECRETARY: And the intrinsic content of the proposal is even indicative of an
ignorance of certain basic principles.

HE-SECRETARY: Or would you really like to see the dignified course of our garden
party disturbed by some kind of dadaistic joking, which would certainly become
the case if such an important, nay, essential point as Great Dancing Floor A were
exposed to boundless intellectualizing? . . . Our colleagues from the Organization
Committee undoubtedly knew why they limited entertainment with funny
objects to the area of Small Dancing Floor C! (26–27)

Hugo's later success lies in his realization that facts mean nothing in this
strange world of *The Garden Party;* only words have value. One cliché can be
defeated only by another, which explains why Plzák can so easily assert himself against the dialectics of both the secretaries, who succumb to the language of his "new look."

The He- and She-Secretaries are examples not only of an intellectual
degradation in modern man, but of an emotional one as well. In a conformist
world in which everything is reduced to simple formulae, genuine, spontaneous feelings are impossible. Havel's man is as incapable of true love as is
Beckett's, Ionesco's, or Pinter's. The mechanized man, although often aware
of the inadequacy of his mind, already has a built-in resistance against the
upsurge of the irrational in himself. The pressures of a conformist society,
with its inherent suspicion of any manifestation of individuality which love
might bring to the fore, prevent its development. The social system presented

in the play is shown to be even more destructive to love than that exposed in Western dramas, having created an even more conformist attitude toward the inner life by subjecting it to a constant probing of its function within society as a whole. Plzák, a professed enemy of pedantry and uniformity, makes an eloquent speech in favor of love. His arguments, trivial and vulgar as they are, constitute paradoxically the very assertion of the utilitarian principle: "You know, I can't stand those drybones who bury their heads into the sand because of such problems as make up a little bit of emotional life. Ain't such a thing as love, for example, a damn needy thing, when one knows how to get hold of it. To get hold of these things, that belongs, damn it, after all, also to the edification of man" (31).

The ensuing dialogue between the two young people is a grotesque demonstration of their emotional bankruptcy. They both score well in their theoretical discussion of love in which they can utilize their verbal training, but a different situation develops when they attempt to follow up Plzák's appeal for a "rich emotional life" in practice. Their ability to express their inner feelings has already been so impaired by their constant use of meaningless phrases, that they are unable to say anything coherent to each other. Their attempt at communication results only in verbal dislocations. Their dialogue is constantly marred by the intrusion of inopportune words based on sound similarity and by incorrect metaphorical associations, until it completely disintegrates:

HE-SECRETARY: Your hair is—beautiful—golden—like daredevils—that is to say, daffodils—and your nose is like a red rose—or rather—like a lily of the valley— a white one— . . . And your breasts are like—like—two wells—(Pause) Or rather—excuse me—like balloons—like balloons I wanted to say—excuse me—

SHE-SECRETARY: That's all right—

HE-SECRETARY: And your eyes are like—two balloons—or perhaps like daffodils—

SHE-SECRETARY: And how are things at home?

HE-SECRETARY: Well, you know—nature—or rather lilies—

SHE-SECRETARY: And the balloons? Do they make troubles?

HE-SECRETARY: Not at all, not at all—they are blossoming—

SHE-SECRETARY: Oh, so you are single!

HE-SECRETARY: That is to say they rustle—not the sparrows—moss—moss bustles—like two daffodils—(32)

The fate of the abortive love affair is followed throughout the play. The He-Secretary quickly recovers from the uncomfortable experience, finding his lost equilibrium in the secure routine of his clerical life. The She-Secretary, on the other hand, continues to manifest her grotesque emotional frustration through a verbal vehicle of garbled fragments of the so-called "Vitalist" school of poetry, which flourished in Czechoslovakia especially after the First World War.

Equally degraded is the second "love story" of the play, that between Kalabis and his secretary, Anička. Neither of the two characters is ever on the stage and the only source of information about their relationship is a few fragments of their conversations which "slipped" into three telegrams which Kalabis sent to Pludek-father. Havel uses here in a parodied manner the device of an accidental mix-up of two written texts, usually found in situation comedies (but also in Gogol's *The Inspector General*). Anička, while putting down the text of the telegrams as dictated to her by Kalabis, mechanically includes his declaration of love to her, and after the apparent consummation of the affair, his angry refusal of her expression of affection. The mechanization of man is here hyperbolized in a perhaps not too subtle, yet dramatically effective, way.

A more involved language is spoken by Plzák. It consists of dialectisms . . . as well as lexical vulgarisms. . . . This "popular" diction, which should be the expression of Plzák's liberalism, is intermingled with sentences in a strictly literary language that are somewhat less complex than those of the two clerks; they are reminiscent especially of newspaper jargon. The curious coexistence of the two linguistic strata can be observed in the following passage.

> PLZÁK: If you want under cover of an open discussion to torpedo the amicable atmosphere which I've succeeded in creating here, if it's your intention to undermine the success of our garden party, then there's no place for you in this tightly welded collective. . . . Whoever will mess around here I'll give him such a push with these two paws of mine that he'll spin like a top. . . . It's certainly commendable that you are concerned with the question of art, you mustn't, however, overestimate one-sidedly its importance, since you could fall into an unhealthy, and to the spirit of our garden parties, deeply alien aestheticism. As if we didn't have in technology also a helluva big bag of damn hot questions. (34–36)

Platitude is the most frequently used device for the development of the character of Plzák, who is the prototype of the semi-literate upstart of socialist society. So, for example, the important book which he boasts of being the author of turns out, according to his own description, to be based upon self-evident trivia: "In my book I developed the thesis that every garden party should become the platform for a healthy and, at the same time, disciplined amusement of all officers." On another occasion, when describing the advanced stage of modern society, he is unable to give more than the most commonplace examples: "I maintain that we live in a technical age—magnet—telephone—magnet— . . ." (34). Another device used is comical verbal distortion, for example, "nothing alien is human to me," "Verner" for Jules Verne, etc.

The third act is a bitter satire on bureaucracy in general and on that of socialist institutions in particular. Centralization gave rise to a monstrous proliferation of rules and regulations whose dynamism became a threat to their creators. They finally acquired an abstract existence of their own, and man's preoccupation with them signifies his progressive alienation from reality. They also created their own language, whose use is not a means of communication, but a ritual for an incomprehensible, almost mystical system. There are lengthy dialogues in this act which aim at solving complex bureaucratic problems, but which in actuality consist of nothing but the mechanical interplay of a few abstract notions. Bureaucratic language turned mad can be observed, for example, in the following conversation between the Director and the She-Secretary, built upon a purely grammatical combination of four words and their derivatives: [*liquidation, form, delimitation, norms*]. Almost every sentence contains a syntagm consisting of these words:

SHE-SECRETARY: Do you have the index of liquidation forms?

DIRECTOR: Yes.

SHE-SECRETARY: And the index of delimitation norms?

DIRECTOR: That one I don't.

SHE-SECRETARY: Is this size five? (Points to a coat.)

DIRECTOR: Yes.

SHE-SECRETARY: But the index of liquidation forms without the index of delimitation norms is invalid!

DIRECTOR: Wouldn't it be enough to submit the index of delimitation norms?

SHE-SECRETARY: This would invalidate the whole liquidation.

DIRECTOR: Isn't that a somewhat formal norm?

SHE-SECRETARY: To the contrary: it's a very normal form. . . . If it were a case of another type of liquidation I could perhaps close one eye—

DIRECTOR: What type of liquidation is it, by the way?

SHE-SECRETARY: Liquidation through the process of delimitation. (42–43).

A closer analysis shows that almost every mathematically possible combination of the four words is found here at least once. Other words are simply threaded around these syntagms according to grammatical rules. The minds of the two officials work like perfect computers which, having been fed an assignment, return swiftly all possible combinations.

Hugo's last antagonist, the Director, is a supreme virtuoso of the bureaucratic lingo. Although shrewder and better versed in dialectics than Plzák, even he finally succumbs to Hugo, who quickly masters his language and thereby assumes his identity. At first the Director dominates, but Hugo, step by step, gains control until he virtually displaces the Director with a barrage of words. Yet both men utter exactly the same words, language functioning here purely as a physical force. Nowhere is the triumph of words deprived of meaning in a more naked form than in this passage:

> DIRECTOR: Despite the fact that it is impossible to deny that during the period of struggle against some manifestations of bureaucracy in the activity of the Liquidation Office, the Inauguration Service—thanks to the effort of a few inaugurators who, through the medium of a healthily unconventional and freshly dynamic relation to mankind, succeeded in paving the way to many valuable ideas on this untrodden soil—played—undeniably—
>
> HUGO:—a positive role, nevertheless, anybody—
>
> DIRECTOR:—who would not see these time-limited signs in the perspective of the later development of the Inauguration Service, would fall into the tenets of liberal extremism—
>
> HUGO:—and he who would not see behind these perhaps subjectively positive intentions their—
>
> DIRECTOR:—definitely objective negative impact—
>
> DIRECTOR and HUGO (simultaneously):—which was caused by the fact that as a result of the unhealthy isolation of the entire office some positive elements in the work of the entire Inauguration Service were uncritically overestimated, which led to the fact that in that period—(the Director cannot keep up with Hugo anymore)
>
> HUGO:—when the activization of all positive forces in the Liquidation Office has placed the Liquidation Office again in the forefront of our work as a firm and intelligent bulwark of our unity that it was, unfortunately, the Inauguration Service which succumbed—
>
> DIRECTOR:—to the hysterical atmosphere of poorly thought through excesses—
> . . . (50)

Evidently, in this dialogue, the sound is much more important than the sense. Havel relies to a large measure on non-representational, "anti-theatrical" elements borrowed especially from music. Changes in tempo, repetition, retardation, gradation, etc., with a minimal density of content are essential devices for carrying the movement of the drama. The last quoted dialogue suggests comparison with the development of a motif by voices in succession. The decisive breaking point occurs when both men shout their phrases in unison, after which the succession of voices is reversed. Many other parts of the drama are built upon similar devices. Thus, the whole first act is based on the recurrence of one central motif. The earlier mentioned dialogue about the importance of art versus technology also has a carefully constructed rhythmical development. It consists of a repetition of arguments for and against art and technology which become shorter and shorter, until it climaxes in brief, slogan-like statements in a rapid staccato. . . .

The last act of the play (Hugo's homecoming) contains some of the best examples of absurd dialogue, one being the dispute that develops between the Pludeks over their son's accepting the assignment concerning the liquidation of the Liquidation Office. Most important, however, is Hugo's lengthy tirade, which can be regarded as a clue to the symbolic meaning of the play. In answer to his parents' question as to who he is, Hugo defines his ultimate alienation as follows:

> HUGO: I? Who am I? Now look, I don't like such one-sidedly formulated questions, I really don't! How can one even ask in such a simplified manner? No matter how one answers questions like these—one can never encompass the whole truth, only its limited part: man—that is something so richly complex, changeable, and diversified, that there is no word, sentence, book, nothing at all that could define him in his totality. There is nothing permanent, eternal, absolute in man, he is perpetual change, proudly ringing change, of course! Nowadays, the time of static, unchangeable categories is over; nowadays, A is not just A, and B just B: today we know that A can often be also B, and B at the same time A; that B can be B, as well as A and C; by the same token, C can be not only C, but also A, B, and D, and under certain circumstances, F can be Q or even Y or R! (63)

There can be little doubt that this passage contains a parody of Marxian dialectics, referring to the thesis of permanent change. "All nature," writes Engels in one of the well-known explications of the theory, "from the smallest thing to the biggest, from the sand to the sun, from the protostar to man, is in a constant state of coming into being and going out of being, in constant flux, in a ceaseless state of movement and change."[6] Marx and Engels developed their ideas in a reasonably scholarly way; their popularizers, however, often vulgarized them to a grotesque degree. Stalin's notorious pamphlet, *Dialectical and Historical Materialism,* especially opened the door to a monstrous misuse of dialectics. In the 1940s and 1950s simplified dialectics became the property of all, saturating scientific journals, newspaper articles, and Party proclamations, as well as discussions on the most banal topics. In a world without absolutes, the thesis of permanent change became a method of proving everything as well as denying everything. The idea which was meant to be a weapon against the dogmatism of stilted values developed into a convenient tool for the justification of moral nihilism. In Hugo's mouth, dialectics serve as a theoretical justification of his opportunism. He applied the principle to himself so thoroughly that he changed from situation to situation virtually in front of our eyes.

The Garden Party offers wider possibilities for interpreting it as a parody of dialectics. Besides the thesis of permanent change, the work also seems to burlesque an equally important part of Marxian dialectics, the struggle of opposites, derived from the Hegelian triad. The opposite forces (thesis and antithesis) lead to a synthesis which is qualitatively superior to both, not just a mechanical agglomeration of them. We have a number of syntheses in the work. The competing Liquidation and Inauguration Offices are fused into one big institution. The old bourgeois world of the Pludeks and the new system are synthesized in the very personality of Hugo, who is also a curious fusion of both Plzák and the Director. The syntheses by no means lead to a qualitative improvement, however, but only to magnified absurdity. The dialectical principle can be traced to the very structure of the dialogues. The controversy about art and technology, or the acceptance or non-acceptance of the assignment, for example, all develop into a nonsensical pseudo-synthesis and are excellent examples of a misuse of dialectics, which loom as the prominent intellectual malaise in the drama.

The dialectical mode of thinking is naturally not limited to Communist society. It has its roots in antiquity, from where it reached Marxism through the philosophy of Hegel. From this viewpoint, one may regard *The Garden Party* as performing a critique of an important tradition of Western thought. Like Wittgenstein, or the French existentialists, Havel derides man's obsession with thinking in categories which prevents him from facing ultimate realities and therefore also tending to undermine his ethical self-awareness.

Notes and References

1. Martin Esslin, *The Theatre of the Absurd* (Garden City: Doubleday, 1969), 280.

2. The play premièred at the Theater on the Balustrade in Prague in December, 1963, under the direction of Otomar Krejča. It was translated into English by Vera Blackwell: Václav Havel, *The Garden Party* (London: Cape, 1969). The most important scholarship on Havel in English [before 1980] includes Petr Den, "Notes on Czechoslovakia's Young Theatre of the Absurd," *Books Abroad*, XLI (1967), 157–63; Marketa Goetz-Stankiewicz, "A Revealing Encounter: The Theatre of the Absurd in Czechoslovakia," *Survey*, XXI (Winter/Spring 1975), 85–100; E. J. Czerwinski, "The Invasion: Effects on Theater and Drama in Eastern Europe," in *The Soviet Invasion of Czechoslovakia: Its Effects on Eastern Europe*, ed. by E. J. Czerwinski, J. Piekalkiewicz (New York: Praeger, 1972), 191–210; and my own "Václav Havel and the Language of the Absurd," *Slavic and East European Journal*, XIII (Spring 1965), 42–65, from which substantial portions of this article are derived.

3. Eugène Ionesco. *Amédée, The New Tenant, Victims of Duty,* trans. Donald Watson (New York: Grove, 1958), 158.

4. Jean Vannier, "Langage de l'avant-garde" ["Language of the Avant-garde"] *Théâtre populaire*, XVIII (May 1956): 30–39.

5. Havel, *Protokoly* (Prague: Mladá fronta, 1966), 21. Citations in the text are to this edition by page; all translations of his work are mine.

6. Friedrich Engels, *Dialectics of Nature* (New York: International Publishers, 1940), 13.

9. *Audience* in Jelenia Gòra, Poland, 1998.

10. *Unveiling* in Jelenia Gòra, Poland, 1998.

Havel's *The Memorandum* and the Despotism of Technology

PHYLLIS CAREY

{*Like Wittgenstein or the French existentialists, Havel derides man's obsession with thinking in categories which prevents him from facing ultimate realities and therefore also tending to undermine his ethical self-awareness.*

—*Paul I. Trensky*}

We are looking for new scientific recipes, new ideologies, new control systems, new institutions, new instruments to eliminate the dreadful consequences of our previous recipes, ideologies, control systems, institutions, and instruments. We treat the fatal consequences of technology as though they were a technical defect that could be remedied by technology alone.

—Václav Havel, "World Economic Forum"

In contrasting the drama of Václav Havel and Samuel Beckett, a major influence on Havel,[1] critics are sometimes prone to describe the plays of the former as political and those of the latter as metaphysical. Andrzej Wirth, for example, comments: "In Beckett, the *incommunicado* of the *dramatis personae* is motivated metaphysically. They cannot communicate, because the inability to communicate belongs to their nature as human beings. In Havel's plays, and in most of Eastern European dramaturgy, the *incommunicado* is determined politically . . . the institutionalization of language in closed systems."[2] Mardi Valgemae offers a similar conclusion: "The dramatic worlds of Beckett and Ionesco are microcosms, while the dramatic worlds of Mrožek—and we should add, Havel—are microsocieties."[3]

Such contrasts may be misleading. Beckett's plays have implicit political import as evidenced by their immense popularity in Communist Czechoslovakia, during the political thaw of the 1960s.[4] Beckett's drama portrayed states

This essay was written specifically for this volume and is published for the first time by permission of the author.

of paralysis, futility, and alienation that the Czechoslovaks understood well—both metaphysically and politically. In other words, they recognized these states as realistically present in their societies, but they also grasped their impact as reflecting a lack of spiritual values. As a result of the deep reso-nances with Beckett's drama, from the 1960s on it was impossible, as even a Marxist critic noted, "[to erase] the phenomenon Beckett from our cultural subconscious."[5] In short, Beckett's drama often has political as well as meta-physical relevance in ways that may have been unintentional but which are implicit in the works themselves and which may reflect in some way the social context of an audience.[6]

Analogously, in Havel's plays the "institutionalization of language in closed systems" was and is relevant not only to those in politically totalitarian regimes but also to those in an increasingly technocratic global society. As early as 1984, Havel stressed in one of his philosophical essays that the kind of pervasive domination that characterized Communist control in Czechoslo-vakia was symptomatic of a crisis that threatens all of Western civilization: "I think that, with respect to the relation of Western Europe to the totalitarian systems, no error could be greater than the one looming largest: that of a fail-ure to understand the totalitarian systems for what they ultimately are—a convex mirror of all modern civilization and a harsh, perhaps final call for a global recasting of that civilization's self-understanding."[7] Tracing the source of modern political totalitarianism in its various forms to a scientific material-ism underlying both capitalism and Communism, Havel has consistently attempted to awaken readers and audiences to the subtle, pervasive, and dehumanizing conditioning that accompanies our increasingly technological existence. Such conditioning includes an impersonal objectifying of reality; the reduction of humans to consumers; the measuring of the real exclusively in quantifiable terms; a focus on means as ends in themselves; efficiency and productivity as unquestioned but absolute values; the exploitation of nature and other humans in the name of progress; a standardizing and normalizing of consumers under the guise of a variety of choices; intrusive informational gathering for the sake of data and/or manipulation; and the reliance on tech-nological solutions for the problems caused by the wholesale reliance on the technological. If Havel's drama reflects the political realities of Communist Czechoslovakia, and it does, it also reflects, especially for Western audiences, the succumbing of the individual and society to a world view that increas-ingly disregards human responsibility, a world view that "is a monstrosity which is not guided by humans but which, on the contrary, drags all persons along with its 'objective' self-momentum—objective in the sense of being cut off from all human standards, including human reason and hence entirely irrational—to a terrifying, unknown future" (*Living in Truth,* 147). In other words, it is in some ways a self-imposed totalitarianism of mechanization—physically, psychologically, spiritually.

The Memorandum, Havel's best-known play (it won an Obie Award in 1968 for best foreign play), offers a lens for contemporary global audiences to glimpse the subtle pressures and self-betrayals permeating the human-made systems that have come to circumscribe modern reality. Through its intricate language patterns, the play comically depicts the human collusion in its own enslavement to an impersonal mechanism.

Although its convolutions are complex, the plot itself is simple: Ptydepe, a new language based on scientific principles, is introduced into a large, undefined bureaucratic system headed by one Josef Gross, managing director. Gross, a self-proclaimed humanist, receives a memo written in the new language but is unable to translate it. His efforts to have the memo translated result in a cul-de-sac of bureaucratic protocol. Gross comes to the circular conclusion that "any staff member who has recently received a memorandum in Ptydepe can only be granted a translation of a Ptydepe text after his memorandum has been translated. . . . In other words, the only way to learn what is in one's memo is to know it already."[8] Gross eventually recants his opposition to the language and is demoted to the bottom position of the organization, staff watcher of the other employees. A sympathetic secretary, Maria, translates the memo for him; ironically the memo contains a denouncement of Ptydepe. Gross's replacement, Ballas, former deputy who has orchestrated the implementation of Ptydepe, soon discovers widespread opposition to the language, appoints Gross his deputy and then reinstates him as managing director as he (Ballas) introduces a new synthetic language, Chorukor, at the end of the play. In the meantime, Maria has lost her job for having translated the memo. Through a series of betrayals the play essentially comes full circle with the implication that the vicious cycle, and all its subsidiary vicious cycles, will continue.

The anonymity of the organization at issue and the almost ritualistic behavior of the characters focus attention on processes seemingly devoid of purpose. Helena is a chairman, but she does not know what she is in charge of. The secretaries spend their time going for milk, chocolate, limes, and so on; making coffee; or ironing clothes. Their mechanized routines, like those of their superiors, seem unrelated to any corporate purpose. What is being served for lunch, sexual adventures, and smoking cigars—the small pleasures of life—are recurring topics of conversation, but even these remarks seem to be part of an automatic process. All efforts seem to go into playing the roles that keep the pointless interaction functioning.

The artificial language of Ptydepe foregrounds a focus on methods that have become ends in themselves. Ptydepe, echoing the bureaucratic labels of *Recdep, Teledep,* and *Ficdep* of Orwell's *1984,*[9] is, according to Lear, the instructor of the new language, "built according to an entirely logical principle: the more common the meaning, the shorter the word." "Wombat," accordingly, has 319 letters; "whatever" has only two because it is "the most commonly used term so far known" (*Memorandum*, 17). The fact that "whatever" is almost always a totally ambiguous word is irrelevant to a process that considers words from a quantifiable perspective: amount and efficiency of use determine word length. The process is logical when language is viewed from an exclusively mathematical perspective, but as the play comically illustrates, language in these terms alone reflects the absurdity of a logic cut off from common sense. At the end of the play, Ptydepe is replaced because of its technical flaw, "its uncritical overestimation of the significance of redundancy," resulting in one instance where a brief memo filled 36 single-spaced pages (*Memorandum*, 81).

Perhaps the best—and most hilarious—example of the attempt at controlling language through the application of pseudo-reason and false logic concerns the use of interjections, "the easiest part of Ptydepe," according to Lear (*Memorandum*, 40). Words that might express spontaneous human emotion are subjected to such scientific scrutiny that it would take a computerized memory for one to ever use them according to the linguistic rules. The scientific analysis applied to them differentiates between how and when they are used, resulting in many variants of the simple natural word. "Boo," for example, has six variants depending on the status and the intentions of the employee using it; "hurrah" is a phrase of nine Ptydepe words. Despite the fact that interjections are seen to have derived from the "inarticulate shrieks . . . [of a] primitive creature" (*Memorandum*, 37)—or perhaps because of that assessment—they seem to require the greatest scrutiny in a system where control has become an end in itself, where what is being communicated is less important than how it is to be communicated. In the Ptydepe approach to interjections, the play comically undercuts the creation of immensely complex processes that have no purpose but to propagate more processes. Were Ptydepe to succeed as the official bureaucratic language, few would have the expertise to utter interjections, and those few who persevered to master the designated words would be so much a part of the system that they would most likely lack the spontaneity to ever use such utterances. Moreover, the utterances themselves are far from natural or spontaneous. Technological manipulation of language—currently exemplified in many specialized technical vocabularies—deals with the purely artificial. By its very nature (an ironic phrase in this context), such manipulation of language excludes the natural or transforms it into the artificial.

While the plot of *The Memorandum* twists around the rise and fall of the new language, the body language of the characters actually carries the (equally meaningless) action and humorously highlights the absurdity of attempting to restrict human communication to the mathematical and the logical. Early on Helena, the chairperson, sneaks up on Gross, mistaking him for another character, gestures to Maria to keep silent, and puts her own hands over his eyes, disguising her voice as that of a male. Mistaken identity, the third party as observer, the gender disguise, the ambiguous current status

of the participants of this example of "boo"—all of the nuances of a spontaneous action escape Lear's meticulous analysis of the precision necessary in
uttering interjections in Ptydepe. The concrete example of "boo" farcically
deflates the ostensibly sophisticated linguistic theory, suggesting that its primary function is its underlying mechanism of controlling both human speech
and behavior.

That Ptydepe is a metaphor for attempts to circumscribe human action
and for the abdication of the human to the systems he/she serves becomes
increasingly clear as the play progresses. The most striking example of both
tendencies can be found in Gross's treatment of Maria, the secretary, who,
after translating the Ptydepe memo rather than succumbing to the dead-end
process of getting the proper authorization, is fired from her job. Gross ratio-
nalizes his unwillingness to help Maria get her job back:

> Like Sisyphus, we roll the boulder of our life up the hill of its illusory meaning,
> only for it to roll down again into the valley of its own absurdity. Never before
> has Man lived projected so near to the very brink of the insoluble conflict
> between the subjective will of his moral self and the objective possibility of its
> ethical realization. Manipulated, automatized, made into a fetish, Man loses
> the experience of his own totality; horrified, he stares as a stranger at himself,
> unable not to be what he is not, nor to be what he is. . . . in reality I can do
> next to nothing for you, because I am in fact totally alienated from myself: the
> desire to help you fatefully encounters within me the responsibility thrust upon
> me—who am attempting to salvage the last remains of Man's humanity—
> . . . . a responsibility so binding that I absolutely may not risk the loss of the
> position on which it is based by any open conflict with Mr. Ballas and his men.
> (*Memorandum*, 86–87).

In its dichotomy between word and action, between theory and practice,
between philosophy and life, Gross's self-defense reveals how much he has
become part of the system. Faced with a concrete situation where he could act
humanely, Gross uses existentialist theory to rationalize inaction. On one
level, at least, his words are true; he is manipulated, automatized, totally
alienated from himself. Earlier he had indicted himself and had grovelingly
accepted the position of staff watcher. Immediately after Maria translated the
memo, however, he stated, "Now at last I have an opportunity to prove that I
have more civil courage than I've shown so far. I promise you that this time I
shall not give way to anything or anybody, even at the risk of my position"
(*Memorandum*, 70). As is soon apparent, however, Gross has no civil courage
to assert because he has surrendered his personal identity as a human being.
The play suggests that individual human integrity and the health of society
are inextricably linked.

Echoing Camus and Hamlet, Gross uses language as an abstract analysis
of the plight of modern humanity and an excuse for his own cowardly behavior. He talks about "salvaging the remains," presumably unaware that his

compromises have nullified the principles he asserts, that his philosophy is as remote from his reality as Ptydepe is remote from the conditions of actual life. What is clear is that Gross's identity—like that of the other characters—consists of being a functionary of the bureaucracy. Because Maria responds to Gross as a human and thus oversteps her role as a functionary, she has to be eliminated from the organization. Gross's recanting and his gratitude for being kept in the organization as staff watcher, on the other hand, reveal his total dependency on the system for his identity—even for identity as a would-be dissident; and that dependence in effect effaces his identity as an individual human. Even though he is managing director of the organization, Gross fears upsetting Ballas, the quintessential cog, by overturning Ballas's decision to fire Maria. Instead, Gross says good-bye, encouraging Maria not to "lose your hope, your love of life and your trust in people!" Like Ptydepe, which ignores the concrete acts of communicating in all their complexities, Gross's humanism is simply rhetoric, cut off from the here and now. The seductive thrall of that rhetoric, moreover, appeals even to Maria, who ignores Gross's betrayal of her with the phrase: "Nobody ever talked to me so nicely before." The worship of technique seems to blind even the one character who momentarily transcended the mechanism.

The ease with which humans create systems that end up controlling them is exemplified in the position of the "staff watcher." The staff watcher originated, according to chairperson Helena, who takes full credit for the idea, as a kindness to visitors so that they wouldn't have to hang out in the halls and would be more comfortable waiting in offices with classified data even if none of the staff was present (*Memorandum,* 28). Although the staff watcher was originally conceived as the person on staff who watched for the security of top-secret materials, the position has (logically) evolved into an actual watching of the staff. Replicating comically Orwell's "Big Brother," the staff watcher's main function has become that of official informer, the panopticon that reports betrayals of the system, for example, Gross's taking home a rubber stamp and Maria's translation of Gross's memo. As the play suggests, consumer ease and promises of greater efficiency become a thinly veiled disguise for increasing surveillance and control; the worship of data and its security, the acceptance of efficiency as an unquestioned end in itself, and the fascination with improving methods regardless of ends increasingly seduce humans into surrendering their privacy, their rights, their dignity as human beings.

The interchangeable roles of staff watcher, managing director, and so forth suggest that all are functions of the larger system; which human happens to be fulfilling which function is unimportant. Ballas is a master at watching and manipulating; when it looks as though he may need to assume responsibility for introducing Ptydepe, he accuses Pillar, his sexual partner, in words that describe well Ballas's own role. Ballas says that he himself has "been under {Pillar's} direct surveillance . . . [Pillar] pried into every nook and cranny, was always present, always subtly disguised in the cloak of incon-spicuousness" (*Memorandum,* 78). In parallel fashion to the staff watcher, the characters watch one another, Ballas being the chief watcher and manipula-tor. Helena's seemingly innocent game of blindman's bluff becomes a parody of various kinds of visual dominance and blindsiding that occur in the play. The members of the bureaucracy replicate and reenforce the standardizing surveillance of the system.

While the role of staff watcher is repeated with variations in Ballas and Pillar particularly, repetition in the language and the action create the effect of a self-contained mechanism. Like *Antikódy,* the typographical concrete poems Havel wrote in the early 1960s, the play is almost mathematical in its precision of repetition. The twelve scenes, with the intermission halfway, fol-low a pattern of ABC. Gross's decline in the first half of the play is paralleled by the illusion of Ballas's decline in the second half, although in both cases Ballas's repeated acts of blackmail (*Memorandum,* 33, 75) keep him consis-tently in position as chief manipulator; though the play seems to end where it begins, the repetition has revealed a subtle symbiosis in the main characters: Gross needs Ballas to provide the illusion that Gross is more human; Ballas needs Gross to manipulate. As complementary functionaries, their codepen-dency fuels the rhetoric of humanism versus expediency, a dialogue divorced from action that actually contributes to keeping the mechanism going.

Havel, like Beckett, also uses repetition as a contrapuntal device, reduc-ing language to its sounds and highlighting its mechanical patterns. Midway through the play, Gross asks Helena a series of three questions about translat-ing his memo, repeating each of them at intervals. In the meantime the staff is discussing cigars, coffee, and goose, paying no attention to the managing director's request; when Gross discovers the circular reasoning that makes his memo untranslatable, the three staff members are engaging in an inter-change in Ptydepe, repeating the same words in groups of three. Like a Greek chorus in Babel, the staff's utterly incomprehensible commentary underscores both the circularity and the meaninglessness of the entire process.

In a parallel scene toward the end of the play, the staff members again play the role of chorus, this time reading a protest in unison, calling for an end of Ptydepe and demanding that those responsible be punished. While the traditional Greek chorus frequently drew attention to the universality of a play's implications, Ballas ironically suggests to the staff that all of the work-ers are responsible, but the disjunction between human identity and function is highlighted when the staff demands to know "the actual persons! . . . The names." Ballas, ever the smooth engineer, shifts gears and provides the appar-ently necessary scapegoat—his sexual partner, Pillar, who is immediately replaced to the general relief of the staff by Column, Pillar's structural—and perhaps sexual—counterpart. The mechanism of protest, demand for punish-ment, scapegoating, and a return to the status quo is repeated with variations throughout the play, with various characters—Gross, Maria, and even Ballas—assuming the role of scapegoat. While the process might replicate the mechanism of historical reforms enacted in the post-Stalin period in Communist Czechoslovakia,[10] similar processes can be recognized in corporations and institutions. In contrast to Greek tragedy, where the human takes center stage, the system dominates in *The Memorandum,* the central conflict being the extent to which and the adeptness by which humans adapt to the processes that would control them.

Jeanette Malkin has suggested that "language is the 'hero' and the conqueror" of *The Memorandum.*[11] At best an ironic and absurd "hero" and "conqueror," language seen from the perspective of this play has become an instrument of the system, effectively excluding the human. Like the characters, who are variations on the theme of betrayal, different kinds of discourse in the natural language play various roles, revealing their adaptability to various kinds of systems. Besides the rhetoric of existentialism that fleetingly provides Gross with his illusory identity, the pedantic rhetoric of Lear adapts itself to both Ptydepe and Chorukor, the new artificial language introduced at the end of the play. The most adept at changing discourse—the master technician—is Ballas, the unprincipled chameleon, who alters his rhetoric to suit the occasion. He uses Marxist rhetoric when pushing for the adoption of Ptydepe, for example, "We cannot ignore the stand of the masses. . . . The patience of the masses is great, but it is not infinite" (*Memorandum,* 12–13). When the staff presents its protest, Ballas becomes the master politician, turning his own self-indictment, in contrast to Gross's earlier recanting, into a pseudoreligious, communal guilt from which he subtly distances himself and casts himself as potential savior:

> We meant well, but we did wrong. In short we sinned and now we must accept, courageously and without any feeling of being sinned against, the full consequences of our activities. . . . I have taken certain first steps, . . . specifically aimed toward a bold solution of the very problem which you have now come here to point out to me. . . . And now let me give the platform to Mr. Gross. (*Memorandum,* 77)

For Ballas, adjusting language to fit the occasion for purposes of self-interest is the dominant force; he is a master at doublethink: "the power of holding two contradictory beliefs in one's mind simultaneously, and accepting both of them" (Orwell, 176). When Gross asks him how he can support Ptydepe and yet speak against it, Ballas responds, "Matter of tactics" (*Memorandum,* 11). Ballas consistently exploits the language system for his own ends, no more clearly demonstrated than when he convinces Gross that synthetic languages are actually more humanistic than natural languages. After pointing out the emotional overtones attached to words in the natural language, Ballas asserts,

> It is a paradox, but it is precisely the surface inhumanity of an artificial language which guarantees its truly humanist function! After Ptydepe comes into use, no one will ever again have the impression that he's being injured when in fact he's being helped, and thus everybody will be much happier. (*Memorandum,* 34)

Paradox, to be sure, permeates *The Memorandum*. Ballas's use of language and his actions throughout the play suggest a fundamental paradox: the more humans exalt their own rationality and perfect their technological systems, the more irrational and savage they may become in the process. The "funeral-like procession" of the workers "clutching their knives and forks" at the end of the play symbolically suggests the equation of the human with tools, the death of the human through total subjection to the system. Throughout the play, the characters are concerned about their eating instruments and carry their fire extinguishers with them. The staff watcher lives in a chink of the wall and must crawl out of it backwards on all fours like Willie in Beckett's *Happy Days*. Rather than the highly efficient, sophisticated system it portends to be, as J. V. Clardy notes, the bureaucratic world of *The Memorandum* at times suggests "a pre-cage age."[12]

Although contemporary humans tend to believe that we are far more civilized than our ancestors, the echoes in *The Memorandum* of a presumably bestial period in human existence suggest a savagery underlying our sophisticated, rational know-how, a bestiality not easily recognized because of the assumed superiority of our technological world view. That a technological world view tends to become despotic and normative is evidenced by the fact that the more humans depend on artificial systems, the more they regard the flaws in the systems—or their sometimes disastrous effects—as technical problems that can be remedied by better techniques. In *The Memorandum* the introduction of a new synthetic language, Chorukor, is the solution for the problems created by Ptydepe.[13]

The world of *The Memorandum* is a closed system in a deadly present that promises to continue into the future with only slight variations. The references to existentialism suggest a consciousness of alienation that is already passé, a nostalgic remembrance of a time that seems never to have existed in the increasing adaptation of humans to the processes that use them. Like "the old style" in *Happy Days* and "Oldspeak" in *1984,* the past is irretrievably cut off from the present. In Heideggerian terms, the characters in *The Memorandum* have forgotten that they have forgotten. Although Winnie in *Happy Days* thinks a part of her classics remain, and Gross believes he "salvage[s] this and that" (*Memorandum,* 35), what remains is the seemingly inexhaustible human ability to adapt, individually and communally, to dehumanizing forces.

Contemporary audiences in Western societies can readily relate to the bureaucratic world of *The Memorandum*. The mechanized routines, abrupt and unexplained changes in policy, attempts to make communication more efficient, processes and procedures that make the simplest of tasks enormously complex, office politics, letting people go—all are day-to-day experiences in most of our lives and institutions. While *The Memorandum* reveals the comic absurdity of the systems we create, it also highlights as part of that absurdity the sometimes subtle but often pervasive betrayal of the human in these systems.

We do not tend to think of the technological systematizing that pervades our institutions and our lives in terms of despotism; in fact we are generally far more conscious of the undisputed advances technology offers. And yet *The Memorandum* forces us to examine the depersonalizing and dehumanizing elements that tend to accompany business as usual as the technological holds sway over more and more aspects of human existence. In presenting the effects on the human of a totalized system, the play evokes a hunger for a genuine human response to the other, a responsibility that would begin to transform the system or at least mitigate its effects.

For Havel, the political is inextricably linked with the metaphysical. The brutal forms of political totalitarianism that have characterized our century find some common roots in the dominant worldview that has shaped the modern age in Western civilization. For Havel, theater operates at the crossroads of concrete experience and the worldviews that make those experiences meaningful or absurd. Theater can awaken audiences; it can stir the human spirit. If Gross is incapable of "salvaging the remains" of his human identity, audiences are left with that challenge.

Some 30-odd years after he wrote *The Memorandum,* Havel formulated in a speech at "International Theater Day" his thoughts about the theater as a powerful protest against an often invisible and scarcely recognized form of despotism that many would assert is simply the "real world":

> In today's dehumanizing technological civilization, theater is one of the important islands of human authenticity; that is, it is precisely what—if this world is not to end up badly—must be protected and cultivated. After all, the return of irreplaceable human subjectivity, of the particular human personality and its particular human conscience, is precisely what this world of megamachinery and anonymous megabureaucracy needs. Only man is capable of confronting all the dangers that face the world, confronting them with his renewed responsibility, his awareness of connections—in other words, precisely with something within him that not even the best network of modern computers can replace. The hope of the world lies in the rehabilitation of the living human being.[14]

Notes and References

1. See, for example, Havel's tribute to Beckett in "Václav Havel on Beckett," *The Beckett Circle* 12 (fall 1990): 4. In *Letters to Olga,* Havel notes that when he discovered Beckett

and Ionesco, "I was tremendously excited, inspired and drawn to them, or rather I found them extremely close to my own temperament and sensibility, and it was they who stimulated me to try to communicate everything I wanted to say through drama." See Václav Havel, *Letters to Olga: June 1979–September 1982,* trans. Paul Wilson (New York: Alfred A. Knopf, 1988), 14 November 1981, 248.

      Beckett dedicated his play *Catastrophe* (1982) to Havel when Havel was in prison; Havel wrote *Mistake* (1983) as a response to Beckett's play (see *Index on Censorship* 13, no. 1 [February 1984]: 11–14).

    2.   Andrzej Wirth, "Dramaturgy of Models," *Theatre Byways: Essays in Honor of Claude L. Shaver,* ed. C. J. Stevens and Joseph Aurbach (New Orleans: Polyanthos, 1978), 98–99.

    3.   Mardi Valgemae, "Socialist Allegory of the Absurd: An Examination of Four East European Plays," *Comparative Drama* 5 (1971): 48.

    4.   According to Marketa Goetz-Stankiewicz, "the freer the country became from the political pressures of systematized thinking, the more they liked Beckett." See "A Revealing Encounter: The Theatre of the Absurd in Czechoslovakia" *Survey,* 21, no. 1/2 (94–95) (winter-spring 1975): 89.

    5.   Petr Pujman, quoted in Goetz-Stankiewicz, 89–90.

    6.   The significance of *Waiting for Godot,* for example, to the prisoners of San Quentin in the 1950s and the people of Sarajevo in the 1990s is well documented. In Communist Czechoslovakia, Godot became, among other things, a symbol of a spurious hope based on political salvation from the outside. See, for example, Josef Sládeček (pseudonym), "Nečekání na Godota" ["Not Waiting for Godot"] *Svědectví {Testimony}* 14, no. 54 (1977), quoted in H. Gordon Skilling, *Charter 77 and Human Rights in Czechoslovakia* (London: George Allen and Unwin, 1981), 14; and Havel's use of Godot for political messages in his speech at the Academy of Humanities and Political Sciences (Paris, October 27, 1992), *The Art of the Impossible: Politics as Morality in Practice,* trans. Paul Wilson and others (New York: Alfred A. Knopf, 1997), 103–108.

    7.   Václav Havel, "Politics and Conscience," *Living in Truth,* ed. Jan Vladislav (London: Faber and Faber, 1987), 145; hereafter cited in text as *Living in Truth.*

    8.   Václav Havel, *The Memorandum,* trans. Vera Blackwell (New York: Grove Weidenfeld, 1980), 47; hereafter cited in text as *Memorandum.*

    9.   George Orwell, *1984* (New York: Penguin Books, 1977), 252; hereafter cited in text as Orwell.

    10.   See Paul I. Trensky, "Václav Havel and the Language of the Absurd," *Slavic and East European Journal* 13, no. 1 (1969): 64–65.

    11.   Jeanette R. Malkin, *Verbal Violence in Contemporary Drama* (Cambridge: Cambridge University Press, 1992), 91.

    12.   J. V. Clardy, "Václav Havel's *The Memorandum:* A Study in the Terror of the Czechoslovak Bureaucratic World," *Cimarron Review* 6, no. 7 (1968): 54.

    13.   On a global scale, Havel sees the fall of Communism and the collapse of colonial dominions as evidence of the demise of artificial world orders, but he fears that the new world order will be yet another attempt to solve the problems of the world technologically. See, for example, Václav Havel, "The Philadelphia Liberty Medal," *The Art of the Impossible,* 168–69.

    14.   Václav Havel, "International Theater Day," *The Art of the Impossible,* 163.

Spectacular Pretending:
Havel's *The Beggar's Opera*

PETER STEINER

{*Havel may very well emerge as a kind of prototype of the generative self: creator of signs, pseudonyms, self-interpretations and public meditations.*

—*Michael L. Quinn*}

[Gay's] *Comedy* contains likewise a *Satyre,* which, although it doth by no means affect the present Age, yet might have been useful in the former and may possibly be so in Ages to come. I mean where the Author takes occasion of comparing those *common Robbers to Robbers of the Publick;* and their several Stratagems of betraying, undermining, and hanging each other, to the several Arts of *Politicians* in times of Corruption.

—Jonathan Swift, *Intelligencer* 3

For anybody interested in the social ramifications of literature, John Gay's *The Beggar's Opera* and its numerous adaptations provide an optimal topic of research. Throughout its more than 250-year history this work has negotiated the gulf between the subversive and the sublime, between politics and poetics. From its London première on 29 January 1728, to Bertold Brecht's adaptation produced in Berlin as *Dreigroschenoper* just 200 years later, this play always managed to stir a considerable scandal—as if time could not exhaust the satirical potential of Gay's text that Swift sensed so clairvoyantly.

The next twist in the long history of adaptations of *The Beggar's Opera* to different political contexts, however, was quite unusual in more than one respect. It occurred in a godforsaken Prague suburb, a village called Horní Počernice, on 1 November 1975. That Saturday evening, in the local house of culture, an amateur group staged the première of Václav Havel's version of Gay's play. The invited audience numbered about 300 people, and, judged by Western standards, this was definitely a small potato: a nonprofessional pro-

This is an abbreviated version of a paper delivered at the 10th International Congress of Slavists in Sofia in September, 1988.

duction on the periphery of Prague without advertisement, program, or even reviews in the papers the next day. For Kafka's hometown, however, this was the event of the year: a public performance of a play by a well-known author who, because of his nonconformist stance after the Soviet invasion of 1968, had been banned from the Czechoslovak stage. The question most likely occupying the minds of those who attended the première was whether the permission to produce *The Beggar's Opera* should be attributed to the ignorance and fallibility of the local authorities, or whether the Czechoslovak government, spellbound by the Helsinki Agreement, had benevolently decided to overlook an action with so limited a political fallout.

This charade was further complicated by the fact that Havel's adaptation of *The Beggar's Opera* (in contrast to Brecht's play, which shifted the action to Victorian London) was not modernized and deliberately refrained from any direct reference to Czechoslovak reality. As Havel insisted, "in the text of my play there is nothing that directed against our state, its social order, or public morality."[1] Thus, 10 days after the première, a reporter for the West German weekly *Der Spiegel* who had scooped the story could write: "It is certain that the secret police were also present [at the première]; but, despite general expectations, neither the actors, author, nor viewers have up to now been interrogated. The police censors," he predicted slyly, "will have to study the text of this new piece especially closely to find a legal handle on Havel."[2]

Unfortunately the German reporter, the product of a liberal bourgeois society, was proceeding from hermeneutic assumptions that do not obtain in a one-party state. No textual evidence was necessary in post-1968 Czechoslovakia to deal with a "difficult" writer and, moreover, the police were not particularly good at providing it. Mr. Bolotka, a character from Philip Roth's *Prague Orgy,* is close to the truth when he tells Zuckerman that in Czechoslovakia, "the police are like literary critics—of what little they see, they get most wrong anyway."[3] This is not to cast aspersions against the intelligence quotient of the Czechoslovak security establishment, though it must be said that the local population frequently did so.[4] Rather, a political reading is a particular type of "misprision," to use Harold Bloom's celebrated term. It can be best characterized as the polar opposite of the "close reading" propounded by the New Critics. A political reading is a maximally open reading because it always interprets the text according to the contingencies of a particular social context. As a working hypothesis, one might claim that the more political a reading is, the less it respects such structural properties of the text as grammar, narrativity, or logic, and the more it relies on the vicissitudes of the concrete situation. Given the heterogeneity and fluidity of a situation, it is obvious that not even the police can account for all the ramifications a political reading might have.

The impetus toward open interpretation is especially strong in drama, for among all the literary genres it is the most context-bound. As a compo-

186 of a theatrical performance

nent of a theatrical performance, according to Havel's theoretical essay of 1968, "The Peculiarities of Theater," drama is political in its very essence. "Theater," Havel writes, "[is] an art predestined by its nature to be a concentrated expression of its time because of the *collective nature* of its reception . . . [it functions] as a specific organism incorporated into the social milieu and bound to it in an osmotic process. [It is thus] always hypersensitive to the political and social problems of its time."[5] In moments of political crisis, like that which occurred in Czechoslovakia after the Soviet invasion of 1968, the interaction between theater and society becomes especially palpable.

Since political context is so important to theater, let me briefly describe the situation in Czechoslovakia after Dubček's downfall. The most pressing objective of the new Party leadership was to "normalize" Czechoslovakia, that is, to mold it according to the political model of the Soviet Union. The chief sin attributed to Dubček was his abnegating of power to the people. This claim constitutes the first point of a document approved at the plenary session of the Central Committee of the Czechoslovak Communist Party (CCP) in December of 1970, which became the ideological cornerstone of normalization. "*In 1968 the CCP gradually ceased to be the directive center of the socialist order.* Under the sludge of revisionism it lost the character of a Marxist-Leninist Party, and this loss prevented it from exercising its leadership role in society. By negating the principles of democratic centralism, the Party has gradually lost the capacity for action."[6] To regain this precious capability, the first step of Husák's leadership was to disenfranchise most of the native population, concentrating power in the hands of a tiny number of trusted cadres, the so-called "healthy kernel" of the CCP.

This return to "normalcy" affected the relationship between theater and politics in two complementary ways. If Prague Spring had transformed Czechoslovak citizens from passive objects to active subjects in political life, the opposite occurred in 1969. By eliminating from the decision-making process any trace of popular participation, the Communist leaders transformed the people into the audience of a spectacle. Politics became theater. It is precisely this theatrical metaphor that Milan Šimečka, the most astute observer of the "normalization process," uses to open his pamphlet, *The Restoration of Order*. In 1968 he wrote,

> people suddenly began to perceive politicians . . . as human beings instead of cardboard cut-outs always spouting the same old platitudes. All of a sudden, people could see them cry. Fatigue, moral dilemmas and human weakness were there on their faces for all to see (thanks, of course, to television). Almost in a single moment public life came into existence and many people, for the first time in their lives, began to view politics as the work of human beings instead of a tedious, infinitely boring, inaccessible and anonymous annoyance coming from somewhere on high. Even the first phase of the restoration of order took place on the fully lit stage. People remembered the actors and knew their roles

all too well. Therefore it was with a certain eagerness that they watched how they would act in a completely new play with a completely new director. I think I can state without exaggeration that for the people here the post-1970 events certainly did not appear as an abstract process of "strengthening the leading role of the Party, removing the right-wing elements, purging Czechoslovak culture, deepening cooperation between socialist states," but rather as a historical drama with live characters. It was a play about betrayal, love and hate, about sacrifice and deception, greatness and baseness, revenge and forgiveness, cowardice and heroism, a drama of courage and cunning, decline and fall, about money, envy, and in fact everything that is splendidly human. I do not wish to conceal the fact that I myself viewed the historical events primarily in that manner, and only in that fashion did they fascinate me.[7]

The second effect that Czechoslovak normalization exerted on the social function of theater is a direct result of that just mentioned. If the elimination of the citizenry from the decision-making process rendered politics theater, by the same token theater turned political. This is not to say that by some mistake Party watchdogs failed to censor what was performed on the Czechoslovak stage. Rather, their efforts were frustrated by an unpredictable human factor—the spontaneous reactions of theatergoers. To provide just one example, there is a famous aria in Smetana's *Bartered Bride* in which the singer urges other characters to tear up a "certain agreement." Whenever this aria was sung in the composer's homeland after August 1968, the audience always burst into frenetic applause. The source of their delight was obvious to everyone. For the viewers the words did not refer to the marriage so crucial to the plot of the opera's libretto but to what was on their minds at the moment: the Czechoslovak-Soviet agreement of 1968, which stipulated the "temporary" stationing of the Red Army on Czechoslovak territory. Through this contextualized "misreading," the viewers as a collectivity exercised a right denied to them outside the theater: to publicly voice their attitude toward the puppet government that, in collusion with a foreign power, had usurped control over their lands.

This hermeneutic strategy of Czechoslovak theatergoers, of course, enraged local authorities who, after the scandalous première of Brecht's *Mother Courage* at the Prague National Theater in October 1970, issued a series of directives to correct such unseemly behavior.[8] But at the same time, these liberties with the text perplexed foreign visitors, totally unprepared for such blatant contextualization of theatrical classics. Vivid testimony to this effect is a story told by a Shakespearean actor, Ian McKellen, who in 1969 traveled around Europe with a production of *Richard II*. "The costumes," he says,

were of the actual period of Richard II but the scenery was minimal because it was a touring production. On the whole we concentrated on the humanity of the characters rather than their political nature. We thought of the political factions as a family, Richard II as a man with cousins and uncles and other relatives, and I think it was in that sense that we looked at the politics in it.

However, the Prague performance turned Shakespeare into something completely unexpected.

> When I came to the speech where Richard II returns from Ireland to discover that his nation has been overrun by his cousin Bolingbroke, and he kneels down on the earth and asks the stones and the nettles and the insects to help him in his helpless state against the armies who had invaded his land, I could hear something I had never heard before, nor since, which was a whole audience apparently weeping. It shakes me now to think about it, because in that instant I realized that the audience were crying for themselves. They recognized in Richard II their own predicament of only six months previously when their neighbors and as it were their cousins had invaded their land and all they had were sticks and stones to throw at the tanks.[9]

As my short digression into the curious symbiosis between theater and politics in normalized Czechoslovakia indicates, a lack of direct textual clues is not an obstacle for an audience to perceive a text as referring to their present predicament. Needless to say, a play that compares "several Stratagems of betraying, undermining, and hanging each other, to the several Arts of *Politicians* in times of Corruption" was a perfect vehicle for antigovernment sentiment in post-1968 Czechoslovakia. And given the vast power that the authorities wielded in a country with many Czechs but no balances, it is also obvious that anybody even vaguely suspected of impugning the honor of the socialist government could be dealt with quickly. What, then, was the reason for the momentary hesitation witnessed by the reporter from *Der Spiegel?* In my opinion, Havel's *The Beggar's Opera* put Party ideologues into an embarrassing double bind. If they had punished the instigators of the "travesty," they would have affirmed de facto an unflattering similarity between *Dichtung und Wahrheit* as suggested by the play. If, on the other hand, they had done nothing, the public would have taken their inaction as a sign of weakness, since no Czechoslovak would miss such an opportunity to draw an unfavorable analogy.

Caught between the two equally unpalatable options, the authorities reacted to the challenge of Havel's *The Beggar's Opera* in a fashion that might best be characterized as schizophrenic. On the covert, unofficial plane the authorities employed the time-honored device of turning the victims into villains. Havel and his cohorts, according to rumors emanating from high places, had tainted the political climate and were the direct cause of further tightening of censorship. They had victimized the citizenry.[10] On the overt level, the Party ordered the most prominent participants in Havel's première (whether actors or viewers) to be fired from their jobs, but they instructed employers that the Počernice affair must not be mentioned as the cause of dismissal. Since Havel, as a self-employed writer, appeared immune to this measure, the police, for the sake of justice, revoked his driver's license.[11] By acting in this contradictory way, however, the authorities unwittingly affirmed the deep-seated political message of Havel's play. For *The Beggar's Opera,* without doubt, is a representation of *collective schizophrenia.*

This quasi-medical term has been used in many different ways, and so I would like to explain my understanding of it. Following Gregory Bateson, I see schizophrenia as a particular communication disorder. Human intercourse tends to combine messages of different logical types. To carry out meaningful exchange, participants must be able to distinguish between serious statements and jokes, literal and figurative statements, statements about objects and statements about statements. But a schizophrenic is hopelessly lost in this game. He or she is incapable of logical typing, that is, of properly identifying the level of abstraction of an utterance; this deficiency renders the schizophrenic a contradictory and unpredictable communicant. The cause of the disorder, Bateson maintains, is repeated exposure to double-bind situations during formative years. An authority figure (usually a parent) confuses a child by issuing two incompatible injunctions. The first, on the primary level, induces certain behavior under the threat of punishment. The second, also enforced by punishment, requires, on a more abstract level, behavior that is opposite to that demanded by the first injunction. But can this vicious circle be broken somehow? According to Bateson only by assuming a higher level of abstraction from which the contradictions permeating the primary discourse can be plainly seen. This would be a healthy reaction—to which, alas, the true schizophrenic does not have recourse.[12]

Though the causes of collective schizophrenia are not mental but social, its basic structure remains the same. It involves a hierarchical relation between two groups in which the one with power coerces the powerless to act in a certain way, all the while insisting that the subjects of coercion are free or that the enforced behavior is good for them. At the same time, the powerless are prohibited from expressing their true feelings about this arrangement. The reaction of Czechoslovak authorities to Havel's play—their covert shifting of blame onto the victims and their overt pretense of innocence masking actual persecution—is, I believe, a manifestation of the schizophrenic communicative disorder that characterized Czechoslovak society in a not-so-distant past.

What are the symptoms of this peculiar condition? At the most basic level we should observe that every public statement made in Czechoslovakia either by the government or citizens was always two-leveled. Its true import did not rest in what was said but in what was implied. Havel's 1978 essay "The Power of the Powerless" focuses sharply on this communicative duplicity. Why, the playwright asks, does an ordinary greengrocer put on display among his vegetables the sign, "Proletarians of all lands, unite!"? It is quite obvious that he does not do so because of an irresistible desire to impart this message to his customers because of his political convictions. Like his colleagues, he has received the ready-made slogan from the central office with instructions to put it in a prominent place. His noncompliance with this instruction would cause him difficulties with his employer—he could be fired. Hence the implications of his action are, according to Havel, quite simple. The slogan signifies that, "I, greengrocer XYZ, am here and know what to do; I behave as I am expected; I am reliable and cannot be criticized; I am obedient and, therefore, have the right to a peaceful existence."[13]

Such communicative duplicity, however, requires further explanation. If the government, Havel argues, reversed the informational hierarchy and turned the metamessage into a primary utterance, things might become somewhat sticky. "If the green-grocer was ordered to display the slogan, 'I am scared and, hence, I am totally obedient,' he would not relate to its semantic content in such a relaxed manner, though this content would fully coincide with the hidden meaning of the slogan. The grocer would most likely hesitate to display this unambiguous message about his denigration; he would be embarrassed, ashamed" ("Moc bezmocných," 61). Thus, to save face, the grocer's submission to the system is wrapped in an ideological garment. It is justified as service to the most worthy, progressive cause.

This operation, however, involves a certain manipulation of the concept of ideology. If Karl Marx succeeded in demystifying ideology as a false consciousness serving to justify the ruling class's position of power, his heirs engaged in its remystification. In their parlance, the ideology of Marxism-Leninism is not a lie but the truth. It is not a political ploy but an exact scientific theory, the embodiment of the universal logic of history. This de-ideologization of ideology serves a very specific purpose. It enabled the Czechoslovak Communists, in Havel's words, "to pretend that it pretends nothing." The grocer, it is true, "does not have to believe in all these mystifications. But he has to behave as if he believed them" ("Moc bezmocných," 63). To put this injunction negatively, vis-à-vis his government *he must not pretend to pretend.*

I use this negative formulation advisedly. Aside from an ideological justification for submissive behavior that is reserved for official occasions, Czechoslovak citizens usually offered another justification to their immediate circle of family and friends. This private justification, however, had to be concealed because it directly clashed with the Party's injunction. It claimed that what the greengrocer and his fellow citizens were really doing was *pretending to pretend.* For obvious reasons, everybody implicated in official structures must maintain the façade of pretense. But since only a very few Czechoslovaks were willing to admit to their families or friends that they were cowards or scoundrels, they had to come up with a credible explanation for patent support of the regime. Thus, they declared to those they trusted that the signs of fear and obedience they displayed in public were just a strategic ploy to achieve ends quite contrary to government policy.

Here the gate for collective schizophrenia swings wide open. Since the boundaries between private and public spheres in a totalitarian society are never well defined, Czechoslovak citizens were with astonishing frequency forced to change the logical typing of their utterances. And it was never clear whether their metapretending was really a strategic device or merely another face-saving mechanism to cover actual submission. This is to say, one always had doubts in Czechoslovakia whether one was dealing with heroes or collaborators who, as Havel characterized them in his open letter to [President] Husák of 1975, "have the peculiar ability to persuade themselves again and again and under any circumstances that their dirty work supposedly protects something, or that at least they prevent those who are worse than them from taking over their positions."[14] Under such conditions it ceases to be possible to draw a clear-cut line between the oppressors and the oppressed. In a truly schizophrenic fashion, "everybody," to use Havel's assessment, "is [the system's] victim and support" ("Moc bezmocných," 70).

The all-pervasive fear I am describing was the function of the state's near-absolute power over its citizens. Any human weakness—including parental love—might have been used as an instrument of blackmail: it was a common practice to hold children's futures hostage to the proper behavior of their parents. And since virtually everybody in Czechoslovakia was a civil servant, economic persecution of those who breached the boundaries of the permissible was limitless. These coercive mechanisms, however, would have been virtually useless had the government not had at its disposal the most feared tool of control—an omnipotent and omnipresent secret police. In his letter to Husák, Havel compared this organization to a monstrous spider whose invisible web permeated the entire social fabric. "And," he continued, "though most of the people most of the time do not see this web with their own eyes and cannot touch it, even the commonest citizen knows very well of its existence. At any moment and at any place he or she counts on its silent presence and behaves accordingly: i.e., so as to pass the test of its hidden eyes and ears" ("Dopis Gustávu Husákovi," 23).

As Havel suggests, the effect of a secret police on collective schizophrenia can hardly be overestimated. The agents of such an Orwellian force introduce another level to the game of deception. Those who by pretending to pretend violate the injunction against primary communicative duplicity find their match in those *who pretend to pretend to pretend*—the undercover police, the nameless heroes who with "clean hands, cool heads, and ardent hearts" expose a citizenry's true colors. Yet it must be stressed that the Czechoslovak secret police had a certain compassion for those caught red-handed. They could atone for their unworthy behavior: instead of facing criminal prosecution they could join the crew and themselves become the "hidden eyes and ears" of the state.

Needless to say, it was in the interest of those holding power in Czechoslovakia to convince their subjects of the omniscience of the secret police. To fulfill this task the mass media of the 1970s launched an ambitious campaign to promulgate a new type of positive hero—the double agent who patently would abet the enemies of the state but, in reality, labor on its behalf. The symbol of this undertaking is the shady figure of Jan Minařík, whose story was prominently disseminated by the Czechoslovak propagandists in 1976 through all available channels. A putative Captain of State Security, he left his homeland on a "secret mission" in 1968 and joined Radio Free Europe as a broadcaster, only to redefect in 1975. His subordinate position at the Radio, the evidence furnished by his co-workers for his sudden return, and the forged nature of some of the materials he allegedly brought home all indicate that the story of this spy presented by the Czechoslovak official media is to a large degree deception. True, one can never trust a double agent, but this one looks particularly untrustworthy.[15] Nevertheless, the reason for the media blitz is quite obvious: to increase communicative disorder among the population and in this way dissuade it from quitting the primary game of pretending required by the government. To put it differently, if in this mental poker game the secret police claim to have a royal flush, who is willing to call their bluff? The case of "Captain" Minařík indicates that third-level pretending was not the limit for the deceptive games in post-1968 Czechoslovakia. Theoretically speaking, the lamination of levels of abstraction in intercourse is limitless. But the thicker it gets, the more difficult that logical typing of utterances becomes and the more schizophrenic the communication, until it ceases to make sense for anybody involved.

Before I myself succumb to this disorder, however, let me turn to the text of Havel's play. I shall not dwell on its title, although it is rather curious that the dramatic personae does not contain a single beggar. The plot centers on Macheath, the head of a criminal gang, and on two nuclear families, the Peachums and the Lockits (each composed of a father, a mother, and a daughter). The head of the first family, William Peachum, is also the leader of a criminal gang, whereas Bill Lockit is the chief of police. The antagonistic occupations of the two fathers do not prevent their daughters—Polly Peachum and Lucy Lockit—from being married simultaneously to Macheath. In addition to these main figures, two lesser characters, an independent pickpocket, Filch, and a prostitute, Jenny, are instrumental in the power game unfolding in the play, in which the leading protagonists attempt to gain control over each other.

This cast of characters might suggest the following tensions. Lockit is a policeman, and hence a natural enemy of the two criminals, Macheath and Peachum. These two, on the other hand, though bound by their contempt for the law, are at the same time potential competitors with conflicting goals in mind. Finally, both Polly and Lucy are married to Macheath, which makes the entire situation quite muddy. Parental feelings, ethical norms, love, and jealousy all foster alliances too numerous to be accounted for. The multiplicity of relations among the main protagonists is rich enough to sustain a number of dramatic plots. But what makes Havel's version of *The Beggar's Opera* particularly intriguing is the totally duplicitous behavior of its characters. To achieve their ends they seduce or coerce the others, lie about the motivations for their actions, and constantly shift sides (or, at least, they say they do) as the power configuration changes. Whenever a character steps out of this behavioral pattern by acting spontaneously or by displaying genuine feelings and convictions, he or she is immediately victimized by the others. The play unfolds as a series of gradual revelations about each protagonist, and at each step the levels of pretending are multiplied so that, at the end, in a state of collective schizophrenia, the outcome is utterly unclear.

As the curtain rises, Peachum and his wife discuss the intimate relations between their daughter and Macheath. The father has specifically encouraged Polly to seduce the leader of a competing gang. This plan has succeeded, and Polly announces that she is already married to Macheath. Delighted, Peachum undertakes the next step. As he tells his daughter, her husband is a "rake and spineless cynic" who married her only to gain control over Peachum's business.[16] Appealing to her daughterly love, he urges her to betray her husband and use her new position to gather incriminating evidence that will send Macheath to the gallows. This scheme, however, backfires because Polly has fallen in love with Macheath and wishes nothing but a happy family life. When the incensed Peachum banishes her from his home, her mother suggests that the next plot against Macheath be more radical.

The homeless Polly goes to the robber's tavern—the hangout of Macheath's gang—and urges her husband to flee immediately. Upon leaving her home she had listened behind the door and now worries that Macheath will be trapped. But to her dismay her husband is not at all sympathetic to her story. She should have known from the very beginning, he argues, that her father intended to use her against him. "You should have agreed with everything he said and promised to go along with him so he'd think that his plan was working. And then you'd simply feed him false information, which I would provide, and eventually we'd snare him in his own net. . . . But now you've spoiled everything!" (*Žebrácká opera,* 125). If Polly loves him, as she claims to do, she will go home, make up with her parents, and enact the role he has outlined. Macheath is irresistible, and Polly departs for her parental home as a double agent with her husband's promise that during her absence he will be faithful to her.

Yet the very next female visitor to the tavern attracts Macheath's attention. This is the prostitute Jenny, who tells him that some five years ago he seduced her under false pretenses and then abandoned her. But since he was her first lover she has remained faithful to him and now has come to see him again. Macheath, who does not remember the event, is very much attracted to Jenny and promises to make up for his previous betrayal. But in the middle of the passionate scene that follows, Jenny screams for help and bailiffs enter the room. As becomes obvious, the lady is jailbait, and Macheath is arrested for attempted rape.

During his arraignment the police chief Lockit suggests to Macheath that his case is not as hopeless as it might seem. However, it is not the bribe sensibly offered by Macheath that interests him. Rather, he would like the criminal to become a police informer. Macheath, however, thinks he can get out of jail without resorting to such distasteful tactics. He is secretly married to Lockit's daughter Lucy and is banking on her help. Very soon, Lucy indeed appears in her husband's cell. After a somewhat awkward moment caused by Macheath's yearlong absence from his wife, he succeeds in persuading Lucy that he planned "to make a lot more money on the quiet—a fortune—so that we could move to the country and live together in complete happiness" (*Žebrácká opera,* 138). A rhapsodic description of the life in a manor house that he has imagined for both of them persuades Lucy to arrange his escape.

As the seasoned reader might suspect, Macheath's arrest was engineered by Peachum, who is in cahoots with Lockit. The police chief helped Peachum nab the seducer of his daughter, but not out of kindness. Peachum's organization, it turns out, is nothing but Lockit's instrument for gathering information about the London underworld. And in the course of their conversation, Lockit questions Peachum about the Duke of Gloucester's gold watch, which has recently been stolen. This is a touchy point because the theft was assigned by Peachum to the pickpocket Filch as a tryout for acceptance in the gang— this despite Lockit's explicit injunction against Peachum's hiring new staff. Lockit's ruffled feathers, however, are smoothed when Peachum presents him with a valuable necklace which Lockit, after much persuasion, accepts.

At this point, it seems, the situation is clear: it is a typical case of a mutually profitable collaboration between the mob and the police. But the Duke's watch has added another wrinkle to the story. Filch, who spoke to Macheath after his escape, has learned about Peachum's contacts with the police and is offended. He is an "honest" thief who finds "such trafficking with the enemy disgusting" (*Žebrácká opera,* 143). To appease him, Peachum tells Filch the truth about his police connections:

> Trafficking with the enemy? Perhaps it is. It's a thankless task, sir, but someone has to do it. What would become of the underworld if people like me didn't put their honor on the line each and every day by keeping the lines of communication open, something for which they will very probably never receive recognition? . . . Oh, it's terribly easy to cloister yourself away and cultivate your marvelous principles, but what sense does it make? Only this: to gratify the egotistical self-interest of those who do it. The real heroes of the underground today are a different breed altogether. They may not be constantly flaunting their fidelity to the pure code of honor among thieves, but they do modest, inconspicuous, and risky work in that no-man's-land between the underworld and the police, and they make a real contribution to our objective interests . . .

they expand the range of our opportunities inch by inch, strengthen our security, provide us with important information and, slowly, inconspicuously, with no claim to glory, they serve progress. (*Žebrácká opera*, 143)

Despite this eloquent justification of Peachum's behavior, Filch sticks to his moral principles, quits his job, is promptly arrested for the theft of the Duke's gold watch, and dies on the gallows.

Meanwhile, the escaped Macheath heads toward the house of ill repute where Jenny works so that he might extract revenge on his Delilah. But her attraction is so strong that instead of punishing her he listens to her for a second time. Jenny, as she explains to him, does not work for the police at all. She was coerced to entrap Macheath because her father was sentenced to death, and this was the only chance of obtaining clemency for him. "It was a terrible dilemma," she pleads with Macheath. "I felt that I had to refuse, because I couldn't bring myself to save one man from death by sending another to the gallows. In the end, however, I reckoned that you'd figure a way out of it but father wouldn't. You'd have to know him; he is so helpless" (*Žebrácká opera*, 149–50). The touched Macheath apologizes to Jenny for his black thoughts and consents to wait for her in a little chamber where she will join him at the earliest opportunity. There he is apprehended by Lockit's agents for a second time.

The action now switches to Peachum's household. Polly, as charged by her husband, tells her parents the content of her conversation with Macheath: how he told her to go home, ask for forgiveness, and under the guise of a repentant daughter to spy on Peachum. This idea, she proclaims, is so repugnant to her that she has lost all her former affection for Macheath and to get even with him she is willing to assume the role of a plant in her husband's organization. Fatherly feelings, it seems, are Peachum's Achilles' heel, for he eagerly accepts her confession and rushes to Lockit to ask him for Macheath's release.

After the initial misunderstanding caused by Macheath's escape and new arrest, Peachum presents Lockit with his new plan. Since Polly has volunteered to gather evidence against her husband, it would be advantageous to set Macheath free, and after all the details of his operation become known, to apprehend him with all his accomplices. But Lockit is skeptical. Why is Peachum so eager, he asks, to release a man whose arrest he so recently demanded? Is he trying to get hold of Macheath's property or make Polly happy? Moreover, through an inmate planted in Filch's cell he has learned what Peachum told the pickpocket about his "trafficking with the enemy," and he demands an explanation. Such distrust offends Peachum: "Bill," he addresses the police chief,

Have you any idea at all what it means to spend years fighting against the underworld while you're living in it and cultivating its confidence. . . . Struggling against crime while appearing to commit it? Do you have any inkling of what that means? Wearing two faces for so long? Leading a double life? Thinking in two different ways at once? . . . Constantly trying to fit into a world you condemn and to renounce a world to which you really belong? . . . it's all terribly simple, sitting here in your warm office . . . and handing down your simplistic judgments. But try going out into the midst of life, putting your honor on the line every day of the week by maintaining contacts for which you will probably never receive proper recognition, and undertaking modest and risky work in that dangerous no-man's land between the underworld and the police, fighting slowly, inconspicuously on the side of law and order without any expectation of fame—that is a very different matter. (*Žebrácká opera,* 166–67)

Lockit is touched by Peachum's emotional outburst, and the two hatch a following stratagem.

Peachum is let into Macheath's cell and tells him that if Macheath agrees to merge his gang with Peachum's and assumes the position of deputy, Peachum will prevail upon Lockit to release him. He can do so because he is Lockit's informer. But this fact should not worry Macheath because his collaboration with the police is merely a handy façade for his criminal activities. "Why do you think I cooperate with the police?" he asks Macheath. "Because I love the King? I am just doing what everyone else is doing—in one way or another. Working for my own ends and covering my back at the same time" (*Žebrácká opera,* 172). The hitherto competitors agree to become allies.

No sooner does Peachum leave the cell than an unexpected visitor comes to see Macheath. It is Jenny, who has decided to tell the man she has already betrayed twice why she behaved in such an abominable manner. She has entrapped Macheath, she claims, not just because she works for the police but because of her passionate love for him. "For a long time," Jenny confessed, "I was not even aware of it, but the longer that fire smoldered in my subconsciousness, the more violent the flames that ravaged my consciousness. I was beside myself, I walked about in a daze, hating you and cursing you; my pride became helpless anger and then it happened: I realized if I ever wanted to belong to myself again, I had to destroy you. Yes, my humiliation could only be swept away by bloody vengeance, in a kind of drastic act of self-affirmation. I had to kill you in order to live" (*Žebrácká opera,* 176). The veracity of this story obviously has something to do with Jenny's sex appeal, and the enamored Macheath accepts her explanation. He declares his love to Jenny and assures her that when he is released that day the two of them will run far away, "where no one will ever find us, save for the birds and the stars" (*Žebrácká opera,* 177).

But alas, Macheath is not destined to enjoy this pastoral life. As Lockit questions him, Macheath first denies the deal he made with Peachum and then admits to it. Yet, as Lockit tells him, the deal is off anyway because Macheath has acted in bad faith. He has accepted Peachum's proposal, Lockit insists, "only so you could get out, take control—through a counterfeit merger—of the assets of both organizations, and then you would run off with a certain lady to a place where no one would find you—save for the birds and the stars. . . . In other words when you understood that Peachum was double-crossing you when he said he was double-crossing me, you decided to double-cross him. But—luckily for us and unluckily for you—you yourself were double-crossed shortly thereafter" (*Žebrácká opera*, 180). Since Peachum's plan has obviously been compromised, Lockit returns to his original proposition and asks Macheath to serve as his hidden eyes and ears in Peachum's gang. In a long monologue Macheath ponders the pros and cons of this offer.

> What if I were to turn that offer down? Those around me would understand it as an ostentatious expression of my own superiority and conceit . . . everyone would ask: where does he get the right to be so different from the rest of us . . . and to spit on that minimum of discipline without which no society can function properly? I would be seen as a pompous and arrogant exhibitionist, someone who wanted to play the conscience of the world. . . . And I can understand that: to totally reject the rules of the game this world offers may be the easier way, but it usually leads nowhere. It is far more difficult, and at the same time far more meaningful, to accept those rules, thus enabling one to communicate with those around one, and then to put that ability to work in the gradual struggle for better rules. In other words, the only truly dignified and manly solution to my dilemma is to turn and face life head-on, plunge bravely into its stormy waters, fear not the dirt and the obstacles life places in my way and invest all my strength and all my skill in the struggle to make life better than it is. (*Žebrácká opera*, 182–83)

With these words, the chastened Macheath accepts Lockit's offer, which could not be refused.

At this stage of the play—and we are just a few minutes from the end—the gullible reader might discern a hint of optimism. The law, despite the somewhat dubious techniques it employs, has finally triumphed over the criminals. By striking separate secret deals with both gangsters, Lockit has divided them and turned them into pliable instruments of police control over the mob. Yet, at this very moment another switch takes place that makes us wonder what has actually been transpiring throughout the play. After the now-docile Macheath leaves the scene, the following conversation takes place between Mr. and Mrs. Lockit:

> LOCKIT: Well, Mary, from this moment on, our organization has practically the entire underworld of London under its control.
> MRS. LOCKIT: It took a bit of doing, didn't it?
> LOCKIT: Gaining control of the London Police force was a piece of cake by comparison.

MRS. LOCKIT: I still find it strange, though, Bill. No one knows about our organization, yet everyone is working for it.

LOCKIT: They serve best who know not that they serve. (*Žebrácká opera*, 184)

We realize now that all the elaborate deceptions in which Lockit the police chief engaged were just partial plots in an overarching scheme devised by Lockit the gangster.

This sudden revelation changes our understanding of the play in another, more fundamental way. It is not simply that an additional layer of pretending has been added that shocks us but the recognition that in the universe of discourse depicted by Havel there is no ultimate cap on the levels that deception generates. In light of this, Lockit's supposed triumph appears problematic, to say the least. It is derived solely from his knowledge of what the other characters do or say. But since in the schizophrenic world he inhabits every communication contains a multitude of logical levels without keys to correct ordering, his victory may be as well a self-deception: an incorrect reading of the messages he receives. That cops might be robbers we learn at the end of the play. But we leave the text with the uneasy feeling that the opposite state of affairs—that robbers might be cops—is more than a possibility.

Is there an escape from this paranoid deadlock? Though Havel's play remains silent on this point, its very existence challenges the status quo. Earlier I mentioned that, according to Bateson, the way out of a double bind is through a metastatement that exposes the multilevel contradictions inherent in such a mental trap. Havel's text, which depicts the communication disorder of normalized Czechoslovakia, is a step in that direction. Let me explain what I mean by returning to Bateson. The act of playing, he insists, is the most rudimentary mechanism by which all living beings learn about the variety of logical types involved in their interactions. Playing by definition involves two levels—both an action and a qualifying signal of a higher order that frames it as play. Thus, in play there is an implicit assertion to the effect that "these actions in which we now engage do not denote what the actions *for which they stand* would denote."[17] This observation might sound trivial, but it has important consequences. By creating a fictional universe, play splits reality from its representation and opens the possibility of transcending the immediate givens of a situation, for reflecting about the world in a detached fashion.

Artistic creativity obviously has its roots in this *Spieltrieb*. But it is not simply playing, at least not for Havel. "Art," he argued cogently in his 1967 essay "The Magic Circle," is "play which does everything possible not to be play; play which, just as it begins, 'spoils' play; play which always and ever betrays precisely what it proceeds from."[18] Like play, art thrives on the gap between reality and its representation, but unlike free play it strives to close that gap. Thus, while true play is totally self-sufficient and self-enclosed, art can have social ramifications. Havel's *The Beggar's Opera,* one clearly recognizes, implements this theoretical stance. It is a playful representation of schizophrenia addressed to an audience for which this state of affairs was an everyday reality. By communicating about a communication disorder, Havel theatrically reframes the double-bind predicament of those locked in the primary frame and offers to them for inspection his reframing. *The Beggar's Opera* is both an artistic metastatement and simultaneously a political gesture: an invitation to its audience to break out of the vicious schizophrenic circle by reflecting on their own behavior.

Notes and References

1. Václav Havel, "Fakta o představení Žebrácké opery," *O lidskou identitu* [*On Human Identity*] (London: edice rozmluvy, 1984), 174.

2. "Wenige Schritte," *Der Spiegel,* 10 November 1975: 212.

3. Philip Roth, *Zuckerman Bound: A Trilogy & Epilogue* (New York: Farrar, Straus & Giroux, 1985), 763.

4. See, for example, the great proliferation of "police jokes" in Czechoslovakia in the 1970s. Here is my favorite: "Why do policemen in Prague always walk in threes? Because one knows how to read, another how to write, and the third has to watch them fucking intellectuals."

5. Václav Havel, "Zvláštnosti divadla," *Divadlo* (19 April 1968): 18.

6. *Poučení z krizového vývoje ve straně a společnosti po XIII. sjezdu KSČ: Rezoluce k aktuálním otázkám jednoty strany* (Prague, 1971), 22.

7. Milan Šimečka, *The Restoration of Order: The Normalization of Czechoslovakia,* trans. A.G. Brain (London: Verso, 1984), 17.

8. For more details see "Normalizace v Národním divadle," *Listy* 1, no. 1 (1971): 17–19.

9. John Barton, *Playing Shakespeare* (London: Methuen, 1984), 191–92.

10. For Havel's reaction to these rumors see "Fakta o představení," 173–74 and 179.

11. For more details see "Horní Počernice—všecko vystoupit," *Listy* 6, no. 2 (1976): 26–27; and "Společenská rubrika," ibid., 48.

12. G. Bateson, "Towards a Theory of Schizophrenia," *Steps to an Ecology of Mind: Collected Essays in Anthropology, Psychiatry, Evolution and Epistemology* (St Albans: Herts, 1973), 173–98.

13. Václav Havel, "Moc bezmocných," *O lidskou identitu,* 60; hereafter cited in text as "Moc bezmocných."

14. Václav Havel, "Dopis Gustávu Husákovi," ibid., 24; hereafter cited in text as "Dopis Gustávu Husákovi."

15. For more details about this case see "První a poslední role 'kapitána' Minaříka," *Listy* 6, no. 2 (1976): 7–8; and "Skandál v Římě," ibid., no. 4, 11.

16. Václav Havel, *Žebrácká opera: Na téma Johna Gaye {The Beggar's Opera: on a Theme by John Gay},* quoted from V. Havel, *Hry 1970–1976: Z doby zakázanosti* (Toronto: Sixty-Eight Publishers, 1977), 120; hereafter cited in text as *Žebrácká opera.* For their English translations I am indebted to Paul Wilson whose kind help I am pleased to acknowledge.

17. G. Bateson, "A Theory of Play and Fantasy," quoted from *Steps to an Ecology of Mind,* 152.

18. Václav Havel, "Začarovaný kruh," *Divadlo* (18 January 1967): 3.

Václav Havel:
The Once and Future Playwright

ROBERT SKLOOT

{*Havel has consistently attempted to awaken readers and audiences to the subtle, pervasive, and dehumanizing conditioning that accompanies our increasingly technological existence.*

—*Phyllis Carey*}

In the short space of a few years, we have been witness to a Havel industry. Images of the Czech playwright-politician appear frequently in the West, and his words are quoted often whenever democrats of all kinds convene. His life is held up as an example of resistance to the tyrant's authority and the terrors of the state, and he is celebrated by those who have suffered brutal indignities as well as by those who have suffered not at all.

In 1992, with the fragmentation of his bipartite nation and the [temporary] loss of his presidency, the simple fact of his unwavering commitment to human rights and to policies of tolerance and trust has introduced into the politics of the 1990s a new spirit of both personal courage and political resolve. The mention of Havel's name is, for most observers, an occasion to chart the possibilities of changing old, repressive, tribal ways for new, humane ones, an exercise all the more needed as [some other European] countries hemorrhage in an agony of self-destruction. In this essay, I want to explore the nature of political Havelism by temporarily disengaging it from the newspaper headlines and looking at a number of his plays. In doing so, I want to point out their distinctiveness as well as their problematic aspects and to ask whether, were it not for Havel's political importance, we should attend to (or attend at all) the theater of this astonishingly undramatic actor on the stage of modern history.[1]

One result of Václav Havel's recent celebrity has been references throughout the media to his plays which, it is quite likely, have never been

Reprinted and abridged from *The Kenyon Review* 15, no. 2 (spring 1993): 223–31.

seen or read by most American commentators or journalists. . . . The remainder of Havel's artistic energy has been expended in political essays and correspondence, the latter including *Letters to Olga*[2] (published in English in 1988), *Disturbing the Peace*[3] (in English, 1990) and *Summer Meditations*[4] (in English, 1992). Havel's plays have been generally neglected by most American theaters. Because the predominant concern of most American theater has been, and continues to be, to provide entertainment for the dwindling numbers of middle-class audiences, Havel is not good "box office." For a while, smaller and "engaged" theaters and a few in universities, will produce Havel's plays as a statement of political solidarity with the momentous changes in European politics. At the same time, they will confirm the feebleness of American theatrical art to rouse anyone to thought or action.

Aside from its political context, what is the artistic relationship between Havel's plays and those of his contemporaries? Discerning the thread that binds the plays of [the President of the Czech Republic] to other modern playwrights is important in understanding his theater. One dramatist who comes to mind is Harold Pinter who, not surprisingly, acted in two of Havel's short plays (*Audience* and *Private View* [also translated as *Unveiling*])[5] in 1977 on the British Broadcasting Company. Pinter shares with Havel an interest in how people respond to the space in which they live, particularly the enclosed kind of space which makes Havel's *Audience* and *Largo Desolato*[6] reminiscent of Pinter's *The Dumb Waiter*[7] and, especially, *The Birthday Party*.[8] In the latter, first produced in 1958, Pinter creates the figure of Stanley, the inarticulate recluse who is, depending on the interpretation of the text in production, destroyed by a thuggish, malevolent society or "birthed" into a culture which may not be as corrupt as it is pragmatically brutal. In fact, such opportunities for interpretation separate Pinter's plays from Havel's. Pinter's plays suffer markedly when they are "located"; Havel's, on the other hand, are conceived within a specific political context which is very difficult to separate out from the texts and their implications. Pinter, who writes in a democracy, is interested in existential freedom and is nonideological in his plays; confinement is a condition of life, not of politics. Trying to make his plays overtly political (as in the presentation of McCann's Irishness in *The Birthday Party*) restricts and diminishes them.[9]

Havel, who wrote his plays under tyranny, is deeply ideological in both attitude and experience. His plays embody a knowledge of history and are always attached to a context; Pinter's float free and are open to multiple inferences. For Pinter, the threatening "Other" is whoever happens to be the annihilating force of the moment; for Havel, the Other is always the state which may be, depending on the depth of our compromise with its invidious demands, surprisingly benign. Pinter's people talk elliptically, trying to conceal motive and expressing a wide range of psychological subtexts; Havel's people talk ambiguously, seeking to avoid blame or shame, but expressing a very narrow choice of psychological motive. Both writers do create a very powerful sense of the sinister, and Havel's plays may be called, as Pinter's have been, "comedies of menace." Pinter frequently creates a feeling of threat through the use of an enclosed space; Havel often achieves the same effect by including in his plays a character or two, perhaps silent, who represent the omnipresent repressive state, for example Pillar in *The Memorandum*,[10] the Chaps in *Largo Desolato,* and the mysterious Fistula in *Temptation.*[11]

An even closer theatrical affinity exists between Havel and the English playwright Tom Stoppard, who was born a few months after Havel, also in Czechoslovakia. Kenneth Tynan has written a splendid comparison of the lives, plays and temperaments of the two writers.[12] Suffice to say that the two playwrights share a deep mistrust of all orthodoxy and authority, and an identical delight in the liberating power of satirical language. The beginning of Stoppard's *Travesties*[13] with its multilingual, arch use of language made both artistic and incomprehensible (to the audience) in the hands (or at the scissors) of Tristan Tzara, James Joyce and Vladimir [Ilich] Lenin reminds us of Havel's invention of Ptydepe, the unlearnable bureaucratic babble of *The Memorandum,* written in 1965. And, equally important, the "time slips" in *Travesties* have been an identifying feature of Havel's plays since *The Garden Party,*[14] a theatrical device where one scene or piece of dialogue is repeatedly replayed, perhaps modified by changing who says a certain speech or who performs the repeated action.

In Stoppard's play, the "slips" are "under the erratic control" of Henry Carr, his irascible curmudgeon of a protagonist, and Carr's frequent narrative recapitulations in the performance of *Travesties* are intended by Stoppard to be metatheatrical intrusions. Havel uses the technique more as a metaphorical device, apart from character, in order to signal either a world careening out of control (when the words and actions are accelerated), or one denuded of objective meaning, leaving its inhabitants to their meaningless lives. Stoppard has adapted Havel's *Largo Desolato,* written the introduction to *The Memorandum* in its English translation, and has dedicated his own brilliant political comedy about life under tyranny in Czechoslovakia, *Professional Foul,*[15] to Havel. Geographically speaking, Stoppard is the cultural and national bridge between Havel and Pinter since he was born in Czechoslovakia but relocated to England at an early age. Artistically, he has been more prolific and inventive.

[An early and very strong] influence on Havel, . . . is Eugène Ionesco. With *The Bald Soprano,*[16] first produced in 1950 in Paris and called an "anti-play" by its Romanian-born author, Ionesco began a series of theater pieces extraordinary for their antic humor and complete disregard of what can be called the logical necessities of stage realism. Well into the 1960s, his work endured as one of the dominant influences on European playwriting, and his shadow looms large as a presence in Havel's work. In a brief tribute to Havel, Milan Kundera asserts that

. . . no foreign writer had for us at that time [the 1960s] such a liberating sense as Ionesco. We were suffocating under art conceived as educational, moral or political . . .

One cannot conceive of Havel without the example of Ionesco yet he is not an epigone. His plays are an original and irreplaceable development within what is called "The Theatre of the Absurd." Moreover, they were understood as such by everyone at the time. . . .[17]

Looking at *The Garden Party* with its loopy dialogue, nonsensical action and its fragmentation of character (by the end of the play, the protagonist Hugo Pludek has assumed a second identity of the same name), or noting the pretentious social chatter and bourgeois accumulations in *Private View* [*Unveiling*], it is impossible not to perceive the Ionesco of *The Bald Soprano*, *The Lesson*[18] or *Jack, or the Submission*,[19] the first two of which were produced by Havel's Theatre on the Balustrade in the early 1960s. And Havel's use of doors in *The Increased Difficulty of Concentration*[20] and *Largo Desolato*, in particular as an expression of the intrusions of an erratic, malignant external universe, has Ionesco's type of comic paranoia as its model. Havel, however, adds the political context missing in Ionesco, and Kundera is but one of many observers who see this Absurdism with a political face as a true moment of cultural liberation in the dark history of postwar Czechoslovakian politics.

One additional name must be mentioned in relation to Havel, though not for his structural, scenographic or linguistic similarities. It is a thematic thread that ties Pinter, Stoppard, Ionesco and Havel together with Samuel Beckett who wrote his very short play *Catastrophe*[21] in 1983 to commemorate and excoriate (though subtly, minimally) Havel's lengthy and near-fatal imprisonment. This thematic line can be expressed as the well-worn theme of "respect for individual worth and the individual's need for dignity," though it is the unique genius of each of these five artists that keeps this concern meaningful and frequently moving. The painful and occasionally fanciful existence of Pinter's Stanley, of Stoppard's Henry Carr, of Ionesco's Berenger and of Beckett's Gogo and Didi are all images of their creators' devotion to the irreducible minimum of human freedom, and it is no coincidence that all of them in their personal lives (though some more than others and Beckett least of all) have committed themselves to fighting on several fronts for a humane existence for all the world's abused inhabitants. . . .

Currently, the great attraction to Havel's writing in the West is extratheatrical, based on its antitotalitarian ideology of tolerance and responsibility, as well as Havel's personal drama of exemplary courage in the face of oppression. One curious result of [the break up of] Czechoslovakia is that Havel's political failure [as president of a federal state] now aligns him better with the failure of his plays' protagonists (who share occasional details of a common biography with their author). But if we examine Havel's artistic endeavor apart from his political life, how can we measure his achievement?

Looking at Havel's plays leads even a sympathetic reader to conclude that the stylistic and structural repetitions, for example, the time warps, the repeated gestures and bits of business, the identical dreary "journeys" of the protagonists (Gross in *The Memorandum,* Huml in *The Increased Difficulty of Concentration,* Nettles in *Largo Desolato* and Foustka in *Temptation*) show Havel repeating himself too much. Thus, *Largo Desolato* and *Temptation . . .* reveal a continuing preoccupation with outdated theater forms and an inability to drive his thinking or technique into a more moving, creative expression than it possessed before the time of his imprisonment in 1979. In his brief tribute to Havel, Timothy Garton Ash assesses the situation thus:

> . . . I still cannot avoid a deeper disappointment. The play [*Temptation,* produced in 1986 in Vienna], even as Havel has written it, is weak. And it is weak, it seems to me, for reasons directly related to his situation. For a start, the dramaturgy and stage effects envisioned in his very detailed stage directions are stilted, and if not stilted, then dated—as stroboscopes and smoke, *circa* 1966. Not surprising if you consider that he has been unable to work in the theatre for eighteen years.[22]

In 1986, in a culinary metaphor Brecht would have loved and perhaps agreed with, Ash concludes about *Temptation:* "The thing is overcooked."

The comparison to Ionesco now becomes useful, for it has long been noted that the best efforts of Ionesco are the early, short plays like those mentioned above. Absurdist drama, already a historical detail in the postmodern theater and unknown first-hand to anyone under thirty, was most successful when it remained playfully brief. When lengthy, as is Ionesco's work since *Exit the King*[23] (1962), Absurdism turned turgid and not a little pompous because the fun (often touched with horror) and the spirit of invention were unsustainable. Consider the conclusions of *The Garden Party* and *Temptation,* two Havel plays separated by almost a quarter of a century. The former ends with a character hidden inside a large cupboard (eavesdroppers appear in several Havel plays), making a surprising entrance, walking down to the footlights and directly addressing the audience: "And now, without sort of much ado—go home!" For this play, essentially a cartoon, the ending is abrupt, silly and appropriate. But the ending of *Temptation,* a play that attempts to deal with some of the same themes as *The Garden Party* (the language of bureaucracy, the description of life without commitment), seems to result from an exhausted imagination that has reached a point of no return, and no advance. The concluding dance which Havel describes as "a crazy, orgiastic masked ball or witches' sabbath" is accompanied by excruciatingly loud music and an auditorium full of smoke. The stage direction reads:

> The music suddenly stops, the house lights go on, the smoke fades and it becomes evident that at some point during all this the curtain has fallen. After a very brief silence, music comes on again, now at a bearable level of loud-

ness—the most banal commercial music possible. If the smoke—or the play itself—hasn't caused the audience to flee, and if there are still a few left in the audience who might even want to applaud, let the first to take a bow and thank the audience be a fireman in full uniform with a helmet on his head and a fire extinguisher [a major prop in *The Memorandum*] in his hand.[24]

Temptation explores in greater measure Havel's major theme of betrayal . . . but its satirical attack on a world destined to disappear in flames is too discursive and distended, lacking precision or sting. *Temptation* features the usual Havel touches: repetitive and replayed dialogue or action, long speeches of apology for or exculpation from corruption (Havel's protagonists are frequently compromised intellectuals and/or academics), an environment of bureaucratic time-serving and political cowardice, and ample though insufficient flashes of antic wit. But, unlike Beckett whose work traced an endangered and dying universe with ever greater austerity and concision (including *Catastrophe*), Havel's proliferating scenic and linguistic excesses provide a smaller payoff.

In Tynan's essay referred to earlier, he discusses Stoppard's difficulty in expressing genuine emotion and in creating convincing female characters. These are Havel's problems too, although in his defense it could be argued that in the kind of comic universe he creates, having either would be unusual. Nonetheless Havel's comic plays, essentially cerebral and objective, exclude the opportunity for the expression of deep, genuine feeling. His world is usually one of evasion and avoidance, like the world of classical farce which it frequently resembles in its dependence on rapid entrances and exits through a multiple number of doors. At his weakest, Havel replaces feeling with activity, providing gestures instead of activated concern. When this occurs, as in the recurrent business with PUZUK, the computer in *The Increased Difficulty of Concentration,* the face washing/door slamming of *Largo Desolato* or second dance sequence of *Temptation,* the plays lack, in Tynan's phrase, "the magic ingredient of pressure toward desperation" (Tynan, 110).

The most common Havel story (and clearly a political one) involves the increasing pressure of a (male) protagonist to decide whether or not to betray himself or his friends. Mostly, Havel's characters fail the test miserably. But on the way to failure, the plays suggest a way to a true if limited salvation: the involvement in a genuine experience of love with a woman. Thus, in *The Memorandum,* Gross is attracted to the pure adoration of the office clerk, Maria, but he abandons her at the moment of her greatest need and marches off to lunch with his office staff. That Maria remains "happy" because "nobody ever talked to me so nicely before" does not excuse Gross's avoidance of moral action nor his failure to reciprocate Maria's genuine expression of love toward him. Similarly, at the conclusion of *The Increased Difficulty of Concentration,* Huml almost reaches an expressive emotional reciprocity with Miss Balcar who, at one moment in the final scene, is reduced to tears by her need for Huml despite the gassy academic discourse he puts between them. Though he embraces her and kisses her "gently on her tearful eyes," and she exits "smiling happily," it is clear that Miss Balcar will be the fourth of Huml's failures with women in this play and additional proof of his intellectual and political cowardice.

At the end of *Largo Desolato,* [Marketa] arrives to give Leopold Nettles one final chance for rejuvenation through love. "You have given me back the meaning to my life," she tells him, "which is to give you the meaning back to yours." But their intense embrace is interrupted by the doorbell, and a terrorized Nettles leaves her immediately to chase after and to be humiliated by the two sinister Chaps who inform him that his gesture of "heroism" will no longer be required. Lastly, in *Temptation,* it is Maggie [the Faustian Gretchen figure] who serves as the abused image of innocence when her moment of courage in defending Foustka in front of their hostile bosses ends only in her summary dismissal after Foustka's betrayal of her. She returns later in the play dressed and behaving like a lunatic Ophelia, the one serious moment in the "witches' sabbath," but one deprived of tragic resonance because Havel has her return under peculiar circumstances for a last appearance as one of Foustka's tormentors.

In all of these scenes, I sense that Havel is flirting with a way to express a potentially liberating emotional occasion, liberating to his protagonists and to himself as a playwright of satirical political comedies. But in all of them, he deflects the serious tendencies of the characters and himself, preferring to avoid the entanglements of emotion with a disengaged, objective posture. It would be possible to argue that this lack of emotional commitment is the *result* of the political environment of his country, but I do not believe this is the case. Instead, I see this pattern as a refusal to extend these wonderful comedies into a more profound and troubling territory which would have serious and I think very positive results on Havel's playwriting. Havel turns back to his satire of bureaucratic and academic language in the arias of his cowardly protagonists, preferring the Ionesco "anti-play" to, say, Beckett's "tragicomedy." In this critical context, I would choose the two short pieces *Audience* and *Protest*[25] as Havel's most successful plays, although I have a great liking for the stylish, sustained confidence of the comic ironies of *The Memorandum.* These former plays are relatively brief, with all male characters; they emphasize the anguish of moral action and the fallibility of the human character, and they are very funny.

In the third of his "Six asides about culture"[26] (1984), Havel compares the Czechs with their northeastern neighbors: "We live in a land of notorious realism, far removed from, say, the Polish courage for sacrifice" (Vladislav 126). I understand Havel to refer to the Polish inclination toward the deathly side of human existence rather than his own Czech appreciation of the dark side of human organizations, and to the Polish strain of fatalism which is outside of and resistant to Havel's satirical assault on the notorious political realism of [the Czechs]. Havel has yet to write a play as powerful as, say, Mrożek's *Tango*,[27] that terrifying exposure of malignant brutality which, it should be mentioned, was adapted for the English stage by Tom Stoppard.

In John Webster's early seventeenth-century tragedy, *The Duchess of Malfi*, the title character confronts her state supported executioners and replies to their murderous threats with an ingenious and unlikely metaphor:

> I know that death hath ten thousand several doors
> For men to take their exits, and 'tis found
> They go on such strange geometrical hinges,
> You may open them both ways.

Havel's stage world until now has had the doors but not the death. [It remains an open question whether his future] may include an appointment with the theater where, contemplating the murderous world around him, he will be hard pressed to avoid writing pointedly about how countries and peoples die. In his part of Europe the dire situation isn't, or isn't only, a joke.

". . . if you must have a revolution," wrote Timothy Garton Ash, "it would be difficult to imagine a better revolution than the one Czechoslovakia had: swift, nonviolent, joyful, and funny. A laughing revolution."[28] This revolution culminated in Havel on the balcony overlooking a huge public square, in Prague's open air, unconfined, and recorded by accredited journalists rather than hidden informers. As president, Havel's voice [continues to be] aspiring and consoling, simple and moral, a deliberate rejection of the anxious volubility and fussy cowardice of his absurd protagonists. [Should he return to the theatre some day], he may, in the words of the Israeli novelist David Grossman, "hallucinate another kind of future," or perhaps, another kind of play. For a brief political moment, Havel's was the triumph of life over art, though the future may demand otherwise.

Notes and References

1. For several years, *The New York Review of Books* has featured prominently articles by and about Havel. For a summary of the recent political history of Czechoslovakia, see Paul Wilson, "The End of the Velvet Revolution," *The New York Review of Books* 13 Aug. 1992: 57–64. Wilson has served frequently as Havel's able English translator.

2. Václav Havel, *Letters to Olga,* trans. Paul Wilson (New York: Alfred A. Knopf, 1988).

3. Václav Havel, *Disturbing the Peace,* trans. Paul Wilson (New York: Alfred A. Knopf, 1990).

4. Václav Havel, *Summer Meditations,* trans. Paul Wilson (New York: Alfred A. Knopf, 1992).

5. Václav Havel, *Audience* and *Private View,* trans. Vera Blackwell (London: Cape, 1978). The two plays were published together under the title *Sorry.*

6. Václav Havel, *Largo Desolato,* English version by Tom Stoppard (New York: Grove Press, 1985).

7. Harold Pinter, *The Dumb Waiter* (New York: Grove Press, 1961).

8. Harold Pinter, *The Birthday Party* (New York: Grove Press, 1960).

9. For a recent retrospective view of Pinter's politics, see Benedict Nightingale, "Harold Pinter/Politics," *Around the Absurd: Essays on Modern and Postmodern Drama,* eds. Enoch Brater and Ruby Cohn (Ann Arbor: University of Michigan Press, 1990) 129–54.

10. Václav Havel, *The Memorandum,* trans. Vera Blackwell (New York: Grove Press, 1980).

11. Václav Havel, *Temptation,* trans. Marie Winn (New York: Grove Press, 1989).

12. Kenneth Tynan, *Show People: Profiles in Entertainment* (New York: Simon and Schuster, 1979) 44–123. The essay was written in 1977 and first appeared in *The New Yorker;* hereafter cited in text as Tynan.

13. Tom Stoppard, *Travesties* (New York: Grove Press, 1975).

14. Václav Havel, *The Garden Party,* trans. Vera Blackwell (London: Cape, 1964).

15. Tom Stoppard, *Professional Foul* (New York: Grove Press, 1978).

16. Eugène Ionesco, *The Bald Soprano, Four Plays,* trans. Donald M. Allen (New York: Grove Press, 1958).

17. Milan Kundera, "Candide had to be Destroyed," *Václav Havel or Living in Truth,* ed. Jan Vladislav (London: Faber & Faber, 1987) 259–60; hereafter cited in text as Vladislav. Also note the spirited, disputatious correspondence between Tynan and Ionesco in *The Observer* 22, 29 Jun. and 6 Jul. 1958, and a more serious academic assessment from Paul I. Trensky, "Havel's *The Garden Party* Revisited," *Czech Literature Since 1956: A Symposium,* eds. William E. Harkins and Paul I. Trensky (New York: Bohemica, 1980) 103–18.

18. Eugène Ionesco, *The Lesson, Four Plays.*

19. Eugène Ionesco, *Jack, or the Submission, Four Plays.*

20. Václav Havel, *The Increased Difficulty of Concentration,* trans. Vera Blackwell (London: Cape, 1972).

21. Samuel Beckett, *Catastrophe, Václav Havel or Living in Truth,* 199–203.

22. Timothy Garton Ash, "Prague—A Poem, Not Disappearing," *Václav Havel, or, Living in Truth,* 221.

23. Eugène Ionesco, *Exit the King,* trans. Donald Watson (New York: Grove Press, 1965).

24. Václav Havel, *Temptation,* 102.

25. Václav Havel, *Protest,* trans. Vera Blackwell, *Performing Arts Journal* 35/36 1990: 45–65. [also in *The Vaněk Plays.* See bibliography.]

26. Václav Havel, "Six asides about culture," *Václav Havel or Living in Truth,* 126.

27. Slawomir Mrożek, *Tango,* trans. Ralph Manheim and Teresa Dzieduscycka (New York: Grove Press, 1968).

28. Timothy Garton Ash, "The Revolution of the Magic Lantern," *The New York Review of Books,* 18 Jan. 1990: 51.

Delirious Subjectivity: Four Scenes from Havel

MICHAEL L. QUINN

{*How is one to acquire one's own identity? How is one to create, protect, even enhance it? Under what circumstances can it be lost?*

—*Andrej Krob*}

SETTING THE STAGE: THE NEGATIVE CONCEPT OF DELIRIUM

One of the most interesting products of the contemporary critical focus on semiotics in the formation of subjectivity is the "negative theory" of delirium. Unlike an ordinary analytic theory, which tries to construct coherent references, delirium involves a theory of mistaken references, of incoherence; as a supplement to theories of communication, which are designed to explain how we keep messages straight, this theory explains how sense gets lost, and the interesting things that happen when people lose it.

As a theory of confusion, delirium has several uses, especially philosophical, psychoanalytic and aesthetic ones. As it has emerged in deconstructive philosophical writing, it provides an occasional tropology for the slippage of signs in relation to their conventional functions.[1] For some psychoanalytic theorists delirium is a political solution, a valorized term that opens the utopian prospect of free play to the searching eyes of the anxious subject.[2] In this case delirium serves as an utterly skeptical qualification to the logic of reference, as the shadow-side of a coherent, perhaps oppressive order of determinate things and events that produces symptomatic non-sense.[3] My focus in this essay is on delirium's aesthetic interest, since it provides for both the vivid expression of character and the playful use of signs as they are imaginatively received by an interpreting community.[4]

In *The Logic of Sense* Gilles Deleuze compares the tree of "ordo" with the roots, the "rhizome" of delirium.[5] A logical analysis of representations typically ends in paradox; in delirious analysis the paradoxical "lekta" of representation—its gesture or, in Pierce's terms, interpretant—produces a series of semiotic associations.[6] When these associations fall within the logical status

Reprinted and abridged from *Essays in Theatre / Études théâtrales* 10, no. 2 (May 1992): 117–32.

11. *Protest* at the Burgtheater in Vienna, 1979.

12. *Largo desolato* at the Yale Repertory Theatre, 1990.

13. From a video production of *Temptation*.

of fictions, they have nothing to do with truth claims; their relations are with other signs, and they cease to function as propositions.[7] Even though such a situation causes the subject to lose contact with the phenomenal "manifold of perception," delirious association does seem to involve the mysterious perception of semiotic resemblances, whether of the homonymic type that exists between similar sign materials, or of the synonymic type that relates similar meanings.[8]

Delirious analysis, as a semiotics of mental association like Freud's master tropes of condensation and displacement, may be brought to bear on any subjective context involved in the production and reception of drama.[9] In the authorial context, delirious association provides the source for surrealist playwriting's not-so-random techniques of automatic writing and the journal of dreams; in this form, which communicates without coded associations, the entire appearance of the drama becomes a play of resemblant signs. Yet as a technique of dramatic writing, delirium appears most often as a crucial tool for the representation of character. When the confusion of a central character spins into an aesthetically fascinating dementia, an aesthetics of delirium can be used as a way to express or comprehend the progress of the unravelling mind. The idea of delirium exists as a safe categorical standpoint from which an audience or another character can explain what is being shown after the delirious subject becomes—however poetically—inarticulate.

Václav Havel has, since his first works, written characters whose mental states verge on the delirious. To describe all such moments would require much more than a short essay, so for the present I will describe four representative "moments" of delirium in his plays, together with the subjective situations, both cultural and dramaturgical, that helped to produce them. From this standpoint I am not following the thesis of Deleuze and Guattari, that the whole structure of thought in Western culture is paranoid; I merely intend to use historical circumstance as the subjective, often culturally conditioned scene in which delirium erupts as an important part of dramatic texts or performances.[10] In principle the notion of delirium does not imply any particular politics, but delirious expression does bear with it the conditioning limits of experience and culture, of what can be combined in unverifiable or unlikely scenarios according to the ruling lekta of association that constructs the series.

Only rarely does Havel employ the authorial context in his writing of delirium; the most obvious example is *The Mountain Hotel,* in which the delirium of the authorial persona overpowers the characters by making them all subject to the same repeating semiotic series. More often Havel uses a central moment of delirium—almost a borrowed technical "turn" from the rhetoric of expressionism—as a way of dramatizing the crisis of conscience (of consciousness) in the life of his central character.[11] Fortunately, from the audience's standpoint, he has produced these images of delirium in the context of an "inferential dramaturgy," which interprets the significance of delirium through an ordinary semantic and aesthetic context, encouraging delirious moments to be perceived as a means for the expression of irony and satire. The audience is supposed to be able to understand delirium, and even embrace it in dramatic form, but it is not supposed really to endorse it, and certainly not to imitate it.

SCENE I: MOTOMORPHOSIS

Havel's first use of playful delirium feeds on the formalist tradition of comic theory.[12] I'd like to rehearse this tradition in relation to one of its master tropes, to give an example of the way that even delirious signification establishes a tradition within which its aesthetic uses can become clear.

One of Viktor Shklovsky's favorite metaphors for the art work was a motor car. Writing in 1928, on the cusp of Formalism's official disappearance, he explained:

> If you wish to become a writer you must examine a book as attentively as a watchmaker a clock or a chauffeur a car.
> Cars are examined in the following ways: The most idiotic people come to the automobile and press the balloon of its horn. This is the first degree of stupidity. People who know a little more about cars but overestimate their knowledge come to the car and fiddle with its stick-shift. This is also stupid and even bad, because one should not touch a thing for which another worker is responsible.
> The understanding man scrutinizes the car serenely and comprehends "what is for what": why it has so many cylinders and why it has big wheels, where its transmission is situated, and why its rear is cut in an acute angle and its radiator unpolished.
> This is the way one should read.[13]

Yet from the point of view of delirious analysis, what is most interesting is the way in which the first contacts with the car establish a relation, from which other relations begin to emerge. Shklovsky would have people know how the machine works as such, yet delirious resemblance accommodates the ridiculous efforts of the "stupid" to comprehend the car's significance much more coherently than does their out-of-hand practical dismissal. Only a mad theory of confused association can explain the sorts of uses that automobiles have acquired, for example, in contemporary advertisements for trucks or sports cars, in which the relations of cars to cultural signs of power, pleasure and identity far outweigh their importance as machines for transportation.

The potentially delirious aesthetic play in the metaphor of the motor car was noticed by Shklovsky's friend Roman Jakobson when it occurred as a joke in one of the plays of Prague's Liberated Theater. Jakobson's "Letter to

Voskovec and Werich on the Noetics and Semantics of Fun," written for the
Czech theater's outstanding pair of clowns, gives this example of how a delirious view of the sign for motorcar was staged in one of their revues, as a phenomenal "negative object":

> BUN: Well, you know that big Sentinel sports car? The hood with all that
> chrome, six meters long?
> HAND: Well, yeah, that's my dream!
> BUN: Well, that hood, you see, I don't have that at all. But then again those six
> exhaust pipes, so nice one under the other . . .
> HAND: Well, yeah, I know them!
> BUN: Well, I don't have those, either.[14]

To mistake the sign for the thing it represents becomes, in Jakobson's view, a
convenient vehicle for the disruption of the "automatism of habit," which in
the formalist tradition after Bergson usually implies a laugh. There are many
darker shades of delirium in Czech literature and theory, like the fervent
imaginings of Ladislav Klíma or the "negative objects" in Kafka's works,
(such as *The Castle* or "The Oklahoma Nature Theater" in *Amerika*) but delirium knows no genres, either—even though Havel's early perspective as a
protégé of Jan Werich was doubtless conditioned by comedy. Havel seems to
have inherited both the motorcar and a delirious, comical way of looking at
it.

Havel's first three experiments in the professional theater were formally
complex revues, commissioned for the Theater on the Balustrade by Ivan
Vyskočil, a charismatic cabaret performer who specialized in what he called
the theater of "text-appeal."[15] These were collaborative projects: one was co-
written with Vyskočil, one with Miloš Macourek (an imaginative author of
children's literature), and another, called *The Demented Dove,* dramatized the
delirious transformations of language through the use of verse texts from
writers working in the modernist Czech tradition of Poetism.[16] The first of
these was published as *Auto-Stop* (or *Hitchhike*); it consists of three one-act
plays introduced by a "demonstrator" played by Vyskočil. All three one-acts
are about the impact of the motorcar, but in the central one the demonstrator
takes on the part of a university docent (an assistant professor without tenure)
who is presenting research "On Motomorphosis:" i.e. on an "essentially complex disease process of psychoneurotical origins, consisting in the graduated
and general transformations of persons into an automobile or other kind of
motorized vehicle."[17]

After presenting his dissertation work, docent Macek (which means "tom-
cat") introduces a friendly case-study named Felinka ("feline"?) who drives himself on stage, parks, turns his motor off so that he can talk to the doctor, and
then starts himself back up again so that the audience can ask amusing tech-

nical questions about things like the vibration in his carburetor and the mixture of oil and gasoline in fuel cylinders (since, like most Eastern bloc cars, he has a two-cycle engine). Finally Felinka drives back to his *"ambulance,"* which is the Czech word for both an ambulance and an outpatient clinic. In the next, crucial scene, the enthusiastic docent argues that Felinka's motomorphosis is not merely a delusion, but a real physiological disease, a "pathological process consisting in a complex stalling out of natural physiological functions. . . . Evidently declinating from all normal forms of everyday biology in humans," which is even verifiable "empirically and statistically" (43).

When the audience objects to this bizarre physiological theory, the docent becomes extremely angry, proclaiming that they had better examine their relationship to his contemporary discovery, for they will be unmasked if they are revealed to be "among the members of the union hostile to motorism" (44). In the final scene, the "transformation and conclusion" the audience for the presentation and the docent begin to "sound like klaxon horns," then assemble in formation behind a Mr. Bursik ("Exchange"), and "toodle" offstage together. They have been changed perhaps too literally into the "desiring machines" of Deleuze and Guattari, but in the context of a critical artistic tradition that was clearly moving the metaphor of the motorcar in just that non-sensical direction.

SCENE II: LOGICAL DISAPPEARANCE

This sort of strange episode relates to Havel's study of absurdists like Ionesco—even though it predates *Rhinoceros,* which tells the same story through the more ominously Fascist myth of the savage beast that man can become. The influence of Ionesco asserts itself in Havel's work more obviously in the way Havel's dialogue imitates the theories of the linguistics professor in Ionesco's *The Lesson.* Signs which seem to be the same acquire different meanings in different moments, or their meanings are simply determined subjectively by the force of their speaker's assertions. In Ionesco's work the play's dialogue often suspends its ordinary relation to reality, despite its pretensions to logic.[18] Such a profound loss of connection between signs and their coded references can strike at the very foundations of understanding, including supposedly self-evident notions like Descartes's *cogito.*

In Havel's case the metamorphic "mechanization" of man, seen as a goal in earlier theories like Italian Futurism, is also a metaphor for the forced reorientation of subjectivity that the population in Czechoslovakia experienced after the Nazi occupation in 1938 and the subsequent Communist coup in 1948.[19] As Czeslaw Milosz describes them in *The Captive Mind* (still the classic study of artistic subjectivity in the context of ideological drift), the rigid dialectical and historical requirements of the Soviet ideology established absolute connections between signs and reality that were not subject to judgment; the official ideology became a mechanism which threatened to overpower the traditional critical powers of thought.[20] Consequently the concept of "mechanization" in Havel's work provoked a great deal of explanation in the first phase of his critical reception.[21] The effort to think through the subjective effects of ideological transformation did not yield easily to logical analysis, but rather led Havel to the sorts of paradoxes of being that also provide the springboard for Deleuze's leap into the theory of delirious subjectivity.[22]

The clearest example of this paradoxical problem with identity comes through the self-analysis carried out by Hugo Pludek in *The Garden Party*. This central character has a talent for logical games and an uncanny ability to manipulate discourse into unexpected pseudological formulations and strategies. Leaving the house where he compulsively plays chess with himself (and loses!), Hugo goes to a social gathering where his imitations of official language eventually lead the head of the Inauguration Department to deduce that the Liquidation Department has decided to dissolve his organization. Hugo, when visiting Inauguration the next day, is quick to understand that the liquidation can never begin if there is no Inauguration Department to start it; Hugo ends up in charge of a newly designed central commission that will administer both departments.

This pseudological semiotic game might seem to be a simple indictment of the bizarre Communist practice of strictly categorizing business responsibilities under government bureaus, but Hugo also extends his analysis into an examination of human identity. When the new, powerful Hugo returns home his parents can no longer recognize him, nor does Hugo really know himself; he is caught up in a delirious frenzy of dialectical language, which leads to the kind of semio-poetic analysis in which the connections between signs take on a life of their own apart from their referential uses. In this case the shorthand of representational logic slips into infinite regression:

HUGO: I? Who am I? Now look, I don't like such one-sidedly formulated questions, I really don't! How can you even ask in such a simplified manner? No matter how one answers questions like these—one can never encompass the whole truth, only its limited part: a Person—that is something so richly complex, changeable, and diversified, that there is no sentence, book, nothing at all that could define one in its totality. There is nothing permanent, eternal, absolute in persons, they are perpetual change, proudly ringing change, of course! Nowadays the time of static, unchangeable categories is over; nowadays, A is not just A, and B just B; today we know that A can often also be B, and B at the same time be A; that B can be B, as well as A and C; by the same token, C can be not only C, but also A, B, and D, and under certain circumstances, F can be Q or even Y or R![23]

Hugo's talent for analysis eventually helps him to theorize the delirious erasure of the possibility of his own being. Echoing Hamlet, he concludes: "I don't know whether you want to be or want not to be, and when you want to be and not to be; but me, I want to be always—that's why I must always a little bit not be." This satisfies Hugo's parents, and as the play ends the audience in the theater is subsequently told to "split" (63).

Yet the audience's perception does not split; their identification with the delirious hero does not logically imply their imitation of Hugo's fragmentation into an aspect of political discourse. The coherence of the play's delirious elements depends upon their maintaining an understanding that the signifier for Hugo in the world of the play, the actor playing Hugo, remains recognizable. Hugo may seem to be logical, but he is also so badly mistaken about his place in the world that he is utterly ridiculous, and consequently completely fascinating.

Hugo represents the delirious potential of logic, just as the well-known effects of artificial language in *The Memorandum* represent a linguistic equivalent, in which the principles for the construction of the proposed "official" languages conform precisely to the poles of linguistic confusion and differentiation identified by Karčevski. Because logical arguments can maintain their logical form without maintaining the material correspondences that judgment must establish between signs and their referents, the logical connections between signs do not by themselves provide a secure context for stable judgments of identity. In *The Garden Party* one character goes adrift in an ocean of signs; in *The Memorandum* the whole world of the play risks being similarly overwhelmed by delirious signification.

SCENE III: TIME/SPACE DISCONTINUUM

In *The Increased Difficulty of Concentration* Havel dramatizes the consciousness of a system of order even more vertiginous than language: social philosophy. Eduard Huml, overcome by anxiety, has retreated to his apartment, and Havel's play is cross-cut through time to show his confused interactions with the four women who meet with him there. In this play Havel uses time-sequence displacements to demonstrate confusion—disruptions of regular narrative chronology that also create spatial disturbances as characters move in and out of different doors in different costumes during time-spans that seem impossible. Havel wrote a thesis on this play in which he illustrates the disruptions in a chart, which features a column listing the sequence of chronological events, beginning when Huml has breakfast with his wife, continuing through a series of episodes with a stenographer, mistress and visiting research team, and concluding with his wife's return from work. A parallel column shows the order of events in the plot, beginning and ending with the breakfast scene, and intercutting the action in what looks like a random sequence.[24] In Deleuzian terms, the chart is the rhizome, the root system for an elegant, formally circular play in which the clarity of the dramatic structure is entirely at odds with the hero's confused experience that it conveys. This elegant form is unmistakable for the audience, since the structure is bracketed by the first scene after Huml wakes and its twin, the last scene before he goes to sleep. With time, and consequently the spatial coordinates for time, in such formally imposed confusion, the hero literally cannot tell when and where people are; he lapses into repetitive behavior, confuses the identities of the women in the play, and loses any concept of the relative values of behavior.[25]

At the climax of this formal structure is a crucial scene with the research group. In addition to the leading researcher, Jitka Balcarková—who begins an unlikely affair with the confused Huml at the end of the play—the team includes a computer named PUZUK (the nickname of Havel's younger brother Ivan). This early computer brain is supposed to have enormous powers of calculation and scientific prediction, yet the hermeneutic burden placed upon its sensitive mechanical subjectivity is so great that when it is ordered to perform, it complains that it is tired, and asks for some rest. Later on, forced like Huml to cooperate with the research program despite having made its excuses, the computer becomes delirious, and begins to generate impertinent, surreal and embarrassing questions. Triggered by the machine, Huml's consciousness, too, spins out of control. In a bizarre sequence out of time and space, characters from earlier in the play re-appear in rapid sequence, repeating non-sensical questions that fruitfully combine their lines with others: "Fishing for fresh green apples, are you? Tomorrow I'm going carroting, so there! Give me your mountain dog-plums! Wherein lies the nucleus? Do you piss in public, or just now and then?"[26] The burden of a theory of knowledge which makes the unit of data an absolute fact, but offers only an infinite context for judgment, is too great for either Huml or the little computer to bear, resulting in their parallel episodes of delirious imagination.

Huml, who dictates a lecture throughout the play, had theorized values in the broadest of relativist terms. After this delirious episode Huml can only restore his perspective through a new discovery that he works out in a long speech near the end of the play: the re-discovery of a personal hermeneutic perspective. Centered in the horizon of interactive experience, the human valuation of humans is a matter of shared judgment, and not necessarily an invitation for infinite "factual" ratiocination:

> HUML: I'm afraid the key to a real knowledge of the human individual does not lie in some greater or lesser understanding of the complexity of man as an object of scientific knowledge. The only key lies in man's complexity as a subject of human togetherness, because the limitlessness of our own human nature is so far the only thing capable of approaching—however imperfectly—the limitlessness of others. In other words, the personal, human, unique relation-

ship which arises between two individuals is so far the only thing that can—at least to some extent—mutually unveil the secret of those two individuals. Such values as love, friendship, compassion, sympathy and a unique, irreplaceable mutual understanding—or even mutual conflict—are the only tools which this human approach has at its disposal. By any other means we may perhaps be able more or less to explain man, but we shall never understand him—not even a little—and therefore we shall never arrive at a basic knowledge of him. (56)

Though such a perspective is still vulnerable to problems of interpretation, and especially to any loss of the context for shared communication (either of which could be a pretext for new delirious "miscognitions"), Huml's discovery does solve the problems of spatial, temporal and self perception that can result when the subject exists in semiotic singularity.

SCENE IV: DELIRIUM AND POLITICAL PARALYSIS

Havel's regular theoretical solution to the problem of delirious subjectivity has been a consistent faith in the intuitive hermeneutic power of the audience to infer appropriate judgments of the play's events. In technical articles on playwriting from the 1960s he consistently described conventions themselves as tending to construct "vicious circles"; without the semiotic discretion of the historical audience, any innovation, meaning, and even Deleuzian "sense" would be impossible to communicate.[27] In this regard Havel's conclusions are very much like those of Gadamer, which suggest that interpretation occurs as a negotiation of perspectives on signs.[28] The loss of this audience resource for Havel after the Prague Spring [of 1968] eventually led him to adopt a communicative ethics of dissent that closely resembles a phenomenological version of the late Habermas, in which the crucial concerns are access to communication, the sincerity of communication, and shared rules of legitimate argument.[29] The ability to communicate becomes the foundation for democratic politics.

The political pitfall of delirious subjectivity, then, becomes apparent in Havel's work in the case of isolated characters like Leopold Kopřiva [Nettles], the dissident phenomenologist in *Largo Desolato*. The play begins with three identical scenes:

As the music dies away the curtain rises slowly.
Leopold is alone on stage. He is sitting on the sofa and staring at the front door. After a long pause he gets up and looks through the peep-hole. Then he puts his ear to the door and listens intently. After another long pause the curtain drops suddenly and at the same time the music returns.[30]

The same scene closes the play, modified only to include a curtain call. Leopold, isolated and deprived, exists in a situation in which the only important signs are outside, sensible only through the lens of a peep-hole and the muffled sounds that penetrate the door. Such a situation, the metaphoric equivalent of Havel's imprisonment, provides no reliable or coherent hermeneutic perspective, and requires change.

Left as it is, Leopold's life continues under conditions in which the delirious imaginings of the persecuted subject can only be allayed by the gestures that he gradually adds to his routine in the course of the play: pacing, taking medication, washing, and gasping for air. Even Leopold's monotonous, uneventful life becomes too complex to be tolerated in the context of his delirious situation; his lack of confidence about the truth of signs finds its analogous expression in his lack of personal confidence. Like Huml's, Kopřiva's consciousness yields, late in the play, to a delirious, imagined scene of veiled threats. Other characters appear outside of the plot sequence, speaking lines from earlier in the play that focus on Leopold Kopřiva's self-doubts:

LEOPOLD: I don't exactly know what I was saying—

FIRST SIDNEY: But we know—

(At that moment the bathroom door opens. Bertram is standing in the doorway talking to Leopold.)

BERTRAM: I don't want to be hard on you or hurt you in any way.

(At that moment the kitchen door opens. Edward is standing there speaking to Leopold.)

EDWARD: Were you worried?

(At that moment the door of Suzana's room opens. Suzana is standing there speaking to Leopold.)

SUZANA: Are you sure you didn't get yourself into trouble again somehow?

BERTRAM: I'm not just speaking for myself. . . .

EDWARD: Did you sign anything?

FIRST SIDNEY: We've only taken the liberty of giving you our opinion—

SECOND SIDNEY: The opinion of ordinary people—

FIRST SIDNEY: Lots of ordinary people—

EDWARD: Some hero.

SUZANA: Some hero.

BERTRAM: Some hero.

LUCY: Some hero.

FIRST SIDNEY: You've had enough of me and now you want to get shot of me.

SECOND SIDNEY: Some hero.

FIRST SIDNEY: Did you sign anything?

LEOPOLD: (Shouting) GET OUT! (45–46)

Leopold, paralyzed by dread, fluctuates between a delirium that sometimes becomes a sustained, defensive indifference, but at other times emerges as an indiscriminate desire that has collapsed upon itself, so that he cannot resume his marriage, cannot commit himself to political action, and cannot conceive of meaningful alternatives to confinement. Even formerly convincing political arguments seem questionable, as Leopold admits to an admiring female student:

> LEOPOLD: On the other hand there is the fact—as I've already tried to show in *Ontology of the Human Self*—that there's a certain non-verbal, existential space in which—and only in which—one can get hold of something through experiencing the presence of another person—
> MARKETA: Forgive me, it's exactly that part—it's from chapter four—which made me decide to come and see you—
> LEOPOLD: There you are! But I wouldn't like to raise your hopes unduly, because the fact that I'm meditating on this topic doesn't automatically mean that I am myself capable of creating such a space—
> MARKETA: But you've been creating it for ages—by talking to me at all—by understanding me. . . . (50–51)

Leopold, unlike Huml, does not recapture a hermeneutic perspective, yet it has been taken up by an attentive reader. In this regard Marketa's understanding imitates the receptive understanding of the play's audience, which anchors every instance of delirium in Havel's imaginative work.

Havel uses delirious episodes throughout his later career; even in so apparently documentary a play as *Audience,* the Brewmaster's progressive drunkenness conjures a fluidly discontinuous whirlpool of subjectivity, against which the stoic dissident strives to communicate. In *The Mountain Hotel* the entire play is like Huml's nightmare, a delirious permutation combining characters, scenes, actions and dialogue into new sequences and effects. In *The Beggar's Opera* the delirious moment comes late in the play, when MacHeath finally realizes that his basic assumptions about the world were mistaken; deception is the rule, not the exception that makes truthfulness an issue, and at the end of the play he embraces the delirious implications of moral chaos. In [later plays], like *Temptation* and *Slum Clearance,* the delirious moment is a drunken party—a black mass and a celebration. Many of these moments have proven extremely difficult to stage, especially for the plays written during the time when Havel was without a theater. Earlier plays, carefully revised in rehearsal to respond to the dynamics of audience reception, augmented the coherent context of audience understanding with a strong aesthetic effect.

CURTAIN CALL: HAVEL'S SEMIOTIC SELF

I have argued elsewhere . . . that the reception of Havel's authorial persona has been similarly susceptible to delirious permutations, many of which contributed to the man's unlikely yet all the same inexorable rise to power during the revolution.[31] In "Stories and Totalitarianism" Havel had begun to discover a distinct cultural community in Czechoslovakia's prisons, that still regarded proceedings beyond the prison walls with something like the theater audience's human perspective of hermeneutic engagement:

> While I was in prison I realized again and again how much more present, compared with life outside, the story was. Almost every prisoner had a life story that was unique and shocking, or moving. As I listened to those different stories, I suddenly found myself in something like a pre-totalitarian world, or in the world of literature. Whatever else I may have thought of my fellow prisoners' colorful narratives, they were not documents of totalitarian nihilization. On the contrary, they testified to the rebelliousness with which human uniqueness resists its own nihilization, and the stubbornness with which it holds to its own and is willing to ignore this negating pressure. Regardless of whether crime and misfortune was predominant in any given story, the faces in that world were specific and personal.[32]

Dialogic narrative, and the affirmation of understanding that occurs during its plural, inter-subjective coherence, provides a context for identity and experience that extreme commitments to logic and dogma cannot easily contradict. Havel, known as a historical hero with singular talents, nevertheless theorizes a dialogic construction of the self. . . .

Havel may very well emerge as a kind of proto-type of the generative self: creator of signs, pseudonyms, self-interpretations and public meditations. Certainly his dramaturgy suggests that he manages a careful balance between the expression of delirious characters and the coherent audience interpretation of their playful mental associations. This paradox of aesthetic technique seems sensible in the case of a public figure who asserts a conspicuous lack of desire for power, yet conversely gains power through altruism. The successful subject in postmodern culture is not only reflective, but expressive and receptive, able to balance self-assessment with the ongoing social project of personal interpretation. Canadian philosopher Charles Taylor sums up the contemporary notion of a "dialogic" self in terms that seem to imply just this conclusion about Havel, so I will allow his summary to conclude my argument:

> Much of our understanding of self, society, and world is carried in practices that consist in dialogical action. I would like to argue, in fact, that language itself serves to set up spaces of common action, on a number of levels, intimate and public. This means that our identity is never simply defined in terms of our individual properties. It also places us in some social space. We define ourselves partly in terms of what we come to accept as our appropriate place within dialogical actions. In the case that I really identify myself with my deferential attitude toward wiser people like you, then this conversational stance becomes a constituent of my identity. This social reference figures even more clearly in the identity of the dedicated revolutionary.[33]

Notes and References

1. See for example Derrida's "argument" with John Searle in "Limited Inc a b c . . ." where the two are really at odds from the beginning, since one is charting the possibilities of error, while the other is arguing for the possibility of successful communication. "Limited Inc a b c . . .," trans. Samuel Weber, *Glyph* 2 (Baltimore: Johns Hopkins University Press, 1977): 162–254.

2. This politics of delirium can be found, for example, as an implied alternative to enlightenment in Michel Foucault's *Madness and Civilization: A History of Insanity in the Age of Reason,* trans. Richard Howard (New York: Random, 1965).

3. Some writers, like Julia Kristeva, make the subjective implications of delirium the special responsibility of art, as in her *Revolution in Poetic Language,* trans. Margaret Waller (New York: Columbia University Press, 1984), 215.

4. The most complete overview of this aesthetics of delirium is in the section on poetics in Jean-Jacques Lecercle's *Philosophy Through the Looking Glass* (La Salle, IL: Open Court, 1984.)

5. See Gilles Deleuze, *The Logic of Sense,* trans. Mark Lester with Charles Vitale (New York: Columbia University Press, 1990).

6. See Charles S. Pierce, "Logic as Semiotic: The Theory of Signs," *Semiotics: An Introductory Anthology,* ed. Robert E. Innis (Bloomington: Indiana University Press, 1985), 5.

7. See John R. Searle, "The Logical Status of Fictional Discourse," *New Literary History* 6 (1975): 319–32.

8. See Sergei Karčevski, "The Asymmetric Dualism of the Linguistic Sign," trans. Wendy Steiner, *The Prague School: Selected Writings, 1929–1946,* ed. Peter Steiner (Austin: University of Texas Press, 1982), 47–54.

9. See for example my analysis of delirious signification in *commedia* acting in "The Comedy of Reference," *Theatre Journal* 43.1 (March 1991): 70–92.

10. As a psychologically based technique of writing character, see the analysis by Walter Sokel, *The Writer in Extremis* (Stanford: Stanford University Press, 1959).

11. This delirious analysis of culture is of course the famous thesis of Deleuze and Félix Guattari in *Anti-Oedipus: Capitalism and Schizophrenia,* trans. Robert Hurley, Mark Seem, and Helen R. Lane (Minneapolis: University of Minnesota Press, 1983).

12. I have constructed this tradition from Bergson through the Russian Formalists, Brecht and the Czech Structuralists to Havel in my unpublished study, "The Semiotics of Comic Acting" presented at the American Society of Semiotics meeting in October 1987.

13. Quoted in Peter Steiner, *Russian Formalism: A Metapoetics* (Ithaca: Cornell University Press, 1984), 45–46.

14. My "Jakobson and the Liberated Theater" contains a translation of Jakobson's letter, originally published as part of an anniversary volume marking the tenth anniversary of the theater, *Deset let osvobozeného divadla,* ed. Josef Träger (Prague: Borovy, 1937).

15. See Zdeněk Hořínek, "Hry a příběhy ('Nedivadelní' texty Ivana Vyskočila)" [Plays with Events: (The "Non-Theatrical Texts" of Ivan Vyskočil)], *Divadelní Revue* 1.1 (1989): 58–65.

16. Havel was the dramaturg on this project, "Vyšinuta hrdlička," which gathered texts by 15 writers in a production staged by Jan Grossman at Divadlo na zábradlí, 1963.

17. Ivan Vyskočil and Václav Havel, *Auto-Stop* (Prague: Dilia, 1961); translations from this work are mine and are cited in the text.

18. O. G. Karpinskaja and I. I. Revzin explain how the dialogue eliminates all aspects of coherence except that in the signs themselves; see "A Semiotic Analysis of Early Plays by Ionesco *(The Bald Soprano, The Lesson),*" *Soviet Semiotics: An Anthology,* ed. Daniel P. Lucid (Baltimore: Johns Hopkins University Press, 1977), 199–202.

19. See the many examples of mechanized stage figures in Futurism, as collected and described by Michael Kirby, *Futurist Performance* (New York: Dutton, 1971).

20. See Czeslaw Milosz, *The Captive Mind,* trans. Jane Zielonko (New York: Knopf, 1953).

21. Many excellent Czech critics considered this theme to be the most significant in Havel's early work. See, for example, Jindřich Černý, "Mechanismus života a hry" ("Mechanism in Life and Play"), *Host do domu* 15.8 (1964): 60–62.

22. See Deleuze's sustained treatment of paradox in *Différence et répétition* (Paris: Presses universitaires de France, 1981).

23. Václav Havel, *Zahradní slavnost {The Garden Party}, Ztížená možnost soustředění {The Increased Difficulty of Concentration}.* (London: Rozmluvy, 1986), 62; it seems necessary to mention that the standard English translation by Vera Blackwell does not feature this problem, so I have made my own versions, hereafter cited in the text.

24. Havel's thesis chart actually describes the structure of an earlier draft of the play titled "Eduard," *Diplomní práce,* DAMU, 1966.

25. See my extended analysis of this play and the early draft, "Dramatizing Delirium: Havel's *Ztížená možnost soustředění* and the Don Juan Theme," *Don Juan and Faust in the Twentieth Century,* ed. Eva Šormová (Prague: 1992).

26. I have enjambed several lines from the delirious scene in *The Increased Difficulty of Concentration,* trans. Vera Blackwell (New York: French, 1976), with a couple of small changes; Blackwell's translation is hereafter cited in the text.

27. See for example Havel's "Začarovaný kruh" ("A Vicious Circle") *Divadlo* 1 (1967): 1–9.

28. The standard source, of course, is Hans-Georg Gadamer, *Truth and Method,* trans. W. Gly-Doepel (London: Sheed and Ward, 1975).

29. See, for example, Habermas's "What is Universal Pragmatics?" *Communication and the Evolution of Society,* trans. Thomas McCarthy (Boston: Beacon, 1979).

30. Václav Havel, *Largo Desolato,* trans. Tom Stoppard (New York: Grove, 1985), 1; hereafter cited parenthetically in the text.

31. Michael L. Quinn, "Vaněk for President: Václav Havel and Semiotic Identity," *Small is Beautiful: Small Countries Theatre Conference,* ed. Claude Schumacher (Glasgow: Theatre Studies Publications, 1991), 89–100.

32. Václav Havel, "Stories and Totalitarianism," *Open Letters: Selected Writings 1965–1990,* ed. and trans. Paul Wilson (New York: Knopf, 1991), 338–39.

33. Charles Taylor, "The Dialogic Self," *The Interpretive Turn: Philosophy, Science, Culture,* ed. David R. Hiley, James F. Bohman, and Richard Shusterman (Ithaca: Cornell University Press, 1991), 311.

Life under Absurdity:
Václav Havel's *Largo Desolato*

DOUGLAS SODERBERG

{Havel's plays have been generally neglected by most American theaters. Because the predominant concern of most American theater has been, and continues to be, to provide entertainment for the dwindling numbers of middle class audiences.

—Robert Skloot}

We're still waiting for Godot—some of us more than others. As the 20th century hurtles to an end, artists in particular are anxious, although for them Godot is no longer an old gentleman with ontological answers; he is instead the long arm of the law, the eye at the window, a loud knock at the door. And unlike Joseph K in Kafka's *The Trial,* the artist knows what his crimes are: they are crimes of the imagination.

This, using two literary influences cited by Václav Havel, is a way of describing the dissident experience, the emotional milieu of life under occupation. The dissident writer, of course, must himself express what he wants to say without directly doing so. He develops codes, uses irony, makes his case only by defining the edges. He's a prisoner of his own need to communicate. Havel got three-and-a-half years unusually intensive practice, from October 1979 through January 1983, when he was interred in a Czech prison camp for "criminal subversion of the republic." His letters to his wife, Olga, during that time, ostensibly about very little, were actually carefully camouflaged critiques of the Communist government; they were published in a *samizdat* edition and circulated while Havel was still serving his sentence.

So his letters did get out, they did slip past the warden (whom Havel has described as "having it in for" him). What needed to be said, no matter how convex or tortured, was, in the end, said. Was it a triumph of the freedom of expression? A testimony to the unvanquishability of the human spirit? Only partly so. The experiences of Havel and his countrymen—and of his country—amount to self-censorship. Havel, who characterizes himself as a

Reprinted and abridged from Yale Repertory Theatre magazine, *Yale Reports* (October/November 1990): 1, 3.

mediocre politician, piecemeal philosopher and craftsman-like playwright, is nothing if not self-aware. Less than two years after his release from prison, he wrote a witty, somewhat autobiographical, self-effacing play that addresses the question of self-censorship and identity under duress, *Largo Desolato*. This clever, chilling play (written in just four days) might have been the last word on the subject but was, to no one's surprise, not. The play was published in an underground edition and circulated in Czechoslovakia only privately [Padlock edition, no. 281]. It received its première at the Vienna Burgtheater on April 14, 1985. There had been an official ban on all works by Havel, a ban lifted, finally, with his quick election as president during the frantic, heady revolution in December, 1989.

The time and setting of *Largo Desolato* are unspecified. The story is of one Professor Leopold Nettles, author of cosmological essays that have a devoted following among the intelligentsia. One rousing passage in his latest book, however, has chafed the government. He is accused of "intellectual hooliganism" and, he knows, will go to prison for it. The play shows him battling inner demons, half-listening to an avalanche of proffered advice, and waiting—mostly waiting—for the knock at his door.

Leopold Nettles is a funny, unlikely hero. His surname, in Tom Stoppard's translation, is a joke, a "ticket" name, the use of which was favored by Restoration dramatists; Leopold is the irritant, the sort of fellow who can get under the skin of the public and cause a governmental rash. In fact, the word "hero" is used ironically in the play. Leopold does not act heroically—inertia and fretfulness are not likely to stamp anyone a hero, and yet everyone else in the play, from strangers and colleagues to his wife and mistress, tells him that he is one. And that he must act like one. But he can't. He's a writer, that's all, one who has made perhaps only one mistake, and that is daring to think in a place where it's discouraged. He's no hero. Heaviest is the head that has the crown shoved upon it.

The cautious dissident writer uses analogy as part of his cryptography. For Havel, Leopold represents the corpselike apathy and ennui of the Czech people after the Soviet invasion. His country's morale disheartened Havel so much so that he created in Leopold a comic character, not a tragic one. (Satire is born in much the same way.) Part of the skewed delight in seeing Leopold on stage is his sheer helplessness. There is something pathetically endearing about it. Few people can accurately be described as truly "hapless"; Leopold is one of them. Everything is prescribed for him by powers both present and unseen: what to eat, what to do, when to do it. What to think. He is Buster Keaton under Communist rule, or Didi and Gogo drifting in a void created by someone whose plan they can never understand.

Comic writers such as Beckett and Havel can cause us, often against our wills, to laugh at queasy truths, and from there it's a short jump to where the laughter backfires in our throats. When in the final scene Leopold fulfills the prophecy of one tiny scrap of governmental writing—more words, only more powerful than his own because they have official backing—the laughter shrivels. (The episode parallels one during Havel's prison stay: pressured by the growing support of intellectuals and literati, the state offered Havel parole if he would sign a simple, one-sentence declaration of apology for his anti-Communist activities. Havel refused and was released only some time later for reasons of failing health.)

Largo Desolato can unjustly be lumped together with other plays in the so-called Theatre of the Absurd. This is possible for two good reasons. One, Havel describes himself as an absurdist writer. Talking of his bourgeois childhood, he has said that he "subconsciously felt, or feared, that everyone had—rightly—entered into some kind of conspiracy" against him, and that it contributed significantly to his worldview: ". . . a view which is in fact a key to my plays. It is a view 'from below,' a view from the 'outside,' a view that has grown out of the experience of absurdity. What else but a profound feeling of being excluded can enable a person better to see the absurdity of the world and his own existence?"

Life for him is an "eternal embarrassment" at having no sensation of meaning, no relationship to eternity, no fundamental metaphysical certainty. Absurd theatre takes this amorphous embarrassment and makes it real by staging it. Modern man has had the ground beneath his feet—his identity—pulled away, as though some being had carelessly thrown down a banana peel. Humanity is in a state of crisis.

Another reason the term "theatre of the absurd" (not a conscious movement, but an appellation given later by critical writers) may apply to *Largo Desolato* is that it contains elements from traditionally absurdist drama: repetitions, pseudo-talk, pseudoactivity and a cyclical structure.

But the one thing that propels Havel's play beyond self-conscious absurdism is that those elements which in any other context might be simply "absurd" are, in this case, quite real and rooted in the day-to-day experience of life under a repressive government. The déjà vu of repeated phrases and rhythms and scenes, for instance, echoes the frustration of the dissident thinker. With each new play, essay or speech, he feels that certainly some progress has been made, that he has cracked the wall, so to speak. Maybe he has done so with his comrades—the already enlisted—but he finds the ruling establishment immovable. He is constantly wondering, "Didn't we just settle this?"

The idiocy of pseudo-activity (like walking, or rocking in a chair, or untying and tying one's shoes) and pseudo-talk (making verbal lists, describing minutiae, prattling, talking babytalk) is in *Largo Desolato* given sensible meaning. In *Waiting for Godot,* for instance, the characters wait with neither dread nor joy for something unknown, perhaps just an end to waiting; Leopold Nettles knows for whom he waits, and all his activity, however slight, is an attempt to stave off the inevitable. It's real action with a purpose, not just filler for the void.

Largo Desolato is not, to be precise, the absurd made real. The play depicts reality snarled in the nets of an absurd society. What could be more absurd than a world in which a common childhood paranoia—that one can be punished for one's thoughts—we as adults discover is factual? In a society like ours based on the Bill of Rights, we may easily view this as the ultimate absurdity.

Absurdity is in a sense the dissident writer's métier, his tool and his craft. He attempts to say the (legally) unsayable, to know that which he's forbidden to know. While genuine absurdists like Beckett, Kafka and Ionesco scramble about in circles assuming they are barred from the most fundamental knowledge about themselves and their world, writers like Havel have lived with the fact from 1968 until 1989. Havel weathered it with uncommon grace. He knows himself and sees himself with an ironic eye, never taking himself too seriously. And he knows that, like groups before him, his was not the last to struggle under the weight of state-encouraged self-censorship. His play is a puckish admonition. "I don't give practical advice and I don't make arrangements for anyone. At the most, I occasionally goad into action." He further says that "the only hopes that are worth anything are the ones we discover ourselves, within ourselves, and for ourselves. . . ."

We may laugh at Leopold Nettles. As artists and individuals living in a "free" society, we may be laughing at our own absurd future.

Variations of Temptation—Václav Havel's Politics of Language

Marketa Goetz-Stankiewicz

{By nature Havel is an activist, but his activism is of a special kind. He's a visionary tinkerer; he can imagine the broad outlines of the kind of society he would like to see emerge from the post-Communist ferment, and he has an artist's love of getting involved in the detailed steps necessary to get there.

—Paul Wilson}

If I ignore the trivial truth that art operates by different rules from those of life or of those from thoughts conveyed through essays, I have to point again to the complementary nature of sense and nonsense. The deeper the absence of meaning—in other words of absurdity—the more energetically meaning is thought . . .

—Václav Havel, *Disturbing the Peace*

When approaching a play by Václav Havel, a critic or commentator is bound to have certain preconceptions. He knows that Havel was one of the most famous "dissidents" of the Communist regime in Czechoslovakia, that none of his plays were performed in official theaters there before 1990, that he was harassed and imprisoned several times. (In 1979–1983 he was incarcerated for four years; in early 1989 he was imprisoned again, after being charged with "incitement.") Despite all this (or is it because of it?), his eloquent politico-philosophical essays as well as his plays have been translated into and performed in many languages. Here, critics are bound to argue, we obviously have a literary figure whose life and writings are so closely interwoven with the political situation in his country that we have a ready-made package-deal guide to the interpretation of his works. Journalists, reviewers, and academic commentators have seemed to follow this obvious approach and discussed Havel's writings largely as the direct outcome of what he has been observing in his own society. The "dissident playwright" label has stuck

Reprinted and slightly revised from *Modern Drama* 33, no. 1 (March 1990): 93–105.

hard and fast to Havel's image. But does it do him justice? In this essay I propose to peel off the label and let the readers decide whether they wish to stick it back on after having read my remarks.

In true Havelesque spirit we must first clarify some assumptions: What is "political theater"? Is not drama, dealing mostly with human conflicts and tensions, "political" by its very nature? However, as we wisely put aside this vast question, other related questions begin to sprout like mushrooms after a warm rain.

Let us take some examples. Is *Hamlet* a political play? Brecht certainly thought so. Is Medea's monomania a political statement made by Euripides, as Jan Kott felt it was? Is Hochhuth's *The Deputy* a political play? "Of course," answers the fictional drama critic to whom we now give the floor; "after all, it deals with Pope Pius XII's collaboration with Hitler." Camus's *Le Malentendu (The Misunderstanding)*? "Yes, because it portrays characters whose hope for a better existence drives them to murder." Tom Stoppard's *Professional Foul*? "Yes, of course; the play features a smuggled manuscript, a philosophical text that was considered subversive by a totalitarian government." Peter Handke's *Kaspar*? "Yes indeed, because it shows the process by which an innocent mind is molded to perceive the world in a way approved of by an ailing society." Peter Shaffer's *Amadeus*? "Why certainly; after all, it shows how a genius is ignored by a stupid and bigoted regime while a mediocre musical hack is allowed to flourish."

It is clear that these admittedly random references will not lead us anywhere. But neither, let it be said, do many of the numerous volumes that have been written on "political theater." In his *Geschichte des politischen Theaters* (History of Political Theater), which is useful in our context, Siegfried Melchinger argues that plays from the past deserve to be called "political theater" only if they are still playable, in other words meaningful, today. This, Melchinger stresses, does not mean that "political theater" treats politics in the light of "eternal values";[1] it must concretely show whatever we mean by "politics" (power, ruling systems, war, violence) and must make the audience go through the process of recognizing an experience by seeing it acted out. In Havel's case, the audience that would concretely "recognize" its own experience in his plays was unable to see a play by Havel for twenty years (1969–89). But this does not mean that we, his contemporaries under another political system, do not undergo some process of recognizing our own experience, for if Havel's theater is to be called "political," then only in the broadest sense. To explore this, let us first go back to Havel and to a more hands-on beginning.

In the afterword to a selection of his plays written in 1976 Havel ironically defines the obliquely "political" roots of his writings. He tells us that the "seemingly unfortunate combination of a bourgeois origin and life in a Communist state," though burdening his life with disadvantages, was in fact beneficial in the sense that it allowed him "to see that world, so to speak, from 'below,' " whence "the absurd and grotesque dimensions of the world are most apparent."[2] This wry remark seems to reduce any attempt to argue that Havel is or is not a "political" playwright to an academic game of pigeon-holing, or else it clearly shows that the question is simply pointless. In this spirit I turn to his play *Temptation*.

"The first impulse to write a Faust play," Havel told his friends in 1986 during an evening of informal discussions about *Temptation*, "came in the year 1977 when I was in prison for the first time." Being subjected to lengthy interrogations and particularly harassing pressures during that time, he felt he was "almost physically tempted by the devil."[3] Moreover, by some strange coincidence, the prison authorities handed him Goethe's *Faust* and Thomas Mann's *Doctor Faustus* as reading matter. Gradually he began to feel that he would like to "grasp this material in my own way,"[4] but he had no idea how. During the following years, interrupted by a four-year prison term, he made two attempts to write a Faust play but each time destroyed what he had written. In 1985 he began to read magic literature, assembled for him by his friend, the writer and literary scholar Zdeněk Urbánek (to whom *Temptation* was later dedicated). Still, he tells us, he had no idea how to tackle the theme. Then one day he began "to draw sketches and graphics, schemes of entrances and exits, envisage the structure of the play."[5] This is important in the sense that he did not begin, as Western critics imply, with a political idea but with an artifact for the stage. When Havel finally began writing, he completed the play within ten days—unusually fast for an author who was used to spending two or three years on a dramatic text. Exhausted after its completion, he needed weeks to calm down and let the play go on to "lead its own life," as a text radiating meanings "about which the author cannot know in advance where they will lead and where they will end."[6]

Temptation had its première in German in 1986 at the Akademietheater in Vienna, and in 1987 was performed by the Royal Shakespeare Company in Stratford-upon-Avon; during the Fall of that year it was performed in London, and in Spring 1989 it had its North American première at the Public Theater in New York. Critical reactions to the play are revealing. They vary considerably according to the places from which they come, and tell us more about the assumptions and the receptive climate of these places than about the play itself. The Viennese papers, for example, were mostly concerned with its allegedly unsatisfactory treatment of Goethe and the venerable Faust tradition. Goethe, it was claimed in variations, was put at the service of anti-totalitarian criticism. This, though entirely contrary to Havel's intentions, became the main thrust of the august theater-city's receptive response. The fact that the production was stiff and virtually ignored the play's immense potential for histrionics and humour may have been due to the fact that those responsible for it had made up their minds about two things: firstly, that it was a variation on a German classic; secondly, that it was a political play with an anti-totalitarian message.

The reaction of the British papers and other media to Roger Michell's production of *Temptation* (in George Theiner's translation) was remarkably different. Brought up on Shakespeare, Wilde, Beckett, and Stoppard, the British critics, shrewdly aware that "the play's the thing," comment on the drama as "an intoxicatingly theatrical piece."[7] Although the workings of evil shown are acknowledged to "spring from a totalitarian system," the point is made repeatedly that the play is "not confined to that system";[8] rather it is regarded as "one of the great artistic adventures of our day."[9]

Responding to a flashy but shallower production of *Temptation,* New York critics retired into the safe niche of isolationism and regarded the play largely as sailing under the flag of one who opposes an oppressive political regime. This reaction, as was said before, is to be expected. The playwright himself is acutely aware of the problem, and has repeatedly mentioned his dissatisfaction with being labelled a "dissident": a term, he said, that "implies a special profession."[10] Indeed, when in the past he has been able to see video productions or read reviews of some of his plays abroad he always "preferred those in which the satirical references to the local [Czechoslovakia's] reality were entirely missing."[11] Havel realizes that the drama critics (whom he calls, perhaps with an endearing touch of naiveté, "mostly sophisticated intellectuals") have minds that have become—and here he is by no means naive—confused by various doctrines, ideologies and theories and tend to miss "the essential dramatic quality"[12] of the plays. He comments on directors and producers who, aware of the drabness of life in totalitarian societies, think the plays emerging from there must likewise be drab and gloomy.

Be this as it may, what interests us here is that we also have Czech reactions to the play. These were of course based, until 1990, only on a reading of the text or listening to a tape recording. It is these responses that are particularly interesting for us. In 1986 there appeared (in the Czech *samizdat* series *Nové cesty myšlení* [New Ways of Thought])[13] a volume entitled *Faustování s Havlem* (something like Fausticizing with Havel). It was published on the playwright's fiftieth birthday, which coincided with his being awarded the prestigious Erasmus Prize of the Netherlands. The volume comprises six essays by philosophers, scientists and literary critics none of which discusses what the West has been variously interpreting as the "political" (meaning anti-totalitarian) thrust of the play. Rather they discuss the philosophical, dramatic, literary or metaphysical aspects of *Temptation*. The result is remarkable. One of the most interesting essays from the standpoint of our present context is the philosopher Radim Palouš's contribution "The Temptation of Speech."[14] Here Palouš touches on the tantalizing quality of Havel's work as a contemporary playwright. Havel reveals the vastly different ways in which language may be used: on the one hand to express the highest flights of man's intellect, his ability to reason, to analyze the complexities of physical and spiritual existence, and to define his perception of truth; on the other hand language can serve the ability to conceal and blur the reasoning process, jumble analysis, bury what he knows to be the truth, and mask the putrid lie with the make-up of smooth rhetoric. One might say that Havel's plays are finely choreographed wrestling matches between two types of rhetoric. Although every single one of his plays deals with a critique of language in one way or another, the playwright seems to have given it the most challenging treatment it has yet had in his Faust play, *Temptation*. This, as I hope to show, is "political" theater in its oldest and widest sense.

But first a note on what the play is about. A scientist named Foustka (a Czechified diminutive of Faust) employed in a scientific Institute gets secretly involved with black magic. He is found out because his tempter, a seedy Mephistophelian figure who is working for the Institute as a sort of *agent provocateur*, betrays his secret activities. Foustka tries to explain what the Institute's authorities consider a breach of loyalty to the profession. While all this is going on, Foustka finds himself between two women: his steady woman friend Vilma whose bed he shares once or twice a week, and Maggie, the Institute's secretary who falls in love with him, begins to defend his way of thinking, and as a result loses her job as well as her sanity. At a costume ball held in the Institute's garden things come to a head, Foustka's coat catches fire and everything goes up in smoke.

Like Havel's earlier *The Beggar's Opera*[15] the action is a veritable who-is-who game. Identities are worn and shed like lab coats. Nothing is what it seems to be. No one is who he seems to be. True statements and lies can no longer be differentiated. Uncertainty reigns on all fronts. Although much could be said about Havel's carefully structured game of masks within masks (also a "political" issue), I will limit my remarks to the related and equally carefully structured game of words. It is here, I would argue, that we find the core of Havel's mastery as a dramatist.

We are never told explicitly what kind of scientific research is being carried on in the Institute where Dr. Foustka is employed. However, we do get plenty of information about its general nature: its progressive programs which initiate an "extensive educational, popular-scientific and individually therapeutic activity . . ."[16] These and other vast and obviously laudatory generalizations are spouted by the Institute's Director and his devoted parrot, the Deputy. Nowhere is there mention of any concrete issue or problem; the language keeps us, as it were, at bay. In fact, while seeming to inform, it mystifies; while apparently communicating, it sets up a barrier totally preventing communication. The only times when a specific task or item peeks over this barrier of abstractions is when the Director inquires whether certain things have been attended to. These things turn out to have nothing whatsoever to do with the Institute's nature but rather with irrelevant, indeed strange, but for the audience partly alienating, partly amusing issues, as whether the falcons have been fed or whether the soap has been distributed.

At this point it may be appropriate to remind ourselves of another and older text on temptation, which, though of a different nature, is in essence closely related to Havel's concerns. In C.S. Lewis' *Screwtape Letters* an affectionate uncle, the senior devil Screwtape, teaches his greenhorn nephew Wormwood among other things about the mesmerizing power of generalizations which lull common sense and reason to sleep: "the best of all is to let him [the person to be tempted and thus won for hell] read no science but to give him a grand general idea that he knows it all," due to "the results of modern investigation." As Wormwood has to learn, the purpose of the exercise is "to fuddle him."[17] Once confused by irresistible language he is bound to succumb.

Young Wormwood is a poor student of seduction; as we gather from Screwtape's stern reprovals, he often makes a mess of things. By comparison, Havel's Foustka gets an A+. After his initial talk with his seducer Fistula he seems to have graduated into the master class of rhetoric. Before Fistula's appearance Foustka was a monosyllabic office colleague who stuttered even as he asked the Institute's secretary Maggie for a cup of coffee. At the office party the same evening (after Fistula's first visit) he emerges as an eloquent rhetorician who winds his way through complex philosophical arguments like a fish through water. What has happened? Fistula, a smelly, shabby latter-day devil to Foustka's nervous and hectic Faust, seems to know his client (C.S. Lewis's word is "patient") better than the latter knows himself and has awakened in him talents he did not know he possessed. Goethe's Faust had first to attain youth and vigor before he could seduce Margarete. Two centuries later Havel's Foustka manages to seduce the secretary Maggie with quasi-philosophical language acrobatics. "Have you ever thought," he asks her over a drink at an office party, "that we would be quite unable to understand even the most simple moral action which is not motivated by self-interest, that in fact it would appear to be quite absurd, if we did not admit to ourselves that somewhere within it there is concealed the prerequisite of something higher, some absolute, omniscient and infinitely just moral authority, through which and in which all our actions gain a mysterious worth and through which each and every one of us constantly touches eternity?" (28).

The strategic vocabulary of the passage and its implied progression is obvious. Consider this table:

NOUNS	VERBS	ADJECTIVES	OTHER
self-interest	think	moral (twice)	something higher within us
action	understand	concealed	
authority	gain	absolute	
worth	touch	omniscient	
eternity		mysterious	
		just	

In one grand linguistic swoop we are whirled from action and thought, by means of our own "higher" qualities, to eternity and justice. It is not surprising that Maggie falls for this. After all, she is only one of a long line of female characters who have fallen for the rhetorical feats of Havel's protagonists. The playwright himself likes to remember the shrewd words of a Czech critic who said of his first play *The Garden Party* that "its hero was the phrase."[18] The ability (or temptation?) to let the phrase perform, to play the pliable instrument of language, trying out all its registers while monitoring the listener's reaction, has seized nearly all the protagonists that populate Havel's dramatic universe. For the most part these figures are slaves to the phrase, they are entirely integrated into the social system, spout prepackaged comments and become interchangeable mouthpieces of a certain type of language. A few central characters, however, not quite integrated, troubled, insecure and system-shy, provide us with a fascinating gallery of strategic language acrobats which culminates in Foustka, the scientist/magician whom the devil taught the use of language.

It is obvious that much of this sharp critique of language could be applied to a totalitarian political system. The Czech scholar and essayist Petr Fidelius has written eloquently about the "semantic inflation" which, though an innocuous research subject for academic linguists under certain circumstances, can become a powerful political tool, if used by centrally controlled media. People exposed to the constant onslaught of this tool, namely the language of propaganda, Fidelius argues, gradually begin to live in a lie; a lie not in the moral but in the existential sense: "Life in a lie does not necessarily manifest itself by asserting something that is not true. . . . life in a lie mostly cannot be measured by an average moral yardstick, indeed it frequently gives the impression of being entirely honourable and irreproachable." The horrific result of this is that people, without wanting to, contribute to the general attitude "that it no longer makes any sense to speak about the truth."[19] In the universe of Havel's plays it certainly does not make any sense to speak the truth, for truth is no longer recognizable, having been atomized by false language—a language that no longer has the task of seizing and formulating reality.

Without explicitly mentioning political issues, Havel has provided us with a playwright's version of models of "semantic inflation" of language which has gone dead under the leaden weight of an ideologically controlled bureaucracy. That he manages to do this while combining intellectual content with tension-filled theater, as well as rollicking comedy, is a feat indeed.

At this point we might consider Havel's gallery of language acrobats in order to see whether their rhetoric does not, on closer inspection, turn out to be relevant (even "politically" relevant) to our own society. I have chosen three passages from Havel's earlier plays to serve as illustrations:

> You think one can ask in this simplified way? No matter how one answers this sort of question, one can never encompass whole truth, but only one of its many limited parts. (Hugo Pludek in *The Garden Party*, 1963)

We're living in a strange, complex epoch. As Hamlet says, our "time is out of joint." Just think, we're reaching for the moon and yet it's increasingly hard for us to reach our selves; we're able to split the atom, but unable to prevent the splitting of our personality; we build superb communications between the continents, and yet communication between Man and Man is increasingly difficult. (Josef Gross in *The Memorandum,* 1965)

Among the most basic values of present-day man one can include, for example, work—in other words—the opportunity to do that which would enable man to fulfil himself completely, to develop his own specific potentialities, his relationships with other people, his moral principles—certain convictions regarding his concept of the world, his faith in something to which he can commit his life—full stop. (Eduard Huml in *The Increased Difficulty of Concentration,* 1969)[20]

Hugo Pludek's remark, in our first example, implies that intellectual oversimplification can lead to the erroneous conclusion that one has grasped reality. Who would quarrel with this obviously rational statement? It is only when we place Hugo's remark in the context in which it appears in Havel's play that the picture changes. Having just scored a political victory in a battle of wits with a high official by using a repertory of useful phrases, Hugo has landed a new job in the Ministry of Liquidation. It is also a safe job because, logically, the Ministry of Liquidation cannot be liquidated itself because it is the only appropriate body to undertake liquidations. The linguistic rug has been pulled out from under us. Hugo's initially acceptable words burst like bubbles.

Referring to our second example, imagine the numerous, by no means comic, occasions at which Josef Gross's incontestable statements about communication in the modern world could be uttered with a straight face and applauded by a supportive audience in New York, London or Vancouver, B.C. However, we only need to realize that Havel's character speaks these words while riding the roller coaster of a bureaucratic system built entirely on linguistic prowess and these same words about lack of human communication become potentially sinister.

What contemporary citizen listening to Eduard Huml's dictation to his secretary, in our third example, would fail to nod in agreement with the social scientist's "reasonable" arguments: Values, self-fulfillment, potentialities, relationships, principles, commitment—are these not the right ingredients of an average recipe for what we take to be "the good life"? However, when we remind ourselves that Huml lives in a merry-go-round of eating, dressing, working, as his erotic attachments multiply with mechanistic precision, the language he uses during the dictation is reduced to a burbling sound counterpointing the predictable pattern of events.

All the above statements start out with some kind of common sense proposition which is hardly disputable (although, instructed by Uncle Screwtape, we might have developed a sharpened vision for their dangerous attempts to generalize). Moreover, they seem to be spoken in the spirit of disinterested intellectual pursuits, thus implying that the speaker is engaged in a noble struggle that has never been put in doubt by Western philosophy. We inevitably respect those bold attempts to get answers to questions, regardless of the cost. It is here, I would suggest, that Havel's label as "dissident" playwright definitely peels off. For what he has done is provide us with a variety of language models for this quest-pose which he reveals to be an empty shell. By having his most innocent, humane, and brave characters (it is interesting that they are all women, but that is another story) fall for this pose, Havel has tapped a deep source in Western social consciousness. With surprising consistency and in harmony with his own expanding and maturing perception of today's world, Havel is exploring the secret patterns of strategic language behaviour which we all face in more walks of life than we may be willing to admit.

What is the implied motivation behind the rhetorical feats of Havel's main characters that punctuate his plays? They all talk well, indeed convincingly, if we do not listen too closely. If we do, however, their web of words becomes transparent and another reality appears behind it. In *The Garden Party,* the eager beaver Hugo Pludek's pseudo-philosophic ramblings about the complexity of man and his truths are linked to his desire for a career in the government (the temptation of gaining power). When the hapless would-be-integrated bureaucrat Gross in *The Memorandum* muses about the marvels of technology and the stresses of modern man, he is trying to convince others (and perhaps himself) that a yes-man in society can still preserve his own private vision of values (this is the temptation to combine toeing the line—any line!—with remaining a "thinking man"). Similarly, Eduard Huml, who has an "increased difficulty of concentration," delves into abstract issues of moral philosophy when his private life is in a mess (this is the temptation of trying to have your cake—erotic embraces wherever available—and eat it too, all along retaining one's "good image").

Returning to *Temptation* we find that this "cake"-theme, which has been appearing with increasing insistence in Havel's plays since he began to write, reaches a peak. Double play, the unwillingness to give up one thing for another, the refusal to adhere to a hierarchy of values, the constantly perfected construction of strategic arguments in order to rationalize this form of duplicity—all these are based here on the time-honoured pattern of the Faust story. Although the devil in Havel's play is a shabby informer, Faust has become a mediocre corporation scientist, and evil, in Hannah Arendt's famous words, has become "banal" and, in Havel's own words, "domesticated,"[21] the subtle process of temptation, albeit by less "traditional" means, continues.

Foustka's linguistic seduction of Maggie during the Institute's party—a highly entertaining scene for the audience—is interrupted four times. Twice colleagues ask Maggie to dance; twice Vilma, Foustka's steady woman friend, comments on the growing intensity of the couple's involvement with a cool "Having a good time?" The first time, Foustka can answer self-assuredly: "Maggie and I have been discussing some philosophical questions" (27). The second time, Vilma's identical question finds the two in a passionate embrace. Now Foustka's response is silence. He has achieved his (or Fistula's?) aim. His elegant, passionate speeches about man and the universe have produced the result promised by Fistula (and secretly wished for by himself?): Maggie has indeed fallen in love with him. However, the stages of this process merit a closer look. Maggie's reactions move first from the awkward admission that she has never really thought about things "in this way" and shy admiration, "you know how to put it so nicely" (27), to fervent agreement, "Yes, yes, that's exactly how I've always felt it to be" (28); next, to acknowledging a marvelous discovery in herself, "I've never felt anything like this before" (28); finally to complete emotional abandon, "I love you. . . . Yes, and I'll go on loving you till the day I die" (29). The successful strategy of the rhetorical process can be gauged from the listener's reactions: first, the speaker makes it clear that he is worthy of being listened to; second, he shows that he deserves admiration; third, he finds and stresses a point of recognition, a moment of mimesis; fourth, he causes the listener to experience the uniqueness of this moment in her life; fifth, he makes her the sole accomplice of his thoughts (his last comment is: "who else should I confide in but you?" [29]). Now he has won her entirely.

Yet here we realize with renewed intensity that Havel never permits us to formulate a comfortably assured answer; rather, like Kafka or Beckett, he opens up a myriad of questions which seem to extend out of sight. Shades of implied shades of meaning mock and tempt the reader or audience. As an example I would like to consider briefly the argument of the Czech scholar Radim Palouš, mentioned earlier in these pages. With an eloquence that stems from intellectual passion Palouš sets out to throw a different light on Havel's disturbing graphics of human language. During the successful attempt at seduction by language, Palouš argues, something entirely different gradually happens. Although Maggie, in the tradition of Goethe's Margarete, falls into Foustka's arms and declares her eternal love for him, behind the mask of victorious Eros another process is initiated: the strategic argument designed to win the listener for the speaker has somehow released a "good force," the only truly honest response in the general jumble of lies, masks, and forms of pretense which rule the rest of Havel's play. Thus the weapon handed to Foustka by the evil power has turned out to be a boomerang: it endangers the originator, the devil himself. Maggie perceives only those aspects in Faust's reasoning which awaken her notions of goodness. Intuitively she gravitates to meanings which appeal to her pure spirit, but which she had not been able to formulate herself. Now she recognizes the mute stirrings of her soul in the words expressed (for whatever reason) by someone else. She returns Foustka's talk, in Radim Palouš's words, to "the first and true level of language celebrating the amazing working of the universe as such."[22] So, despite the fact that Foustka achieves his purpose—Maggie falls in love with him—he has won a Pyrrhic victory in the sense that he has got more than he bargained for: she loves him forever. Also, and more significantly, despite the fact that she fell for the tool provided by evil, this fall inadvertently provided her with a weapon against the falsehood around her. Out of temptation through language there emerged language as the carrier and formulator of notions of truth and goodness.

No matter how resourceful and, under the circumstances, reassuringly noble Palouš's argument is, it does push a point. True, Maggie remains a character untouched by evil, an unblemished carrier of truth. However, when Palouš speaks of "the first and true level of language," he himself takes a quasi-metaphysical leap which would convince neither the literary theorist nor the moral philosopher. As for the average member of the audience concerned with political issues, Maggie's "positive" stance is of doubtful value. After all, she ends up in an asylum.

Nevertheless Palouš's argument shows what intellectual adventures the play has in store for us. Several other essays from *Faustování s Havlem,*[23] though pursuing entirely different lines of thought, testify similarly to the play's challenging wealth. It is due, I would argue, to the mysterious quality of Havel's plays, revealing a deep kinship, as I said earlier, with Kafka and Beckett. We know that in both these latter cases, attempts at "interpretation" of meaning are bound to finish up in a similar *cul de sac.* But there is something else in *Temptation* that is likely to give future critics much food for discussion. Embedded in the play is a textbook on the complexities of temptation by language or—the other side of the coin—seduction by language. There are three key scenes of dialogue between Fistula, the tempter, and Foustka, the tempted. Or is this the wrong way of putting it? Should one say Fistula, the stimulator, and Foustka, the stimulated? After all, the former tells us that he is not much of a tempter but that at most he "occasionally provide[s]. . . . a stimulus" (35). These three debates are like sparkling linguistic fencing, in which, although the stimulator at first clearly has the upper hand, the stimulated gradually rises to the occasion and finally outdoes his opponent (or does the latter merely let him score a point because he has already taught his lesson and thereby achieved his purpose?). With an intellectual playfulness and unerring sense for the histrionic that might deceive us about the seriousness of the topic discussed, the playwright takes us through a spectrum of philosophical questions about truth and falsehood, reason and rationalization, good and evil. These debates represent something unique in contemporary theater in the sense that they provide what Havel himself thinks good theater should be, namely "an adventurous journey," which playwright and audience experience simultaneously and which is "equally surprising, tantalizing and disturbing for us all."[24]

But we must return to our initial question: Is Havel to be regarded as a "political" playwright in the sense that he is an eloquent critic of totalitarianism? Yes, because he defines, with intellectual and dramatic energy, the rigid social structures dictated by a coercive ideology which pulverize and absorb personal identity. However, as I have tried to show, there is much more. By showing us how disturbingly close our most cherished linguistic formulations are to the dark realm of confusion and danger, Havel casts a giant question mark over some of the assumptions underlying the time-honored patterns by which we are accustomed to live. If we find that he formulates his own thoughts on the power of theater in a possibly rather utopian manner, we might remember that he wrote them from prison, half-way through his long incarceration:

> I would say that it is precisely this joint participation in an unusual journey, this collective uncertainty about where the journey is leading, this delight in discovering it together and finding the courage and the ability to negotiate and enjoy new vistas together—it is all this that creates a remarkable and rare sense of community among the participants, this exciting sense of mutual understanding, of a "new brotherhood."[25]

It is, I would argue, a welcome and rare challenge for theater-audiences in the West today to let themselves be taken on an exploratory adventure of this kind offered by a contemporary playwright.

Notes and References

1. Siegfried Melchinger, *Geschichte des politischen Theaters* (Frankfurt am Main, 1974), vol. I, 243.
2. Václav Havel, "Dovětek autora" ["Author's Afterword"], *Hry 1970–76* (Toronto, 1977), 302. My translation.
3. Václav Havel's comment in the discussion "O *Pokoušení* s Václavem Havlem" ["About *Temptation* with Václav Havel"] which appeared as Appendix in *Faustování s Havlem* in the samizdat series *Nové cesty myšlení* [*New Ways of Thought*] (Praha, 1986), p 198.
4. Ibid., 199.
5. Ibid., 200.
6. Ibid., 203.
7. Michael Billington, "A Tempting Fate," *The Guardian*, 2 May 1987, 12.
8. Zina Rohan, "Havel's I: a Critical Triumph," "Central Talks and Features—Topical Report," BBC World Service Broadcast, 4 May 1987.
9. Michael Coveney, "*Temptation* / The Other Place," *The Financial Times*, 1 May 1987.
10. Václav Havel, "The Power of the Powerless," trans. Paul Wilson, *Václav Havel or Living in Truth*, ed. Jan Vladislav (London, 1987), 78. Reprinted in *Open Letters: Selected Prose 1965–1990*, ed. Paul Wilson (London, 1991), 125–214.
11. "O *Pokoušení* s Václavem Havlem," 224.
12. Ibid., 224.
13. See note 3.

14. Radim Palouš, "Pokoušení řeči" ["The Temptation of Speech"], *Faustování s Havlem.*
15. *Žebrácká opera* [*The Beggar's Opera*], *Hry 1970–1976.*
16. Václav Havel, *Temptation,* trans. George Theiner, *Index on Censorship,* (December 1986), 24. Page references to this edition are cited parenthetically.
17. C.S. Lewis, *The Screwtape Letters* (London, 1956), 14.
18. Václav Havel, *Fernverhöre: Ein Gespräch mit Karel Hvížďala,* trans. into German Joachim Bruss (Reinbek, 1987), 236. My translation.
19. Petr Fidelius, "O zacházení se slovy" ["On handling words"], *Svědectví* [*Testimony*], 17, 68 (1983), 708. My translation.
20. Václav Havel, *The Garden Party,* trans. Vera Blackwell (London, 1969), 73; *The Memorandum,* trans. Vera Blackwell (New York, 1980), 86; *The Increased Difficulty of Concentration,* trans. Vera Blackwell (London, 1972), 19.
21. Václav Havel, in "O *Pokoušení* s Václavem Havlem," 232.
22. Radim Palouš, "Pokoušení řeči," 11.
23. This collection includes some challenging interpretations. What is refreshing about them is that, despite their learnedness, they are not highly specialized "professional" pieces of writing, but rather resourceful, generally cultured responses to the text. Ivan M. Havel's "Fistula's Monologue," Zdeněk Neubauer's "Faust's Secret Mistress," and Martin Palouš's "Theater for Life and Death" [author's translation of titles] deserve special mention here.
24. Václav Havel, *Letters to Olga,* trans. Paul Wilson (New York: Alfred A. Knopf, 1988), 252, 253.
25. Ibid., 253.

HAVEL IN THE MINDS
OF HIS COUNTRYMEN

◆

"That Bourgeois Brat!"

Josef Škvorecký

{[Havel] said he was encouraged by two things brought to light by the revolution: the totalitarian system had not been able to erase human striving for something higher; and the humanist and democratic traditions of Czechoslovakia were seemingly only asleep.
—Rob McRae}

With my own ears, I heard this about our present president from a highly placed and clearly irritated official of the then Writers Union's Central Committee. It happened sometime in 1967 as Havel was waiting at the door with a petition he had used since the end of the 1950s to pester the union's officials; the highly placed official was even more annoyed than usual.

I met Havel at the Writers Union once more: I had never been a member of the Writers Union—they accepted me, I think, during Dubček's time, but I don't even know this for sure. At this time I represented the translators' subdivision as its chairman. Whom Havel represented, I don't know; qualms of conscience, perhaps. On the agenda that day was the case of Jan Beneš, who had been arrested because he sent articles to Tigrid's *Svědectví [Testimony]*. Under the union's bylaws, it was a cut-and-dried case: a member convicted of anti-state activity was to be expelled from the Union. I don't even know any longer whether Beneš was actually convicted or just arrested, since in those times anyone who was arrested for such an activity was also convicted as a matter of course. These bylaws were written in no uncertain terms; however, at that time, shortly before the fall of Novotný's regime, no one wanted to understand their wording.

And so a lengthy discussion ensued and went on and on; all the hot dogs were eaten and all the beer was drunk, and still no one wanted to obey the bylaws. It took almost six hours—or was it eight? The debate seemed endless. After a very long time, one of the most devoted Party members stood up and angrily proclaimed: "If you, comrades, do not expel this Beneš, I will can-

Translated from Czech by Zdenka Brodská and Mary Hrabik Samal for this volume. Originally published in *Milý Václave . . . [Dear Václav . . .]* (Prague: Divadelní ústav a Nakladatelství lidové noviny, 1997), 56–59. Reprinted by permission of the publisher.

cel my membership in the union. That guy squeals on his Dobříš colleague-writers!"

After this a few of the devoted Party members dared to raise their voices, and the voting began. Everyone, it seemed to me, voted for Beneš's expulsion. I myself didn't raise my hand, but I was terribly afraid. Is anyone against the expulsion? Two hands went up. One was the hand of Heda Volanská, and the other belonged to Václav Havel. I confess I lacked the courage to join them. At least, I raised my hand when the chair asked who abstains.

Years passed, and Václav Havel became one of our authors; that is, my wife published his *Plays 1970–76* and later his *Letters to Olga* through our Sixty-Eight Publishers. Then Václav Havel slowly became known and famous throughout the world. Václav Táborský found some willing allies among the professors of York University in Toronto, and together they pushed through an honorary doctorate for Havel. Later throngs of degrees, medals, and honors were heaped upon Havel, but this doctorate was the first. Who in the world, however, would know the mere half-century-old York University in Toronto? When I later read the list of Havel's degrees that European academic institutions with incomparably more famous pedigrees had awarded him, I did not find the name of York University in that faraway Canadian province. Still, it was the very first honor, and for me made memorable by the fact that my wife, as his publisher, accepted the doctoral diploma on behalf of Havel, who was in prison at that time. After the ceremony, another fresh honorary doctor, the jazz legend Oscar Peterson, leaned over to my wife and whispered into her ear: "Tell Mr. Havel, I'm with him all the way!"

My own university, the University of Toronto, also tried to help Havel. North American institutions of higher learning have created the position of writer-in-residence, a job which carries no special duties and supports the writer financially for one year. In Havel's case, it would have been something more. I contacted my friend professor Sam Solecki of the English Department, who then chaired the committee that selects writers-in-residence; Havel received an invitation from the University of Toronto for a one-year stay at Massey College, which housed the offices of the University's guests. Havel replied with a beautiful thank-you letter, but refused the invitation because he feared—quite rightly—that the Party-government would let him come to Toronto but not return to Prague, as had happened to Kohout and Gruša. He did not want to go into exile.

The university at least made possible that the English version of Havel's *Beggar's Opera* had its world première in the theater of the drama department at Scarborough College, one of our institution's colleges. The play was translated and directed by Michal Schonberg, a professor in the department who later became well-known in Prague for a book on the history of Prague's Osvovozené divadlo [the Liberated Theater] and a book-length interview with Jiří Voskovec. It was a fine student performance, played with the same gusto as the amateur actors performed the same play in a village near Prague and almost paid for it with imprisonment. So in this way, Torontonians in Ontario made their mark in the history of our president's work.

I tried once more to honor the dissident when I nominated him for the Robert F. Kennedy Human Rights Award. It was shortly before the fall of the Party-government and Havel's ascension to Prague's Castle. I had been a member of the committee for this award for many years, and many times I had nominated dissidents (Karel Srp and the Jazz Section, Marta Kubišová and other female dissidents) for this award. It seemed that I might succeed this time, but the massacre on Tiananmen Square intervened and I failed again.

I personally saw Václav Havel after more than 20 years when he visited our publishing house on Davenport Avenue in the spring of 1990. He was already president then, and I had to let the police dog, whose task was to find hidden explosives, sniff me. And then I saw Havel a couple of times in Prague and America, but unfortunately, it was always at one or another official function.

I am pleased that we published his two books when it was otherwise impossible. And I am happy that when it was possible to do what not so long ago was simply unthinkable, he conferred on my wife and me the Order of the White Lion.

May God keep him for us!

14. Visiting Sixty Eight Publishers in Toronto, 1990.

15. Jangling keys to the crowd during the Velvet Revolution, 1989.

The Jubilee

VÁCLAV BĚLOHRADSKÝ

{. . . for Havel, ideological thinking, as it seeks to provide a system for understanding human action, is fundamentally inconsistent with his conception of human action and thought.

—Dean C. Hammer}

From a rock concert to a student demonstration, from *The Garden Party* to the President's speeches. What is Václav Havel's "Living in Truth?"

In an agricultural museum exposition at the castle Kačina close to Kutná Hora, I discovered the ancient ten commandments for millers. I liked the tenth commandment best: "Thou shalt take flour made from grain that has been brought and thou shalt not covet what has been scattered." It is a wise commandment; most marriages, friendships, and nations fall apart because people want back what has been scattered. We must never ask the return of what has been scattered, but we have to recall it often since it is impossible to grasp the full meaning of any human work or deed without reminding ourselves of the long-ago-scattered "historical context" with which they used to torture us in school when explaining works of art. Jakobson was well aware of the context's enormous power when he wrote, "If Mácha were living today, maybe he would have preferred writing lyrical poetry just for himself and published his diary instead." Then, we would have associated Mácha with Joyce or Lawrence, and the critics would have written that all these authors strove for "an unfalsified image of man."

I would like to recall here the scattered context of a rare and profound experience in my life; it was my encounter with Havel's essay "The Power of the Powerless" in my Italian exile. In 1979 the small publishing house CSEO in Bologna had published it as a book. CSEO was a bit like *samizdat;* it did not have any permanent employees and lived on charity and the enthusiasm of its founding father Ricci. It specialized in dissident literature, but was not very

Translated from Czech by Zdenka Brodská and Mary Hrabik Samal for this volume. Originally published in *Milý Václave . . .* [*Dear Václav . . .*] (Prague: Divadelní ústav a Nakladatelství lidové noviny, 1997), 26–29. Reprinted by permission of the publisher.

successful because after years of terrorism and strikes, Italians were leery of politics until "The Power of the Powerless" came out of the blue like a thunderbolt; more than 30,000 copies were sold, which was almost a miracle for such a small publishing house. The big newspapers ignored the book, of course; who—at that time—would have been interested in the fate of a bourgeois offspring who was constantly in and out of prison? They took note only when that bourgeois offspring became president, but that's the way it is in the democratic West.

I remember the day when the walls of the Catholic University in Milan were covered with quotes from Havel's book. Students were most fascinated with two themes: first, with the idea that totalitarianism is nothing but an image of the West in a convex mirror. "And in the end, is not the greyness and the emptiness of life in the post-totalitarian system only an inflated caricature of modern life in general? And do we not in fact stand (although in the external measures of civilization we are far behind) as a kind of warning to the West, revealing to it its own latent tendencies?"[1] I still know this sentence by heart because we discussed it in many seminars. It is true, however, that this critical approach to the West evaporated quite quickly from our cultural and political scene, having been hysterically veiled over by a one-sided effort to become a part of the "Western European structure" and to secure our democracy in this way. All those "structures," however, be they Western, Eastern, state, or privately owned, have one thing in common: they are contradictory to "living in truth" or to "the intentions of life"; precisely for this reason we use that ugly word "structures" in referring to them.

Second, the idea of a hidden sphere of life—those intentions of life, the natural need to live in harmony with oneself that can never be easily and completely manipulated—fascinated the students. "Under the orderly surface of the life of lies, therefore, there slumbers the hidden sphere of life in its real aims, of its hidden openness to truth. . . ." ("Power," 148). At that time, the democratic post-industrial society had started to become hopelessly complex, computerized, bureaucratized, and indifferent to natural speech; as public space became crowded with ephemeral images, the post-industrial society changed into *societé du spectacle,* a society of show and performance. Young people were more and more ecologically sensitive; they keenly perceived how democracy had become dependent on a meaningless imperative of constant economic growth, on the blind faith that the increase of goods, opportunities, and information will solve the problems caused precisely by this increase of goods, opportunities, and information. This was, of course, only a different form of Havel's "life within the lie." Italian students of 1979 saw their fathers, free citizens of the West, as very similar to Havel's famed green-grocer, who placed the slogan: "Workers of the world, unite!" in his shop window into the midst of the onions and carrots because "these things must be done," and these details "guarantee him a relatively tranquil life 'in harmony with society' " ("Power," 132). The ideology of growth includes a similar slogan: it offers the illusion that it is in harmony with the order of universe and humankind.

The expression "living in truth" is dangerous because everyone would like to limit it to his life and his truth. Havel, however, writes that living in truth "can be any means by which a person or a group revolts against manipulation: . . . from a rock concert to a student demonstration" ("Power," 150–51). Life is ruled by "an elemental need to live in harmony with oneself at least to a certain degree," but how can a finite, faulty, and mortal being live in harmony with itself? It can do so only by constant modification of its life goals and maps of the world, images and interpretations, meanings of signs which it employs. Karel Čapek has written about how strong one's indifference has to be in order for one to ignore one's own life experience when it contradicts absolute thought. The word "truth" in our Western context is often only a different denotation for this strong indifference.

When does a person live in truth in Havel's sense of the word? Not when he respects some dogma; he lives in truth only when he crosses the boundaries of his own version of the world, finds himself on an alternative map of reality, and is constantly forced to justify his own positions.

In "The Power of the Powerless," I like this sentence best: "People feel more and more urgently that the less a policy is based on a concrete human 'here and now' and the more it is bound to some abstract 'there' and 'one day,' the easier it can become just another variant of human enslavement" ("Power," 161). I endow this sentence with a more general meaning: people take refuge in an abstract "there" to escape the overwhelming multitude of experiences, tension among the different versions of the world, simply the marketplace of free speech.

From *The Garden Party,* with which Václav Havel astonished us in December of 1963, to his presidential speeches, the struggle with various petrified forms of the abstract "there" and "one day" is a constant source of Havel's commitment as a man, artist, and politician.

Notes and References

1. Václav Havel, "The Power of the Powerless," *Václav Havel, Open Letters: Selected Prose 1965–1990,* selected, edited, and translated by Paul Wilson (London: Faber and Faber, 1991), 145; hereafter cited parenthetically in text as "Power."

Reflections on Václav Havel

Jiřina Šiklová

{. . . here was a man—on his fourth day in office and not yet familiar with the silver tea service and the comforts of power—willing to risk the loss of his newfound privilege for something as plain and unprofitable as the truth. For an American politician, Havel's opening statement would have been—quite literally—impossible.
—Lewis Lapham}

Do you know a children's game called Secretary? The first player writes something on a given subject, then the second player, the third, the fourth and so on without anyone knowing what the others had written before him. Then they read it all, and often have a good laugh.

I am writing this article in a similar manner. Its topic has been given: A Critical Reflection on Václav Havel. I accepted this task although I did not know what my predecessors had written. Besides, I do not even know if I will succeed. I simply do not want to criticize Havel! I resent that constant barrage aimed at him because of his advisors, sweaters or trousers. On the other hand, to be on the side of those in power was always out of fashion in the Czech lands!

It often begins right in the morning. The phone rings: "Have you seen the papers? How could Havel have signed that decree, resolution, bill on lustration, church, reprivatization, separation? Has he taken leave of his senses? Why is he under Klaus's thumb? He messed up everything, did not stand up for his dissident friends, and now is completely alone in that government. He surrounds himself with friends instead of professionals!" Or: "He kicked out his friends from the Castle and took in the old bureaucrats! Is it possible he does not know that so and so and so and so are former Communists?" Very often it ends in shouting: "Tell him to do . . . ! He should do this . . . ! And you still stand up for him! Don't try to explain anything, you really do! We did not make the revolution to install the capitalism of the nineteenth century here! I am so unhappy—only now, have I lost all my idealism!"

Translated from Czech by Zdenka Brodská and Mary Hrabik Samal and reprinted from *Listy* (April 1994).

At the same time, however, the very same people bring me Havel's books and photographs to have them autographed. They are very surprised when I tell them that the Castle is as close or as far for me as for any other Prague visitor.

And exactly because of this, I can defend the new establishment, even if it is not customary to do so in this nation. I do not belong to any political party, I work for the university, "Charles the Fourth" pays my salary, and on top of everything, I can now retire any day! Moreover, I do not need anything from Havel.

But, does he need me to stand up for him? Václav Havel, the politician, the writer, the man, certainly does not. As a sensitive human being, maybe he does! Everyone needs that! First of all, we need to realize why we focus our complaints and discontent at him and why we do not overlook in him one tenth of what we would in a different politician.

I remember a meeting of Charter 77 signatories held not long after the 1989 revolution. It took place in Dana Němcová's Ječná Street apartment. Václav Havel was already president, and one of his very close friends, laughing heartily, greeted him in the hall saying: "The powerless greet the powerful." Václav Havel visibly resented that.

He was sitting on the floor in a very disciplined and non-presidential manner, chain-smoking, as he waited for a long time till Jan Ruml, the Charter 77 spokesperson then, let him speak. The encounter in the hall, I suspect, unnerved him more than if he were to address the American Congress. And then, he spoke about that remark explaining in a very complicated way why he had accepted the presidency.

I felt sorry for him. At the same time, however, I appreciated the fact that he valued his relationship with his friends more than his newly acquired post. It was clear to me that as a president, he would suffer a lot.

"You will have to grow a hide as thick as an elephant's, my dear," I thought, "and when after much self-control you have developed it, the very same people will reproach you saying that you have changed, blown them off, had no time for them, that you have become formal, repetitive, different."

The previous regime made us act as immature adolescents, who expected that someone else would make decisions, and if anything were to go wrong, they would have the right to be forgiven and not to be personally held responsible. Discontented people always idealize the past or future and view the present as just temporary. We have idealized Masaryk's Czechoslovakia, the West and, especially ourselves: "We are so wonderful and capable that we will create an ideal state with a perfect government, with a president, who is a philosopher, with a parliament full of representatives, whose ideas are sparkling and witty." If this ideal does not materialize, then we feel aggrieved because our self-image has been proven wrong. And this is hard to forgive.

Politicizing, baseness, corruption—all of this is foreign to us. The former regime did this, and we were, according to the present musings, just its victims.

Our present attitude to the first post-November government of the Civic Forum and to President Havel reminds me a little of adolescents who grew up in a family with constantly arguing parents. In their desire to escape this situation, they dream of marriage in such idealized and absolutely unrealistic terms that they will blame their spouses for its failure as they did their parents for their unhappy childhood. They live with the feeling that they have been wronged because their demands were so obviously justified. And we do the same thing: we literally demand from our first post-revolution government and our President something which is unattainable.

As usual, we did not achieve Paradise on Earth. Moreover, I really do not know why precisely these generations, who were deformed by their own collaboration with all possible regimes, should enter the promised land. I expected that everything would be much worse. Thanks to Václav Havel and the government of the Civic Forum, we have cleared the most dangerous hurdle without serious harm. Is this too little? I think it is a lot!

I vividly remember the week after November 17, when every day I spoke at meetings of students at different colleges. It was the same everywhere; the most frequent question being: "Who is Václav Havel?" And I gave them his biography and told them what he wrote in his plays and essays. . . . Everything by heart. . . . No one knew or read him at that time, but all of a sudden, all began to love him. We were as overgrown adolescents who are in dire need of a great love to purify themselves and to get rid of their own meaningless past. This feeling is disproportionate; it is not yet a relationship among equals; it is just a narcissistic reflection of oneself in some other person. In our case, that other person was the Civic Forum and Václav Havel.

That sacrificial lamb, the government of the Civic Forum, ended after two years. It was unable to fulfill the overblown expectations since they were totally unrealistic. The problems on our horizon are very similar to the problems in every marriage or in every normal society. We are not even worse than the others. We are better, but it is not enough for us because it differs so from our expectations and self-image. Thank God, that there is no other revolution on our horizon! The road ahead of us is going to be tiring, boring, long, and it cannot be shortened! We do not have any kulaks, bourgeoisie, imperialists or class enemies to blame. Besides, we all somehow collaborated with or at least got along in the previous regime. Yet we cannot blame ourselves, discard the dreams and take reality for what it is; perhaps, this is possible only in a second or third marriage. But how can the shattered self-image be reconciled with reality without much pain? By blaming those who led us and did not realize our beautiful, wonderful, holy ideals! They are to be blamed! That's why we judge more severely the government of the Civic Forum and the dissidents, including Havel, than the Communists. To have been an active member of the Civic Forum and not to have left in time is, perhaps, worse than to have sat in Jakeš's Politburo. We even do not remember him any more, and we, perhaps, reproach the rest of the *Apparatchiki* only because they used to steal more.

Really being an adult means to have the ability to see our parents' faults, understand their actions and weaknesses, and despite all that to accept and love them without reproach and pathos. They are only human! They did what they could! Till we reach this adulthood, we will continue to repeat the ritual of worship and rejection and seek a scapegoat, whose role a charismatic person such as Havel can certainly play.

In spite of his efforts, Václav Havel is not easily understood either as an author or as a president. It is especially true for the nation, which constantly refers to T. G. Masaryk but so far has not managed to publish his collected works! In the past, it was forbidden; today, no one would buy them! Havel is unintelligible because of his character; normal people cannot identify with him as they can with the very popular Vladimír Dlouhý, the politician who fulfills all the requirements for a solid leader. He is the same as the others. Dlouhý has always publicly stated that he was a member of the Communist Party not because he agreed with its ideas, but because he wanted to have a university education, to travel abroad and to prepare himself for the role he is playing today. If the revolution had not occurred, he would have served the former regime as well, and his decisions would have been professional. Unlike Dlouhý, Václav Havel used to say that a man should not live a life of lies and hypocrisy; a person should not say "yes" to the powers-that-be just to make his life easier.

It is nice to listen to Havel because everyone is aware he must agree with him, especially when one thinks about children! Subconsciously however, our citizen is actually happy when he discovers some flaw in Havel, which he then can analyze, repeat as gossip and excitedly discuss. It makes our citizen somehow better and at the same time soothes his conscience.

I do not remember T. G. Masaryk, but I think people also did not read him, and they loved him unreservedly only after his death. An ideal is such a lovely thing! It does not require a lot of space; it can fit into a very small apartment of a prefabricated house.

Havel's closest dissident friends who were in the first post-revolutionary government with him take pot shots at him. They reproach him because he does not want to be partisan, he does not agree with them and this is why they now do not sit in the parliament and government. Again—it is Havel's fault. He should have made them into a political party, stated clearly for whom he would vote and the Civic Forum would be sitting in the parliament now. If Havel had done so, he would perhaps not be so lonely today, but he would not be himself. He simply did not want to do that. He has always been a loner; he did not want to have some political party behind him; he acted as he acted; he might have made a mistake.

It is the basis of democratic thinking to accept the other person as a different being and appreciate his or her dissimilarity. Although it is very healthy, do not ask a lion to eat oatmeal!

Havel's very probable loneliness, the necessity to obey rituals given by his being a president, is another reason why I cannot reproach him, but rather wish to understand him and even to embrace him from apart. Paradoxically, he lost the freedom of a dissident in November 1989; he lost a way of life he loved; moreover, he is certainly well aware that he plays a role of a master of ceremonies, and he is not happy about that. Hegel once wrote that awareness of his own position and meaning puts a slave above his master. This thought alone can be enough for a man; it can give him the strength to fulfill his mission in life. I do not know what this famous slave would say to Hegel, but I think that, in spite of Hegel's reasoning, he would bitterly resent his station in life. Havel certainly knows that if he were not to act in the conventional manner, he would harm this nation and its people. Does it make him happy, though? Ask Georg Friedrich Hegel—he should know!

Sometimes, even foreign journalists come to my place in Prague. Before the presidential election, there were many of them, and almost everyone asked me if I wished Havel to be elected president. I gave a stereotypical answer to this stereotypical question: "As a person, who loves him, I do not wish it! Were he to be elected president, he will suffer, lose his friends and his privacy, he will not have time to write, and what is worse, he will muse on his worldly glory as on an absurd Garden Party. As a citizen, mother of two and grandmother of five, I wish him to be elected because his personage will serve as a kind of guarantee that this land is peaceful and appropriate for foreign investment."

I thought of my own and my family's interest above all and wished Havel to play the role of a sacrificial lamb. Only a very stupid person can envy a president his fame, receptions, fanfares, glorious meetings and all that drill.

In 1990 in Paris, I closely watched two days in the life of Václav Havel. I would not like to change places with him—not even for a week. Am I supposed to criticize him for what he does? I will spoil this game and do it gladly!

In a few years, when everything has quieted down, people will find their place and have more faith in themselves, and the words of Martina Spinková, mother of five, will become true. She was visiting my son's cottage in Jelenov with her large family. All were young Catholics; the yard was full of small children, and I had to serve dinner on the ping-pong table. We ate spaghetti with ketchup and bad-mouthed Husák and Jakeš in traditional manner. Martina Spinková stopped this current of abuse: "Do not complain, in the future, our descendants will envy us because we lived in the times of John Paul II and Václav Havel."

I agreed with her then and still do now, wholeheartedly!

Timely Reflections on a
Seemingly Untimely Playwright

Andrej Krob

{Comic writers such as Beckett and Havel can cause us, often against our wills, to laugh at queasy truths, and from there it's a short jump to where the laughter backfires in our throats.

—Douglas Soderberg}

Some time ago I invited a friend for a beer. Because he thought it timely we drank not 1 but 10 glasses together. A regular who joined our table shared with us this piece of pub-acquired wisdom: "What was drunk yesterday or will be drunk tomorrow is untimely; only what we manage to drink today is timely." Of course, we paid his bill since every ounce of wisdom comes at a price.

As a director, now and then I have to deal with theater experts who doubt the timeliness of Havel the playwright. Facing them is difficult. By now I have lived in one household with the characters of his plays for some 20 years; naturally our relationship has grown and changed over time. However, when someone begins to express reservations about the characters today it upsets me; I even feel offended on their behalf.

How does one acquire such housemates? An author creates an abstract image of a human being, the director and actor add specific physical features, and then all together, they exclaim: *Ecce homo!* To confirm their very existence, its timeliness, or timelessness indefinitely, the characters then have to go every evening to their play as if they were going to work. Their creators refuse to change anything in their sad ordained destiny, which had been determined for them in advance. The characters' only asset is their immortality. Characters in a play do not die; they only fade into oblivion.

I admit that there are a lot of things that I am happy not to know. It is enough for me just to surmise something about them; I consider it much

Translated from Czech by Zdenka Brodská and Mary Hrabik Samal for this volume. Originally published in *Milý Václave . . . [Dear Václav . . .]* (Prague: Divadelní ústav a Nakladatelství lidové noviny, 1997), 82–84. Reprinted by permission of the publisher.

more adventurous and mysterious. For example, I surmise that the theater seeks to capture the timely moment, but also the timely thought. I also suspect that Havel's *The Garden Party,* which is my most recent and timely production [Krob has since directed two Havel plays in Poland], is a play about life with stupidity and all the consequences of such a life. The play is not only for those who recognize their own past in it and weep, but also for those who do not and laugh. True enough, an invincible stupidity, which is challenged by nothing and thus is unable to learn from anything, plagues one of the play's characters, Ferda Plzák. Nothing can totally annihilate this stupidity; only its form can be altered. Although the leading protagonist of the play, Hugo Pludek, is not one iota smarter than his opposite, Plzák, he is teachable. He can temper his intransigence and learn to employ tactical maneuvers. By keeping his eyes and ears open, he can change his style. His vincible stupidity makes him capable of learning and instinctively recognizing opportunities. It also endows him with an instinct for self-preservation. This stupidity can be preposterous, but precisely because of this, it can be even more dangerous.

Granted, that a particular era has inspired the author of *The Garden Party.* What playwright of the absurd would forgo such ample inspiration for the setting of his play? Some prosper fabulously in this ambiance because others cannot. A world in itself in the midst of the world for all. . . . Not everyone needs to experience this kind of peculiarity for himself or herself. No one strives for anything in this world because it offers nothing. In spite of this, it can originate and function on the ruins of utopias of a better world—a nameless world where no one makes any effort, where only those without a name prosper. . . . It is almost impossible to doubt its timeliness. The closing monologue of the bourgeois youth who, besides having mastered chess, probably knows all the world's phone directories by heart, is not just a skillful and witty play on words. It defines a certain manner of living, provides a manual for a certain skill and gives a lesson in diplomacy, that is, how to say deliberately something other than what one really thinks when it is difficult to tell a lie from the truth and when decency is a synonym for stupidity. Shakespeare's Hamlet will ask ad infinitum if he should or should not be. In this matter, Havel's Pludek possesses absolute certainty. He knows how TO BE in all situations. Maybe the Czech advantage has always been that in as far as we dared to ask questions similar to Hamlet's, there was always someone who had an appropriate and timely answer for us.

At the time when *The Garden Party* was written, there was much talk about the loss of identity or alienation. For what does one need oneself? How is one to acquire one's own identity? How is one to create, protect, even enhance it? Under what circumstances can it be lost? To betray oneself, one has to have something that can be betrayed. A person has to have his or her identity to deny it. Hugo Pludek cannot deny his own identity since he has never had any. The author has given bodily features to his own line of reasoning just because he wanted to demonstrate its independence from a material substance. Ultimately, the material substance called Hugo Pludek doesn't know where it belongs. Its spirit, however, marches on to its goal without the nameless bodily substance interfering in or profiting from this process. The vacuous words do not need interpretation. Having been liberated from dependence on a person, the word is interpreting itself. This is a remarkable, but inverse, victory of spirit over material substance.

Today, it appears that no one is losing his or her identity. That massive pressure, which weighted so heavily on the individual, has disappeared. Everyone makes his or her own decisions; if we are alienated or have lost something, it is the doing of our own free will. It is much more difficult to discover oneself, and at the same time, it is so much easier to lose oneself.

If at the same time we seek to uncover and describe mysterious strength that is the source of our talent and gives meaning to our very existence, we are betraying ourselves since we are accepting rules which demand at all cost the rationalization of the non-rationalizable, that is, the origin and source of our mind's indescribable doings. Based on our own experience, not on something we mindlessly took over from someone else, the course of our own life gives our talent a much more rational substance and makes it indescribably wiser because it can accept only what we have grasped wholly and want to use deliberately. In such a manner, our personality is formed as is the strength to defend it.

Our identity is constantly threatened today. We save what we consider eternal in the computers' memories' gigantic brains, those preserving cans of immortality, within the centralized depositories of all the boxes filled with our fetishes. There we assemble the evidence of our existence for the future. The world's experience is being endlessly renewed there, but it moves further and further away from us; thanks to our own inventiveness, it makes up its own universe based on our ideas. As time goes by, we understand this universe less and less. The more remote it becomes, the less it needs us.

I suspect that Havel's plays are also about this . . .

Some time ago I again went for a beer. My friend did not have time, so I got drunk alone. "What isn't happening here and now, doesn't necessarily have to be untimely since it's happening somewhere else." The regular offered his ounce of pub wisdom and paid my tab. "Nowadays, they don't pay for wisdom: it's listeners that they pay for," he added. How the world has changed, I said to myself. With a heavy heart, I left behind the identity which I had so lightheartedly dissolved in the beer.

Actually, I did not want to persuade anyone about anything. I was just meditating under my breath . . .

HAVEL ON THE ROLE
OF THE PRESIDENT

◆

16. Walking through the meadows, 1996.

17. With Marketa Goetz-Stankiewicz, 1989.

The Role of the Czech President

Václav Havel

The standing of the first Czech president will differ from the standing of the last Czechoslovak president not only in that he will be the head of a different kind of state; the function of the Czech president is also defined differently in the constitution, and his role will differ as well because the political situation in the country is radically altered. Since the last elections, a new phase in the political development of the country has set in . . . a phase of stabilizing parliamentary democracy based on clear competition between political parties of various colors and stripes, and on a clearly emerging separation of political powers. The post-revolutionary period is over, and the president will no longer find himself in the strange role of leader of the nation or the symbol of a new epoch, and he will no longer be compelled, or even be able, to get mixed up in everything and thus be responsible for everything.

With these circumstances in mind, it would be rather foolish to expect a candidate for the office of Czech president to come out with a coherent political program. The Czech president will not be a chief executive or a leader of the parliamentary majority but merely an indirectly elected public servant with a very specific position and mission. He will, of course, have favorite issues of his own that he will wish to pursue through the power of his influence, but he will not be able to promise, in the form of a political program, solutions to matters outside his competence. Only one thing can legitimately be expected of him: his ideas about what the constitutional and political status of the president means, about the ways in which—if elected—he would attempt to fulfill that meaning, and about the values he would seek to defend, safeguard, and promote as the head of state.

According to the constitution, the government assumes or loses power by being granted, or refused, the confidence of the assembly of elected representatives. The president, on the other hand, is elected by both houses of Parliament, and, even more important, he is not directly responsible to them for his activities and is therefore unrecallable.

Václav Havel, "Role českého prezidenta," written for the journal *Mladá fronta Dnes;* reprinted in *Václav Havel 1992 & 1993* (Praha/Lytomyšl: Paseka, 1994), 36–44, translated from Czech by Paul Wilson for this volume. Reprinted by permission of Aura-Pont.

What does this unrecallability mean? Essentially, that while governments can change, the assembly of representatives can be dissolved, and elections can put an entirely new political team in place—depending on the changing mood of the population—the president will remain in office for five years. At the same time, the president will not be a mere passive observer of political change but will be its main actor. After all, he has the authority to appoint a government and, under certain circumstances, to dissolve the representative assembly. This means that his importance will clearly grow in times of political change or crisis because he alone will have the power to intervene in such situations and be the bridge over the crisis or settle it. In any case, this is why he is unrecallable: if his period in office were dependent on the changing political situation or mood, he would scarcely be able to play this role.

The president's unrecallability, combined with the powers already mentioned, is also the key, in my opinion, to understanding his special constitutional and therefore political role: he should guarantee or mediate the continuity of state power, and therefore represent the identity and integrity of the state (after all, he represents the state abroad). In other words, he is a constant of the constitutional and political system, a kind of fixed point, an instance of the last court of appeal or the last resort, a permanent certainty amidst the dynamics of democratic evolution.

. . . The president should turn his attention mainly to matters of basic and long-term significance that concern the very existence and democratic essence of the state, the stability of its political system, the values on which it is founded, constitutionality and constitutional order, and of course, the authority of the state abroad. He should not enter into everyday, temporary political conflicts as a party to the disputes, as a rival or protagonist on the political stage. For this reason he should not identify too closely with any of the existing political parties. The execution of everyday policies is, in any case, the task of the government, or rather of the political parties that form the governing coalition, not of the president. The president should probably not appear on television every day with solutions to all the current problems but rather should be a presence in the background, a guarantor of the legitimacy of the solutions found.

On the other hand, it would be irresponsible of a president to merely "float above the waters." His involvement in everyday politics, however, should be of a rather specific kind: he should operate here as an inconspicuous moderator of political negotiations, occasionally as a consensus-seeker, a behind-the-scenes instigator, someone who creates room for understanding to take place, who is an integrating agent, something like a guardian of the political culture. Rather than concentrating on the technical aspects of disputes, he should focus on the method or the style of their settlement. Simply put: instead of being a player, he should see that the rules of the game are observed.

. . . The president, in my opinion, should watch that the political parties do not yield to the temptation to see the state as their privileged domain and thus begin subtly to stifle natural and free forms of association and assembly by attempting to bring them under their control (a process observable in some parliamentary democracies). Therefore, because he will be in touch with political parties, the president should not neglect contact with all the other organizations of a nonrepresentational nature (from the churches to the trade unions). Through these contacts with the whole of civic society, he would continue to emphasize that genuine democracy can only develop in a climate of multilayered and genuinely independent social associations and that only the richness and the variety of those associations can ultimately create a truly inspirational environment for the political parties as well, which, though they are the basic instrument of democracy, are not its be-all and end-all.

The authority of the president should be rather more statesmanlike than political and it should fully only come to the fore in extreme situations, when the president can act as a kind of referee, arbitrator, or problem solver. The import of his words should, at the same time, come more from the importance he gives to his function and less from the political forces or groupings that happen to be supporting him at the moment.

An important task of the president is concern for the political atmosphere in the land, the climate of public life. I am persuaded that the general political stability and the orderly development of the country depend more on this climate than many are willing to admit. Emphasis on the moral aspect of citizenship, the moral source of politics, the spiritual and intellectual dimension of social coexistence, the role of the state as public servant (which of course it can only fulfill if it enjoys a certain authority), appeals to responsibility, to tolerance, to mutual understanding—all of this will be, I am firmly convinced, a permanent and important responsibility of the president, flowing directly from his political position as defined in the constitution. The effect of this work of political enlightenment is never visible at once; it is indirect, long term, and often very hard to demonstrate. All the more reason why this task is the one relatively the least dependent on the moods of the moment.

In general, the president should concentrate on systemic themes relating to a general system of values, and, as it were, climatic; in other words, precisely that which relates to the basic existential questions of the state, its democratic identity, and its political stability.

Among the primary things a president should take a permanent, intense interest in is human rights. Here he can become closely involved in individual cases without interfering in the competence of other constitutional institutions or becoming inappropriately involved in the political controversies of the day. This task flows directly from the responsibilities that a head of state should definitely have to guard and endorse—the basic humanistic values on which the state is founded.

As I have already indicated, what is generally understood by a political program—that is, a collection of concrete aims from all areas of social life—cannot be the common denominator of the president's activities. To have such a program and push for its implementation is the job of political parties and ultimately of the government that embodies this program in their government declaration. In the president's case, something essentially different should be this common denominator: a common spirit. It should be a spirit of respect for people and for human dignity, respect for the democratic essence of the state and its long-term interests, the spirit of global responsibility for matters concerning the human community. This spirit can hardly be materialized in a collection of theses. It can only be demonstrated through the way one acts, through one's public appearances, through one's approach to various tasks, through the architecture of one's public activities, one's style of work, one's distribution of emphases.

Every president will naturally have his own very concrete ideas about how to solve a particular problem, how to proceed in a particular area, from foreign policy to political, economic, social, educational, or security policies. No one can prevent him from articulating his opinions during meetings or public appearances. Nevertheless, every president should place certain restrictions on himself in this regard and to weigh carefully when, how, and in what way he should express them so as not to destabilize the situation by entering inorganically into spheres that go beyond his immediate competence, or by casting doubt on the electoral programs of those who were given the confidence of the electorate in direct, general elections. To find the right balance between the responsibility to speak the truth according to his best lights and the responsibility to respect the democratic division of power and the political mandate of the other constitutional institutions will never be easy, and the final authority in the creation of this balance will obviously always be a quantity as "unscientific" as ordinary sensitivity for a situation or simply good taste.

The president has the right to return laws to Parliament for reconsideration. It is an important right. Its importance lies not just in the fact that it is the only safeguard or brake that the executive has against Parliament. What is more important is that this right can deepen the cooperation and the good relationship between the president and the Parliament: Parliament will undoubtedly have an interest in the president's not returning their laws, and therefore it will probably inform him of them before they are put to a final vote, or even in some cases unofficially consult with him about them. In this way, the president will, in a sense, be brought nearer the legislative process, indirectly drawn into it, initiated into its atmosphere. His signature on the law will then be far from a purely formal act, but rather an act of genuine identification with the law. As one who represents the state externally, he will thus far more immediately be able to stand behind the legislative process in his country and will not be able to offer the excuse that he has no influence on the laws.

Just as the suspensive veto can significantly bring the president and Parliament closer together, the principle of countersigning . . . can bring him significantly closer to the government. He and the government in a certain sense are mutually dependent on each other: the president will need the government's cosignature for many of his tasks, and the government will need the president's signature for many things. This eliminates the danger of a double-track system, because both institutions will simply have to cooperate with each other every day, regardless of how little they may want to do so. In some areas—in foreign policy, for instance, or matters concerning the army—the official policies of the country will be more or less a vector of these two forces (the minister of foreign affairs may deal with foreign policy in the spirit of government policies, but the president represents the country abroad and therefore bears responsibility for this policy; likewise, the minister of defense operates in harmony with the will of the government, but he cannot very well go around, or not respect, the commander-in-chief of the armed forces).

In both principles (the veto and the power to countersign) the constitution creates a good opportunity for efficient cooperation between the president and Parliament and the president and the government. Thanks to this the president can have—albeit indirectly—a considerable influence on the policies of the state. I don't think, however, that he should abuse this influence, to stubbornly push through his own ideas and thus in fact force or blackmail those who are direct representatives of the political will of the people. I merely feel that in cases of necessity he could use his influence to hold the long-term, general interest against any eventual momentary and particular interest that the government and the Parliament might have a tendency to push forward, especially before elections. Such an intervention in a situation would correspond to the role that a president should, in my opinion, play in the future, that is, the role of the guardian of the intellectual, spiritual, and political values on which the state is founded, its long-term perspectives, its international prestige, its capacity at times to sacrifice its momentary interests to the general interests and the interests of future generations.

My recent brief stay in the sphere of high politics has convinced me that in a democracy, at least 50 percent of politics is psychology. A politician can have enthusiasm, all the legal powers he wants, as many good intentions as he wants, be as right as he wants, have as much expertise and as many expert advisers as he wants—and all of that together need not give him the slightest influence, never mind success, if he does not know how to deal with people (both individuals and the public) and cannot persuade them to support his cause. For this reason, the Czech president will not have an easy time of it; his influence on things will clearly not be automatic, and he will have to work hard to win his place in the sun through the authority of his personality and the credibility of his daily work. I think, however, that this is all to the good.

Glossary

♦

Amadeus: Miloš Forman's [see entry] award-winning 1984 film, based on Peter Shaffer's play about the rivalry between Salieri and Mozart.

Apparatchik: Full-time Party worker, member of the Party bureaucracy, or a Party propagandist in the Soviet Union.

Arendt, Hannah: (1906–1975) Political theorist and philosopher, one of the first to apply the phenomenological method to politics. Presented the idea of "the banality of evil" through her account of Adolf Eichmann's trial (1963). Her best-known book is the monumental *The Origins of Totalitarianism* (1951).

Aron, Raymond: (1905–1983) Distinguished French sociologist, philosopher, and political commentator known for his skeptical views on ideological orthodoxies. Leading columnist of *Le Figaro*. His articles were syndicated throughout Europe.

Bartered Bride, The: [*Prodaná nevěsta*] (première in 1866) A comic opera in three acts by Czech composer Bedřich Smetana (1824–1884).

Beckett, Samuel: (1906–1989) Nobel Prize-winning Irish playwright, director, poet, essayist, and novelist who wrote in both English and French. He is best known for his plays, such as *Waiting for Godot* (1954), *Endgame* (1957), *Krapp's Last Tape* (1959), and *Happy Days* (1961), in which he explores the existential plight of twentieth-century humanity. In 1982 he wrote and dedicated his play *Catastrophe* to Havel; later (1983) Havel dedicated *Mistake* [*Chyba*] to Beckett.

Bellow, Saul: (b. 1915) American novelist known for his characterizations of urban humanity, particularly Jewish intellectuals attempting not to succumb to the general malaise. His novel *Herzog* appeared in 1964.

Beneš, Jan: (b. 1936) Czech writer, persecuted under the Communist regime; emigrated to the United States in 1969.

Bloom, Harold: (b. 1930) Sterling Professor of Humanities at Yale and Berg Professor of English at New York University. His numerous works include *The Anxiety of Influence* (1973) and *The Western Canon* (1994).

Böll, Heinrich: (1917–1985) German prose writer; his themes concern World War II and the postwar scene in Germany. His numerous works include *The Clown* [*Der Clown*] (English translation 1965) and *Group Portrait with a Lady* [*Gruppenbild mit Dame*] (English translation 1973).

Brecht, Bertolt: (1898–1956) German playwright, poet, and "practical man of the theatre." He founded the famous Berliner Ensemble in 1949. His conception of "epic theater" contrasts with traditional theatrical forms. His most famous plays are *The Threepenny Opera* [*Die Dreigroschenoper*] (1928) (English translation 1955) based on John Gay's *The Beggar's Opera* and performed with Kurt Weill's music, *Mother Courage and her Children* [*Mutter Courage und ihre Kinder*] (1941) (English translation 1955), and *The Life of Galileo* [*Leben des Galilei*] (1943) (English translation [the so-called Laughton version] 1951).

Brezhnev, Leonid: (1906–1982) Communist Party leader in the Soviet Union during the Prague Spring. Succeeded Khrushchev as first secretary. President of the Soviet Union 1972. The Brezhnev doctrine was a geopolitical doctrine based on domination through overwhelming power, creating the illusion of stability.

Camus, Albert: (1913–1960) French novelist, playwright, essayist. Born in Algeria, he lived in France from 1942. Awarded the Nobel Prize for literature in 1957. Among his best-known works are *The Stranger* [*L'étranger*] (1942) (English translation 1946) and *The Rebel* [*L'homme revolté*] (1951) (English translation 1953).

Captive Mind, The: Prose text by Polish writer Czeslaw Milosz [see entry] published in 1953 (English translation in the same year), reflecting the problems of intellectuals under Stalinism.

Castle, The: [*Das Schloß*] Franz Kafka's renowned novel written in 1922 (English translation 1930).

Černý, Václav: (1905–1987) Eminent Czech historian, writer, literary critic, and translator. Charter 77 signatory. His memoirs reflect the history and state of Czech culture.

Charles IV: (1316–1378) German king and king of Bohemia from 1346–1378, and Holy Roman Emperor from 1355–1378. Under his rule Prague became the political, economic, and cultural center of the Holy Roman Empire.

Charter 77: Czech human rights movement formed in 1977, initiated by Václav Havel who was also its spokesman several times. It rapidly became the focal center of the peaceful activities of Czechoslovak dissidents. In the charter the group appeals to the nations of the world to influence Communist rulers everywhere, especially with respect to human rights in the spirit of the Helsinki Agreement. For a detailed study of the charter movement see H. Gordon Skilling, *Charter 77 and Human Rights in Czechoslovakia* (1981).

Civic Democratic Party: [ODS: Občanská demokratická strana] Czech political party established by the Democratic right wing of the Civic Forum after it split in 1991. The party advocates a rapid transition to a market economy with wholesale privatization of state assets. Headed by Václav Klaus [see entry].

Civic Forum: [OF: Občanské forum] Czech political movement that spearheaded the opposition to Communist rule in 1989 and won the multiparty election in June the following year. The movement split in early 1991 when the Civic Movement [OH] [see entry] and the Civic Democratic Party [ODA] were formed.

Civic Movement: [OH: Občanské hnutí] Czech political party that arose out of the left of center section of the Civic Forum when it split in 1991. Its leader was Jiří Dienstbier [see entry].

Comenius, Jan Amos: [Komenský, J. A.] (1592–1670) Czech philosopher. Considered the Czech counterpart of Descartes. Tended to humanism, nonviolence, and a harmonic coexistence with the order of nature.

Darkness at Noon: A celebrated novel by Arthur Koestler (1905–1983), published in 1940. The novel did much to draw attention to the nature of Stalin's regime.

Descartes, René: (1596–1650) French philosopher. Main figure in the seventeenth-century intellectual revolution which laid down the foundations of what is thought of as the modern scientific age.

Dichtung und Wahrheit: [*Poetry and Truth*] Wofgang von Goethe's famed autobiography. It deals with Goethe's early life up to his departure for Weimar in 1775.

Dienstbier, Jiří: (b. 1937) Czech journalist, publicist, politician, and writer. In 1969 expelled from the Communist Party. Charter 77 signatory and spokesperson. Imprisoned 1979–1982. Cofounder (with Václav Havel) of the underground publication *Lidové noviny* [*The People's News*] in 1988. 1989–1992 minister of foreign affairs of the Czechoslovak Federal Republic. Heads the Civic Movement. Currently Ambassador Extraordinary to the United Nations for Human Rights.

Dlouhý, Vladimír: (b. 1953) Czech economist and politician. Federal minister of the economy 1990–1992. Minister of trade and industry of the Czech Republic 1992.

Dobříš, Castle: A castle in the country near Prague where under Communism writers who wrote in the required socialist realist style were put up for certain periods in order to be able to write and create in peace and quiet.

Dubček, Alexander: (1921–1992) First secretary of the Communist Party of Czechoslovakia. Coined the slogan "Socialism with a human face." Presided over attempts to restore basic civil freedoms and an independent judiciary during the Prague Spring in 1968. Forced out of office in 1969. After the Velvet Revolution in November 1989 he reemerged from historical oblivion.

Erasmus, Desiderius: (1466–1536) A key figure in Renaissance humanism. Critic of scholastic theology and contemporary mores. One of the greatest scholars of his time.

Fidelius, Petr: (b. 1948) Pseudonym of Karel Palek. Published in *samizdat* [see entry] from the late 1970s onwards. Chiefly concerned with semantic research into the language of Communist propaganda. Editor of the journal *Kritický sborník* [*Critical Collection*]. Three of his long essays are collected in the volume *Řeč komunistické moci* [*The Language of Communist Power*] 1998.

Forman, Miloš: (b. 1932) Czech film director. Left Czechoslovakia for the United States in 1969. Director of such award-winning films as *One Flew Over the Cuckoo's Nest* (1975) and *Amadeus* (1984) [see entry].

Futurism: An early twentieth-century avant-garde movement in the arts that began in 1909 with a manifesto by the Italian poet Marinetti, who also coined the term.

Gellner, Ernest: (1925–1997) Professor of sociology and economics at the University of London and William Wise Professor Emeritus of Social Anthropology at the University of Cambridge. After 1989 taught at the Central European University in Prague. Author of numerous books, the best known of which are *Words and Things* (1959) and *Nations and Nationalism* (1983).

Gruša, Jiří: (b. 1938) Czech writer and dissident under Communism. Active in *samizdat* publications. Arrested and deprived of Czechoslovak citizenship in 1981. Lived in the Federal Republic of Germany after 1981. His best-known work is the novel *The Questionnaire* [*Dotazník*], *samizdat* publication 1975 (English translation 1980). Ambassador of the Czech Republic to the Federal Republic of Germany 1992–1997. Ambassador to Austria 1998.

Habsburg Empire: Royal German family, one of the principal sovereign dynasties of Europe from the fifteenth to the twentieth century. The Habsburgs ruled over a large part of Central Europe (including Hungary and today's Czech Republic) from 1526 until the end of World War I in 1918.

Hájek, Jiří: (b. 1913) Czech politician, dissident; signatory and 1977–1978 and 1979 spokesman of Charter 77. From 1988 chair of the Czechoslovak Helsinki Committee. Author of several works on social and political issues.

Handke, Peter: (b. 1942) Linguistically innovative, widely translated Austrian prose writer and playwright. His best known play is *Kaspar* (1968) (English translation 1969).

Hašek, Jaroslav: (1883–1923) Czech, truly bohemian writer best known for his gargantuan masterpiece *The Good Soldier Švejk* [see entry].

Hegel, Georg Wilhelm Friedrich: (1770–1831) Great German idealist philosopher. His contribution to political philosophy is the idealist theory of the state.

Helsinki Agreement: An international agreement adopted by the states participating at the Conference on Security and Cooperation in Europe. Signed by 33 European countries, the United States, and Canada on 1 August 1975. It was a nonbinding declaration covering issues of security as well as economic, scientific, technological, environmental, and human rights matters.

Hochhuth Rolf: (b. 1931) German playwright sometimes described as the founder of documentary theater. Noted for his political skepticism. Best-known play is *The Deputy* [*Der Stellvertreter*] (1963) (English translation 1964), concerned with the Vatican's relation to Nazism.

Hrabal, Bohumil: (1914–1997) Czech prose writer. To make it possible for his work to be published (though only in censored form), he acknowledged in a 1975 television interview that the Party line was right. His renowned comic picaresque novel *I Served the King of England* [*Obsluhoval jsem anglického krále*] (published semi-officially in 1982) has been translated into English by the translator of Václav Havel's speeches, Paul Wilson (1989). Hrabal is also the author of the novel *Closely Watched Trains* [*Ostře sledované vlaky*] (1965) on which the script for the well-known film was based.

Hus, Jan: (1372/3–1415) Czech religious reformer and renowned Czech patriot, declared a heretic by the Council of Constance and burned at the stake. Inspired the religious and political movement of the Hussites.

Husák, Gustáv: (b. 1913) General secretary of the Central Committee of the Communist Party of Czechoslovakia 1969–1987. President of the Socialist Republic of Czechoslovakia 1987–1989.

Husserl, Edmund: (1859–1938) German philosopher (born in Moravia, now in the Czech Republic). Founder of phenomenology, a new description and analysis of consciousness.

Ionesco, Eugène: (1912–1994) French/Romanian playwright and leading exponent of the theater of the absurd. His best-known plays are *The Bald Soprano* [*La cantatrice chauve*] (1950) (English translation 1958) and *Le Rhinoceros* (1958) (English translation the same year).

Jakeš, Miloš: (b. 1922) Czechoslovak party official. Succeeding Gustáv Husák, he became first secretary of the Communist Party in 1987. Stepped down after the Velvet Revolution [see entry] in November 1989.

Jakobson, Roman: (1896–1982) Russian-born, one of the foremost twentieth-century linguists and principal founder of the European movement in structural linguistics known as the "Prague School." Professor at Columbia University (1943–1949) and at Harvard University (1949–1967).

Jaruzelski, Wojciech: (b. 1923) Polish military, Party, and government official. Prime minister of Poland 1981–1985. President of the state council or head of state 1985–1989. President of the Republic (a newly created post) 1989–1990.

Klaus, Václav: (b. 1941) Founder of the Civic Forum Movement and its chairman 1990–1991. Minister of finance 1989–1992. Prime minister of the Czech Republic 1992–1997. Speaker of Parliament 1998.

Klíma, Ivan: (b. 1931) Czech writer; dissident forbidden to publish from 1969 until the demise of Communism. His short stories and novels circulate widely in English translation. Among his best-known works are the volumes of short stories *My First Loves* [*Moje první lásky*] (English translation 1986) and *My Golden Trades* [*Moje zlatá řemesla*] (English translation 1992), and the novels *Judge on Trial* [*Soudce z milosti*] (English translation 1991), *Love and Garbage* [*Láska a smetí*] (English translation 1990), and *Waiting for the Dark, Waiting for the Light* [*Čekání na tmu, čekání na světlo*] (English translation 1994).

Klíma, Ladislav: (1878–1927) Czech philosopher and novelist. Some of his essays were published in *samizdat*. Built on the thought of Schopenhauer and Nietzsche, and anticipated both existentialism and phenomenology.

Klímová, Rita: (1931–1993) Democratic Czechoslovakia's first post-1989 ambassador to the United States (1990–1992).

Kohl, Helmut: (b. 1930) Chancellor, Federal Republic of Germany, since 1982. Reelected as chancellor of reunited Germany, a post he kept until 1998 when he was defeated in the election.

Kohout, Pavel: (b. 1928) Czech writer, dissident, Charter 77 signatory. Forcibly prevented from returning to Czechoslovakia, he lived in Vienna until 1989. Now divides his time between Prague and Vienna. Widely translated; writes in German as well as Czech. His best-known plays are *August August August* (1967) and *Fire in the Basement* [*Požár v suterénu*] (English translation 1986). His best-known novels available in translation are *The Hangwoman* [*Katyně*] (English translation 1981) and *I am Snowing* (*Sněžím*) (English translation, 1994).

Kołakowski, Leszek: (b.1927) Leading Polish philosopher and man of letters. Left Poland in 1968 after being expelled from the Communist Party and from his chair at Warsaw University. Settled in Oxford, teaching at All Souls' College and at the University of Chicago. His major work is *Main Currents in Marxism* (3 vols.) (1978), which is a testimony to his seeing Marxism as a sterile doctrine inimical to freedom.

Konrád, Györgi: (b.1933) Hungarian writer. Arrested as a result of his essays "Die Intelligenz auf dem Weg zur Klassenmacht" ["The intelligentsia on the road to class power"] in 1974 but released after a week as a result of worldwide protest. His best-known works available in English translation are the novel *The Case Worker* (English translation 1974), the essay "Antipolitics" (English translation 1984), and *The Melancholy of Rebirth: Essays from Post-Communist Central Europe 1989–1994* (English translation 1995).

Kott, Jan: (b.1914) Polish writer, professor of literature, and literary critic. Author of many books and essays on theater and literature of which the best known is the seminal *Shakespeare Our Contemporary* (English translation 1965).

Kubišová, Marta: (b.1942) Czech pop singer who achieved national fame during the 1960s. Charter 77 signatory. After the Soviet invasion in 1968 she was blacklisted and forbidden to sing publicly until 1989.

Kulak: Wealthy peasant in the Soviet Union. The kulaks were liquidated under Stalinism.

Kundera, Milan: (b.1929) Renowned Czech/French writer. Expelled from the Communist Party in 1948 and from his post as professor at the Prague Film Institute in 1970. Permitted to leave the country in 1975. Since then has been living in France. Two of his bestseller novels are *The Book of Laughter* *and Forgetting* [*Kniha smíchu a zapomnění*] (English translation 1978) and *The Unbearable Lightness of Being* [*Nesnesitelná lehkost bytí*] (English translation 1984). Later works include *Immortality* [*Nesmrtelnost*] (English translation 1991) and *Identity* [*L'identité,* written in French] (English translation 1998).

Landovský, Pavel: (b.1936) Czech actor and dramatist. Charter 77 signatory. After living in Vienna throughout the 1980s, he returned to Prague. One of his most memorable roles is the Brewmaster in Havel's *Audience.*

Lesson, The: [*La legon*] (1951). A one-act play by Eugène Ionesco [see entry] (English translation 1958).

Mácha, Karel Hynek: (1810–1836) Is considered the greatest poet of Czech romanticism.

Macourek, Miloš: (b.1926) Czech writer, dramaturge, author of children's books and numerous film scripts.

Masaryk, Tomáš Garrigue: (1850–1937) Czech philosopher and statesman. Led the movement for Czech and Slovak independence from the Austro-Hungarian Empire. Became Czechoslovakia's revered first president in 1918.

Massey College: Residential college for senior scholars and graduate students within the University of Toronto. Built 1960–1963.

Mazowiecki, Tadeusz: (b.1927) Polish lawyer and journalist. Veteran politician of the opposition. Adviser to Lech Wałesa [see entry]. Editor of several Catholic publications, then of *Tygodnik Solidarność* [*Solidarity Weekly*]. Prime minister of Poland 1989–1991.

Milosz, Czeslaw: (b.1911) Renowned Polish poet living in the United States. Awarded the Nobel Prize for literature in 1980. [Also see entry *The Captive Mind.*]

Mitterand, François: (1916–1996) President of France 1981–1995. Led the country to closer political and economic integration with Western Europe.

Morgenthau, Hans Joachim: (1904–1980) German-born American political scientist and historian noted as a leading analyst of the role of power in international politics.

Munich: The Munich Agreement, signed on 29 September 1938 by the prime ministers of Germany, Italy, France, and Britain, stipulated that Czechoslovakia must cede the Sudetenland [see entry] (comprising almost half the territory of Bohemia) to Hitler's Germany. The Czechoslovak government was forced to abide by the agreement.

Němcová, Dana: Czech dissident. Actively espoused Charter 77 and in consequence sentenced to two years imprisonment on a charge of subversion. Václav Havel was sentenced to four and a half years during the same trial.

Normalization: The official term for the government's so-called restoration of order that included efforts to stamp out any remnants of the Prague Spring after the occupation of Czechoslovakia in 1968. Dissident writers, artists, and intellectuals were not only banned but also harassed and frequently imprisoned.

Novotný, Antonin: First secretary of the Czechoslovak Communist Party, president of the republic from 1957. Removed during the political thaw at the end of 1967. Replaced by Alexander Dubček in January 1968.

Palach, Jan: Czech student who immolated himself by fire in January 1969 in Prague's main square as protest against the Soviet occupation of Czechoslovakia in August 1968.

Palouš, Radim: (b.1924) Czech philosopher, dissident, Charter 77 spokesperson. After the downfall of Communism Chancellor of Charles University in Prague.

Patočka, Jan: (1907–1977) Czech philosopher, student of Husserl and Heidegger, proponent of phenomenology. In his 70th year he assumed the difficult role of spokesperson of Charter 77 for whose activities he provided the philosophical basis. Died suddenly after a lengthy police interrogation in March 1977. His collected works are being published.

Pinter, Harold: (b. 1930) English playwright, scriptwriter, short-story writer, novelist, poet, actor, director. His best-known plays are *The Birthday Party* (1958), *The Dumb Waiter* (1960), *The Caretaker* (1960), and *The Homecoming* (1965). His latest play is *Ashes to Ashes* (1998). In 1977 Pinter acted the part of Vaněk in Havel's *Audience* and *Private View* [*Unveiling*] for the British Broadcasting Company.

Plastic People of the Universe: Czech rock band. The trials and convictions in 1976 of Ivan Jirouš, a poet and the band's musical director, and other rock musicians were one of the initial stimuli for Charter 77.

Politburo: [Politytcheskoye Byuro] The office of the Central Committee of the Communist Party of the Soviet Union, which directly established all policies for the Party, the government, and the administration of the Soviet Union as well as the satellite Communist Parties and governments.

Prague Orgy, The: A novel by American writer Philip Roth (1985).

Prague Spring: The culmination of the reform process which began in the early 1960s in Czechoslovakia. An effort, under Alexander Dubček [see entry], to restructure Marxist-Leninist Socialism in a way more suitable to Czechoslovak historical, cultural, and economic circumstances. Its watchword was "Socialism with a human face."

Přemyslids: First Czech royal house, founded, according to legend, by the plowman Přemysl. The members of the Přemyslid dynasty ruled Bohemia and the lands associated with it from about 800 to 1306.

Rebel, The: [*L'homme revolté*] An essay (English translation 1953) by Albert Camus [see entry] where he traces the origins and development of revolt.

Rhinoceros: Internationally renowned play by Eugène Ionesco [see entry]. The play expresses the author's horror of ideological conformism.

Rorty, Richard: (b.1931) American philosopher, professor at the University of Virginia. A noted pragmatist, he practices a sustained critique of the foundationalist, metaphysical aspirations of philosophy. Among his works are *The Consequences of Pragmatism* (1982) and *Achieving Our Country: Leftist Thought in Twentieth-Century America* (1998).

Ruml, Jan: (b.1953) Publicist, dissident, and Charter 77 signatory. Active in *samizdat.* Imprisoned 1981–1982. Until 1989 held various manual jobs. After the collapse of Communism, deputy interior minister 1990. Interior minister of the Czech Republic 1992. Leader of Unie Svobody [The Freedom Union]. Elected Senator 1998.

Samizdat: Originally a Russian term, it gradually acquired wider meaning: the unofficial reproduction of unpublished and unpublishable banned writings. In Communist Czechoslovakia it started during the gloomy period of normalization [see entry], when a small circle of forbidden authors began to exchange their writings as typescripts, bound and numbered. Thus, under the general editorship of the writer Ludvík Vaculík, the now renowned *Edice petlice* [*Padlock Edition*], consisting by the late 1980s of over 360 titles, came into being. Gradually numerous other book series and journals began to appear. In addition to literature, they dealt with topics such as philosophy, religion, history, politics, economics, art, and others.

Schwarzenberg, Karel Jan von: (b.1937) Descendant of one of the leading princely families of Bohemia, Austria, and Southern Germany. The Schwarzenbergs had to flee to Austria after the Communist takeover in 1948 and lived there until 1989. After the Soviet-led invasion of Czechoslovakia in 1968, Karel von Schwarzenberg offered one of his castles near Nuremberg in Germany to what became the renowned Documentation Center of *samizdat* writings. Became Chair of Helsinki Federation for Human Rights 1990. For a period chief of staff in the President's office 1990–1992. President Havel revived for him the title of Chancellor.

Seifert, Jaroslav: (1901–1986) Czech poet, writer of feuilletons, and translator from the French. Of strong influence on all aspects of subsequent Czech poetry. Awarded Nobel Prize for literature in 1984. Charter 77 signatory. Only some of his works were published under Communism.

Shaffer, Peter: (b.1926) British playwright. Author of the play *Amadeus* (1980) on which Miloš Forman based his 1984 film of the same name [see entries]. His other well-known plays include *Five Finger Exercise* (1958) and *Equus* (1974).

Shklovsky, Borisovich Viktor: (1893–1984) Russian writer and leading exponent of the school of formalism. His most important theoretical writings were collected in the volume *O teoriyi prozy* [*About the Theory of Prose*], written during and after World War I.

Šimečka, Milan: (1930–1990) Philosopher and essayist. Imprisoned for a year in 1981. Active in *samizdat*. After the collapse of Communism, he was briefly chairman of the board of advisers to President Havel. Among his writings, initially published in *samizdat,* is the well-known *The Restoration of Order* [*Obnovení pořádku*] (English translation 1984).

Slánský Trial: Rudolf Slánský (1901–1952) secretary-general of the Czechoslovak Communist Party, 1946–1951. Was arrested on Stalin's orders, sentenced in a show trial in 1952 during which he admitted his "crimes committed in collaboration with Western imperialist capitalism." He was executed soon after.

Sorel, Julien: The ambitious working-class hero of Stendhal's novel *The Red and the Black* [*Le rouge et le noir*] (1830) (First English translation 1926).

Srp, Karel: Czech jazz musician.

Stakhanovites: Soviet superworkers. The term takes its name from Alexei Stakhanov, a miner who, inspired by a Communist Party call for increased productivity, exceeded the quota expected of him by 1,300%.

StB: [Státní bezpečnost] The plainclothes Czechoslovak State Police under Communism.

Stoppard Tom: (b. 1937) English playwright born in the Czech Republic. The best known among his numerous plays are *Rosencrantz and Guildenstern are Dead* (1967), *Jumpers* (1972), *Travesties* (1975), *Professional Foul* [dedicated to Václav Havel] (1978), *Hapgood* (1988), and *Arcadia* (1997). Stoppard's English version of Havel's *Largo Desolato* appeared in 1987.

Stroheim, Erich von: (1885–1957) Austrian actor, director, and writer. Emigrated to the United States in 1914 where he worked in Hollywood as actor and later director. The film *Greed* (1924), dealing with the power of money to corrupt, is considered his directorial masterpiece.

Sudetenland: Sections of northern and western Bohemia and northern Moravia. Annexed by Hitler in October 1938 [see entry Munich]. Marks the beginning of the Second Republic of Czechoslovakia, which lasted only until March 1939, when the whole of Bohemia and Moravia were occupied by Germany. The German population living in the Sudetenland prior to its expulsion by the Czechs in 1945 was referred to as Sudeten Germans.

Svědectví [Testimony]: Eminent Czech emigré journal published in Paris and edited by Pavel Tigrid [see entry]. Published in the United States 1956–1960 and from 1960 in Paris.

Švejk, the Good Soldier: Renowned novel by Jaroslav Hašek [see entry]. Written in the 1920s, it soon swept Europe with the hilarity and pungency of its antimilitaristic and antibureaucratic satire (the first unabridged translation into English by Cecil Parrott appeared only in 1973).

Taylor, Charles: (b.1931) Canadian philosopher and political theorist. Professor of philosophy at McGill University. Author of many publications, the best known of which are *Hegel* (1975) and *The Malaise of Modernity* (1991).

Tigrid, Pavel: (b.1917) Czech writer, journalist, and editor. Left Czechoslovakia in 1948. For 35 years chief editor of the eminent emigré quarterly *Svědectví* [*Witnessing*] in Paris. After the downfall of Communism he returned to Prague and became adviser to President Havel, then minister of culture of the Czech Republic (1994–1996). Currently deals with Czech-German relations.

Tomášek, František: (1899–1992) Czech cleric, named cardinal at 1976 papal consistory. Until 1991 archbishop of Prague.

Trahison des clercs, La: [*The Betrayal of the Intellectuals*] A renowned study by the French author Julien Benda published in 1927 (English translation 1928).

Tvář: Czech journal, published 1964–1965 and 1968–1969. Nonideological and envisioned as a forum for young writers, the journal was one of the first to be closed down in the process of normalization. An annotated selection of its content was published in a volume (Prague: Torst 1995).

Tynan, Kenneth: (1927–1980) British drama critic. Wrote for a variety of papers, most influentially for the *Observer* (1954–1963). Published numerous books on theater. Conceived and partly wrote the review *O Calcutta* (1969).

Urbánek, Zdeněk: (b.1917) Czech writer for many years at the heart of the Czech dissent. Translator of Shakespeare into Czech. Some of his writings are collected in *On the Sky's Clayey Bottom: Sketches and Happenings from the Years of Silence* (English translation 1992).

Velvet Revolution: The name for the three-week period of peaceful demonstrations in Prague in November and December 1989. On 28 November a student demonstration was forcefully suppressed. Subsequently the Velvet Revolution culminated in the collapse of the Communist rule and the formation of a new government.

Vyskočil, Ivan: (b.1929) Czech playwright (also psychologist), carrying on the tradition of the Liberated Theater [see entry Werich]. Numerous stage adaptations, cabaret texts, collaborations with other playwrights (for example, *Autostop* with Václav Havel in 1961). Active as author, actor, and director in the renowned Theater on the Balustrade.

Waldheim, Kurt: (b.1918) President of the Republic of Austria 1986–1992. Secretary General of the United Nations 1972–1981. Focal point of a critical controversy when it was disclosed that his past included some collaboration with the Nazis.

Wałesa, Lech: (b.1943) Founder of the Polish Solidarity trade union. Awarded the Nobel Peace Prize in 1983. President of Poland 1990–1993.

Warsaw Pact: Former regional defense alliance of the East European Communist countries led by the Soviet Union. Conceived as a counterweight to NATO. To cut short the liberalization that took place during the Prague Spring, Warsaw Pact troups occupied Czechoslovakia in August 1968 [see entry Prague Spring].

Weber, Karl Emil Maximilian (Max): (1864–1920) German economist and sociologist who, together with Durkheim, is considered one of the fathers of sociology. His major work, unfinished at his death, is *Economy and Society* [*Wirtschaft und Gesellschaft*] (English translation in 3 volumes 1968).

Weil, Simone: (1909–1943) French philosopher and mystic. Maintained total noncommitment as regards religious or political institutions. Her best-known works, published posthumously, are *Waiting on God* [*Attente de Dieu*] (1950) (English translation 1951) and *Oppression and Liberty* [*Oppression et liberté*] (1955) (English translation 1958).

Weizsäcker, Richard, Freiherr von: (b.1920) *Bundespräsident* of the Federal Republic of Germany (1984–1994).

Werich, Jan: (1905–1980) Actor and author. Copartner of the duo Voskovec and Werich (with Jiří Voskovec [1905–1981]). In 1925 one of the founders of the renowned Czech Liberated Theater, which became the center of Voskovec and Werich's hilarious but dark-edged satirical work.

Wiesel, Elie: (b.1928) Andrew W. Mellon Professor of the Humanities at Boston University. Awarded the Nobel Peace Prize in 1986. Among his works are *A Beggar in Jerusalem* (1969) and *All Rivers Flow to the Sea* (1995).

Wittgenstein, Ludwig (Josef Johann): (1889–1951) Austrian philosopher. Taught at Cambridge University from 1929, professor from 1939. His most influential contributions to philosophy are in language and logic, reflected in his *Tractatus Logico-Philosophicus* (1921) (published in German and English 1922) and the posthumously published *Philosophical Investigations* [*Philosophische Untersuchungen*] (1953).

ENGLISH-LANGUAGE BIBLIOGRAPHY

◆

PRIMARY SOURCES IN ENGLISH

PROSE WRITINGS AND SPEECHES

Books

The Anatomy of a Reticence. Stockholm: Charter 77 Foundation, 1986.
The Art of the Impossible: Politics as Morality in Practice: Speeches and Writings, 1990–1996. Trans. Paul Wilson and others. New York: Alfred A. Knopf, 1997.
Cards on the Table. Scheinfeld, Germany: Documentation Centre for the Promotion of Independent Czechoslovak Literature, 1988.
Disturbing the Peace: A Conversation with Karel Hvížd'ala. Trans. Paul Wilson. New York: Alfred A. Knopf, 1990.
Letters to Olga: June 1979–September 1982. Trans. Paul Wilson. New York: Alfred A. Knopf, 1988.
Open Letters: Selected Writings 1965–1990. Selected and edited by Paul Wilson. New York: Alfred A. Knopf, 1991.
Summer Meditations. Trans. Paul Wilson. New York: Alfred A. Knopf, 1992. Also Vintage Books, 1993.
Toward a Civil Society: Selected Speeches and Writings 1990–1994. Trans. Paul Wilson and others. Prague: Lidové noviny, n.d.
Václav Havel or Living in Truth. Ed. Jan Vladislav. London: Faber and Faber, 1987.

Individual Essays

"The Age of Chicanery: Technical Notes on My House-Arrest." *Encounter* (September 1979): 33–40.
"Anatomy of a Reticence." Trans. Erazim Kohák. Stockholm: The Charter 77 Foundation, 1985. [Pamphlet: *Voices from Czechoslovakia.*] Also published in *Cross Currents: A Yearbook of Central European Culture* 5. Ann Arbor, 1986. (*Samizdat*, 1985.) Also in *Open Letters*, 291–322.
"The Anatomy of Hate." *Diogenes* 176 (winter 1996): 19–24.
"The Anatomy of the Gag." Trans. Michal Schonberg. *Modern Drama* 23, no. 1 (March 1980): 13–24 (original Czech edition, 1966).

"Anti-Political Politics." *Civil Society and the State: New European Perspectives.* Ed. John Keane, 381–88. London: Verso, 1988.

"A Call for Sacrifice: The Co-Responsibility of the West." *Foreign Affairs* 73, no. 2 (March/April 1994): 2–7.

"Democracy's Forgotten Dimension." *Journal of Democracy* 6, no. 2 (1995): 3–12.

"The End of the Modern Era." *New York Times,* Sunday, 1 March 1992, sec. E, 15.

"The Hope for Europe." *The New York Review of Books* 43, no. 8 (20 June 1996): 38–41.

"Last Conversation" (1977). Trans. Milan Pomichalek and Anna Mozga. *Good-bye Samizdat: Twenty Years of Czechoslovak Underground Writing.* Ed. Marketa Goetz-Stankiewicz, 211–14. Evanston, Ill.: Northwestern University Press, 1992.

"Letter to Dr. Gustav Husák, General Secretary of the Czechoslovak Communist Party." *Survey* 21, no. 3 (1975). Also in *Encounter* (September 1975) and *Open Letters* as "Dear Dr. Husák," 50–83.

"Light on a Landscape." Trans. Milan Pomichalek and Anna Mozga. [Chapter: Playwright's Comments.] In *The Vaněk Plays: Four Authors, One Character.* Ed. Marketa Goetz-Stankiewicz, 237–39. Vancouver: University of British Columbia Press, 1987. [Czech original untitled—this is the translators' title.]

"Meeting Gorbachev." Trans. George Theiner. *Granta* 23 (1988): 11–15. (*Samizdat,* 1987.) Also in *Open Letters,* 351–54.

"Much Ado . . ." *Index on Censorship* 5, no. 3 (1976): 55–56. [Letter to Prague officials on the police actions against amateurs who performed his *Beggar's Opera.*]

"Mystery and Meaning." *American Theatre* 11, no. 8 (1994): 120.

"NATO's Problem is a Hesitant West." *New Perspectives Quarterly* 13, no. 3 (1996): 44–45.

"NATO's Quality of Life." *New York Times,* 13 May 1997, sec. A, 15, 21.

"The Need for Transcendence in the Postmodern World." *The Futurist* 29, no. 4 (1995): 46–49.

"A Neglected Generation." *Acta* 2, no. 5–8 (1988): 21–24.

"A New European Order?" Trans. Paul Wilson. *The New York Review of Books* 42, no. 4 (2 March 1995): 43–44. [Speech at the Conference on Security and Cooperation in Europe, Budapest, December 1994.]

"The New Measure of Man." *New York Times,* Friday, 8 July 1994, sec. A, 15.

"The New Year in Prague." Trans. Paul Wilson. *The New York Review of Books* 38, no. 5 (7 March 1991): 19–20.

"New Year's Address." [January 1990] *The Spectator* (27 January 1990). Also in *Open Letters,* 390–96.

"On Dialectical Metaphysics." Trans. Michal Schonberg. *Modern Drama* 23, no. 1 (March 1980): 6–12. [Original Czech edition, 1966.]

"On Kafka." *The New York Review of Books* 37, no. 14 (27 Sept. 1990): 19.

"On Rita Klímová (1931–1993)" [Obituary.] With Paul Wilson. *The New York Review of Books* 41, no. 3 (3 Feb 1994): 6.

"Our Shared Responsibility for Future Democracy." *Visions for the 21st Century.* Ed. Sheila M. Moorcroft, 39–41. Westport, Conn.: Praeger Publishers, 1993.

"Politics and Conscience." Trans. Erazim Kohák and Roger Scruton. *The Salisbury Review* 3, no. 2 (1985). Also in *Open Letters,* 249–71.

"Politics and the Theatre." *Times Literary Supplement* (28 September 1967): 879–80.

"The Politics of Responsibility." *World Policy Journal* 12, no. 3 (1995): 81–87.

"Post-Modernism: The Search for Universal Laws." *Vital Speeches* 60 (1 August 1994): 613–15.

"The Power of Folly." *Cross Currents: A Yearbook of Central European Culture* 6 (1987): 47–52.

"The Power of the Powerless." *The Power of the Powerless: Citizens Against the State in Central-Eastern Europe.* Ed. John Keane. London: Hutchinson, 1985. Also in *Open Letters,* 125–214.

"Reflections on the Theatre." *Index on Censorship* 12, no. 2 (1983): 31–32. [Abridged version of the first part of an article published in *Kritický sborník* 4 (1983), printed here from a *Samizdat* typescript.]

"The Responsibility of Intellectuals." *The New York Review of Books* 42, no. 11 (22 June 1995): 36–37.

"Second Wind" (1976). Trans. Paul Wilson. *Good-bye Samizdat: Twenty Years of Czechoslovak Underground Writing*. Ed. Marketa Goetz-Stankiewicz. Evanston, Ill.: Northwestern University Press, 1992, 205–10. Also in *Open Letters*, 3–9.

"Six Asides About Culture." Trans. Erazim Kohák. In *A Besieged Culture: Czechoslovakia Ten Years After Helsinki*. Ed. A. Heneka et al. Stockholm/Vienna: The Charter 77 Foundation, 1985. Also in *Open Letters*, 272–84.

"A Soul of the Soul." *Media Studies Journal* 9, no. 3 (1995): 25.

"Stories and Totalitarianism." Trans. Paul Wilson. *Index on Censorship* 17, no. 3 (1988): 14–21. Reprinted in slightly different form in *Idler* 18 (July/August 1988). Also in *Open Letters*, 328–50.

"Testing Ground." Trans. A. G. Brain. *The Independent* (3 July 1989). Also in *Open Letters*, 373–76.

"There Is no Godot." *World Press Review* (January 1993): 56.

"Thinking About František K." Trans. A. G. Brain. *Listy: The Journal of the Czechoslovak Socialist Opposition* 1 (1988). Also in *Open Letters*, 363–72.

"Thriller." Trans. Paul Wilson. *Idler* (June/July 1985). Also in *Open Letters*, 285–90.

"A Time for Transcendence." *New Age Journal* (September/October 1994). Reprinted in *Utne Reader*, no. 67 (January-February 1995): 53, 112–13.

"Václav Havel Speaks to Fulbrighters." [Fulbright Prize Address.] *Fulbright Association Newsletter* 19, no. 4 (1997): 5–8.

"Words on Words." Trans. A. G. Brain. *The New York Review of Books* 36, no. 21–22 (18 January 1990): 5–8. Also in *Open Letters* as "A Word About Words," 377–89.

DRAMA

Conversation: A One Act Play. Trans. George Theiner. *Index on Censorship* 5, no. 3 (1976): 41–50. [also translated as *Audience*.] This play has been translated by different translators. Here it appears under the title the translator used. The title used by another translator is in brackets.

The Garden Party. Trans. and adapted by Vera Blackwell. London: Jonathan Cape, 1969. [Original Czech edition, 1963.]

The Garden Party and Other Plays. New York: Grove Press, 1993. Contains *The Garden Party* (1963), trans. Vera Blackwell (1969); *The Memorandum* (1966), trans. Vera Blackwell (1967); *The Increased Difficulty of Concentration* (1968), trans. Vera Blackwell (1976); *Audience {Conversation}* (Prague: Samizdat, 1975; *Svědectví* 12, no. 51; *Hry* (Toronto: Sixty-Eight Publishers, 1977), trans. George Theiner (1976). *Unveiling (Private View)* (Prague: *Samizdat*, 1975; Toronto: *Hry*, 1977), trans. Jan Novak (1986). *Protest* (*Samizdat*, 1978), trans. Vera Blackwell (1984). *Mistake* (1983), trans. George Theiner (1983).

The Increased Difficulty of Concentration. Trans. Vera Blackwell. New York: Samuel French, 1976. Jonathan Cape: 1972. [Original Czech edition, 1968.]

Largo Desolato. English version by Tom Stoppard. New York: Grove Press, 1987. [First edition in German translation. Reinbek: Rowohlt Verlag, 1985.]

The Memorandum. Trans. Vera Blackwell. New York: Grove Press/Evergreen, 1980. Grove, 1967. [Original Czech edition, 1966.]

Mistake. Trans. George Theiner. *Index on Censorship* 13, no. 1 (February 1984): 13–14. [1983— in response to Samuel Beckett's dedication of his *Catastrophe* to Havel.]

Protest. Trans. and adapted by Vera Blackwell (1984). In *DramaContemporary: Czechoslovakia*. Ed. Marketa Goetz-Stankiewicz. New York: Performing Arts Journal Publications, 1985: 69–90. [Czech edition, 1978.]

Redevelopment or, Slum Clearance. English version by James Saunders from a literal translation by Marie Winn. London: Faber and Faber, 1990.

Selected Plays 1963–1983. London: Faber and Faber, 1992. Contains *The Garden Party* (1963), trans. Vera Blackwell (1969), 1–51; *The Memorandum* (1966), trans. Vera Blackwell (1967), 53–129; *The Increased Difficulty of Concentration* (1968), trans. Vera Blackwell (1976), 131–82; *Audience {Conversation}* (1975), trans. George Theiner (1976), 183–211 [original Czech edition, *samizdat* 1975]; *Unveiling {Private View}* (1975), trans. Jan Novak (1986), 213–37 [original Czech edition, *samizdat* 1975]; *Protest* (1978), trans. Vera Blackwell (1984), 239–66 [original Czech edition, *samizdat* 1978]; *Mistake* (1983), trans. George Theiner (1983), 267–73 [original Czech edition, *samizdat* 1983].

Selected Plays 1984–87. London: Faber and Faber, 1994. Contains *Largo Desolato* (1984), trans. Tom Stoppard (1987), 1–60 [original Czech edition, *samizdat* 1984]; *Temptation* (1986), trans. George Theiner (1986, 1988), 61–135 [original Czech edition, *samizdat* 1985]; *Redevelopment* [also translated as *Slum Clearance*] (1987), trans. James Saunders (1990), 137–207 [English version by James Saunders from a literal translation by Marie Winn] [original Czech edition, *samizdat* 1987].

Sorry. . . : Two Plays. Translated and adapted by Vera Blackwell. London: Eyre Methuen in association with the BBC, 1978. Contains *Audience [Conversation]*, 7–35; *Private View [Unveiling]*, 37–64.

Temptation. Trans. George Theiner. London and Boston: Faber and Faber, 1988. This translation first appeared in *Index on Censorship* 15, no. 10 (November/December 1986): 22–43.

Temptation: A Play in Ten Scenes. Trans. Marie Winn. New York: Grove Weidenfeld, 1989.

Three Vaněk Plays. London: Faber and Faber, 1990. Contains *Audience; Unveiling; Protest.*

Tomorrow! Trans. Barbara Day. In *Czech Plays.* Selected and introduced by Barbara Day. London: Nick Hern Books, 1994. 1–26. [original Czech edition published anonymously, 1988.]

The Vaněk Plays: Four Authors, One Character. Ed. Marketa Goetz-Stankiewicz. Vancouver: University of British Columbia Press, 1987. Contains *Audience,* trans. Jan Novak (1986), 1–26; *Unveiling,* trans. Jan Novak (1986), 27–49; *Protest,* trans. Vera Blackwell (1984), 51–75.

INTERVIEWS

"An Apolitical Politician." Interview with Valerie Masterov. *Moscow News* (10 July 1997): 1.

"Breaking the Ice Barrier." Interview with BBC, 1977. *Index on Censorship* 7, no. 1 (January-February 1978): 25–28.

"A Conversation with President Havel." Interview with Adam Michnik. *World Press Review* 39, no. 3 (March 1992): 14–16.

"A Conversation with Václav Havel." Interview with Andrzej Jagodzinski. Trans. Daniel Bourne. *Artful Dodge* 26–27 (1994): 23–29.

"Europe at the fin de siècle." Interview with Maximilian Schell. *Society* 32 (September-October 1995): 68–73.

"I Take the Side of Truth." Interview with Antoine Spire. *Index on Censorship* 12, no. 6 (December 1983): 3–7. Also in *Open Letters,* 237–48.

"Metamorphosis in Prague: The East Is Green for Havel." Interview with Leonid Shinkarev (30 June 1989). *The Unesco Courier* (June 1990): 4–10.

"My Temptation." Interview with Karel Hvížd'ala. *Index on Censorship* 15, no. 10 (November-December 1986): 19–43.

"Out of Unity, Discord." Interview with Igor Blazevic. *Index on Censorship* 23, no. 3 (July-August 1994): 59–65. Also in *New Statesman and Society* (22 July 1994): 32–33.

"An Uncertain Strength: An Interview with Václav Havel," Interview conducted in Prague with Dana, Emingerová and Luboš Beniak. Trans. Paul Wilson. *The New York Review of Books,* no.14 (15 August 1991): 6.

"A Vote for Nostalgia." Interview with Charles Lambroschini. *Index on Censorship* 25, no. 3 (May/June 1996): 76–77.

"We Must Respect Russia's Interests, but Russia, Too, Must Respect How We Will Decide Our Future." Interview with Viktor Loshak. *Moscow News* (10 June 1994): 6.

Notes on Contributors

♦

Timothy Garton Ash is a historian, publicist, and writer on current affairs. He is a fellow of St. Anthony's College, Oxford. Specializing in Central European history, he has written widely on the culture and political developments of countries in this area. Among his publications are: *The Polish Revolution: Solidarity 1980–82* (1983), *The Uses of Adversity: Essays on the Fate of Central Europe* (1989), *The Magic Lantern: The Revolution of '89 Witnessed in Warsaw, Budapest, Berlin and Prague* (1990), and *The File: a Personal History* (1997). He is a frequent contributor to *The New York Review of Books*.

Stanisław Baranczak has been a professor of Polish language and literature at Harvard since 1981. He is a graduate of Adam Mickiewicz University in Poznan, Poland, where he taught at the Institute of Polish Philology. He was fired by the university in 1977 as retaliation for being a founding member of the human rights group KOR and publishing books without the censors' permission. His books include *A Fugitive from Utopia: The Poetry of Zbigniew Herbert* and *Breathing Under Water and Other East European Essays* (1990) as well as translations of *View with a Grain of Sand: Selected Poems* by Wisława Szymborska (translated with Clare Cavanagh) and "Laments" by Jan Kochanowski (translated with Seamus Heaney).

Václav Bělohradský is a professor of sociology and politology at the University of Trieste. During the 1960s he studied philosophy at Charles University. He emigrated to Italy in 1970. His essays were published in *samizdat*. Since 1990 he has also been lecturing at Charles University in Prague and contributes to Czech papers and journals of opinion. Among his publications are *The Eschatological Crisis of Non-Personality* (1982) and *The Natural World as a Political Problem* (1981).

Jean Bethke Elshtain is Laura Spelman Rockefeller Professor of Social and Political Ethics at the Divinity School, the University of Chicago. Among her numerous books are *Public Man, Private Woman: Women in Social and Political Thought* (1981), *Democracy on Trial* (1993), and *Real Politics: Political Theory and Everyday Life* (1997). She is also a regular contributor to the *New Republic*.

Dean C. Hammer is associate professor of government at Franklin and Marshall College in Lancaster, Pa. He is author of *The Puritan Tradition in Revolutionary, Federalist, and Whig Political Theory: A Rhetoric of Origins* and has published essays on political theory, classics, and philosophy.

Andrej Krob is a Czech theater director. He directed the famous première (and only performance during the Communist regime) of Havel's *The Beggar's Opera* in a village near Prague (1975). He performed physical labor under Communism, and is now a theater director in Prague where he has directed remarkable and iconoclastic revivals of Havel's plays.

Lewis Lapham was editor of *Harper's Magazine* from 1976–1981 and has been editor since 1983. He is author of several books, including *Fortune's Child* (1980), *Imperial Masquerade* (1990), *The Wish for Kings* (1993), and *Hotel America: Scenes in the Lobby of the fin de siècle* (1995). His latest book of essays is *Waiting for the Barbarians* (1997). In 1995 he received the National Magazine Award for three essays appearing in *Harper's Magazine.* He has also written for *Life, Commentary, National Review, Fortune, Forbes,* the *American Spectator,* the *London Observer,* the *New York Times,* the *Wall Street Journal,* and other journals. He has lectured at many leading universities.

Rob McRae is a Canadian diplomat and former political philosophy professor, who has served on assignments in Belgrade, Prague and London. He is currently Deputy Permanent Representative at the Canadian Joint Delegation to the NATO, Brussels. His other books are *The Matter with Truth* (1990) and *Philosophy and the Absolute* (1985).

Michael L. Quinn was assistant professor at the School of Drama, University of Washington from 1989–1994. He wrote "The Semiotic Stage: Prague School Theater Theory" as well as many articles on directing, acting, and dramatic literature. At the time of his death he was completing a book manuscript, "Václav Havel and the Drama of Identity," and was editor of *Theater Survey.* An annual writing prize was established in his name at the University of Washington School of Drama.

Stephen Schiff is a staff writer for the *New Yorker* and the former critic-at-large of *Vanity Fair.* He was a finalist for the Pulitzer Prize in criticism in 1983. He wrote the screenplay "Lolita" for the film adaptation of Vladimir Nabokov's novel. His screenplay "The Deep End of the Ocean" was filmed for release in the fall of 1998. He was the film critic of National Public Radio's "Fresh Air" (1987–1996), and a correspondent on the CBS-TV prime-time news magazine "West 57th" (1988–1990).

Jiřina Šiklová is professor and Chair of sociology at Charles University and a publicist. Under Communism during the 1970s and 1980s she was employed as a hospital assistant in gerontology. Having been fired for political reasons, she worked as a cleaning woman. Very active during the years of dissidence, she was imprisoned in

1981–82. Since 1990 she has lectured in many countries and contributed to Czech and international journals. Her main concerns are the place of women in society and human rights in general. She has been nominated as the Czech woman of the year.

H. Gordon Skilling is professor of political science (emeritus) at the University of Toronto and founder and first director of the Centre for Russian and East European Studies there. He is a specialist on Czechoslovak politics and Czech history, and author of *Czechoslovakia's Interrupted Revolution* (1976), *Charter 77 and Human Rights in Czechoslovakia* (1981), *Listy z Prahy* (1988), and *T. G. Masaryk, Against the Current, 1882–1914* (1994) [translation into Czech: *T. G. Masaryk, proti proudu* (1995)]. He is also editor or coeditor of several books including *Czechoslovakia, 1918–88: Seventy Years from Independence* (1991) and *Civic Freedom in Central Europe: Voices from Czechoslovakia* (1991).

Robert Skloot has been professor of theater and drama at the University of Wisconsin-Madison since 1968, and since 1996 Associate vice chancellor of academic affairs. He was director of the university theater and chair of the department of theater and drama from 1990–1993, and editor of *The Theatre of the Holocaust* (1982) and *The Darkness We Carry: The Drama of the Holocaust* (1988). He has published numerous articles on modern drama and theater and has been the recipient of Fulbright lectureships to Israel, Austria, and Chile.

Josef Škvorecký is a Czech-Canadian writer, and author of many novels, of which the best known (all available in English) are *The Cowards* [*Zbabělci*] (English translation 1972); *The Miracle Game* [*Mirákl*] (English translation 1990); *The Engineer of Human Souls* [*Příběh inženýra lidských duší*] (English translation 1984), for which he received the Canadian Governor General's Award for Best Fiction; *Dvořák in Love* [*Scherzo capriccioso*] (English translation 1986); and *The Bride of Texas* (*Nevěsta z Texasu*] (English translation 1996). He has also published several volumes of short stories, nonfiction works, and the autobiography *Headed for the Blues: a Memoir* [*Neully: paměti, úvahy, příběhy*] (English translation 1996). In 1971 Škvorecký and his wife, the writer Zdena Salivarová, founded Sixty-Eight Publishers, which for over 20 years published banned Czech and Slovak books, including the first volume of Václav Havel's plays. In 1990 they were awarded by President Havel the Order of the White Lion. In 1980 Škvorecký received the Neustadt Prize for Literature, and in 1992 he was appointed to the Order of Canada.

Douglas Soderberg studied playwriting at Carnegie-Mellon University (MFA, 1981) and dramaturgy at the Yale School of Drama. His plays have been presented in the United States as well as in Bonn, Moscow, Calcutta and other cities abroad. He has been artist-in-residence at the University of Minnesota at Duluth and taught playwriting. His play *The Roots of Chaos* is published in *The Best Short Plays of 1986*. He acted as production dramaturge for the Yale Repertory Theater's production of Havel's *Largo Desolato* in 1990.

Peter Steiner has taught at the University of Michigan and Harvard and is now associate professor at the University of Pennsylvania. His major publications deal with various issues of Slavic literary theory. He was coeditor of *The Sign: Semiotics Around the World* (1980) and is author of *Russian Formalism: A Metapoetics*, 1984. The essay on Havel is a chapter from his projected book on "Politics or Poetics: Modern Czech Fiction in Its Social Context."

J. P. Stern was born in Prague; after the German occupation of his country his family moved to England. He was head of German studies at University College, London (1972–1986) and, among other honorary positions, fellow of the British Academy. His numerous publications and editions include studies on Ernst Jünger and Lichtenberg. The most important works among his broadly sweeping publications are his essays on nineteenth-century German literature, *The Mind of Nietzsche* (1980), *Hitler, the Führer and the People* (1975), and *The Heart of Europe: Essays on Literature and Ideology* (1992), a volume he completed a short time before his death in 1991.

Paul I. Trensky was born in the Czech Republic. He is professor at Fordham University in New York where he teaches comparative literature and drama. He published numerous essays on Russian, Czech and comparative literature. His principal works are *Czech Drama since World War II* (1978) and *The Fiction of Josef Škvorecký* (1990). Since 1990 he has also been very active as drama critic for the Prague theater journal *Svět a divadlo* [*The World and the Theatre*].

Paul Wilson is a writer and translator; he was producer with the CBC current affairs show, "This Morning." He has written on Havel and the Czech political and cultural scene and has translated many of Václav Havel's essays, letters, and speeches into English. His most important books of translations are *Letters to Olga, June 1979– September 1982* (1988), *Open Letters, Selected Prose 1965–1990* (1991), *Summer Meditations* (1992), and *The Art of the Impossible: Politics as Morality in Practice. Speeches and Writings 1990–1996* (1997). He has also translated novels by Josef Škvorecký and Bohumil Hrabal. Currently he is Senior Editor of *Saturday Night* magazine.

Kenneth S. Zagacki is associate professor of communication studies at Louisiana State University in Baton Rouge. He has published numerous essays on political communication and on the relationship of rhetoric to philosophy.

Index

◆

1984 (Orwell), 175, 181

Abraham, F. Murray, 4
Agnes, Princess, 33
Albright, Madeleine, 128
Allen, Woody, 76
Amadeus (Shaffer), 76, 229, 267
American Public Broadcasting System, 94
Amerika (Kafka), 213
Anti-Semitism, 40, 109, 137–38
Apparatchik(i), 120, 252, 267
Arafat, Yasser, 84
Arendt, Hannah, 87, 122, 236, 267; Elsh-
    tain on (and Havel), 116, 123
Aron, Raymond, 62, 267; on totalitarianism
    134; on political oppression, 136
Austria, 66, 84, 106–7, 109
Austro-Hungarian Empire, 107, 109. *See also*
    Habsburg Empire

Bald Soprano, The (Ionesco), 54, 161, 162; its
    influence on Havel, 202
Baltic States, 82
Baranczak, Stanislaw, 5, 6, 44–55, 57
Bartered Bride, The (Smetana), 187, 267
Bateson, Gregory, 189, 198
Bayard, Caroline, 147; on Havel and post-
    modernism. 143–44; on intellectual
    144–45
Beatles, The, 79
Beatty, Warren, 91
Beaumarchais de [Pierre-Augustin Caron], 94
Beckett, Samuel, 1, 13, 15, 165, 267; as
    "absurdist" writer 227; in Czechoslova-

kia, 173–4; kinship with Havel,
    237–38; and Havel's theater, (Carey)
    179, 181, (Skloot) 203, 206
Beggar's Opera, The (Gay), 12
Bellow, Saul, 96, 267
Bělohradský, Václav, 15, 75, 247–49
Beneš, Edvard, 33–34
Beneš, Jan , 243–44, 268
Beniak, Luboš, 79
Bergson, Henri, 213
Berlin, 184
Birthday Party, The (Pinter): compared with
    Havel's plays, 201
Bizet, Georges, 95
Black, Shirley Temple, 80
Blackwell, Vera, 3
Blake, William, 66
Bloch, Ernst, 9, 41
Bloom, Harold , 185, 268
Bohemia, 33, 44, 80, 86, 89, 107, 109
Böll, Heinrich, 1, 34, 70, 268
Bond, Cliff, 100
Bratislava, 42
Brecht, Bertolt, 12, 39, 94,187, 229, 268;
    and his *Dreigroschenoper*, 184, 185; his
    Galileo on heroes, 61
Breughel, Pieter, 80
Brezhnev, Leonid, 47, 268
Brzezinski, Zbigniew, 62, 66
Bristol Old Vic, 3
Burke, Kenneth: on comedy 131–32; on
    irony 134; on "identification," 136
Bush, George, 79
Byron, Lord George Gordon, 70

Camus, Albert, 54, 122, 177, 268; and
   political theater, 229
Canada, 100
Canadian Broadcasting Corporation, 21
Čapek, Karel, 249
Captive Mind, The (Milosz), 268; on Soviet
   ideology, 214–15
Cardenál, Ernesto, 45
Carey, Phyllis, 11–12, 200; on *Memorandum*,
   173–83
Castle, The (Kafka), 39, 41, 213, 268
Catastrophe (Beckett), 1, 203, 205, 231
Central Europe, 16, 24, 54, 59; its sense of
   irony, 48; Havel on, 118; and
   post–Cold War, 127
Černý, Václav, 268
Chairs, The (Ionesco), 41
Chapman, John Jay, 91
Charles IV, 268
Charter 77: 23, 47, 115, 159, 269; founding
   of, 35; Havel's work with, 106–9;
   meeting after 1989, 251
Chekhov, Anton, 161
Chorukor (*Memorandum*), 40–41, 175
Churchill, Winston, 44
Civic Democratic Party (ODS), 25, 29, 269
Civic Forum (OF), 22–26 *passim;* 66, 91, 99,
   269; and first stages of new order, 252–53
Civic Movement (OH), 24, 269
Civil society, 21; Havel on, 28; need for cre-
   ation of, 150
Clardy, J.V.: on *Memorandum,* 181
Clinton, Hillary, [photo] 128
Clinton, William Jefferson, 67; [photo] 128
CNN, 76
Cold War, 129; post–Cold War world 127;
   Havel on, 133
Comenius, Jan Amos , 42, 269
Communism, 9, 11, 15, 22, 24, 25; and
   population, 251; collapse of 23
Communist Party, 23, 24; and Havel, 25–26
Communist takeover of 1948: 24, 34, 47,
   78, 99, 214. *See also* Czechoslovakia
Constitution: Communist, 153; Czech,
   drafting of 81, Czech (Havel on), 119;
   United States, 94
Copenhagen, 63, 64
Copland, Aaron, 96
*Cross Currents: a Yearbook of Central European
   Culture,* 4
Czech Drama Since World War II (Trensky), 4
Czechoslovak Republic: Communist coup

d'état (1948), 34; Communist régime
   in, 93, 94; interwar period in, 110;
   under Masaryk, 9, 12; its democratic
   revolutions of 1918 and 1989
   (Skilling), 105, 110; Czech-Slovak relations in, 26–27, 101; political thaw in,
   13, 15. *See also* Munich Agreement and
   Soviet invasion
Czechoslovak Television, 94
Czechoslovak Writers' Union, 15, 23, 47,
   243
Czech Republic, 21; Havel on role of its
   president, 16, 261–65

Darkness at Noon (Koestler), 38, 269
Darwin, Charles, 51
Deleuze, Giles, 13, 209, 211; and theory of
   "delirious" subjectivity, 214–15
Deputy, The (Hochhuth), 229
Derrida, Jacques, 11; on Western philosophy
   144; on politics of subversion 147–48
Descartes, René 214, 269
Dialectical and Historical Materialism (Stalin),
   170
Dichtung und Wahrheit (Goethe), 188, 269
Dienstbier, Jiří, 35, 50, 69, 269
Dior, Christian, 86
Dlouhý, Vladimír, 253, 270
Dobříš, Castle, 244, 270
Doctor Faustus (Thomas Mann), 230
Domingo, Placido, 95
Don Giovanni (Mozart), 95
Dreigroschenoper, Die (Brecht), 12, 184
Dreyfus, Alfred, 70
Dubček, Alexander, 99, 243, 270; after
   Soviet invasion, 186
Duchess of Malfi, The (Webster), 207
Dumb Waiter, The (Pinter), 201. *See also* Pinter
Dürrenmatt, Friedrich, 94
Dvořák, Antonin, 86, 94; his New World
   Symphony, 96
Dylan, Bob, 92

East Berlin, 83
East Germany, 34, 37
Elshtain, Jean Bethke, 8, 9–10, 44; on
   Arendt and Havel, 116; on Havel's
   first speech as president, 114–15; on
   Havel's political thought 112–26 *pas-
   sim;* on Rorty, 114–15, 123; on theory
   and practice in politics, 113–15. *See also*
   Havel, Václav

Engels, Friedrich, 41, 170
Erasmus, Desiderius, 270; his vision of folly, 131; on three judgments of folly, 134
Erasmus Prize, 231
Esslin, Martin, 159
Euripides, 229
Europe: Havel on, 124
Exit the King (Ionesco), 204

Fanfare for the Common Man (Copland), 96
Farrell, T.B., 127
Fascism, 110
Faust (Goethe), 230, 233, 237; the Faust theme in *Temptation* 14–15, 232, 236
Fidelius, Petr, 234, 270
Flack, Roberta, 94
Folly and Insanity in Renaissance Literature (Grassi and Lorch), 131
formalism, 212
Forman, Miloš, 77, 94, 95, 270; on emigration, 78
Foss, Lukas, 96
Foss, S. K., 129
Foucault, Michel, 11, 13; on globalizing discourses 148–49
France, 70, 83
Freimanová, Anna, [photo] 90
French Revolution, 124
Freud, Sigmund, 114, 211
Futurism, 214, 270

Gadamer, Hans-Georg, 218
Gandhi, Mahatma, 78; and Havel, 34
Garton Ash, Timothy, 5, 9, 112; on intellectuals and politics, including Havel-Klaus tension, 6–7, 57–71; response to Klaus at PEN conference, 59–64; on moral conscience, 130; on *Temptation*, 204; on Velvet Revolution, 207
Gay, John, 12, 184
Gellner, Ernest, 65, 270
Genet, Jean, 160
Germany, 6, 42, 59, 80, 159; and Havel's visit, 83; its political debates, 70; Nazi Germany and Czechoslovakia, 33–34, 110; and President Weizsäcker, 67–68
Gillespie, Dizzy, 94
Glucksmann, André, 1
Goebbels, Paul Joseph, 45
Goethe, Johann Wolfgang von, 230, 233, 237
Goetz-Stankiewicz, Marketa, 41, 127; Intro-

duction, 1–18; on theme of temptation in Havel, 228–40; [photo] 260
Gogol, Nikolai, 167
Gorbachev, Mikhail, 34
Goya y Lucientes, Francisco, 80
Grass, Günter, 70
Grassi, Ernesto,134; on folly, 131; on empathy, 137
Grossman, David: on Havel, 207
Gruša, Jiří, 244, 270
Guattari, Felix, 211, 214
Guimond, Pierre, 100

Habermas, Jürgen, 218
Habsburg Empire, 271; compared with Soviet Empire, 9, 106–7, 110
Hájek, Jiří, 35, 47, 271
Hamburg, 3
Hamlet (Shakespeare), 177, 229; and *Garden Party*, 216; and Havel, 17; speech to the players, 21; in Havel's plays, 235; and Hamlet's question, 256
Hammer, Dean C., 8, 247; on Havel and democratic discourse, 10–11, 143–56
Handke, Peter, 229, 271
Happy Days (Beckett), 181
Harvard University, 60
Hašek, Jaroslav, 34, 271. *See also* Švejk
Havel, Ivan M., [photo] 210
Havel, Václav: on Central Europe, 118; his character, 48–49, 85; on Communist oppression, 138; on Communists, 25–26; compared with Arendt, (Elshtain), 116, 123; on his own conscience, 86–87; on conscience and politics, 108, 120, 174; on crisis of modern man, 108–9; on Czechoslovakia as a federalist state, 27–28; on Czech-Slovak relations, 27–29; on dialectic, 123; his "drama" (Wilson), 22–24; on folly, 132; on global responsibility 264; on history, 133; on human identity, 112, 146; on ideological thinking and ideologies, 145–46, 152–53; Luers on, 85; and Masaryk (Skilling), 105–11; his office, 79–81; his paradoxes, 17, (Barancak), 46–47; on party politics, 28; on politics, 117, 119, 124–25, 151, 263; contrasted with Patočka, 119; [photos, individual] 246, 260; his political persona (Schiff), 78–79; on his political vision, 154; his postmodernism,

Havel, Václav *(continued)*
  10–11, 37–38; premières of his plays, 3; on his presidency, 85–86; on the president's power, 82; prizes received, 3; on progress, 118; on racial hate, 137–38; on restructuring and market economy, 150, 153–54; on results of Soviet rule, 101, 150; his rhetoric of folly and irony (Zagacki), 129–30; his "role," 6, 7,15, 22, (Garton Ash), 67–69; on the role of the president, 16, 261–65; Rorty on, 115; and Sisyphus, 6, 17, 177; his special brand of responsibility, 10, (Elshtain), 120, 264; on Sudeten Germans, 42; as target of criticism and hope (Siklová), 250–54; on the theater, 182, 186; topicality of his theater, 16; on totalitarian systems and modern civilization, 174; translations of his plays, 3; on utopianism 122; on values, 139, 263; Western images of, 200

PLAYS
Audience, 3, 6, 201, 203–6 *passim;* analyses of (Stern), 39–40, (Baranczak) 49–52; "delirious" episodes in, 220; "he can we can't theme," 51–53; [photo] 172
Autostop (with Vyskočil), 213–14
The Beggar's Opera, 13, 16; analyzed (Steiner), 184–99; and collective schizophrenia, 189–91; its "delirious" moment, 220; fluid identities in, 232; performance in Toronto, 244; its première, 12, 184–85; reaction of authorities to, 188–89
Conspirators: and self-generated movement of human relations, 40
The Demented Dove (in collaboration), 213
The Garden Party, 11, 13, 16, 23, 38–39, 202–4 *passim;* 247, 249; analyzed (Trensky), 159–71; director on, 256–57; as family drama, 162; on identity, 256–57; its language, 11, 161–66 *passim;* 235; as political satire, 163–64, 170–71; and regression 215–16; its rhythm, 169; as satire on bureaucracy, 168–69; as topical for today, 257
The Increased Difficulty of Concentration, 3, 13, 204, 205; "delirious" subjectivity in, 216–18; Huml and Western consciousness, 235–36

Largo Desolato, 1, 3, 4, 13, 38, 49; and theater of absurd, 226–27; and theme of betrayal, 37; and "delirious" subjectivity, 218–20; Havel on, 53; [photo] 210; and self-censorship, 225; and Vaněk plays, 50
The Memorandum, 3, 87, 204–6 *passim*; analysis of (Carey) 173–83; and institutionalization of language, 174; and social mechanisms, 311–12; and Obie Award, 159; artificial language Ptydepe and other devices, 40–41, 49–50, 175–77, 179, 216; and seduction theme, 235–36
The Mistake, 3
The Mountain Hotel, 13, 40; "delirious" episodes in, 211, 220
Private View see *Unveiling*
Protest, 3, 6, 206; "he can we can't" theme, 50–52; [photo] 210
Slum Clearance [*Redevelopment*], 3, 42; "delirious" episodes in, 220
Temptation, 3, 4, 6, 37, 87, 202–6 *passim;* betrayal theme in, 205–6; "delirious" moment in, 220; Garton Ash on, 204; [photo] 210; and New York critics, 231; seduction theme in, 14–15; temptation theme in 228–39
Unveiling [*Private View*], 3, 6, 50, 203–6 *passim;* "he can we can't" theme in, 51; and Ionesco, 203; [photo] 172; and Pinter, 201; Vaněk plays: their authors, 50; Vaněk as character, 49–54, *passim*

PROSE
Anticodes, 179
The Art of the Impossible, 87
Disturbing the Peace, 46, 80, 87, 201; on absurdity, 228; on first imprisonment, 36–37; on folly, 132; his double role, 48
"Letter to Gustáv Husák," 38, 47; on coercive mechanisms of Communist regime, 191
Letters to Olga, 1, 10, 35–37 *passim;* 46, 80, 81, 201, 244; thoughts on betrayal in, 37; as genesis of a secular saint, 87; on human identity, 112; on responsibility, 120–21; in *samizdat,* 224; on theater, 239
"The Magic Circle," 198–99
Open Letters, 87
"Paradise Lost," 124–25

"The Peculiarities of Theater," 186;
"The Power of the Powerless," 12, 15, 54–55, 63–64; on communicative duplicity, 189–91; and Italian students, 247–49; on life's plurality, 145; on Marxist-Leninist system, 152; on network of power relations, 25
"The Role of the Czech President," 16, 261–65
"Six Asides about Culture," 206–7
"Stories and Totalitarianism," 221
Summer Meditations, 5, 22–24 *passim;* 67, 201; political credo in, 28; rejection of utopia and ideological systems, 145–46; on responsibility, 112
Toward a Civil Society, 62–63, 66
"The Trial," 34–35

SPEECHES
Speech to the International Conference on Anti-Semitism in Post-Totalitarian Europe (1992), 137–38
Copenhagen Speech (1990): on politics (Garton Ash on), 63–66 *passim*
Speech to Czech Parliament (1993), 150
Speech to the Czechoslovak Federal Assembly (1990), 27–28
First Speech as President of Czechoslovakia (1990), 115–16
Speech at George Washington University (1993), 150
Speech at the Hebrew University in Jerusalem (1990), 135
New Year's Address, January 1, 1990, 25; on truth, 92–93; on a 'humane Republic,' 101–2; on the legacy of the past, 115–16
Speech at New York University, 64
Speech receiving Sonning Prize. *See* Copenhagen Speech
"The State of the Republic" (1997): critique of the market place and belief in an open Civil society (Wilson on), 21, 29
Speech at International Theater Day: on theater, 182
Speech to the United States Congress (1990), 83, 93–94, 132–36 *passim*
Welcome Speech to PEN Congress (1995): on intellectuals and politics, 58, 64
Speech to World Economic Forum: on technology (1992), 173

Havlová, Olga, 36, 80; [photos] 128, 246
Havlová, Dagmar, [photos] 56, 128
Hegel, Georg Wilhelm Friedrich, 144, 254, 271; and dialectics 170–71
Heidegger, Martin, 35, 87, 118, 181
Helsinki Agreement, 107, 185, 271
Herzog (Bellow), 96
Hilsner, Leopold: Masaryk and the Hilsner case, 109
History of Sexuality, The (Foucault), 149
Hitler, Adolf, 33, 42, 45, 229
Hochhuth, Rolf, 229, 271
Honegger, Gitta, 14
Howe, Irving, 87
Hrabal, Bohumil, 67, 86, 271
Hungary, 29, 34
Husák, Gustáv, 36, 47–50 *passim;* 61, 99, 254, 271; and Castle Gardens, 99; Havel's letter to, 38, 47, 191; and normalization 186
Hus, Jan, 42, 100, 271
Husserl, Edmund, 35, 118, 272
Hvížd'ala, Karel, 87

Inspector General, The (Gogol), 167
Intellectuals and politics: discussion of at PEN Congress, 58–61. *See also* Garton Ash, Timothy
Ionesco, Eugène, 6, 13, 41, 165, 214, 227, 272; his dramatic characters, 160–61; and Havel's plays, 54; 202–6 *passim;* (Skloot) influence of, 202, 203
Italy, 15, 247–49

Jack, or the Submission (Ionesco), 203
Jackson, Andrew, 99
Jakeš, Miloš, 252, 254, 272
Jakobson, Roman, 13, 247, 272; and Liberated Theater, 212–13
Jaruzelski, Wojciech, 84, 272
John Paul II, Pope, 42, 44, 254; [photo] 56
Johnson, Paul, 60
Joyce, James, 202
Juncker, Klaus, 3, [photo] 32

Kafka, Franz, 2, 6, 15, 41, 62, 185, 224, 227; and Beckett, 14; and Havel 237; and "negative" objects, 213
Kant, Immanuel: on philosophers, 67
Karčevski Sergei, 216
Kaspar (Handke), 229
Keaton, Buster, 225

Kellenberger, J., 130
Killer Sneers, The (Ionesco), 161
Kissinger, Henry, 62, 91, 96–97
Klaus, Václav , 21, 25, 61, 64, 77, 250,
    272; disagreements with Havel (Wilson), 29; on intellectuals, 58–59; tension between prime minister and president (Garton Ash), 66–69 *passim. See
    also* Garton Ash, Timothy
Klestil, Thomas, 66
Klíma, Ivan, 86, 272; on intellectuals, 61,
    64; at PEN conference 59–61 *passim;*
    on PEN, 69
Klíma, Ladislav, 213, 272
Klímoví, Rita, 272; on Havel, 83; on
    nation's guilt, 78
Koestler, Arthur, 87
Kohl, Helmut, 68–69, 273; [photo] 56
Kohout, Pavel, 86, 244, 273; as author of a
    Vaněk play, 50
Kołakowski, Leszek, 44, 273
Kondracke, M., 127
Konrád, György , 58–59, 61, 273
Koscak, Mikhail, 93
Kott, Jan, 229, 273
Kriseová, Eva, 4
Krob, Andrej, 209, 255–7; as director of
    Havel's plays, 16; [photo] 90
Kubišová, Marta, 245, 273
kulak, 273
Kundera, Milan, 1, 42, 273–274; on Havel,
    202–3

Lamr, Aleš, 79
Landovsky, Pavel, 50, 274
Lapham, Lewis, 8, 9, 250; on Academy
    Awards ceremony in Havel's honor,
    91–97
Laterna Magica Theatre: the "Revolution of
    the Magic Lantern," 7, 33, 57, 68, 70;
    and the Civic Forum, 91
Leipzig, 106
Lenin, Vladimir Ilich (Ulyanov), 202
Lesson, The (Ionesco), 203, 214, 274
"Letter to Voskovec and Werich on the
    Semantics of Fun" (Jakobson), 212–13
Lewis, C. S., 233
Liberated Theater (Prague), 212–13, 244
Lincoln, Abraham, 44
Living in Truth (Vladislav, ed.), 174
Logic of Sense, The (Deleuze), 209
London, 184

Lorch, Maristella, 131, 134
Luers, William, 84; on Havel, 85
Lukács, George, 41
Lyotard, Jean-François, 144

Maastricht, 62, 65
Mácha, Karel Hynek, 247, 274
Macourek, Miloš, 213, 274
Madison, James, 154
Magic Lantern Theater. *See* Laterna Magica
Maids, The (Genet), 160
Malkin, Jeanette, 180
Mann, Thomas, 230
Mao Tse-tung, 45
market economy: Havel on, 153–54
Marx, Karl: and dialectics 170–71; and
    concept of ideology, 190
Marxism, 129; Havel on Marxism, 136; the
    Marxist project (Elshtain), 113; Marxism-Leninism, 144, 190; Marxist-
    Leninist Party, 186
Masaryk, Tomáš Garrigue , 42, 99, 251,
    274; compared with Havel, 9;
    (Skilling) 105–11 *passim;* Havel on
    101; as symbol, 253; on statesmanship
    and philosophy, 65–66
Massey College, 244, 274
Max, Peter, 79
Mazowiecki, Tadeusz, 88, 274
McKellen, Ian: on Czech audience, 187–88
McRae, Rob, 8, 243; on Havel's first day as
    president—a view from the crowd,
    98–102
Melchinger, Siegfried, 229
Michell, Roger, 231
Mikkelsen, Ole, 100
Miller, Arthur, 1, 95
Milosz, Czeslaw , 122, 274. *See also Captive
    Mind*
Minařík, Jan, 192
Misunderstanding, The (Camus), 229
Mitterand, François, 79, 274
Mladý Svět, 79, 135
Morgenthau, Hans, 116, 274
Moscow, 36, 83
Mother Courage and her Children (Brecht): performance in Prague, 187
Mozart, Wolfgang Amadeus, 94, 95
Mrożek, Slawomir, 173, 207
Mucha, Alfons, 80
Munich, 83, 274–275
Munich Agreement (1938), 5, 31, 83, 110;

and Czechs, 33–34. *See also* Czechoslovakia
Musil, Jiří: defines changes Czech society
faces, 150

nationalism, 17
NATO, 100
Navrátil, Augustin, 33
Nazism. *See* Germany
Němcová, Dana , 251, 275
Nero, 45
Netherlands, 231
New Critics, 185
Newman, Paul, 94–95
New Testament, The, 130, 139; Paul on empa-
thy, 137
New York, 36, 159
New Yorker, The, 44
New York Times, 84
normalization, 275; Milan Šimečka on,
186–87
Nové cesty myšlení, 231
Novotný, Antonín, 243 , 275

Obie Award: for *Memorandum*, 159, 175
Opletal, Jan, 31
Orange Tree Theatre (London), 3
Order of the White Lion, 245
Ortega, Daniel, 45
Orwell, George, 60, 62, 64, 87, 122, 178
Oxford University, 60

Palach, Jan, 31, 100, 275
Palouš, Radim, 275; on *Temptation,* 231,
237–38
Paseka Publishing House, [photo] 90
Patočka, Jan, 10, 35–37 *passim;* 59, 87, 275;
and Charter 77, 47; and Havel, on the-
ism, 119; as Havel's mentor, 46; and
Heidegger's phenomenology, 87; Rorty
on, 115
Peck, Gregory, 94, 96
PEN, 6–7, 57–71 *passim*
Peterson, Oscar, 91
Philosophy Today, 143
Pierce, Charles S., 209
Pinter, Harold, 3, 13, 87, 165, 203, 275;
compared with Havel, 201–02
Pistek, Theodor, 76
Pius XII, Pope, 229
Plastic People of the Universe, 34, 109, 275
Plato, 81; and philosopher-king, 67

Plečnik, Josip, 75
Poetism, 213
Poland, 29, 34, 44; and Lech Wałęsa, 65,
88; Havel performed in, 256
Poles: compared with Czechs, 206–7
Politburo, 275–76
political theater: nature of (Goetz-
Stankiewicz), 228–30; and Havel's the-
ater, 239
post-Communism, 22, 24. *See also* Havel,
Václav
*Postmodern Condition: A Report of Knowledge,
The* (Lyotard), 144
Postmodernism: and Havel, 10–11, 37–38,
143–56. *See also* Havel, Václav
Prague Castle: on day of Havel's election
(McRae), 98–102
Prague National Theater, 185
Prague Orgy, The (Roth), 185, 276
Prague Spring (1968), 3, 5, 24, 34, 47,
173–74, 276; cut short by invasion,
186; and loss of audience for Havel's
plays, 218
Přemyslids, 75, 276
Professional Foul (Stoppard), 1, 202, 229
Ptydepe (*Memorandum*), 12, 40–41, 50,
175–81 *passim*
Public Against Violence (movement), 23
Public Theater (New York), 3, 4
Pynsent, Robert B., 4

*Questions of Identity: Czech and Slovak Ideas on
Nationalism* (Pynsent), 4
Quinn, Michael L., 13–14, 184; on theory of
negative delirium and Havel's plays,
209–23

Radio Free Europe, 31, 192
Rebel, The (Camus), 54, 276
Reed, Lou: and Czech *samizdat*, 77, 84
*Reluctant President, The: A Political Life of
Václav Havel* (Simmons), 4
Restoration of Order, The (Šimečka) , 186
Rhinoceros (Ionesco), 54, 161, 214, 276
Richard II (Shakespeare): performance in
Prague, 187–88
Rolling Stones, 77, 84, 118
Rome, 33
Rorty, Richard, 1, 10, 118, 276; on contin-
gency, 114–15; on dignity, 118, 129;
on teleology of progress, 123. *See also*
Elshtain, Jean Bethke

Roth, Philip, 87, 185
Rowohlt Publishers, 3
Royal Shakespeare Company, 3, 230
Ruml, Jan, 251, 276
Rushdie, Salman, 58, 60
Russell, Bertrand, 62

Saint-Germain (Treaty of), 34
Salzburg Festival (1990), 83–84
samizdat, 57, 106, 231, 247, 276; in book-
    stores after Communist demise, 86;
    and Havel's writings, 107; and *Letters to
    Olga,* 224; and Lou Reed's experience,
    84
Sarandon, Susan, 95
Sartre, Jean Paul, 7, 62, 70
Schiff, Stephen, 7, 9, 105; on Havel as newly
    elected President, 75–89
Schonberg, Michal, 244
Schwarzenberg, Karel von, 76, 277; meeting
    with Havel, 79–80
Screwtape Letters, The (C.S. Lewis), 233, 235–36
Seifert, Jaroslav, 277
Sellers, Peter, 76
Shaffer, Peter, 229, 277. *See also Amadeus*
Shakespeare, William, 45, 94, 231, 256; on
    the Prague stage, 187–88
Shapiro, Michael J., 147
Shaw, George Bernard, 40
Shevardnadze, Eduard, 66
Shklovsky, Borisovich Viktor, 13, 212, 277
Šiklová, Jiřina, 15–16, 98; on Havel as sym-
    bol for criticism and hope, 250–54
*Silenced Theatre, The: Czech Playwrights with-
    out a Stage* (Goetz-Stankiewicz), 4, 41
Šimečka, Milan: on normalization, 186–7,
    277. *See also Restoration of Order*
Simmons, Michael, 4. *See also Reluctant Presi-
    dent*
Sisyphus, 17, 177
Sixty-Eight Publishers, 15, [photo] 246; and
    Havel's *Plays, 1970–76,* 244
Skilling, H. Gordon, 9, 31; on Havel and
    Masaryk, 105–11; [photo] 32
Skloot, Robert, 6, 13, 224; on Havel's plays,
    200–208
Škvorecký, Josef, 15, 86, 91; on memories of
    young Havel and later, 243–45,
    [photo] 246
Škvorecký, Zdena, [writes under the name of
    Zdena Salivarová] 244–45, [photo]
    246

Slánský, Rudolf, 40, 277
Slovakia, 26–28 *passim;* 33, 45, 77; in inter-
    war period, 110; Slovak nationalism,
    23, 26; Slovak sovereignty, 111
Slovaks, 77; Havel on Czechs and Slovaks,
    78, 101–2; Czech and Slovak history,
    105–6; their dissident intellectuals, 59
Smetana, Bedřich, 187
Society for a Merrier Present, 79
Socrates, 35
Soderberg, Douglas, 12, 14, 255; on *Largo
    Desolato,* 224–27
Sorel, Julien, 160, 277
South Africa, 147
Soviet Empire: compared to Habsburg
    Empire: 9; (Skilling) 106–7
Soviet Invasion (1968), 3, 31, 47, 59, 185,
    225; Forman on results of, 78; resis-
    tance against, 38
Soyinka, Wole, 58
Spiegel, Der: on Havel's *Beggar's Opera,* 185,
    188
Spinková, Martina, 245
Srp, Karel, 245, 277
St. Paul, 130, 137, 139
Stakhanovites, 75–76, 277
Stalin, Joseph, 45, 82, 170, 180
Stalinism, 13
StB, 100, 278
Steiner, Peter, 12, 159; on *Beggar's Opera,*
    184–99
Štěpánová, Bára, 79, 81
Stern, J. P., 5, 143; on Havel and his con-
    text, 31–43
Stockhom, 3
Stoppard, Tom, 1, 49, 87, 229, 231, 278; on
    absurdity, 40; comparison with Havel,
    13, (Skloot) 202–5. *See also Professional
    Foul* and *Travesties*
Stratford-on-Avon, 3
Streep, Meryl, 91
Stroheim, Erich von, 82, 278
Sudeten Germans: their expulsion, 33–34,
    83; and Havel, 42. *See also* Havel,
    Václav
Sudetenland, 278
Sullivan, Dale, 139
Svědectví, 243, 278
Švejk, 34, 38, 55, 278
Sweden, 59
Swift, Jonathan, 184
Szelényi, Ivan, 61

Táborský, Václav, 244
Tango (Mrożek), 207
Taylor, Charles, 278; on dialogic self, 221
Teresa, Mother, 128
Thatcher, Margaret, 60, 69
Theater of the Absurd, 49, 54, 160–61; versus political theater, 14; and Havel's theater 87; Vannier on, 161
Theater of Protest: and Havel, 49
Theater on the Balustrade, 3, 47, 213
Theiner, George, 3, 231
Three Penny Opera, The (Brecht), 184
Tiananmen Square, 34, 245
Tigrid, Pavel, 243, 278
Titian, 80
Tomášek, František, Cardinal , 33, 99, 278
Toronto, 15
Totalitarianism, 22, 25. *See also* Havel, Václav
Trahison des clercs, 61–62, 122, 278
Travesties (Stoppard), 202
Trensky, Paul, 4, 11, 173; on the *Garden Party*, 159–71
Trial, The (Kafka), 14, 224
Trieste, 3, 15
Tříska, Jan, 14
Trump, Ivana, 91
Turkey, 59
Tvář, 47, 279
Tynan, Kenneth, 279; Havel and Stoppard compared, 202; on Stoppard, 205
Tzara, Tristan, 202

United States, 78; and the Soviet Union, Havel on, 133; United States Congress and Havel, 83; U.S. ceremony honoring Havel, 91–97; Havel on the United States and post–Cold War, 132–34
University of British Columbia Press, 50
University of Toronto, 244–45
Urbánek, Zdeněk, 230
Utopianism: Havel on, 122

Václav Havel (Kriseová), 4
Valgemae, Mardi, 173
Vaněk Plays, The: Four Authors, One Character, (Goetz-Stankiewicz), 4
Vaněk Plays (Václav Havel's), 6
Vannier, Jean, 161
Velvet Revolution, 5, 23, 24, 59, 75, 225, 279; description of (Stern), 31–33; and first interim government, 26; high

moments of (McRae), 98–102; Havel during, [photo] 246; two democratic revolutions compared (Skilling), 109–10
Velvet Underground Revival, 84
Verne, Jules, 167
Versailles (Treaty of), 34
Vico, Giovanni Battista, 131
Victims of Duty (Ionesco), 161
Vienna, 3, 106, 107
Vienna Akademietheater, 230
Vienna Burgtheater, 225
Virilio, Paul 147
Vitalist School of Poetry, 167
Volanská, Heda, 244
Voskovec, Jiří, 213, 244
Vyskočil, Ivan, 213, 279

Waiting for Godot (Beckett), 226
Waldheim, Kurt, 279; Havel and the "Waldheim issue," 83–84, 151–52
Wałęsa, Lech, 65, 88, 279
Wall Street Journal, 93
Walters, Barbara, 96, 97
Warsaw Pact, 24, 279; its regimes, 86
Weber, Max, 61, 279
Webster, John, 207
Weil, Simone, 122, 280
Weizsäcker, Richard von, 67–69 *passim,* 280
Wenceslas, King, 31
Werich, Jan, 213, 280
Wiesel, Eli, 94, 280
Wilde, Oscar, 231
Wilson, Paul, 5, 7, 16, 228; an assessment of as person and leader, 21–30
Winn, Marie, 3
Winter's Tale, A (Shakespeare), 45
Wirth, Andrzej, 173
Wittgenstein, Ludwig, 171, 173, 280
Wolfe, Tom, 92
World War II, 83, 93, 133

York University (Toronto), 244
Yugoslavia, 65, 75, 137

Zagacki, Kenneth S., 10, 21; on Havel and the concept of folly, 127–42
Žantovský, Michael, 76–80; (Schiff) on Havel as president, 83–84; as Schiff's escort in the Castle, 76
Zappa, Frank, 42, 77, 84
Zurich, 3

The Volume Editors

◆

Phyllis Carey is professor of English at Mount Mary College, Milwaukee, Wis., where she currently chairs the English Department and teaches composition and literature courses. She is coeditor (with Ed Jewinski) of *Re: Joyce n' Beckett* (1992), (with Catharine Malloy) *Seamus Heaney: The Shaping Spirit* (1996) and editor of *Wagering on Transcendence: The Search for Meaning in Literature* (1997). She has published essays on Václav Havel, Samuel Beckett, and James Joyce, as well as interviews with Czeslaw Milosz and Seamus Deane.

Marketa Goetz-Stankiewicz is professor (emerita) of Germanic Studies and Comparative Literature at the University of British Columbia. She is the author of *The Silenced Theatre: Czech Playwrights without a Stage* (1979) and editor of *DramaContemporary: Czechoslovakia* (1985), *The Vaněk Plays: Four Authors, One Character* (1987), and *Good-bye, Samizdat: Twenty Years of Czechoslovak Underground Writing* (1992). She has published numerous essays on modern Czech, German, and comparative literature in a variety of books and journals.

The General Editor

◆

Robert Lecker is professor of English at McGill University in Montreal. He received his Ph.D. from York University. Professor Lecker is the author of numerous critical studies, including *On the Line* (1982), *Robert Kroetch* (1986), *An Other I* (1988), and *Making It Real: The Canonization of English-Canadian Literature* (1995). He is the editor of the critical journal *Essays on Canadian Writing* and of many collections of critical essays, the most recent of which is *Canadian Canons: Essays in Literary Value* (1991). He is the founding and current general editor of Twayne's Masterwork Studies and the editor of the Twayne World Authors Series on Canadian writers. He is also the general editor of G. K. Hall's Critical Essays on World Literature series.